Managing Learning in Virtual Settings:
The Role of Context

António D. de Figueiredo
Universidade de Coimbra, Portugal

Ana P. Afonso
Universidade de Coimbra, Portugal

Information Science Publishing
Hershey • London • Melbourne • Singapore

Acquisitions Editor:	Michelle Potter
Development Editor:	Kristin Roth
Senior Managing Editor:	Amanda Appicello
Managing Editor:	Jennifer Neidig
Copy Editor:	TechBooks
Typesetter:	TechBooks
Cover Design:	Lisa Tosheff
Printed at:	Yurchak Printing Inc.

Published in the United States of America by
  Information Science Publishing (an imprint of Idea Group Inc.)
  701 E. Chocolate Avenue
  Hershey PA 17033
  Tel: 717-533-8845
  Fax: 717-533-8661
  E-mail: cust@idea-group.com
  Web site: http://www.idea-group.com

and in the United Kingdom by
  Information Science Publishing (an imprint of Idea Group Inc.)
  3 Henrietta Street
  Covent Garden
  London WC2E 8LU
  Tel: 44 20 7240 0856
  Fax: 44 20 7379 3313
  Web site: http://www.eurospan.co.uk

Library of Congress Cataloging-in-Publication Data
Managing learning in virtual settings : the role of context / Antonio Dias
   Figueiredo and Ana Paula Afonso, editors.
      p. cm.
   Summary: "This book emphasizes the role of context in the development
and management of virtual learning environments"--Provided by publisher.
   Includes bibliographical references and index.
   ISBN 1-59140-488-6 (hc) -- ISBN 1-59140-489-4 (sc) -- ISBN 1-59140-490-8
(ebook)
   1. Distance education--Computer-assisted instruction--Management. 2. Web
-based instruction--Management.   I. Figueiredo, Antonio Dias, 1946-   .
II. Afonso, Ana Paula, 1973-   .
LC5803.C65M36 2006
371.35'8--dc22
                                        2005013547British Cataloguing in
Publication Data
A Cataloguing in Publication record for this book is available from the British Library.

Managing Learning in Virtual Settings: The Role of Context

Table of Contents

Preface

The Book

Managing Learning in Virtual Settings: The Role of Context stresses the dimension of context in a world dominated by the centrality of content, guiding the reader in developing insight on balanced, organic, and successful learning environments and strategies that go largely beyond the dimension of content. It is aimed at all kinds of educators and administrators of education, researchers, e-learning system managers, instructional designers, e-learning-based professional companies, corporate training departments, and all publics interested in e-learning and Web-based learning. Through 17 chapters, divided into an introduction and two parts—"Concepts" and "Experiences"—it discusses the basis for the development and management of learning contexts, with contributions from domains as diverse as learning theories, philosophy, psychology, sociology, epistemology, anthropology, organizational learning, communities of practice, and others. It emphasizes the role of context in the development and management of virtual learning environments and attempts to open up new threads in clarifying the influence of contextual issues on learning, while covering a balanced combination of all the dimensions and components of the learning context.

The Issues

Most of the literature on e-learning, Web-based learning, and other kinds of learning in virtual settings concentrates on the delivery of content, relegating to a lesser role the contexts and the activity-rich, interaction-rich, and culturally rich learning environments that the use of technology is making possible and where new principles and practices can and should be explored. Striking a balance on such a scenario, this book is specifically devoted to the issues of context. It is an interdisciplinary book providing a broad and multidisciplinary vision of learning contexts. It does so by offering a sound body of theory on a multiplicity of domains relevant to the understanding of learning contexts, while illustrating and complementing this theory with a variety of real-world experiences. In the choice of its authors, it combines academic knowledge with practitioner experience, putting together visions that come from different professional cultures and parts of the world.

Organization of the Book

This book is made up of 17 chapters, organized into an introductory chapter followed by two parts: Section I—Concepts, with nine chapters; and Section II—Experiences, with seven chapters. A brief description of each chapter follows.

Chapter I

In the introductory chapter, titled *Context and Learning: A Philosophical Framework*, António Dias de Figueiredo and Ana Paula Afonso present a simple model for the description of learning events and a philosophical framework for the clarification of the nature of learning contexts. The model describes a learning event as involving the learner, interacting with content and context. The philosophical framework differentiates between positivist and constructivist paradigms by formulating three questions, to which each paradigm responds with four principles. The three questions and resulting eight principles are then summarized on a table that can be easily recalled by the reader whishing to analyze the two radically different interpretations of context. The implications of these distinctions are then analyzed, namely in what regards the management of learning contexts, the duality between content and context, and the challenges of designing learning contexts.

Section I: Concepts

Chapter II

In *Virtual Settings: E-Learning as Creating Context*, Philip Duchastel and Markus Molz maintain that contextual analysis and contextual design of virtual and semivirtual learning environments are essential. They conceptualize learning as a confluence of four co-evolving contextual realms of reality—the realm of subjective experience, the realm of information, the institutional realm, and the realm of community—which they organize into a fourfold model of multiple embedded contexts. In spite of their shift of emphasis to context, they insist that content remains essential in any design paradigm, though at a higher level of abstraction and moving to expected outcomes rather than encapsulated in a consolidated expression. They discuss the relationship between interaction and activity, recalling that it is the nature of the interaction rather than the activity itself that molds learning. Finally, they examine design issues raised by their model and work toward a paradigm of contextual design for learning, which they complete centering on open high-level issues that must be addressed in conceiving a well-balanced learning architecture.

Chapter III

Licínio Roque and António Dias de Figueiredo, in *Context Engineering for Learning: A Sociotechnical Approach*, analyze the problems related to the role of context in learning and development, individual and organizational, influenced by anthropology, activity theory, and actor-network theory. Bearing in mind that a virtual learning context is a special case of an information system, they present the context engineering (CE) approach to information systems development (ISD) as a framework to think and organize the development of virtual contexts for e-learning. This approach proposes to achieve an understanding of development as a sociotechnical phenomenon within a cultural and historical envelope and to provide a framework focused on the relationship between a model of context and its mediators. The authors then attempt to translate this approach to the development of virtual learning contexts into fundamental ideas and guiding principles, elaborating on some of the learning and development issues that arise.

Chapter IV

In *The Role of Context When Implementing Learning Environments: Some Key Issues*, Bernard Blandin emphasizes the role of sociology in clarifying what is at stake when implementing new learning environments. He starts by setting the theoretical scene around a vision of learning as a situated activity. He then confronts the theoretical background with empirical research that studies the influence of contextual issues on learning. He proposes a heuristic model for the design of learning environments that takes context into account, namely in its organizational component. He discusses some implementation issues, arguing that the success of a new learning environment is conditioned by change and adaptations of its organizational context. He closes with a discussion of new learning environments under the light of the sociology of innovation, suggesting pragmatic guidelines for the successful development of such environments, inspired by a range of theoretical approaches, from socioeconomical theories and psychosociological theories of influence to organizational learning theories and theories of sociotechnical networks.

Chapter V

Ellen Christiansen, in *Space as Learning Context: The Role of Dwelling in the Development of Academic Education*, argues for the role of space, or "dwelling," in educational settings, claiming that to support self-regulated learning, space has to be laid out in ways that let the learners feel included, guided, and able to transform. She stresses that the important divide with respect to space in education is not between virtual and physical but between empowering and disempowering settings. In her view, course designers should be aware of the ways that support the students in making themselves a dwelling out of the space allocated. She illustrates with a classroom and a workshop as examples of dwellings where self-regulated learning occurs and explores a metaphor where the design of an educational setting is seen as both a window and a mirror. Finally, she comments on the role of the managers of educational settings when supporting the development of self-regulated learners by means of space design, warning that at this level guidance needs to take full predominance over control.

Chapter VI

In *The Dynamics of Online Collaboration: Team Task, Team Development, Peer Relationship, and Communication Media*, Ke Zhang and Xun Ge propose a framework to help understand and manage the complex dynamics of online collaboration from four perspectives: team task, team development, peer relationship, and communication media. Team task covers four key types of tasks (discussion, problem solving, decision making, and production) as well as task complexity, viewed from the point of view of the cognitive demands it puts upon collaboration. Team development discusses the stages and temporal rhythms of team development, the diverse needs for moderation they elicit, and the relevance of peer control, external moderation, and team contacts. Peer relationships are analyzed from the point of view of affective conflicts and cognitive conflicts and lead to recommendations on how to build up healthy team relationships. Finally, communications media are examined in light of rational media theories (media richness theory and social presence theory) and social constructivist media theories, in an interesting attempt to get the best of both.

Chapter VII

Mark Schofield, Andrew Sackville, and John Davey, in *Designing for Unique Online Learning Contexts: The Alignment of Purpose, Audience, and Form of Interactivity*, stress the importance of designing learning environments for interactivity and they argue for the problematization of design at the levels of purpose, audience, and form. They put forward a model for the design of effective online learning environments inspired by the metaphor of a bespoke tailor that makes a jacket for a client, making sure that the jacket fits the body and that subsequent tailoring and adjustments can be made. The jacket surrounds the online learning experience and includes the technology and tools used, the models of pedagogy, the parameters of interactivity, and the conceptions of learning community. The body fits inside the jacket and comprises the conceptualization, design, and delivery of the online learning experience. Tailoring the jacket to fit the body, even when the body changes, calls for meticulous interactivity analysis and constructive alignment of outcomes, pedagogy, and assessment.

Chapter VIII

In *Communities as Context Providers for Web-Based Learning*, Ana Paula Afonso provides an evolutionary vision of community by elaborating on three approaches of community: a deconstructivist approach, a (socio)constructivist approach, and a contextual approach. The chapter stresses the lack of consensus around the concept of community and its more recent deployment in the educational domain. It elaborates on how the educational use of virtual settings has neglected the construction of the learning context and tries to show the existence of a broad and solid body of knowledge that may provide useful insight to overcome the limitations of many online learning experiences. The author proposes learning communities as a framework for a contextual approach to the management of learning in virtual settings.

Chapter IX

Laura G. Farres and Colla J. MacDonald, in *Activity Theory and Context: An Understanding of the Development of Constructivist Instructional Design Models*, propose a conceptual framework for examining constructivist instructional design model development. Considering that each constructivist instructional design model tends to offer a unique approach to e-learning, based on its own context of development, the aim of the framework is to help identify the unique contribution afforded by each model. This leads to a better understanding of the context of every model, which, in turn, enables the clarification of the ways in which it can be applied. The framework uses activity theory as a lens from which to understand each context, arguing that activity theory provides a suitable framework for natu-ralistic inquiry within complex settings, and establishes a language from which better comparisons of context can be carried out. The framework is then applied to two real constructivist instructional design models for e-learning, which illustrate how it can be used to examine the similarities and uniqueness of the models.

Chapter X

In *The Distance from Isolation: Why Communities are the Logical Conclusion in E-Learning*, Martin Weller argues that the popularity of the Internet stems from three of its key design features—openness, robustness, and decentralization—which have developed into social features and become embodied in cultural values. Taking as a reference some sociologically successful developments—Napster, blogging, and open source software development—he argues that an analysis of the presence or absence of the three core values is useful in predicting what developments, tech-nologies, and approaches might be successful for a generation of learners that have been enculturated into such values. Bearing in mind the benefits of communities in learning processes, he then uses the three core values perspective to examine the potential of communities in e-learning. He closes with a discussion of the realization of such communities by means of a five-stage model of community evolution that facilitates analysis through a dynamic balance of people, process, and technology.

Section II: Experiences

Chapter XI

In *Narrative Designing for Context in Virtual Settings*, Patricia Arnold, John D. Smith, and Beverly Trayner focus on the role of narrative in negotiating and revealing contexts. Drawing on Bruner's work on narrative and on situated theo-ries of learning, the authors explore how narrative can help reveal individual and community contexts, resorting to the narrative genre themselves, in the shape of three stories of learning in designed and emerged virtual settings. They conclude by translating these stories into guidelines for the design of virtual learning set-tings.

Chapter XII

Kathy L. Milhauser, in *The Voice of the Online Learner*, introduces a new per-spective in this book: that of the online learner. Through four biographical stories, she explores the process of transformative learning undergone by the learners of a strongly contextual online course, upholding that learners are the best designers of their own learning. The author then concludes with the discussion of a set of key elements of transformative online learning environments, building on the experience of designers and on the postulates of constructivism, social constructivism, constructionism, and situated learning.

Chapter XIII

In *Learning Agency in New Learning Environments: An Australian Case Study of the Influence of Context*, Hitendra Pillay, John A. Clarke, and Peter G. Taylor explore the Bandurian concept of learner agency, broadening it to the more inclusive concept of learning agency. In the chapter, the authors explore this concept empirically using data collected in a longitudinal study about the students' approaches to learning, their perceptions of the learning environments, and their epistemological reflections on themselves as learners. After an exhaustive analysis of the data, the authors conclude by suggesting that the individuals' approach to learning arises from mutual interaction between individual and contextual agency.

Chapter XIV

Michael Forret, Elaine Khoo, and Bronwen Cowie, in *New Wine or New Bottles: What's New About Online Teaching?*, present a case study on the nature of successful online tertiary teaching and learning, while arguing that quality pedagogy, either face-to-face or virtual, is founded on a well-considered view of learning. They first develop a sociocultural view of learning, building on the principles of constructivism, socioconstructivism, and situated theories of learning, from which they identify a set of key characteristics of quality pedagogy, whose applicability is shown to be supported by their research findings.

Chapter XV

In *Quality Assurance During Distributed Collaboration: A Case Study in Creating a Cross-Institutional Learning Community*, Rita M. Vick, Brent Auernheimer, Marie K. Iding, and Martha E. Crosby describe the design of a cross-institutional hybrid asynchronous-synchronous course, with a deeper focus on its synchronous part—that is, the nature and level of interactivity in this hybrid virtual learning environment. They then elaborate on the use of local and global virtual learning communities to stimulate a collaborative learning environment. The case concludes with the empirical analysis of students' interactivity and satisfaction levels based on qualitative and interpretative analysis. The authors also provide an insightful discussion on the lessons learned from this experience.

Chapter XVI

Sulayman K. Sowe, Athanasis Karoulis, and Ioannis Stamelos, in *A Constructivist View of Knowledge Management in Open Source Virtual Communities*, address the domain of free or open source software development (F/OSSD) as an example of an online learning community. They elaborate on a constructivist view of knowledge management within these communities, exploring the learning activities that take place in these online collaborative environments. Their focus is on the resources and activities that promote collaborative learning and on the process of learning transfer from the virtual to the real-life setting. The chapter concludes with some proposed guidelines regarding educational issues in F/OSSD.

Chapter XVII

In *Building a Learning Community Online*, Tessa Owens and Petra Luck bring a different perspective to this book by introducing the subject of work and gender into the learning domain. Their case study describes the experience of an e-learning project aimed at working students from the nursery sector that promoted the emergence of a community of practice. The authors conclude by considering that the problem-based learning approach used provided an appropriate learning context and that the context of gender further enhanced its value.

Mailing List

A mailing list, context@dei.uc.pt, has been set up for reader interaction with the authors and editors of this book and between themselves on the topics of the book. To subscribe to this mailing list, please send a message without subject to majordomo@dei.uc.pt and write in the body of the message: subscribe context@dei.uc.pt. You will receive an acceptance message as soon as your subscription is approved.

António Dias de Figueiredo, Universidade de Coimbra, Portugal
Ana Paula Afonso, Universidade de Coimbra, Portugal

Chapter I

Context and Learning:
A Philosophical Framework

António Dias de Figueiredo, Universidade de Coimbra, Portugal

Ana Paula Afonso, Universidade de Coimbra, Portugal

Abstract

This chapter presents a philosophical framework to help understand the essence of learning contexts. It starts with a brief historical account of the emergence and evolution of the problems of context in learning, and of their increased relevance as learning activities migrate to the online world. It then presents a simple model for a learning event—involving learner, content, and context—from which it analyzes the answers to three key philosophical questions that discriminate between the positivist and the constructivist worldviews. These answers are expressed in the form of four foundational hypotheses or principles for each worldview, which help analyze the resulting two radically different interpretations of learning con-

texts. The implications of these distinctions on the management of learning contexts, on the perception of the duality between content and context, and on the approaches to the design of learning contexts are then analyzed.

Introduction

The problems of context in learning have been around for at least 200 years. In fact, they only started becoming serious when the school systems of the Industrial Age were created in response to the requirements of mass education, and, as a result, learning started taking place increasingly out of context. Up until then, a significant part of what people learned was learned just-in-time, in the context of real-world problems, rather than just-in-case, as a deliberate accumulation of knowledge. When faced with problems that they did not know how to solve, people were taught, in context, by other people, so that from then on they were able to solve similar problems on their own. Their knowledge was, thus, for the most part, the accumulation of knowledge gained trough their real-world experiences. Even when wishing to become professionals, they started out as apprentices and learned a craft in the context of their master's workshop. True enough, some learning did occur partly out of context, such as when people listened to the narratives and debates of the elderly or more experienced, but most of their learning did, indeed, take place in context.

When mass schooling started to materialize at the dawn of the Industrial Age, the ruling values became those of the mechanical world. To be perfect in those days was to operate like a machine. So, the factories, following the management principles of Frederick Taylor, became machines, and the workers, so well pictured in Charlie Chaplin's Modern Times, became parts of those machines. The same organizational principles applied to schools, the assembly lines that mass-produced humanpower for the industrial society. The bells ringing, the aligned rows of desks, the breakup of knowledge into artificial disciplines, the memorization and reproduction of texts, and the "acquisition" of knowledge with no visible application all resulted from this mechanistic drive.

In the meantime, the metaphors of the ruling mechanistic language started describing knowledge as not something that could be built by the learners themselves in appropriate contexts but as "content," some sort of mechanist fluid that could be "transferred" from the textbooks and the minds of the teachers into the empty minds of the learners. The sociable, contextual principles of apprenticeship learning, which had pervaded for centuries, had been replaced by something thought to be more effective—knowledge "transfer." As knowledge was broken down into disparate subjects, most of them without visible application, and started being massively transferred, mostly by telling and questioning, real learning contexts gradually disappeared from education.

Although this kind of mechanistic education quickly gained the favor of the industrial society, it did not stay unchallenged for long. As early as 1899, John Dewey started opposing mechanistic schooling, advocating the values of inquiry, participation, and collaboration and writing that school work should be a mode of activity "which reproduces, or runs parallel to, some form of work carried on in social life" (Dewey, 1899, p. 92). In his confrontations with the proponents of a traditional, "curriculum-centered" education he criticized a view where the child was expected simply "to receive, to accept" (Dewey, 1902, p. 276). In 1929, Alfred North Whitehead (1929), in The Aims of Education, also criticized an education that was built upon "inert ideas" (p. 13), maintaining that the key problem of education was that of "keeping knowledge alive" (p. 17), and calling for the eradication of the "fatal disconnection of subjects" (p. 18).

Still Dewey and Childs (1933) insisted that education had the responsibility for preparing individuals "to share . . ., instead of merely equipping them with an ability to make their private way in isolation and competition," and claimed that "the ability and desire to think collectively, to engage in social planning . . . is a requirement of good citizenship." In the late 1930s and early 1940s, Kurt Lewin stressed the significance of learners playing an active role in discovering knowledge for themselves and the powerful influence of the social environment of the learner in promoting change (Lewin & Grabbe, 1945). Between 1930 and 1935, the Russian psychologist Lev Vygotsky produced a series of essays that, following their translation into English (Vygotsky, 1978), strongly influenced educational thought worldwide by asserting that knowledge results not from a transmission process but from the internalization of social interactions. The reflections of Thomas Kuhn on "knowledge as a social artifact maintained by a community of peers" (Kuhn, 1962), of Michael Polanyi on "knowledge as action" (and knowing as distinct from knowledge) (Polanyi, 1966), and of Donald Schön on "reflection-in-action" (Schön, 1983) all contributed, among many others that would be too numerous to recall here, to strengthen the perception of the fundamental role of context in learning.

In the last decade or so, a number of very inspiring books that concentrate explicitly or implicitly on learning contexts have appeared, some of which will be mentioned later in this chapter (Brown & Duguid, 1991; Chaiklin & Lave, 1996; Cole, 1986; Forman, Minick & Stone, 1993; Lave & Wenger, 1991; Light & Butterworth, 1992; Nardi, 1996; Wenger, 1998).

Unfortunately, however, the mechanistic vision of learning as the "delivery of content" still dominates to a large extent the educational processes of the present day. So, one of the major concerns of this chapter, and of this book, is to make clear that beyond the delivery of content, we need to take systematically into account interaction and activity, the learning contexts, and the completely renewed social and cultural frameworks that our education is calling for and that technologies are now capable of offering. We do not deny that part of the future of learning and education is to be found in the production of content, that is, chunks of structured information that can be stored and delivered across networks. We argue, however, that a significant part of the future of learning and education—the most important part of it—is to be found on context, that is, on making learning happen within activity-rich, interaction-rich, and culturally rich social environments that never existed, that the intelligent use of technology is making possible, and where different paradigms apply.

In the next paragraph we will comment on the extension of this concern to the online world of virtual settings for learning. A longer paragraph will then follow, presenting a philosophical framework for understanding the essence of learning contexts. The implications of this framework will then be analyzed, namely in what regards the management of learning contexts, the duality between content and context, and the challenges of designing context. The chapter closes with some concluding remarks.

Virtual Settings

Conventional learning and education take place in tangible settings—such as classrooms, training rooms, or the workplace—where the social interaction that supports learning happens face-to-face. As learning extends from these tangible settings into the indefinite space of the Internet, the social interactions cease to happen face-to-face. They become "virtual," in the sense that their existence and development are not physically visible anymore but are inferred from mediated evidence. Those indefinite spaces where e-learning and Web-based learning happen are described as virtual settings. The difficulty with the organization and management of learning contexts in virtual settings is that, although they share their principles with tangible settings, they have significant differences of degree, for example, in the strongly mediated nature of the activities and social interactions that need to be developed and managed. The intensive use of technology as a mediator (besides the traditional mediation of language), the decisive importance of the social dimension, and the paradoxical absence of presence (when the social dimension is so critically important) make virtual settings much more sensitive to the interpretation we make of context. This is why the philosophical framework proposed here, although applicable to any kind of learning situation, face-to-face or online, is thought to be particularly useful for those concerned with the management of learning contexts in virtual settings.

Steps to a Philosophy of Context

When we try to grasp the essence of context, for example, in relation to learning, we find ourselves in the position of the blind men of the Indian parable, who attempted to make out what an elephant was by placing themselves around the animal and each one of them touching a different part. One, feeling the side, concluded that it was a wall; another, touching the tusk, claimed it was a spear; a third one, holding the trunk, declared it was a snake; a fourth one, patting a leg, argued it was a tree; still another, grasping the ear, maintained it was a fan; the last one, holding the tail, insisted it was a rope. None of them got the perception of the whole. Our wish, in this book, is to move some steps toward the understanding of learning context as a whole.

In his Philosophical Investigations, Ludwig Wittgenstein (1953) argued that to find out what a word means, one must have mastered the language game to which the word belongs; meaning does not lie in naming objects, but in use. For example, only people familiar with chess will be able to understand the meaning of the word "pawn." We face a similar challenge with the word "context." In an exploratory attempt to grasp its meaning, in the language game of this chapter, we will adopt a simplified model that relates the learner with content and context, in a learning event (cf. Figure 1). This offers a common ground where the word starts being used. The rest of the chapter, as well as the whole book, will hopefully lead, through further use of the word "context," to the construction of increased meaning. On the model, we will postulate three exploratory definitions:

- A learning event is a situation where an individual learns.
- Content is information that has been structured and encoded as text, multimedia materials, the spoken word of the teacher, or any other means.
- Context is the set of circumstances that are relevant for the learner to build her knowledge.

In this simplified model, the action of the teacher, if there is one, will be seen partly as content and partly as context, and the technological infrastructure, if there is one, will be seen as belonging to the context. A learning event can be of any length and

Figure 1. A simple model relating learner, content, and context in a learning event

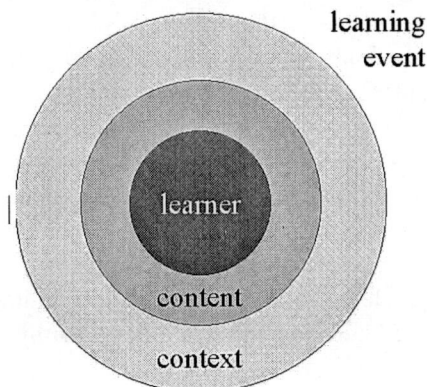

intensity, and may be intentional or nonintentional. A course, a lecture, the discussion of a case, and the instant insight sparked by a serendipitous incident will all be considered learning events. Understood as encoded information, content can be transferred and exchanged. The learner may learn in the absence of content just by interacting with context (which happens, informally, most of the time outside the school). It is important to note that in the small world represented by the model of Figure 1, the learner is engaged in activities involving content and context. Even when these activities are mechanistic, such as listening to a lecture or carrying out drill-and-practice, they are nevertheless activities. It is also important to note that this small world may be inhabited by other actors besides the learner, such as colleagues or partners, when the learning event takes place in a classroom or in a community of practice.

With context understood as the set of circumstances that are relevant in a learning event, a classroom, for instance, is a learning context. A Web site offering online courses is also a learning context. Within a classroom, a lecture, a laboratory assignment, a shared project, and the discussion of a case study all are learning contexts. All kinds of teaching and learning strategies correspond to learning contexts. Many of the most dynamic fields of current research in learning and education, such as computer-supported cooperative learning (CSCL), situated learning, or learning communities, are concerned with learning contexts. Hundreds of expressions currently used in education—such as project-based learning, problem-based learning, inquiry-based learning, action learning, situated learning, reflective learning, learning by doing, incidental learning, learning from mistakes, case studies, scenario building, interaction, community models, simulations, debates, directed dialogues, Socratic dialogues, question posing, panel discussions, and role playing—do pertain to the issues of learning contexts. The advantage of concentrating on context as a whole—the major motivation of this book—rather than on the multiplicity of its manifestations, currently studied by disparate research groups and communities, is that by doing so, it becomes possible to articulate the multitude of distinct concepts, theories, and practices into a single, coherent, and operational worldview.

The perception of context in learning and the relevance attached to it depend very much on the philosophical paradigm adopted. To simplify our reasoning, we will consider just the two categories of paradigms that are more commonly referred to in the literature: the positivist and the constructivist. In order to differentiate between the two, we will look into the ways in which they answer three key philosophical questions: the ontological, the epistemological, and the methodological (Guba & Lincoln, 1994). The ontological question inquires about what can be known. The epistemological question asks what is knowledge, or what knowledge we can get. The methodological question inquires about how we can build that knowledge. Another key philosophical question is often taken into account, the ethical question: what is the worth, or value, of the knowledge we build (Piaget, 1967, p. 6)? In spite of the relevance of this fourth question in other circumstances, we will leave it unaddressed here to keep this chapter within manageable proportions.

The Ontological Question

The positivist paradigm answers the ontological question with the realist hypothesis: there is a reality out there that is independent from our thoughts and beliefs about it. This reality, tangible or immaterial, holds a degree of stability that makes it potentially knowable and explainable by immutable laws, whatever its complexity. For instance, if I see a tree before me, it is because it has a real existence, independent of my imagination, and because the image I get from it is a faithful copy of the original tree. I am certain that the attributes this tree has today are more or less the same that it will have tomorrow, or that any change of attributes that may occur will be easily knowable and explainable. In summary, the realist hypothesis responds to the ontological question by saying that we can know all the external reality, visible or invisible, that surrounds us, is independent of us, and is driven by immutable laws.

The answer of the constructivist paradigm to the ontological question is given by the phenomenological hypothesis, which believes that things can only be known through their interactions and that our perception of the world, both in its tangible objects and abstract objects (like mathematical formulas), is built in, and by, our conscience (Hegel, 1979). For instance, a "circle" is not a "fact" existing in reality (no perfect circle exists), but it is not a product of our mind either. We build the notion of a circle from the round objects we see around us, and then we attribute to those objects the ideal form we have created from them.

As noted by LeMoigne (1999, p. 71), the phenomenological hypothesis has been insightfully expressed by Jean Piaget (1936) in The Construction of Reality in the Child: "intelligence begins neither with knowledge of the self nor of things as such but with knowledge of their interaction, and it is by orienting itself simultaneously toward the two poles of that interaction that intelligence organizes the world by organizing itself" (p. 311). In this sense, the act of knowing an object is inseparable from the act of knowing ourselves: we do not know the things themselves (as in the ontological view of positivism), but the interactions of those things with us and our context. Or, as put by Gaston Bachelard (1938), "Nothing comes of itself. Nothing is given. Everything is constructed" (p. 14). The phenomenological hypothesis expresses three corollaries about knowable reality (LeMoigne, 1999, pp. 73-74):

- The irreversibility of cognition. The concepts of action and inter-action lead to the concept of temporality. Temporality is irreversible, as metaphorically held by Heraclitus, the Greek philosopher: "You cannot step twice into the same river."

- The dialectics of cognition. It is through the interactions between organized and organizer that the knowledge of the phenomena is attained. Blaise Pascal, the 17th-century French philosopher, referred to "any thing being caused and causing, helped and helping, mediate and immediate" (Pascal, 1670).

- The recursivity of cognition. There is interdependence between the phenomenon we perceive and the knowledge we build about it, so that from the representation we get of the phenomenon we build an active representation that transforms that knowledge, producing a new representation, and so on, recursively. We can see this principle puzzlingly pictured in some of M. C. Escher's illustrations, such as "Drawing Hands" and "Three Spheres."

In summary, the phenomenological response to the ontological question is that what can be known is what is constructed by us from our perceptions of reality. It becomes known as we interact with it, which changes our own perceptions and our knowledge, so that, as we keep cointeracting, we see it in new perspectives, in a recursive and irreversible process that hopefully leads us to increased knowledge.

The Epistemological Question

We will now analyze the answers of both paradigms to the epistemological question "What is knowledge? What knowledge can we get?" Positivism responds to this question with the deterministic hypothesis, which claims that all things happen through antecedent causes: "Everything that happens is fully determined by what has gone before it: every event has antecedent causes which were sufficient to ensure its occurrence" (Mautner, 2000). As put by Descartes (1961) in the Discourse on Method, all realities, even the most complex, can be decomposed in "long chains of reasons, all simple and easy," so that, provided "one always kept to the order necessary to deduce one thing from another, there would not be anything so far distant that one could not finally reach it, nor so hidden that one could not discover it" (p. 66). The belief in the deterministic hypothesis expresses not only the possibility of describing a reality independent of the subject (as postulated by the realist hypothesis), but also the possibility of explaining it in a unique and permanent way.

The clarification of the deterministic hypothesis calls for the elucidation of the nature of causes. Aristotle proposed, in Physics 2.3 (350 BCE), that we discriminate between four kinds of causes: material causes, the materials out of which things are made (such as the bronze in which a statue was cast); formal causes, the statements of essence (such as the sketches that led to the statue); efficient causes, the agents or forces that produced the changes (such as the sculptor who made the statue); and final causes, or purposes for which things exist (such as the intent of representing justice through the statue made). The positivist paradigm takes efficient causes as the only ones capable of producing change and, hence, of explaining reality. From a positivist point of view, final causes are irrelevant. In summary, the positivist answer to the epistemological question is that knowledge is what we can learn by exploring the causes of the problems we face; the only knowledge we can get is that resulting from our inquiries into the efficient causes of the problems we face.

Constructivism responds to the epistemological question with the teleological hypothesis, claiming that knowledge is what gets us somewhere and that knowledge is constructed with an aim. This is a natural consequence of the phenomenological response to the ontological question, which attaches a key role to the subject in the construction of knowledge. As remarked by LeMoigne (1999, p. 77), Heinz von Foerster, one of the founders of Cybernetics, once observed that the question "why?" could have two completely distinct kinds of answer: "because" and "in order to," noting that the intelligence of a cognitive being is often better activated by the second answer. As stressed by LeMoigne, "To know something in terms of plausible aims is at least as reasonable as to know it in terms of probable cause, especially if we cannot grant that a phenomenon has a clear cause" (p. 77).

The Methodological Question

The last question to be addressed is the methodological question, "How can we build knowledge?" As explained by LeMoigne (1999, pp. 24-32), positivism responds to the methodological question with two principles: the principle of analytical modeling and the principle of sufficient reason. The principle of analytical modeling, first formulated by Descartes as the second precept of his Discourse on Method, states that to explain any reality (following the epistemological hypothesis of determinism) we must "divide each difficulty . . . into as many parts as possible and necessary to resolve it better" (Descartes, 1961). The principle of sufficient reason, formulated by Leibnitz, upholds that there is no effect without a cause or no change without a reason for change.

The response of constructivism to the methodological question also comes as two hypotheses, both recognizing (in agreement with the teleological hypothesis) that we need knowledge not just to understand but also to build the reality we experience: the principle of complexity and the principle of intelligent action. The principle of complexity acknowledges the need to recognize reality as complex systems in a constant state of flux, embodying characteristics of both stability and change, where the whole is more than the sum of the parts (the whole hardly knowable without knowing the parts, and vice versa), where chaos lives coupled with order, and where parts interact with each other in the shared construction of reality, with an emergent and largely unpredictable character that is supported, to some extent, by processes of self-organization and co-creation. This principle was already contained, to some extent, in Blaise Pascal's words quoted earlier, which can now be quoted in full: "The whole is more than the sum of the parts. . . . Any thing being caused and causing, helped and helping, mediate and immediate and all (things) being maintaining each other through a natural and insensitive link, which binds the most faraway and the most different, I take for impossible to know the parts without knowing the whole as to know the whole without knowing the parts" (Pascal, 1670). In fact, the notion of complexity can be traced back to as early as the year 500 BC, when Heraclitus suggested that the secrets of the universe were to be found in hidden tensions and connections that simultaneously created patterns of unity and change (Morgan, 1986). It was only in our times, however, that researchers started systematically devoting their inquiries to complexity: Bateson's (1972) ecological view of systems evolving with self-generated changes in identity, David Bohm's (1980) concepts of implicate and explicate order, Maturana and Varela's (1980) notion of autopoiesis and circular chains of interaction, Prigogine's (1984) dissipative structures, and Edgard Morin's (1990) change of paradigmatical value induced by open systems, to name but just a few.

The principle of intelligent action, quoted by LeMoigne as being contained in Dewey's definition of "intelligent action" (Dewey, 1933) establishes that human reason can, in a reproducing way, elaborate and transform intelligible representations of the phenomena of dissonance to which it is confronted, creating responses in the form of "intelligent actions" adapted to reduce these dissonances (LeMoigne, 1999, p. 83). This principle finds one of its more suggestive expressions in the work of Donald Schön (1983) on "reflective action" and "reflection-in-action." In reflective action, which is typical of the work of practitioners, work progresses through a trajectory of trial and error, reformulating problems as they are solved, in a permanent dialogue between the problem solver and the problematic situation being solved, which is influenced by and influences the intervention. Action research, as a mode of inquiry, is also solidly grounded on the principle of intelligent action.

To facilitate the ensuing discussion of how the worldviews of positivism and constructivism affect the perception of context, we summarize them in Table 1.

Table 1. A table comparing positivism and constructivism in light of three key philosophical questions

QUESTIONS	ANSWERS	
	positivism	constructivism
ontological question what can be known?	realist hypothesis	phenomenological hypothesis
epistemological question what is knowledge?	deterministic hypothesis	teleological hypothesis
methodological question how can we build that knowledge?	principle of analytical modeling	principle of complexity
	principle of sufficient reason	principle of intelligent action

Two Visions for Context

From the philosophical considerations noted earlier in this chapter and recalling the simplified model of Figure 1, we may now attempt to typify the interpretations of context that make more sense for each paradigm. We do not attach any value judgments to them, in the sense of advocating that one is "better" than the other. Although we feel much more comfortable with the meaning we extract from the constructivist paradigm, we reckon that, in the language game that leads to increased meaning, the reader may feel happier with one or the other, or may even prefer to switch between them until he or she deems that a satisfactory meaning is being achieved. Also, the degree of complexity of the learning event at hand may dictate that we choose one or the other paradigm. Generally, simpler and more mechanistic contexts are easily handled within the positivist view, whereas socially more complex contexts can hardly be dealt with outside a constructivist perspective.

Within the positivist paradigm, context is viewed as occurring in a realist world, and so it is external and clearly independent of the learner and the activities in which the learner is engaged. In this sense, context is understood as the environment where the activities take place, the word "environment" being interpreted in the purity of its etymological origin (from the French environnement, meaning what is "around"). Thus, for instance, if the learner is learning in a classroom, the context may be seen as the room, with its desks and other equipment, the learner's colleagues, and the teacher and the rules that determine how activities must progress in class, which are all viewed as external and surrounding the activities of the learner.

For the positivist worldview, context is also delimited, in the sense that we feel capable of recognizing where it begins and where it ends. The school where the classroom is situated, the community where the school is located, the country, and even the part of the world (Central Africa is, no doubt, a context different from the Western Europe) may be seen as successive layers of context surrounding the activities of the learner. Michael Cole noted that this concentric description of contexts stressed the notion of context as "that which surrounds" (Cole, 1986, p. 133).

The positivist paradigm also implies, from its realist and deterministic hypotheses, and from its principle of sufficient reason, that context can be seen as stable and driven by immutable laws. We can predict its evolution over time and space, even if it changes. This means that a positivist context is stable and predictable and that its behavior can be characterized in advance. As an example, when developing content for a given course, we take context into account beforehand in the elaboration of our materials, and we then forget about it, trusting that its behavior will always be as expected. After the course has been planed and materials developed, context becomes of little relevance. The role of colleagues and classroom equipment (such as computers and Internet connections), for example, are seen as predictable, previously planned, and properly taken into account, so that content can remain stable and be explored more or less independently from context.

The principles of analytical modeling and of sufficient reason also reinforce the already mentioned independence between the activities of the learner and context. Activities occur within the context, but independent of it and following a trajectory that has been planned. Learners participating, for instance, in the discussion of a case study, are seen as carrying out their discussion using some content (the text of the case study and the required reading material) within a fixed context: the classroom and the teacher moderating the discussion.

Turning now to the constructivist paradigm, we notice that context cannot be located and delimited. Following the phenomenological hypothesis, context is only perceived through its interactions with the learner. In fact, these interactions organize the context, as it is perceived by the learner, as much as they organize the learner's experience. To a large extent, context is the interactions. Context is what the learner feels as the context of the learning experience. Simone de Beauvoir, the French philosopher, writer, and social essayist, reminds us that even the Bible expresses this kind of thinking. When asked "Who is my neighbor?" Jesus did not respond with a definition, but with a parable, the parable of the Good Samaritan. What the parable says, in essence, is that it is we who decide who our neighbors are. Even if they are our enemies, as was the case in the parable, if we decide that they are our neighbors, then they will become our neighbors. As she put it, "We are not the neighbor of anyone, we make someone our neighbor by making ourselves his/her neighbor through an act" (Beauvoir, 1944, p. 245).

The notion of context as environment does not make any sense in a constructivist world, and this is why the word "context" has been chosen. Indeed, "context" comes from the Latin origin contexere, "to weave together." In the case of learning, this stresses that context is seen as being woven together with the act of learning, rather than around it, as conveyed by the word "environment." The metaphor of weaving together is beautifully illustrated in the "analogy of a rope" proposed for context by Roy Birdwhistell and described by McDermott (1993, p. 274). A rope is made up of individual fibers, which are discontinuous. When the fibers are twisted together, they make up threads, and the threads twisted together make up the rope. The rope is not "around" the fibers. The rope is the fibers and the relationships that hold them together. We cannot remove all the fibers from the rope and say, "Here are the fibers; here is the rope!" The discontinuous fibers give sense to the rope and the rope gives sense to the fibers. They generate each other, just as learning activities and their context.

In the constructivist worldview, context is not stable but permanently changing. It changes because it is a network of interactions that happen, in spite of us, under the influence of other actors in the context, and it changes as a result of the interactions we maintain with it. The way in which we perceive it in its changeability is the way in which it helps building our learning experience. Thus, context is dependent on the activities of the learner. Activities do not occur inside the context, as was the case for the positivist paradigm; activities are part of the context. From the constructivist perspective, the discussion of a case study does not occur inside a context; the discussion of a case study is part of the context, and an essential one, for that matter, since it helps in creating a set of circumstances that are relevant for the learner to learn what had been planned.

A constructivist context can be predicted and characterized in advance only to some extent. The more open-ended or socially complex the activity is, the less we can predict its development. This is very suggestively expressed by Etienne Wenger in his call for a balance between the designed and the emergent in communities of practice—a balance between the amount of time allocated to planned learning and the time given to spontaneous learner activity, which recognizes that it is important to plan in advance the unfolding of the learning activities but that excess planning may kill any opportunities for novelty in the learning process (Wenger, 1998, pp. 232-233).

The concept of concentric contexts does not make much sense in the constructivist paradigm either. As stated in the simplified definition proposed for the model of Figure 1, context is what is relevant for the learner to build his or her knowledge, and that may change from moment to moment. This is why we have argued earlier that context is what the learner feels as the context of his or her learning experience. By extension, when a designer is designing a learning context, we may say that the context is what the designer feels to be relevant for the learning experience of the learner.

Implications for Learning

Managing Learning

The logic of managing learning also depends very much on the paradigm from which learning is approached. The determinism of the positivist worldview demands that management and control be clearly located. It may be located on the teacher (in a conventional teacher-centered classroom), on the learner (if a learner-centered approach is being followed), or on programs and materials establishing successive steps and control points for the learner's progress, but it is always clearly located in an unquestionable vision of command and control. Control may be delegated and moved around, but it will always be clearly located.

In the constructivist world, where to learn is to construct one's own knowledge, "managing learning" can only be understood as a metaphor. No one can manage the learning of someone else. What one can do is manage the learning contexts for someone else to learn. As stated earlier, a constructivist context can only be partially predicted and characterized. So, it cannot be fully managed according to plan. Managing context, in a constructivist world, is an adaptive exercise. As Jim Highsmith put it, "While battlefield commanders plan extensively, they realize that plans are just a beginning. . . . Battlefield commanders succeed by defeating the enemy, not conforming to a plan. . . . I cannot imagine a battlefield commander saying, 'We lost the battle, but by golly, we were successful because we followed our plan to the letter' "(Highsmith, 2002). Managing learning in a constructivist world is, thus, a mixed approach of prescription and emergence: prescription, to provide directions that create a vision, clarify aims, and maintain coherence, relevance, and appeal; emergence, to leave room for visionary initiatives and the emergence of creative trajectories, such as when they result from collective learning and shared culture building.

An example, from the field of group facilitation, which is of particular relevance when managing learning in communities of learners, may help in clarifying our view. The well-known concept of "stages of group development" proposed by Tuckmann and Jensen (1965), which, in its original formulation, discriminated between four stages of group development—forming, storming, norming, and performing—recognizes that the context of a group goes through four quite different stages (one might say, four different contexts). Although those stages are, in essence, very different, the transitions between them are sometimes so fuzzy that only experienced moderators succeed in noticing that they are happening. It becomes clear that in this case we can plan for each stage and, maybe, for the transitions, but, since the pace at which the stages occur is hardly predictable, there is still a lot of management and improvisation to do. In fact, if the moderator is not experienced enough, the group may cease to exist when the second stage is reached. We may go to some length in managing the process if, as proposed by Blanchard, Carew, and Parisi-Carew (1993), we resort to "Situational Leadership"®, a team management approach comprising four phases—directing, coaching, supporting, and delegating—specifically intended to feed group development through Tuckman's four stages. This only confirms, however, the need to adjust management to the evolution of context.

The fuzziness of the transition between phases points to another aspect of the management of constructivist contexts that seems worthwhile mentioning here: the partial replacement of the "process view" of learning contexts, strongly imbued with deterministic connotations, by a "pattern view", more adjusted to a vision inspired by the principle of complexity. This suggests that it makes sense to envisage the management of complex learning contexts as being, in some measure, the management of patterns of context.

Content vs. Context

If we concentrate on the two outer layers of the model of Figure 1, we are left with content and context. In the positivist perspective, and in agreement with the principle of analytical modeling, these are two completely distinct entities satisfying the definitions given earlier in the chapter. In the constructivist perspective, however, the boundary between the two becomes fuzzy. In fact, part of the content may

Figure 2. The duality between content and context

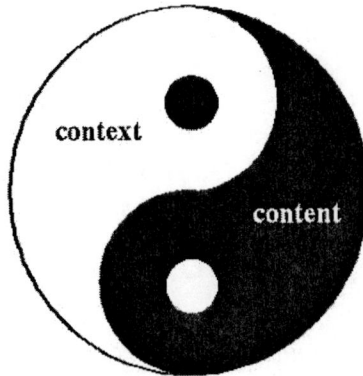

be consigned to the status of context, and vice versa. An inspiring metaphor for this process of cogeneration is the yin–yang duality, or rotational symmetry, of the old Chinese Book of Changes, representing the archetypal opposites that guide change (cf. Figure 2).

This means, in our case, that context holds in itself the seed of content and content holds in itself the seed of context, so that, like brightness and darkness, or day and night, one generates the other and one may not exist without the other. To illustrate this notion with a simple example, we may think of a community of learners, scattered across the country, following an online course that supports collaboration and gives them access to a large digital library. During the course, they have to carry out various individual and collective activities assigned to them. The context, in this example, is, for each learner, a complex set (or "network," as we will call it later) of items, activities, and people, such as the collaboration mechanisms of the platform (e-mail and mail lists, and Weblog, whiteboard, and mind-map editors), the digital library (its multimedia materials, books, journals, and papers, in addition to its access protocols), the activities assigned to the learners, the other learners in the community (with whom intense collaboration is maintained), the protocols and netiquette supporting the collaboration, and the coordinator and e-moderators of the course. The content is, for each learner, the materials specifically produced to support the course, in addition to any materials the learner decides to download from the library, to work on. As the learners may choose from the library any materials they wish, this means that what is seen as content by one learner may be seen as context by another. Also, what is seen as content by one leaner will very likely become context when he or she puts it away after use and may become content again if the learner decides to use it again.

It may be easier to understand, now, while evoking the wholeness imparted by the duality of content and context, the sense of mutilation of reality felt by constructivist educators and researchers when they watch learning and e-learning being simplistically described, by some of their positivist colleagues, as the mere "transfer" of "content" in the full ignorance of context.

Designing Context

We did not explore, up to now, the implications of the teleological hypothesis. It is, however, a foundational hypothesis of the constructivist worldview, as we may realize by noticing that the word "constructivism" has the same root as "construction" or "constructing." It may be helpful at this stage to point out briefly the main difference between the natural sciences and what Herbert Simon (1969) called "the Sciences of the Artificial." The natural sciences are, in a few words, the sciences that explain the world. The sciences of the artificial are, conversely, the sciences of what is made by human beings.

The sciences of the artificial are closely related to what Giambattista Vico (1993) called, in the 17th and 18th centuries, the sciences of ingenium, or of the human genius. They are also close to the epistemological traces we can extract from Leonardo da Vinci's Notebooks (1998), written in the 15th and 16th centuries by the great master of disegno (or design) of all times. If we pay closer attention to the epistemology of natural sciences and of the sciences of the artificial, as they have been practiced in the last hundred years, we notice that the former (e.g. physics) have been following a deterministic and clearly positivist perspective, resting upon the inquiry into efficient causes. The latter (e.g., engineering), on the contrary, and in spite of their traditional dependence on the former, have taken a much more teleological and constructivist approach. Donald Schön (1983), in The Reflective Practitioner, even called for an "epistemology of practice" or "epistemology of reflection-in-action" to be ascribed to them. They are much more concerned with the final causes, and their major concern is not to explain (although they can explain) but to build. They are eminently teleological.

Thus, when taking a constructivist approach to learning contexts, it makes sense if we take a teleological mind-set. In this case, our answer to the question "Why a learning context?" will not start with "because," followed by an analytical explanation of what we expect to get from context, so that the learners can learn; it will start with "in order to," followed by an explanation of the context that we must design and build for the learners to learn better. Learning and education is not just about explaining how people learn (in the explanatory attitude of the natural sciences), but also about use of the human genius (in the teleological attitude of the sciences of the artificial) to design and build systems that make possible for people to learn what they want and need to learn.

This takes us to the issue of designing learning contexts. Of course, to design for learning is by no means an exclusive concern of constructivist educationalists. "Instructional design" or the "design of instruction" has been around for many years, and a considerable part of it (although not all of it) rests upon behaviorist, mechanist, and positivist visions of learning that ignore or simplify context—disregarding its absolutely unavoidable social dimension. The genuine constructivist approaches, on the contrary, take context in all its complexity, exploring the social and cultural dimensions in depth.

Part of the research in this direction concentrated on communities of practice situated in social and organizational contexts (Brown & Duguid, 1991; Lave & Wenger, 1991; Wenger, 1998). Another part of research has been inspired by concerns with social cognition motivated by the resurgence of interest in the work of Lev Vygotsky (1978) and by the recognition of the inextricable link between contextual constraints and the acquisition of knowledge, such as with social constraints combining with physical contexts (Light & Butterworth, 1992). On an adjacent key, work on the social and cultural foundations of the developmental process, as resulting from the application, extension, and progress of the work of the Soviet sociohistorical school of Lev Vygotsky, Alexei Leont'ev, Alexander Luria and their colleagues has been explored by Forman et al. (1993). In 1996, three very influential books were published, building partly on the foundations of the former but exploring additional threads, including the utilization of activity theory: one by Michael Cole (1986), who proposes a new concept of cultural psychology, and two edited, respectively, by Chaiklin and Lave (1996) and Nardi (1996).

In order to avoid going over the concepts and principles so powerfully formulated by these authors, we have opted for devoting some of the remaining lines of this chapter to two less explored threads in the search of sound approaches for the design and management of learning contexts: actor-network theory and design patterns.

Actor-network theory (ANT) is a social theory widely used as an intellectual framework to help in understanding networks of interests where individual actors form alliances, mobilize other actors, and resort to artifacts to reinforce their alliances and satisfy their interests (Callon, 1986; Callon & Latour, 1981; Law, 1992). In this theory, an actor is any element, human or nonhuman, that intervenes in the network, creating relationships of mutual dependence with other actors and translating its wishes in appropriate languages. An actor-network is a heterogeneous network of aligned interests that interconnects the various (human and nonhuman) actors. In the example given earlier, of a community of learners following an online course that supports collaboration and gives them access to a digital library, the actor-network includes all the items and people, such as the collaboration mechanisms of the platform they use (e-mail and mail lists, in addition to Weblog, whiteboard, and mind-map editors), the digital library (and its multimedia materials, books, journals, and papers and its access protocols), the codes of behavior and netiquette supporting the collaboration, all kinds of content, all the learners in the community, and the coordinator and e-moderators of the course.

Two important concepts of actor-network theory are those of translation and inscription. Translation is a process of reinterpretation, representation, or appropriation of interests by an actor, so that they can be followed by the other actors in the network (Aanested & Hanseth, 2000). In order to make translation possible, a medium or "material" is needed where the translation is inscribed (Callon, 1991, p. 143). Inscription is the way in which patterns of use are incorporated in technical artifacts (Monteiro, 2000). In the given example, the procedures for online collaboration may be translated into some form of netiquette, which is, in turn, inscribed in one of the top Web pages of the course. The concept of inscription does not necessarily imply deterministic consequences, since there is no assurance that the patterns incorporated in the artifact are interpreted as desired and predicted, and followed by the other actors (Monteiro, 2000).

In the perspective of actor-network theory (Monteiro, 2000), the design of a learning context is a process of translation. The designers start by translating the learning objectives into a number of requirements. The requirements are then translated into a combination of activities and materials that make up the context. The design process attaches to the various actors (the learners, the teachers, the protocols, the content) specific roles that they are expected to play during the learning process. In other words, the designers perform the inscription, into the learning context, of a program of action that is supposed to be fulfilled by the actors. Designs are, of course, based on scenarios imagined by their authors. In many cases, they fail to anticipate what will happen in reality. The actors may then reject the program of action and refuse to play their roles, and they may even use the context to develop an antiprogram of action. A classical example is that of computer-based educational applications that include a leaner mode and a teacher mode, which are often found to be much more challenging and pedagogically successful when the learners use them in the teacher mode.

With design understood as a process of translation, it will be helpful to know how to carry out this process. A very lively description of how to go about this is given by Michel Callon (1986) in a paper where he distinguishes between four phases in the process: problematization, interessement, enrolment, and mobilization. In problematization, the focal actor (the designer is also an actor in the network) defines, for the other actors, identities and interests consistent with his or her own and creates a context that forces their acceptance. This context is called an obligatory passage point. In the example of the community of learners following an online course, a regular online meeting that everyone must attend or the organization of a learning portfolio that everyone must build are examples of obligatory passage points. Interessement is the set of activities and processes that attempt to induce the actors into accepting the roles that have been assigned to them by the focal actor. Enrolment is the acceptance, by part of the actors, of the commitment to carry out a set of tasks, recognizing the interests that have been assigned to them by the focal actor. Finally, mobilization is the generalization of adherence of all the other actors to the commitment to carry out their tasks, so that that their acting becomes generalized and predictable and is in agreement with the intents of the focal actor.

From this necessarily very concise introduction of actor-network theory, it is hoped that the interested reader may now, with a deeper incursion into the theory, consider interpreting, designing, and managing learning contexts as actor-networks. Another approach to the interpretation of contexts, which by no means contradicts the previous one, is likely to be found in the concept of design "patterns" exposed by Christopher Alexander (1979) in his book The Timeless Way of Building. Described as an original approach to the theory and application of architecture, this book offers, however, a most inspiring model for the development of any complex sociotechnical system. One of its most well known consequences outside the field of architecture is the concept of design patterns in software engineering. The philosophy of The Timeless Way supports the view that buildings and towns should grow naturally, rather than be strictly planned, and that patterns, or common features and relationships abstracted from previous successful solutions, should be allowed to gain life. Of course, the concepts of buildings and towns can be understood as mere metaphors and the whole philosophy be translated into the reality of designing learning contexts.

To illustrate the concept of pattern with an example from the domain of architecture, we may notice that a window is not, by itself, beautiful or ugly. A window that looks beautiful in a catalog may turn out to be an ugly window when combined with a façade that does not match it, a wall angle that does not favor it, or a beam of sunlight that it is unable to catch. A window is beautiful when it integrates in harmony the reality to which it belongs, which becomes, as a whole, much more beautiful, thanks to that window. The same happens with learners, and educators, and classrooms, and online virtual settings. None of them is anything without the others, and the beauty is in the harmony of the whole, the beauty is context!

Conclusion

This chapter has proposed a model for the description of learning events and a philosophical framework for the clarification of the nature of learning contexts. Both the model and the framework have been made very simple, so as to facilitate the clarification, in the presence of real-world learning situations, of the perspective the reader is, conscientiously or unconscientiously, taking. The model describes a learning event as involving the learner at the core, interacting with content and context. The philosophical framework differentiates between the positivist and constructivist paradigms, and has been formulated as three questions to which each paradigm responds with four principles. The three questions and eight principles are then summarized on a table that can be easily recalled by the reader wishing to understand, in almost any situation, on which side of the fence he or she is standing. Some of the implications of the framework are then illustrated, namely in what regards the management of learning contexts, the dialectics between content and context, and the challenges of designing learning contexts. These three implications are not, by any means, comprehensive, so that the reader is left with an intellectual tool that can be used extensively in the future in exploring a multitude of other implications relating to the nature and role of learning contexts, as well as their design, management, and exploration.

References

Aanested, M., & Hanseth, O. (2000). Implementing open network technologies in complex practices: A case from telemedicine. In R. Baskerville, J. Stage, & J. I. DeGross (Eds.), *Organizational and social perspectives on information technology* (pp. 355-369). New York: Springer.

Alexander, C. (1979). *The timeless way of building*. Oxford: Oxford University Press.

Bachelard, G. (1938). *La Formation de l' Esprit Scientifique*. Paris: Presses Universitaires de France.

Bateson, G. (1972). *Steps to an ecology of mind*. New York: Ballantine Books.

Beauvoir, S. (1944). *Pour une Morale de l'Ambiguïté suivi de Pyrrhus et Cinéas*. Paris: Gallimard.

Blanchard, K., Carew, D., & Parisi-Carew, E. (1993). *The one minute manager builds high performing teams*. London: Harper Collins.

Bohm, D. (1980). *Wholeness and the implicate order*. London: Routledge.

Brown, J., & Duguid, P. (1991). Organizational learning and communities of practice: Toward a unified view of working, learning, and innovation. *Organizational Science, 2*(1), 40-57.

Callon, M. (1986). Some elements of a sociology of translation: Domestication of the scallops and the fishermen. In J. Law (Ed.), *Power, action and belief: A new sociology of knowledge* (pp. 197-225). London: Routledge.

Callon, M. (1991). Techno-economic network and irreversibility. In J. Law (Ed.), *A sociology of monsters. Essays on power, technology and domination* (pp. 132-164). London: Routledge.

Callon, M., & Latour, B. (1981). Unscrewing the big Leviathan: How actors macro-structure reality and how sociologists help them to do so. In K. D. Knorr-Cetina & A.V. Cicourel (Eds.), *Advances in social theory and methodology: Towards an integration of micro and macro-sociologies* (pp. 277-303). London: Routledge.

Chaiklin, S., & Lave, J. (Eds.). (1996). *Understanding practice: Perspectives on activity and context*. Cambridge: Cambridge University Press.

Cole, M. (1986). *Culture psychology: A once and future discipline*. Cambridge, MA: Belknap Press of Harvard University Press.

Da Vinci, L. (1998). *The notebooks of Leonardo da Vinci*. In I. A. Richter (Ed.), Oxford: Oxford University Press.

Descartes, R. (1961). *Discours de la Méthode* (avec introduction et notes par Etienne Gilson). Paris: Librarie Philosophique J. Vrin.

Dewey, J. (1899). The school and society. In J. A. Boydston (Ed.), *Middle Works of John Dewey* (Vol. 1, pp. 1-109). Carbondale, IL: Southern Illinois University Press.

Dewey, J. (1902). The child and the curriculum. In J. A. Boydston (Ed.), *Middle Works of John Dewey* (Vol. 2, pp. 271-291). Carbondale, IL: Southern Illinois University Press.

Dewey, J. (1933). *How we think: A restatement of the relation of reflective thinking to the educational process.* Boston: D.C. Heath.

Dewey, J., & Childs, J. (1933). The socio-economic situation and education. In W. Kilpatrick (Ed.), *The educational frontier.* New York: Appleton-Century.

Forman, E. A., Minick, N., & Stone, C. A. (1993). *Contexts for learning: Sociocultural dynamics in children's development.* New York: Oxford University Press.

Guba, E. G., & Lincoln, Y. S. (1994). Competing paradigms in qualitative research. In K. D. Denzin & Y. S. Lincoln (Eds.), *Handbook of qualitative research.* Thousand Oaks, CA: Sage.

Hegel, G. W. F. (1979). *The phenomenology of spirit* (A. V. Miller, Trans.). Oxford: Oxford University Press. (Original work published 1807.)

Highsmith, J. (2002, October). What is agile software development? *CrossTalk, 15*(10), 4-9.

Kuhn, T. (1962). *The structure of scientific revolutions.* Chicago: University of Chicago Press.

Lave, J., & Wenger, E. (1991). *Situated learning. Legitimate peripheral participation.* Cambridge, MA: University of Cambridge Press.

Law, J. (1992). Notes on the theory of the actor-network: Ordering, strategy and heterogeneity. *Systems Practice, 5,* 379-393.

LeMoigne, J.-L.. (1999). *Les Épistémologies Constructivistes* (2nd ed.). Paris: Presses Universitaires de France.

Lewin, K., & Grabbe, P. (1945). Conduct, knowledge, and acceptance of new values. *Journal of Social Issues, 1*(3), 53-66.

Light, P., & Butterworth, G. (Eds.).(1992). *Context and cognition: Ways of learning and knowing.* Hillsdale, NJ: Lawrence Erlbaum.

Maturana, H., & Varela, F. (1980). *Autopoiesis and cognition: The realization of the living.* London: Reidel.

Mautner, T. (2000). *The Penguin dictionary of philosophy.* London: Penguin.

McDermott, R. (1993). The acquisition of a child by a learning disability. In S. Chaiklin, & J. Lave (Eds.), *Understanding practice: Perspectives on activity and context* (pp. 269-305). New York: Cambridge University Press.

Monteiro, E. (2000). Actor-network theory. In C. Ciborra (Ed.), *From control to drift: The dynamics of corporate information infrastructures.* Oxford: Oxford University Press.

Morgan, G. (1986). *Images of organization.* London: Sage.

Morin, E. (1990). *Introduction à la pensée complexe.* Paris: ESF.

Nardi, B. A. (Ed.). (1996). *Context and consciousness: Activity theory and human–computer interaction.* Cambridge: MIT Press.

Pascal, B. (1670). *Pensées.* Paris: Arthème Fayard et Cie.

Piaget, J. (1936). *La construction du réel chez l'enfant.* Neuchâtel: Delachaux et Niestlé.

Piaget, J. (1967). Logique et connaissance scietifique. In *Encyclopédie de la Pléiade.* Paris: Pléiade/Gallimard.

Polanyi, M. (1966). *The tacit dimension.* Gloucester, MA: Peter Smith.

Prigogine, I. (1984). *Order out of chaos.* New York: Random House.

Schön, D. (1983). *The reflective practitioner: How professionals think in action.* New York: Basic Books.

Simon, H. A. (1969). *The sciences of the artificial.* Cambridge, MA: MIT Press.

Tuckman, B. W., & Jensen, M. A. (1965). Developmental sequence in small groups. *Psychological Bulletin, 63*(6), 384-399.

Vico, G. (1993). *On humanistic education* (Six inaugural orations, 1699-1707). Ithaca, NY: Cornell University Press.

Vygotsky, L. S. (1978). *Mind in society: The development of higher psychological processes.* Cambridge, MA: Harvard University Press.

Wenger, E. (1998). *Communities of practice: Learning, meaning and identity.* New York: Cambridge University Press.

Whitehead, A. N. (1929). *The aims of education.* London: William & Norgate.

Wittgenstein, L. (1953). *Philosophical investigations* (G. E. M. Ascombe, Trans.). New York: Macmillan.

SECTION I

CONCEPTS

Chapter II

Virtual Settings:
E-Learning as Creating Context

Philip Duchastel, Information Design Atelier, Canada

Markus Molz, Diversity Dynamics Development Consultancy, Germany

Abstract

A fourfold model of the main contextual factors to be taken into account in learning is presented, with the view to examining how they interrelate and how they impinge on learning. We further consider the traditionally central factor of information (content) to help us see how it should be positioned within the more open context of e-learning. It is the advent of e-learning, and technology more generally, that is enabling a shift in the interaction, away from the delivery of information to access to information and away from interaction limited to the classroom setting to various virtual communities. The point of the shift is to reengage the learner in more personalized learning that can be more interesting and meaningful. It thus overcomes the receptive learner stance encouraged by the impersonal delivery of information and encourages instead an active interactive stance in which the learner accesses information as per the current learning needs.

Introduction

"Context principle (C): Context is relevant for learning and the construction of meaning. Therefore, context must be taken into explicit consideration when planning instruction. Most designers accept some version of the Context Principle either explicitly or tacitly. . . . Differences involve what might be considered a relevant context" (Spector, 2000a, p. 523).

It is indeed a foundational claim of instructional design that context influences learning. After all, Gagné's theory of learning and the design principles derived from it (see Driscoll, 2000) are explicitly based on a set of conditions of learning that represent internal and external factors impinging on learning. It is by tweaking these conditions of learning that one fashions a learning environment to optimize learning.

And yet, contextual factors generally play second fiddle in the fashioning of learning environments, giving pride of place to general instructional procedures and to content, that is, the knowledge that is to be learned. This reductionist tendency has been labeled "context stripping" (Richey & Tessmer, 1995).

This is certainly due to the impetus of positivistic science to look for general laws. But we should not forget that content factors are indeed important in their own right, as forcefully pointed out by Gagné in emphasizing the hierarchical nature of content mastery, whereby all prerequisites must first be mastered before attacking a more advanced skill.

Likewise, another leading theorist of the time, David Ausubel, also built a theory of learning around contextual factors that were knowledge based. He emphasized the importance of the learner having the knowledge context of what was to be learned for maximum benefit to be derived from the learning (Ausubel, 1963).

It is quite clear that factors related to how the learning content is structured and presented for learning favor or impede learning depending on how they are taken into account (Duchastel, 2003). This is what today has become the learning objects issue to be juggled with developing learning architectures (Ip & Morrison, 2001).

But what about the factors included in the educational setting? These are indeed given less attention in most circumstances. "What is more amazing than the wealth of educational resources that we have produced and accumulated is how far we have not come in improving learning and instruction" (Spector, 2000b). This harsh conclusion of an acknowledged expert in the field of instructional design and evaluation lets us ask the question how important the neglected physical, psychological, social, and organizational context factors are in sustaining learning in the 21st century? That is what will be considered here.

We will present a basic model of the main contextual factors to be taken into account, with the view to examining how they interrelate and how they impinge on learning. We will consider once again the central factor of information (content) to help us see how it should be positioned within the general ensemble. We will discuss design issues and work toward a paradigm of contextual design for learning. And we will conclude with some open high-level issues that remain challenges for us in the field and that must be addressed in moving toward a well-balanced learning architecture as we engage in design for e-learning environments.

The Multiple Contexts of Learning

If we attempt to analyze the contexts of learning, we come to partition contextual factors in a number of realms that are generally present in any instructional situation, even if often not explicitly acknowledged.

Learning in the most basic sense of the term results from the disequilibrating and reequilibrating interaction between what an individual (the learner) experiences as his or her inner world of feelings, thoughts, and intentions on the one hand and information from the immediate physical environment or various mediated symbolic forms on the other. In order to be called learning, "such changes should persist over time and across a variety of situations" (Learning Principle; Spector, 2000a, p. 523).

Behaviorists have been stressing the influence of the environment and treating the inner world as a black box. Cognitivists, however, are stipulating mental structures and their innate predispositions and developmental potential, which can be triggered but not changed by the environment. Evidently both parts are playing a major role in learning.

The sociohistorical turn initiated by Vygotsky pointed out, finally, that individuals are always using one or another kind of language as a tool for participating in the culture of their respective communities. Communities are using and producing objective artifacts and institutional structures, which in their turn enable and constrain their further development.

Learning and cognition are always situated in one or another kind of culturally organized setting. Sociocultural sectors, such as education, business, mass media, civil society, or research and research disciplines, may be more or less intertwined, thus facilitating or limiting cross-sector transfer and application of knowledge (Choi & Hannafin, 1995).

Learning in the collective perspective means growing social participation, whereas learning in the individualistic interpretation means growing knowledge.

These perspectives are fundamentally irreducible to each other while being complementary to understand and enhance learning (Sfard, 1998). These have been artificially opposed during the historic unfolding of lines of reasoning in learning philosophy and theory (Case, 1996; McKeough, 1991). In practice they are not opposed, as Mike Spector states by the "Integration Principle (I): human experience does not come neatly compartmentalized. It must be considered and understood in the context of a setting that typically includes the following: other individuals, a variety of goals (some of which might not be explicit and might conflict with others), various artifacts and technologies, activities, and cultural, organizational and societal influences" (Spector, 2000a, p. 523).

All these features come together to form a learning environment, or in other words the context for learning. In a more organized fashion, learning can be conceptualized as the confluence of the four coevolving realms of reality as represented in Figure 1 (following the holonic all-quadrants model of Wilber, 2000).

We will show now that each of these four realms of reality is a context embedded in a context embedded in still another context, and so on.

Experiential Context

The starting point of learning is necessarily the realm of subjective experience (Experience Principle; Spector, 2000a). Experience is enabled and constrained by identification. Identification goes through stages of decentration (from egocentric to ethnocentric to world-centric and beyond) allowing for broader and deeper modes of experience. It seems as if there is no end to unlimiting the experiential context of human beings. While coping with experiences (designed for learning or not), a unique biography of individual learning and development is created, with cognitive, affective, and conative aspects coevolving closely intermingled. Through each qualitatively new developmental stage, self-management and world-view are expanded, and motivation is altered accordingly.

It is a truism that motivation is crucial for sustaining learning over a period of time and must be directly addressed in the design of learning environments (Duchastel, 1997a). Its importance is generally recognized in instructional design theory, although often not dealt with as encompassingly as it should be in practice. Whether a learner feels overwhelmed, bored, or stimulated by a learning task depends basically on prior knowledge and skills, specific and general. This is the traditional stance to determine type and amount of necessary support and guidance. In e-learning an appropriate level of ICT skills is of course of vital importance. But there are much more individual characteristics playing a role in shaping motivation: the learners' attitudes toward learning in general, and the learning object in particular; their learning style and their value hierarchy; their personal interests, goals, and talents; and so forth.

Figure 1. The four quadrants of learning

	internal	external
individual	1. Experiential Context	2. Information Context
collective	4. Community Context	3. Institutional Context

Information Context

Information also will always appear contextualized, that is, framed by a certain situation (even decontextualized information appears in a particular situation, a situation that is lacking the appropriate context to make sense of the information). Indeed, knowledge is contextualized information: it is context that provides meaning to information. Pieces of information are embedded in larger structures of information, like phrases, which are parts of paragraphs, which are part of chapters, which are part of books, which are part of series, and so forth. With hypermedia there is now a tremendous amount of mutual same-level embedding of information, making evident the self-referential nature of meaning making. Real or virtual artifacts can allow for different degrees of interaction: just one-way perception as in static information, simple or complex but predefined interaction (from multiple choice to microworlds), and finally the possibility to design new objects in an open manner by using flexible tools (Jonassen, 1994).

The information interaction context can be as broad as all available resources on the Internet or as restricted as one single linear paper. Both extremes can be helpful for learning, depending on other context factors, such as the learning goals, the habits and key skills of the learners, the available time frame, and the prescriptions of the instructional approach that has been selected. Less savvy learners in complex information contexts can take advantage of prompts for metacognitive activity, navigation and search facilities, structured content and semantic learning aids, and easily accessible expert, teacher, or peer support. However, there are no cumulative and linear relationships between these different types of learning aids, learner characteristics, and the learning outcome.

Institutional Context

The institutional context relates to the socioeconomic system and the power relationships in which the learning takes place. The type of framework found in classrooms, schools, school systems, educational policy strategies, and so on (some being very open, others being very structured), certainly exerts an enabling or constraining influence on how different types of learners engage in learning. First, there are the material conditions to consider, such as location, buildings, equipment (ICT and other), and the student–teacher ratio, allowing for more or less efficiency, flexibility, and comfort of teaching and learning. Second, aspects of institutional policy also fall into this category, such as staff and student selection, evaluation procedures, the ratio between prescription and personal choice in the curriculum, the institutional strategy concerning e-learning, international collaboration, innovation (which may or may not exist), the potential or the lack of it to deliver grades or certificates, and the programme evaluation standards (external, internal) to be respected. Third, there is a societal perspective: the comparative prestige, the fees (and who is in charge), the degree of competition between educational institutions of the same type, the recognition of the educational programmes by the labor market, and so forth. (Torres & Antikainen, 2003).

The institutional context factors determine basically the composition of groups of learners and teachers (heterogeneity/homogeneity, equality/inequality, inclusion/exclusion) in any phase of the educational programme (e.g., Dorn, 1996; Gamoran, 1986) and the conditions under which learning takes place. A good deal of these institutional context factors can hardly be influenced by developers of learning environments, but they need to be taken into account carefully and systematically. To the extent, however, that e-learning goes beyond one single institution, region, or nation, unprecedented arrays of choice arise. Institutional settings are so tremendously different across the globe, and e-learning can exploit this diversity as strategic potential to optimize learning much more easily than learning that is not enhanced by ICT.

Community Context

It is the community context, finally, that has been the most discussed in recent educational theorizing (e.g. Salomon, 1993; Wenger, 1999; Wilson & Ryder, 2001). Likewise, it is the community context that is at the center of technological means of creating, within the design of e-learning environments, networks of interchange between learners (Laister & Koubek, 2001; Seufert, Lechner & Stanoevska, 2002; Wolf, 2001).

Each type of group (rather task-oriented or rather based on affective relations, face-to-face or virtual, with synchronous or asynchronous, oral or written communication) shows up with particular opportunities and problems with regards to certain kinds of learning objectives. ICT today frees instruction from being closely location bound, thus opening new fields for instructional innovation (Aviram, 1992). For a couple of social psychological reasons, however, as Ohlson & Ohlson (2000) argue convincingly, distance matters! In particular, common grounding is difficult to achieve in virtual-only communication. Group cohesion is an important factor for successful cooperative learning and inquiry if group think is prevented. Learning communities can vary considerably in size, location, and survival, from small, local, ad-hoc groups to large-scale, global groups with an extensive history, ending up in communities of communities. The longer a community exists and the more intense communication is going on, the more likely a particular community culture will appear, which can help to bridge the cultural diversity of the members as a common reference.

More and more virtual communities indeed have to cope with international, cross-cultural, and multilingual communication (McLoughlin, 2001). Binational settings offer different learning opportunities and ask for different educational approaches than multinational settings. Although challenging, these types of context are very well suited for the development of the key competencies the global knowledge worker needs, provided appropriate instructional strategies have been implemented (e.g. Oubenaissa, Giardina & Bhattacharya, 2002). Anyway, the neat barriers between work and learning fade away (Goodyear, 1999).

Interaction for Learning: From Delivery to Access, from Classroom to Community

An important point to consider in discussing context is the relationship between interaction and activity. There has been much criticism, and rightly so, of the forced passivity of much learning in institutional contexts that seek to contain costs of instruction by grouping students in large classes that do not favor interaction and that impose an instructor-centric mode of instruction.

As recent educational philosophies have once again emphasized active engagement in learning (long after Dewey's initial advocacy for doing so, among others), and as technology has facilitated such a move, the learner-centric view of instruction has seen a resurgence in educational circles (Grabinger, 1996). Discussions of action, experiential, and problem- and project-based learning scenarios are common nowadays in educational discourse (e.g., Ip & Naidu, 2001), even if the teaching body as a whole has yet to embrace these educational approaches as fully as many would like.

A more active student operating in a learner-centric environment is naturally a more interactive student. Indeed, it is the nature of the interaction rather than the activity itself that molds learning. This is well illustrated by the poor style of learning that we see in e-learning training programs that simply invite the learner to respond by clicking an advance button on the screen, and conversely, by the extremely rich learning environments in which the learner is invited to make decisions in realistic scenarios that reflect real-life contexts (Schank, 2002).

It is thus interaction with information artifacts and with teachers and co-learners in a permeable institutional setting that will most impact the learner. And it is the advent of e-learning, and technology more generally, that is enabling a shift in the interaction, away from the delivery of information to access to information and away from interaction limited to the classroom setting to various (virtual) communities.

In whatever form it takes, whether it is through human contact or contact with written or other external representations, it is information with which the learner interacts in forging ahead in building understanding and in memorizing factual elements.

We must therefore agree that factors related to content and its presentation do remain important. Indeed, in instructional design, content presentation captures much attention in the development cycle and design advice often centers on such factors (e.g., much of the research-based principles offered by Clark and Mayer, 2003, focus on these factors for designing e-learning).

Even here, internal experiential context plays a role, however. The following is an example: Clark and Mayer (2003) present the Redundancy Principle (presenting words in both text and audio narration can hinder learning), but suggest exceptions to the redundancy principle in special situations, such as when learners might have trouble processing spoken words (as in the case of those coming from a different linguistic background, for instance).

It is not always easy to separate internal and external context factors, nor is it ever desirable to develop content without attention to factors involved in the setting and the usage of the materials being developed. Research-based design guidelines, however, often rest on a body of knowledge that was developed in very constrained circumstances where research process imperatives win out over practical ones that would support the ecological validity of the research. Design experiments and developmental research would take practical concerns and contexts into account from the very beginning. They are much too rarely undertaken, however (Kelly, 2003).

Be that as it may, generally we all agree that some structure is needed to essentially guide learning efforts. Lest effort on the part of the learner become diffused in all directions as a topic is explored, some degree of orientation is offered by the curriculum and the instructor that interprets this curriculum. This is of utmost importance for beginners and should fade out for advanced learners taking over the control in the perspective of lifelong self-regulated learning (Visser, 2001).

The question of what goals and what content are appropriate for schooling is at the heart of great debates in educational circles and is perhaps the central problem with education today, as suggested by Egan (1997), who has pointed out the conflicts between the multiple goals being pursued.

It remains, however, that technology generally opens up the educational setting to a wider range of resources than those that were traditionally provided, going ever more global in this direction. The impact of this has been the shift mentioned earlier from delivery to access of information (Kirschner & Valcke, 1994)—and hence from a loosening of the constraints associated with contextual factors related to the curriculum to a wider diversity not only of information resources made available, but also of actors engaged in the context.

When a student actively engages more with peers in an e-learning course than with the course instructor, one sees loosening up taking place. This also happens when the student contacts potential community people that can be of service in a learning project. The community of learners and the community of practice shape a new cultural context for learning far different from the traditional, class-bound context of the past (Pea, 1994).

The shift from delivery to access that we see in e-learning is thus having a major impact on the fourfold learning context and hence on the nature of interactions taking place, with learning benefiting from this enhanced level of interaction when properly designed and coached.

It is this very shift that is involved in passing from an instructor-centric to a learner-centered mode of instruction, which lets the student take much more initiative in fashioning his or her own learning under the watchful eye of the instructor or some other mentor. With the learner at the center, the instructor becomes one element of the community context among many others, albeit a most important one in most cases (and even a crucial one in many cases).

The point of the shift is to reengage the learner in more personalized learning that can be more interesting and meaningful. It thus overcomes the receptive learner stance encouraged by the impersonal delivery of information and encourages instead an active interactive stance in which the learner accesses information as per the current learning needs.

This shift increases the complexity of the learning situation. The (lifelong) learner has to be encouraged to become in some sense his or her own instructional designer. Greater attention than before must therefore be given to the internal contexts, one's individual aspirations and experience, and the makeup of the learning communities.

Wider and more open, flexible contexts (Hannafin, Hannafin, Land, & Oliver, 1999) bring with them more options for the learner (more varied information to access, a greater community network to be dealt with). However, for optimal learning, this requires additional structure and guidance on a meta level that is generally not yet sufficiently taken into account (e.g., assistance in reflection on motivation and on learning strategies, strategic development of learning communities, frictionless integration of virtual learning environments into institutional and global information infrastructures).

Design Paradigm

Even if the field of instructional design currently shows an abundance of perspectives (Reigeluth, 1999) that need to be brought together into a unified model (Duchastel & Molz, 2004; Molz et al, 2003), it behooves us to consider the impact of the shift mentioned earlier and of the growing technology options on the design process. It sometimes feels as if our grounding in traditional tenets of instructional design is losing grip on the greater complexity of e-learning.

When we accept the greater importance of the role of multiple embedded contexts in the four realms described in the first section, we must consider the question of where you start in designing instruction. Do you really put the learner in the center and start from working on personal learning history, interests, and motivation? Or rather, can we start off by consciously stressing the design of the community context factors? Or should we perhaps stick to the more traditional decisions regarding content selection and structuring? Could we still continue to separate instructional design from organizational design and reform of the institutional context? (see Bereiter, 2002, for a profound discussion of each of these points and their interrelationships).

This thorny issue (see Duchastel, 2003, for a perspective on it) is in reality without a solution, for the internal and external, individual and collective contexts are but the two (times two) sides of the same coin (holon). In learning, the student engages in experiential processes stimulated by and generating information content, which is the fallout and the basis of communication in communities with a certain social structure (Spector, 2000a). One realm without the others does not exist.

And yet, there may be a preferred way to approach the design task, as is exemplified in the allied field of information design, where we see interaction design contrasted with information design itself (Shedroff, 2001).

The traditional preference in instructor-centric instruction is generally for a content-first approach. The core task is for the instructor (or the course developer) to consolidate a pedagogical ensemble of content to communicate to the student, for that remains the central activity of this form of pedagogy.

As we engage the shift to a learner-centered mode, however, along with the more open and flexible contexts that it brings about, consolidated content loses some of its importance, for there is an opening of access to multiple other sources of information, in either other channels of communication or other actors in the learning context. The added complexity of this opening up of information access leads us to emphasize processes, as well as motivational and sociocultural issues.

It is important to reiterate that content (information design) remains a strong focus in any instructional design paradigm, for it is (in the extended sense of the term) the very stuff of learning. Forgetting this principle will lead to chaotic learning processes whose lack of focus will lead directly to a lack of practical results. The necessary reorientation is not about neglecting existing strength of instructional design but to strengthen neglected realms of design.

In sum, then, the e-learning instructional designer will architect a manifold learning context out of the many technological and human options that can populate an open and flexible learning environment. In the first realm the designer will take care to create learning environments that allow learners to find and reflect on personalized learning opportunities and task the learner in order to keep the learning focused on the learning goals (in this approach, one moves away somewhat from explicit content in order to focus on goals to be achieved and on tasks to be engaged in by the learner [see Duchastel, 1997b; Duchastel & Turcotte, 1996]).

As far as the second realm is concerned, the designer will basically put in place the information access and communication tools that will be needed by the learner. In the third realm the designer has to link up with organizational development in order to prevent upcoming instructional approaches from lacking coherence and support. And finally, in the fourth realm the designer needs to open or create options for the learner concerning communities to participate in and to stimulate learning communities to become engaged with real-life communities, transcending the classroom and becoming useful contributors to a society in profound transformation (Shneiderman, 1998). Overall, the instructional designer needs to take care to pass over to the learners themselves, step by step, more and more responsibility and competence in all these design tasks in all the realms.

This shift in paradigm brings about added scope for innovation in pedagogy. Technology easily enables the replication of traditional instructional functions online. But which are valuable to replicate, and which should be left behind? This is an issue for designers and for instructional theorists. Instructional content remains in the picture, but it takes on a different form: its level of abstraction increases and it shifts to expected outcomes rather than being encapsulated in a consolidated expression of content.

Many educators simply attempt to replicate online a form of teaching that was suitable in one context and that overly and unnecessarily constrains the new, much more open context. Many e-learning platforms pander to this traditionalism in the academy in seeking to expand their level of acceptance in the marketplace. Learning is often not well served in these circumstances.

What would serve it better is capitalizing on the more flexible environments offered by technology in order to truly put the learner at the center of the design, and finally to become a fully participating codesigner. Technology in itself is necessary but insufficient for innovation; what is required is true pedagogical innovation—but this remains the swan song of instructional design confronted with the forces of academic traditionalism and the habits of fixed roles.

Our considerations of instructional design of contexts would be incomplete without mentioning the importance of contexts of instructional design. The very same four realms discussed earlier influence to what extent and in which manner design tasks are really done (Tessmer & Wedman, 1995): clarity of the task (explicit and hidden agendas), allocated resources (time, money, staff) and other institutional factors (type, size, strategy of the organization), characteristics of the development team and their professional community (size, roles, history, face-to-face or virtual communication), and finally characteristics of the individual designer (competencies, experiences, preferences, commitment). We can conclude that instructional development models need to become as context sensitive as the learning environments they are to generate. Process and product need to reflect each other.

Conclusion

What emerges from this refocus of pedagogical concern on instructional contexts is the complexity of interaction between content and experience, individuality and community, communication and structure, and standards and openness. All these aspects are equally essential for learning to blossom. We need to continue exploring the many facets of their mutuality and experiment with instructional designs that extend the context frontiers of each, all the while searching for the proper mix to encourage and optimize learning. Contextual analysis and contextual design of (semi)virtual learning environments turn out to be truly essential and need to be taken seriously (see the early warnings of Jacobson & Spiro, 1994, and Richey & Tessmer, 1995).

Where are we headed with this opening up of the learning environment and with an associated reconsideration of instructional design? As e-learning blends in ever more with traditional forms of learning and as we continue to digitize not only information but learning contexts as well, there is no end in sight of this opening up of pedagogy. From pretty monolithic forms of instruction dominating schools, universities, and further education organizations, we have come to the many forms of current e-learning and blended practice, and we will see this diversity continue to expand further as ever broader and more varied context factors are brought into the picture.

In the course of this challenging evolution, we should never forget the "Uncertainty Principle (U). Basically, this principle is a reminder that the instructional enterprise is complex and our knowledge of relevant aspects is incomplete. We do not know in a complete and comprehensive way all of the factors and mechanisms involved in learning. . . . In short, we may know less about learning and instruction than we are inclined to believe" (Spector, 2000a, p. 524). Theorizing about contextualization is itself in need of contextualization!

References

Ausubel, D. (1963). *The psychology of meaningful verbal learning.* New York: Grune & Stratton.

Aviram, A. (1992). Non-lococentric education. *Educational Review, 44*(1), 3-17.

Bereiter, C. (2002). *Education and mind in the knowledge age.* Mahwah, NJ: Erlbaum.

Case, R. (1996). Changing views of knowledge and their impact on learning. In D. R. Olson & N. Torrance (Eds.), *The handbook of education and human development: New models of learning, teaching and schooling.* Oxford: Blackwell.

Choi, J. I.,& Hannafin, M. (1995). Situated cognition and learning environments: Roles, structures, and implications for design. *Educational Technology Research & Development, 43*(2), 3-69.

Clark, R., & Mayer, R. (2003). E-learning and the science of instruction. San Francisco, CA: Jossey-Bass/Pfeiffer.

Dorn, S. (1996). *Creating the dropout: An institutional and social history of school failure.* Westport, CT: Praeger.

Driscoll, M. (2000). *Psychology of learning for instruction* (2nd ed). Boston: Allyn & Bacon.

Duchastel, P. (1997a). A motivational framework for Web-based instruction. In B. Khan (Ed.), *Web-based instruction: Development, application and evaluation.* Englewood Cliffs, NJ: Educational Technology.

Duchastel, P. (1997b). A Web-based model for university instruction. *Journal of Educational Technology Systems, 25*(3), 221-228.

Duchastel, P. (2003). Learnability. In C. Ghaoui (Ed.), *Usability evaluation of online learning programs.* Hershey, PA: Idea Group.

Duchastel, P., & Molz, M. (2004). Learning and design—The quest for a theory of learning. *Educational Technology Magazine, 44*(1), 45-48.

Duchastel, P., & Turcotte, S. (1996). On-line learning and teaching in an information-rich context. *Proceedings of INET'96.* Montreal, Canada.

Egan, K. (1997). *The educated mind.* Chicago: University of Chicago Press.

Gamoran, A. (1986). Instructional and institutional effects of ability groups. *Sociology of Education, 59*(4), 185-198.

Goodyear, P. (1999). Seeing learning as work: Implications for understanding and improving analysis and design. *Journal of Courseware Engineering, 2,* 3-11.

Grabinger, R. S. (1996). Rich environments for active learning. In D. H. Jonassen (Ed.), *Handbook of research for educational communications and technology.* New York: MacMillan.

Hannafin, M. J., Hannafin, K. M., Land, S. M., & Oliver, K. (1999). Open learning environments: Foundations, methods and models. In C. M. Reigeluth (Ed.), *Instructional design theories and models* (Vol. 2). Mahwah, NJ: Erlbaum.

Ip, A., & Morrison, I. (2001). *Learning objects in different pedagogical paradigms.* ASCILITE 2001. Retrieved December 12, 2003, from http://users. tpg.com.au/adslfrcf/lo/LO(ASCILITE2001).pdf

Ip, A., & Naidu, S. (2001). Experienced-based pedagogical designs for e-learning. *Education Technology, 61*(5), 53-58.

Jacobson, M. J., & Spiro, R. J. (1994). A framework for the contextual analysis of technology-based learning environments. *Journal of Computing in Higher Education, 5*(2), 3-32.

Jonassen, D. E. (1994). *Technology as cognitive tools: Learners as designers. IT-Forum.* (Paper 1). Retrieved from http://it.coe.uga.edu/itforum/paper1/ paper1.html

Kelly, A. E. (2003). Research as design. Theme issue: The role of design in educational research. *Educational Researcher, 32*(1), 3-4.

Kirschner, P., & Valcke, M. (1994). From supply-driven to demand-driven education: New conceptions and the role of ICT therein. *Computers in Human Services, 10*(4), 31-53.

Laister, J., & Koubek, A. (2001). *3rd Generation learning platforms. Requirements and motivation for collaborative learning.* Final paper of the INVITE project. Retrieved December 12, 2003, from http://invite.fh-joanneum.at/download/icl_tj_paper_final.pdf

McKeough, A. (1991). Three perspectives on learning and instruction. In A. McKeough, & J. L. Lupast (Eds.), *Toward the practice of theory-based instruction.* Hillsdale, NJ: Erlbaum.

McLoughlin, C. (2001). Inclusivity and alignment: Principles of pedagogy, task and assessment design for effective, cross-cultural online learning. *Distance Education, 22*(1), 7-29.

Molz, M., Eckhardt, A., Schnotz, W., Niegemann, H., & Hochscheid-Mauel, D. (2003). Deconstructing instructional design models. Towards an integrative conceptual framework for instructional design. In H. Niegemann, R. Brünken, & D. Leutner (Eds.), *Instructional design for multimedia learning.* Münster, NY: Waxmann.

Ohlson, G. M., & Ohlson, J. S. (2000). Distance matters. *Human-Computer Interaction, 15*(2/3), 139-178.

Oubenaissa, L., Giardina, M., & Bhattacharya, M. (2002). Designing a framework for the implementation of situated online, collaborative, problem-based activity: Operating within a local and multi-cultural learning context. *International Journal of E-Learning, 1*(3), 41-46.

Pea, R. D. (1994). Seeing what we build together: Distributed multimedia learning environments for transformative communications. *Journal of the Learning Sciences, 3*(3), 285-299.

Reigeluth, C. (Ed.). (1999). *Instructional design theories and models: A new paradigm of instructional theory* (Vol. 2). Mahwah, NJ: Erlbaum.

Richey, R. C., & Tessmer, M. (1995). Enhancing instructional systems design through contextual analysis. In B. B. Seels (Ed.), *Instructional design fundamentals. A reconsideration.* Englewood Cliffs, NJ: Educational Technology.

Salomon, G. (Ed.). (1993). *Distributed cognition. Psychological and educational considerations.* Cambridge, MA: Cambridge University Press.

Schank, R. (2002). *Designing worldclass e-learning.* New York: McGraw-Hill.

Seufert, S., Lechner, U., & Stanoevska, K. (2002). A reference model for online learning communities. *International Journal of E-Learning, 1*(1), 43-54.

Sfard, A. (1998). On two metaphors for learning and the dangers of choosing just one. *Educational Researcher, 3,* 4-13.

Shedroff, N. (2001). *Experience design.* Indianapolis, IN: New Riders.

Shneiderman, B. (1998). Relate-create-donate: A teaching/learning philosophy for the cyber-generation. *Computers & Education, 31*(1), 25-39.

Spector, J. M. (2000b). Trends and issues in educational technology: How far we have not come. *ERIC IT Newsletter, 12*(2). Retrieved December 12, 2003, from http://suedweb.syr.edu/faculty/spector/publications/trends-tech-educ-eric.pdf

Spector, M. (2000a). Towards a philosophy of instruction. *Educational Technology & Society, 3*(3), 522-525.

Tessmer, M., & Wedman, J. (1995). Context-sensitive instructional design models: A response to design research, studies, and criticism. *Performance Improvement Quarterly, 8*(3), 38-54.

Torres, C.A., & Antikainen, A. (Eds.). (2003). *The international handbook on the sociology of education: An international assessment of new research and theory.* Lanham, MD: Rowman & Littlefield.

Visser, J. (2001). Integrity, completeness and comprehensiveness of the learning environment: Meeting the basic learning needs of all throughout life. In D. Aspin, J. Chapman, M. Hatton, & Y. Sawano (Eds.), *International handbook of lifelong learning.* London: Kluwer.

Wenger, E. (1999). *Communities of practice. Learning, meaning and identity.* Cambridge, MA: Cambridge University Press.

Wilber, K. (2000). *A theory of everything. An integral vision of business, politics, science and spirituality.* Boston: Shambala.

Wilson, B., & Ryder, M. (2001). *Dynamic learning communities: An alternative to designed instructional systems.* Retrieved January 12, 2003, from http://carbon.cudenver.edu/~mryder/dlc.html

Wolf, K. D. (2001). Internet based learning communities – Moving from patchwork environments to ubiquitous learning infrastructures. In S. Dijkstra, D. Jonassen, & D. Sembill (Eds.), *Multimedia learning. Results and perspectives.* Frankfurt/Main: Lang.

Chapter III

Context Engineering for Learning:
A Sociotechnical Approach

Licínio Roque, Universidade de Coimbra, Portugal

António Dias de Figueiredo, Universidade de Coimbra, Portugal

Abstract

The authors present a view of the problems related to the role of context in learn-ing and development, individual and organizational, influenced by readings in anthropology, activity theory, and actor-network theory, and of how they relate to the problems of developing e-learning experiences. Next, they briefly present the context engineering approach to information systems development as a frame-work to think and organize the development of virtual contexts for e-learning. This approach proposes to achieve a critical understanding of development as a sociotechnical phenomenon within a cultural and historical envelope to provide a framework of development problems focused on the relation between a model of context and its mediators. It also proposes to use contextuality as the key to per-form emancipatory movements while operating on sociotechnical networks. The authors then attempt to translate the fundamental ideas and guiding principles of this approach to the development of virtual learning contexts, elaborating on some of the learning and development issues that arise.

Introduction

In this inquiry, we focus on the role of context as the centre of a developmental approach to learning, by both the individual and the organization. Why are we interested in context? In spite of common experience suggesting that the learning processes are highly contextual, we are puzzled to see context so often absent from the public discourse about education and learning media and tools. Figueiredo (2000) reflects on context and why it is being largely overlooked in the current content-delivery hype on mediated learning. Context does not fit well within the traditional mechanistic paradigm of classroom education, and the transposition of the paradigm to new online media may disastrously lead to the entire loss of the contextual dimensions in the process.

Maximizing the return on investment in learning resources has long been a fundamental aspect and the economic justification for organizing schooling and training activities the way we are used to see them. But, depending on how we conceive of the quality and effectiveness of the learning experience, other aspects may become relevant. Moreover, to our current knowledge, more participatory learning contexts are barely scaleable. The scalability of social contexts, such as classroom activities and workshop environments, while maintaining their value as learning settings for participatory or interactive experiences, is limited, among other factors, by each actor's attention span. Attention to the activities and learning trajectory of each individual learner—part of each active subject's personal context—requires trained human skills and humanpower. Only a naïve transmissive view of learning can rejoice with the hypothetical scenario of one-dimensional people sharing a known and normalized history of previous experiences, getting knowledge poured into their heads through online content delivery pipes. In fact, practical experience tells us that learning is highly context dependent, as there is much more to learning than learning objects or subject matters.

We are concerned with the role of context in learning and with the uses of contextualization as a way to promote individual and collective development in virtual settings. As a departure point, we propose an operational view of context as the scaffolding of content by enacting activities that can reify interesting learning situations and, as such, provide useful environments for the individual or collective construction of meaning. In this perspective, the production of mediators to support the development of learning activities in virtual settings shows much in common with other information systems development (ISD) efforts, provided that we are able to characterize the target activities in question. This characterization helps to model the context that is the target of the ISD efforts and is to be enabled by the deployment of suitable mediators. This prompts us to search for an understanding of the context of the learning activities in virtual settings and of the mediators in these contexts.

After running through some of the problems and approaches to the phenomena of context and contextualization, from anthropology and linguistics to psychology and sociology, we will conjecture on the idea of designing contexts for learning and on the instrumental role of the design of interactive mediators as effective and material supports to these contexts. The relevance of these references to the study of learning activities and of their mediation in virtual settings calls for a firm grasp of the role played by context, or the lack of it, in these activities. Consequently, it is important for us to become more aware of the roles played by mediating instruments and of their influence in ascribing roles and in promoting rules, norms, and practices. Like language and through language, these mediators influence modes of practical action and, as such, the performance of the activities that form the learning context. We may also inquire into their influence in the establishment and deletion of social relationships resulting from mediating the actions in that context, as well as of the part played by these relationships in the unfolding of those actions. On this conjecture, we will then attempt to translate the context engineering (CE) sociotechnical approach to information systems development (Roque, Almeida, & Figueiredo, 2004) to frame the development problems for enabling learning in virtual settings.

The Essence of Context

Problems of Context

In a seminal essay on the problem of meaning in primitive languages, Bronislaw Malinowski (1923) elaborated two important themes that were to figure prominently in the study of context: (1) that language is embedded within a context of situation, and (2) that language must be conceptualized as a mode of practical action. Such a perspective on language as "an indispensable element of concerted human action" led him, at a later date, to articulate a view of meaning as something embedded within trajectories of action and the word as a means of bringing things about, a handle to acts and objects. He also told us that "meaning . . . does not come . . . from contemplation of things, or analysis of occurrences, but in practical and active acquaintance with relevant situations. The real knowledge of a word comes through the practice of appropriately using it within a certain situation."

The concept of context resists a single technical definition and poses significant challenges as one proceeds from one research area to another. Sharfstein (1989) tells us about his working definition of context as that which envelops the object of interest and that which, by its relevance, helps in explaining it. And he adds that, by definition, context is what is relevant for what we aim to explain and excludes all other, however near they may be found, that do not offer the required explaining power. He proceeds, explaining the difference between contextualism, relativism, and skepticism in terms of the degree of argument and elaborates on what he calls the problem of context. A purely philosophical approach would be caught between the illusion that full knowledge of circumstances would enable perfect explanations and that such omniscience would be logically inconceivable, since knowledge itself depends on limiting conditions that make it worth, and, as such, omniscience seems humanly improbable.

From the Latin contexere (Dilley, 1999), which means weaving or joining together, alluding to a process of weaving words to produce elaborated speech, to search for context would be to establish connections between elements enabling the construction of explanations for a situation. Dilley tells us that context has long been a key concept in studies of language and anthropology. He adds that for a time its use remained mostly tacit and, in the attempt to produce contextualized versions of their knowledge, several authors from cultural anthropology forgot about the nature of context itself and considered it static, clear, self-sufficient, and even self-evident, requiring no extra dwelling. Fabian (in Dilley, 1999) says that these studies reveal the underlying positive view of context. Yet, context is itself a subject of interpretation, prior or subsequent to that of the contextualized object. The context is itself a choice and, when explicit, a human construction. Context is, thus, part of the problem, in the way that we chose to interpret our own rules. There are at least two approaches to context in anthropology: context as connections to be established by the interpretative act; and context as the object of study, itself subject to analysis. Dilley cites Wittgenstein's advice to seek not for the meaning of the word but for the uses of the concept.

Introducing a set of studies on the role of context, Duranti and Goodwin (1992) refer to several understandings of context and its use. The most common would be the dichotomy between focal event and context. In this understanding, focal event is the object or event of interest to be explained and context is the environment that is brought into the explanation. Context is, thus, a frame that surrounds the event being examined and provides resources for its interpretation. The notion of context thus involves a juxtaposition of two entities, a focal event and a field of action within which the event is embedded. A relationship between two orders of phenomena that mutually inform each other to comprise a larger whole is absolutely central to the notion of context. From a comparison with the relationship between organism and environment, borrowed from cybernetic theory, a parallel is drawn to the problem of delineating where the system ends and where the environment begins; that is, to the problem of what is the context that informs certain behavior. Making use of Bateson's (1972) metaphor of a blind man with a stick, crossing the street, the authors expose a number of issues central to the analysis of context. First, the importance of taking as a point of departure, for the analysis of context, the perspective of the participant(s) whose behavior is being analyzed. What analysts seek to describe is not what they consider context, but rather how the subject, himself or herself, attends to and organizes his or her perception of the events and situations that he or she is navigating through. Second, the metaphor illustrates how what a participant treats as relevant context is shaped by the specific activities being performed at that moment. Continuing, they explain how "one of the great difficulties posed in the analysis of context is describing the socio-historical knowledge that a participant employs to act within the environment of the moment." Moreover, "in so far as participant's articulation of their environment is shaped by the activities of the moment, the context that is relevant to what they are doing changes radically when they move from one activity to another. . . . The dynamic mutability of context is complicated further by the ability of participants to rapidly invoke within the talk of the moment alternative contextual frames" (Duranti & Goodwin, 1992). This is one of the key insights from Gumperz's notion of contextualization cues (Gumperz, 1992).

In conclusion, such phenomena demonstrate the importance of the following: "first, approaching context from the perspective of an actor actively operating on the world within which he or she finds him- or herself embedded; second, tying the analysis of context to the study of the indigenous activities that participants use to constitute the culturally and historically organized social worlds that they inhabit; and third, recognizing that participants are situated within multiple contexts which are capable of rapid and dynamic change as the events they are engaged in unfold." Within social situations, a key constituent of the environment are the other human beings, who are active agents with their own plans and agendas. People become environments for each other.

One of the recurring themes being addressed by Duranti and Goodwin (1992) is the capacity for human beings to dynamically reshape the context that provides organization for their actions within the interaction itself. The dynamic and socially constitutive properties of context are inescapable. "Each additional move within the interaction modifies the existing context while creating a new arena for subsequent interaction." Moreover, as strategic actors, individual participants can actively attempt to shape context in ways that further their own interests. In so far as the processes to which context is relevant are social and interactive, one party's proposals as to what should constitute the operative context might fail to achieve ratification by others. Miscommunication and active challenges to a proposed redefinition of the situation are possibilities. In brief, context is viewed as a socially constituted, interactively sustained, time-bound phenomenon.

Context as Activity

Activity theory proposes the study of human behavior situated in a social, cultural, and historically constituted context that focuses on mediation as a basic and fundamental property of human action. Originated with the study of language and signs within learning contexts (Vygotsky, 1986), activity theory takes the mediated human activity as a fundamental unit for contextual analysis. Vygotsky proposes the "zone of proximal development" (ZPD) as an alternative construct to the subject-independent notion of learning levels. To account for the specificity of learning conditions underlying each individual learning step, in particular in what regards the "learning space" between the subject's previous performance and what he or she can achieve with the collaboration of a more experienced person, the ZPD construct helps to map a subject-specific notion of development.

Engeström (1987) proposes a model of activity that is an extension of the original subject—object instrumental mediation by explicitly considering the community dimension and thus revealing a richer set of relations and respective forms of mediation. This model can be used as a guide for the analysis of different types of mediators in individual and social human activity. The artifacts, considered as instrumental mediators that let the user relate to the object of interest and thus to achieve an outcome, are now accompanied by social rules governing the relation of the subjects to the community and by a division of labor organizing the relation between community members and the object of the activity. These are the three prime relations that can more easily be brought into explanations about any human activity, from this activity system model.

Engeström goes on to explore the relations and possible contradictions between the constituent elements of activity systems and between activity systems themselves. He exposes another construct that can be useful to interpret what goes on in human organized activity as change takes place through development efforts. With the notion of expansive learning, he builds the cycle of expansive transition, a model that can be used to interpret learning as transitions in activity systems networks, as change occurs to adjust to or try to solve contradictions. With this model, he later elaborates a methodological proposal for achieving the transformation of work (for a late version see Engeström, 1999). This model assumes development to work from some previous form of activity and understands development as an adjustment within an established network of activities and as a cyclic on-going process of movement and adaptation.

Remembering the materialism of the mediations of human activity underlying this theory, we are compelled to understand developmental interventions as making available new, and used, forms of mediation of human activity. These can range from mental instruments, such as constructs, ideas, methods and models, sign systems, and languages, to physical artifacts. On our bodies of knowledge, these mediators are usually arranged into disciplinary sets that get communicated for the apprentice to train with. The notion of expansive learning presupposes that these forms of mediation are not necessarily known and may get developed along the transition process, thus possibly enriching or reformulating the body of knowledge. This goes from the general view of learning what is socially accepted as known to what could be considered as a more culturally advanced step that includes the knowledge creation process, either explicitly, or is embedded in the production of material and ideal artifacts, roles, rules of social governance, organizational or performative practices, and so forth. If we understand networks of activity systems as models for human organizations, then we can also interpret organizational transformation through cycles of expansive transition by which individual activities are transformed and by which they adjust within the context of neighboring activities, possibly in ways not anticipated (Almeida & Roque, 2000). In the process, we can draw some conjectures about development assumptions and why they, supposedly, so often fail: assuming the deterministic nature of process and outcome; ignoring on-going changes in motives and goals; ignoring actors, human and nonhuman, and their vested interests within the larger social net; and accepting a partial perspective of the phenomena and thus ignoring the multiplicity of the disciplinary agencies involved in the transformation (Almeida & Roque, 2002)—in sum, ignoring the influence of some influential part of the current context in the formal, material, and effective constitution of development and, as such, the influence of the current form of activity, and respective activity network, which is the context within which the "learning intervention" will be interpreted.

Context as Heterogeneous Sociotechnical Network

A perspective of context as social network offers the ability to build understandings based on interactions between social actors. Actor-network theory (ANT) offers a language base for the explanation of social phenomena supported on relationships between human and nonhuman actors and on the constitution of the actors themselves. It enables the exploration of both micro- and macrosociologies, of the actor as network and of the network as actors, as a minimal ontology for an ethnomethodological approach (Latour, 1999a).

The ANT body of knowledge grew from various sociological studies of science and technology in diverse domains and offers a basic terminology that has enabled the construction of elaborate explanations for sociotechnical and historical development events. It enables the analysis of sociotechnical contexts that views technology not as neutral to human values and interests, but as influencing relationships of power and of people with their environments (Callon, 1991). Latour (1991) explains the use of the sociotechnical network as a model of the ensemble of relations that influence but do not determine a program of action.

One central notion is that of the actor as author of inscriptions that get translated by other actors. The concept of inscription refers to patterns of use, or programs of action, that can be embodied in technical artifacts. A translation is a work through which actors modify, displace, and translate their various and contradictory interests (Latour, 1999b). By considering the actor as a network and centre for translations, the theory opens the ground for actor heterogeneity. Each actor's translations get influenced by the heterogeneous network of relationships it interprets. Both human and nonhuman actors may influence a program of action by their translations of each other's inscriptions. Neither a pure human voluntarism nor a technological determinism is assumed, but only the interplay between actors' wills or inscribed interests can account for the emergence of complex social reality. The force of older and newer inscriptions, for example, their material strength or their convincing argument, as well as their interpretative flexibility within previous alignments, influences their translations by other actors. Alignments provide stability regions, here called translation regimes, which foster specific translations and action programs while inhibiting others.

Akrich (1992) talks about inscriptions and translations in the context of design. Inscriptions refer to the way designed artifacts carry with them the patterns of use that foster specific action programs. From the standpoint of the designer, these instruments are vehicles of expression that will intervene socially when successfully inscribed in sociotechnical networks. An engineer, although apparently involved in mere technological matters, becomes also a sociologist, moralist, and politician and influences interpersonal relationships through media that assume values, convey roles, and influence power. Within this framework, Latour (1991) explains how trajectories of development cannot be viewed in a single social context. One must try to understand the simultaneous production of "text" and "context." According to this, any division between a social component and a technical or scientific production is necessarily arbitrary. The same author argues that the only nonarbitrary division should be between successive versions of statements (i.e. technical objects) more or less loaded with inscriptions and translations, and that we should learn to follow and document.

A technical trajectory is thus understood as a series of design and user acts, inscriptions, and translations, which produced the current actor-network that configures a certain mediator, be it a physical or an intellectual tool, a rule, a method, or practice. It is argued that for each technical trajectory there is a symmetric trajectory in context, corresponding to the transformations on the relationships between diverse actors and the focal object. Such an exercise would consider a set of relationships of variable geometry as the subject in interaction with an object, also an actor-network of variable geometry. Both suffer transformations in what seems as a cultural-historical process. Against visions of society or object as immutable, ANT proposes a view of a path of innovations where all actors coevolve. This dissolution between what changes and the environment in which it changes makes more flexible what can and cannot be realized. This difference becomes a matter of positioning on a developmental trajectory. Irreversibility becomes a matter of alignment of interests between human actors and their intermediaries. Nothing is intrinsically realistic or unrealistic because social reality is not a finite state, but a phenomenon always requiring maintenance.

This sociological perspective can help us understand the impact traditional methods, tools, and social and organizational arrangements can have when these actors exert their influence on the conception of learning in virtual settings. The inertia imposed by currently accepted methods and established practices that have firm relationships with performing actors is significant and noticeable in the "more of the same" approach that is followed on many projects. As such, someone interested in innovating in the context of e-learning will have to consider who the stakeholders in traditional education are and how their positions transfer to this new context. Authors, editors, publishers, teachers, and learners all have vested interests. What do they have to win or lose? What methods and practices, roles and rules, andideal and material artifacts align with or embody such interests? How to perform the translations required for the new virtual learning settings, eventually and successfully leaving behind the excess baggage of traditional methods? The problem, thus, seems that of designing a trajectory for change that can mobilize critical actors to achieve a stable translation regime that favors new concepts, new relationships, and possibly new roles and value propositions for social transformation to occur and stabilize.

The Context in Learning Experiences

With the views on context previously exposed, learning can be understood as establishing relations with the technical constructs, both ideal and material, that make up specific disciplinary traditions. Learning implies the actor becoming able to actively include such relations in personal and organizational discourse, as well as becoming able to perform with these constructs to achieve proposed or intentional goals within the context of established or recognizable patterns of activity. The activity perspective—focused on learning-by-doing—could lead us to consider the planning of activities as contexts for learning. Action plans could be elaborated by the master and act as mediators to inform the learner of desirable action patterns to be performed and of the performance that would favor the construction of personal, action-oriented knowledge congruent with the disciplinary tradition. In a social or organizational context where these action plans are readily available and accompanied by the master's couching or supervision, as the situation unfolds, we would have situated learning and a community-based approach where the learner would become a member of a community of practice.

Becoming a member of a community of practice also means participating in a sociotechnical network, sharing social connections with technological artifacts, and interpreting, as performing actors, the roles and action plans inscribed by the designers. Learning technical competences would thus entail a dimension of role-playing, as well as a dimension of authorship, because interpretation often involves a translation to each individual's context of values, interests, and conditions for action. The social network perspective can help us focus on the web of mediators as actors that would contribute to the development of associated higher mental functions. As designers of learning contexts, we would be driven to focus on the conception of forms of activity that could serve as test-beds for the development of personal or collective instruments for the desired performances, while fostering the emergence of desired roles and patterns of organization among performers that might be reifications of established practice or new findings that get successfully inscribed within the accepted disciplinary tradition.

What does it mean to design learning experiences, and how do we take the problems of context into consideration? In fact, how do we take context as a complementary approach to content design? How can we design virtual contexts for learning? Such are the questions that we pose to ourselves as we begin to take on the endeavor of expanding our knowledge of the role of context in molding the learning experience and its results. Will we be able to systematically design and develop virtual contexts for specific learning purposes? From a viewpoint of contexts as learning activities, we can confidently say that it has been done successfully in the past. As part of designing learning activities in virtual settings, we would have to consider actual and desirable forms of mediation, such as technical instruments, norms, and procedures, which could be enacted as parts of a meaningful whole. To what extent different people may attribute similar or different meanings to events, to media, and to their roles may depend largely on their perception and understanding of the context, as we have introduced it here. As masters in the master/disciple dichotomy, we will probably be seen, mostly, as providers or as managers of virtual contexts. From this standpoint, some immediate questions arise. Will we have to, or even be able to, account for the specificity of each learner's perspective of the learning experience even as we attempt a design-for-all approach? Should we, instead, focus on development for specific niches of previous experience and intended effect? Will we be able to account for the dynamic mutability of each learner's context during the actual learning experience? Will we be able to account for its multiplicity as each person is influenced by diverse historical and cultural backgrounds? Under what conditions should we be concerned with such and other questions when attempting the development of virtual contexts? What approach should we follow for this development?

The Context Engineering Approach in a Nutshell

Motivation, Goals, and Fundamental Concepts

While dealing with the role of context and change in the practice of information systems development (ISD), of which the development of virtual learning settings can be thought of as a paradigmatic case, we begin the synthesis of a sociotechnical approach to ISD (Almeida & Roque, 2000, 2002; Roque et al., 2002, 2004). In this synthesis, we have taken the neohumanist paradigm of social sciences (originated by Burrel and Morgan) as a starting point (Hirscheim, Klien, & Lyytinen, 1995). Roughly, it proposes a critical or conflicting view of the situation as the motive for development and change as emancipation and a subjectivist view of the nature of knowledge underlying the formulation of action or intervention. To this, we added a requisite of usefulness toward the interpretation of practice, arriving at the following goals:

- to build a framework that enables us to understand and conceive of the development activities supported on the dialectic relationship between context and the mediators of the activities that mould this context;

- to achieve an understanding of development as a sociotechnical phenomenon within a cultural and historical envelope; and

- to deal explicitly with contextuality as the key to performing emancipatory movements.

These goals can be understood within the previously exposed conceptions of context and contextualization in action and language use, which, in turn, provide the fundamental concepts at the centre of our concerns while analyzing organizational discourse and formulating transforming actions. The context engineering (CE) approach was then systematized under a previously proposed framework (Iivary & Lyytinen, 1999; Iivary, Hirscheim, & Klein, 1998, 2001) of goals, main concepts, general principles, and process-oriented principles.

It is in the context of the previous discussions on context that we wish to pose the hypothesis of adopting the CE approach to ISD as a form of social engineering useful when developing contexts for learning. As social actors wishing to produce sociotechnical inscriptions, we envision context as media. These media are made up by social relationships that we intend to shape by intervening in the material mediators supporting these relationships or constituting their expressions. These media may span from computational, psychological, sociological, organizational, managerial, or discernable from any relevant disciplinary tradition.

Thus, should we, as ISD practitioners, be able to re-centre our attention on developing the relations that make up each actor-network in our context, as well as the network that delineates the context itself, with all its consequences? We think this perspective promises to be more inclusive than any purely technical and objective one, as that of designing computational artifacts. This sense grows as we acknowledge the diversity of forms of mediation that make up actual social networks and that can be the target of this development. To summarize, this conception is based on some fundamental concepts:

- a view of context both as a dynamic figure/ground dichotomy and as an autopoietic flux of interactions that shape understandings;

- the pervasiveness of mediation in human activity and of mediators as development targets;

- an understanding of the role of human activity as unit of context, for sense making or interpretation of each other's actions;

- sociotechnical networks as media and relationships as the fabric of reality that the developer aims to influence and shape; and

- heterogeneous social engineering as phenomenon and development hypothesis.

From this ontological positioning, we then conjecture a form of engineering that takes the social relationships as its media, weaving heterogeneous sociotechnical networks within a historical and cultural perspective.

A Framework of Movements

Several authors have reflected on the special character of design activities in several fields from architecture to engineering. Alexander (1964) talks about the search for a solution as a process of fitting diverse factors within a professional language. Schön (1983) talks about reflection-in-action as the essential character of any design activity, the "conversation" that the professional establishes with the situation, and engineering as a movement-testing experience. From the reflection on our practice along several ISD projects, and guided by the conceptual foundations previously discussed, we arrived at the methodological framework depicted in Figure 1.

This is not intended to be an algorithmic proposal, as in the proposals of traditional methods, but as the schematic representation of the relationship between a set of essential movements centered on the problems of context in development. These movements reflect the dialectics of development that occurs between context and artifacts and is then generalized for any kind of mediator. The model is partly inspired by a minimalist desire for time-compressing the traditional engineering cycles (analysis, design, construction, test, deployment) that take place between the diagnostic of the situation and the generalization of the new form of activity, while articulating it with the learning model expressed in the cycle of expansive transition (Engeström, 1987) (from need-state to generalization and consolidation).

This framework intends to bring to the fore the dialectical relationship between particular conceptions or models of context and its role in the formulation of interventions, such as the design of artifacts, and vice versa, considering the role of media interventions in the emergent flow of the ongoing conception of context as intersubjectivity. This diagram reflects, yet, the typical source of the information used in each activity, at each movement's starting point, and the main product, at its arrival, here expressed as models of context and of mediators. The framework shares a hermeneutic-like structure, as the model of context represents our sociotechnical whole and each mediator is a focal part of this whole, brought to the fore for specific disciplinary action, within that context.

With its focus on context, the framework divides our development concerns into six main activities—diagnostic, innovation, creation, evaluation, adaptation, and generalization—and a consolidation phase. When interpreted as the basis for a method to manage contextual change, these activities may be understood as six movements or "operators" to be juggled in a planned or contingent manner. Either way, the main contribution of this framework may be that of raising the importance of explicitly dealing with the formulation of context as an intersubjective understanding of the situation underlying the development, that is, how the actors involved see their context as a common ground. Building on these assumptions, we propose a set of activities to represent the essential movements within this framework.

Diagnostic – It is a movement we perform to obtain a shared understanding about the current (organizational) context. What activities do we perform, and how? What are the relevant actor-networks and their development trajectories? The outcome of this activity is a representation of the context, as a starting point for development. We have tried mapping activity systems, actor-networks, and value nets for strategic analysis as representations of context (Parolini, 1999). The subject of this activity may be as complex as the object itself and can be understood as an actor-network that, at least temporarily, shares relationships with the network that is the object of analysis. Social and disciplinary rules influence the subject's relation to the community, and practices and interests relate the community to the object of the activity. The pressure for a definitive version of context may depend

Figure 1. The context engineering framework of contextual movements

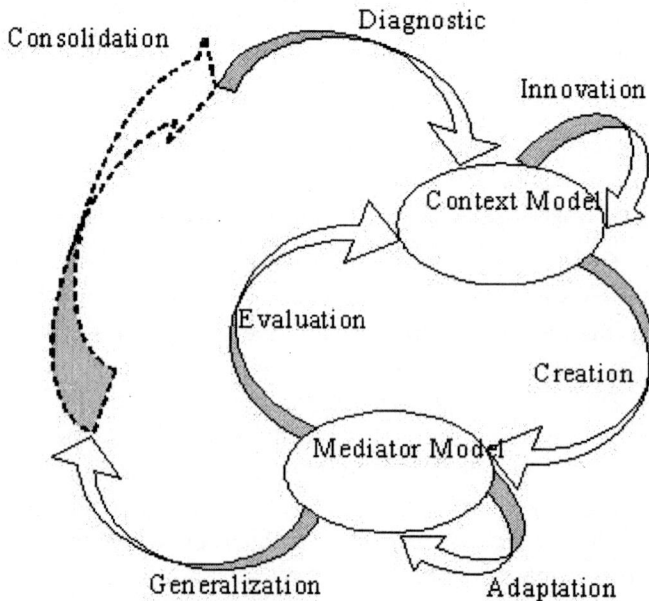

on the perception of its impact and life span as the process cycles between a view of context and of the mediators and through generalization and consolidation. If we think of it as just a starting point to be followed by innovation attempts, this pressure may be significantly relieved.

Innovation – This movement aims to propose new activities and networks. It is an attempt at conceptually thinking out of the box. Team members may ask questions oriented toward considering new technology adoption, but the main focus is the new forms of activity. The motive should be to build a model for organizational transformation, and the outcome the idealized form of the expected new context (or activities) that could be useful for creating appropriate artifacts. Mapping and building an understanding of the underlying actor-networks and their historicity can help figure out what could be plausible moves.

Creation – The objective is to produce artifacts for the projected new context or activities. This is traditionally the role of software engineering and interaction design methods within ISD frameworks, which corresponds to the specification and production of prototypes and microcosms for experimentation. During this process the situation is translated into idealized inscriptions to achieve desired goals. User involvement can be fostered by producing experimental prototypes that can be used for enacting the final form of activity and letting the user become truly capable of expressing his or her views in an explicit way that would have otherwise stayed tacit under conversation. This would enable the goal of user requirements construction and valuation, and ultimately emancipatory expression.

Evaluation – This movement is performed in order to achieve a decision on whether we should revise our knowledge of the context, refine the mediator for the selected context, or proceed toward the generalization of its use. This decision depends on the nature and relevance of the information the team gathers while performing the evaluation, and that, in turn, is likely to be influenced by the specific approach to evaluation (what you are looking for). Evaluation can be traced back to a dual view: either we are seeking a mediator to fulfill a predefined set of requirements or we are interested in a valuation of the transformation produced by its introduction. In the second view, a significantly broader appreciation of its impact can be achieved.

Adaptation – This movement is performed in order to produce a change in the artifact without implying a redefinition of the modeled context. The adaptation might be accomplished by the team or by the users, since it might be an adaptation of the artifact or an adaptation of the previously intended use, or both, in any case possibly leading to a reevaluation of the artifact and associated context. This represents the kinds of innovations that happen daily and maybe silently, sometimes only noted and valued when their accumulation involves a broader rethinking of the activities.

Generalization – This movement involves the deployment of the mediator's models from the microcosm where they were developed and on to the target settings, so that their use can be consolidated. Note that by deploying artifacts and other mediators we are also, tacitly or explicitly, deploying the new form of context that must interact and possibly compete with the current, established set of activities. The relationships between proposed mediators and other new and old forms of activity should be considered as they may influence generalized adoption. In this process, relationship alignments may be key for the effective inscription on the social network.

The *consolidation phase* represents the adjustment of the new form of activity within the context of the neighboring activity systems, as suggested by the expansive learning cycle (Engeström, 1987). This phase represents the process of adaptation that occurs after the generalization of the new instruments when a new form of activity emerges through its interaction with the neighboring activities, possibly in unanticipated ways. Translation regimes favor specific translations and the predictability of adoption; such may be the role of tutoring as well as the user's supportive relationship with more experienced users.

These activities aim at work with both context and mediator models as microcosms to understand the impact of the introduction of mediators in communities of practice, along the actual development of those mediators, acting as classes of methodological movements available to information systems (IS) practitioners. By working with both, models of context and mediators, this framework demands rapid and cheaper iterations to continually evolve them and account for the pace of changes in organizational environments. Each ISD process iteration could be a combination of these activities on a sequence unique for each particular situation that derives from the specific demands of the situation and actual evolution. Considering the possibility of different development rhythms between mediators and/or situations and their interdependence, interesting research questions can arise. The movements can also be viewed as a taxonomy of methodological research challenges requiring more detailed work.

Engineering Contexts for Learning

Exercising the Approach

In this section we attempt to translate the context engineering guiding and process principles to the development of e-learning activities. To that effect, we explore e-learning contexts as specific cases of ISD contexts. First, we explicitly acknowledge the conjecture that we actually can design e-learning activities, or activities for learning in virtual settings. Our position is that we can build an operative understanding of media scaffolding for e-learning within the context engineering approach. From this conjecture other relevant questions arise: Can we engineer virtual contexts for e-learning? What does that mean, and how do we do it?

From the ontological viewpoint of context engineering, e-learning occurs within a heterogeneous sociotechnical network composed of relationships between learning objects, practices, and traditions related to a disciplinary community, within time and spatial frames or encounters, molded by event models and technological media. The extent to which an individual's learning experience is influenced by the mediating actor-network may be difficult to grasp, and impossible to determine, even from his or her own subjective position. Learning, as the establishing of meaningful relationships, by the learner, within that disciplinary network, possibly emerges as both a result of accidental encounters as well as of intentional actions. The role of information systems in this emergence, even if just by providing inter-action support and thus mediating the establishment of relationships, may significantly influence the outcome. Additionally, information systems may embody technical or learning objects that are intended to be the targets of the learning activity, among others, by

- providing experimentation models (e.g. scale models or simulations) from which the learners can interactively develop other models or theories,

- providing the social locus for interactively building community discourse and sustaining verbal or other forms of context for the coordination of learning activities, and

- conveying so-called content objects as digested forms of knowledge (e.g. libraries of learning objects, such as books, articles, film, presentations, and animations).

By mediating interactions among the learning agents, information systems also embody practices and regulatory norms inscribed upon them by their designers, as expected, and privileged patterns of individual and social behavior. These may stem from idealized forms of activity that may be viewed as providing useful contexts for learning awareness or developing specific capabilities. From the viewpoint of context engineering, it is the developer's concern to explicitly formulate models of such contexts in relation to the intended learning goals and to devise appropriate mediations to support them. So, it also becomes the concern of someone developing e-learning media to think of

- social norms defining roles and influencing behaviors that can be communicated or enacted by the actors directly involved in the learning experiences, and

- organizational practices governing patterns of activity that can be enacted to the benefit of the development of capabilities or competences (models for such activities have been proposed and benefits are known; they include brainstorming, inquiry, open dialog, presentation, critical argumentation, etc.).

These are forms of mediation in human activity that influence the conception of information systems artifacts and may be objects of development in the broader view of sociotechnical intervention. As with technical objects, they concur to establishing relationships that result from learning agendas, but, if misaligned with the learning purpose, they can also hinder the process. Thus, they should be explicitly accounted for when proposing learning scenarios, and they should be called up at the service of the learning experience.

Developing e-learning contexts means, first of all, defining value proposals that they embody from personal, economic, and moral stances. Do learning activities have something special to them? Developing contexts for learning in the individual, organization, and society also means coping with the inherent emancipatory goal in learning for those appreciating the products of the development effort. This implies enabling them to transcend their current performance by helping them fulfill or traverse their individual zones of proximal development. From a social constructivist standpoint, by deploying mediations the developer aims to empower the learner to make her journey through sociotechnical scaffoldings. Next we will examine the implications of the context engineering guiding and process principles to the development of e-learning contexts.

Guiding Principles

CE proposes a view of information systems as sociotechnical phenomena, not only of the social interaction between human actors but also of their interaction with artifacts and of their influence on the emerging organizational patterns of behavior. The sociotechnical constitution and genesis of collective patterns of behavior, which we understand as the object of development, constitutes the context for the learning experience.

CE proposes a view of development as emancipatory movement. Departing from a critical and subjective perspective of development phenomena, but not restricted to it; for example, recognizing the materiality in the diverse forms of mediation, development will be guided by the emancipatory role. But information systems developer as emancipator may be contradictory. A participatory exercise whereby learners are able to mobilize media to achieve self-development can lead to true emancipation. For this, learners must be able to use the diverse forms of media in ways that further their learning goals, even if unanticipated by the designer. General-purpose instruments, like e-mail, seem to best accommodate these motives. ISD is then viewed as a process instrument and not an end in itself.

Recognize human and nonhuman actors, or *heterogeneous symmetrical interactionism*. If we recognize the materiality in the diverse forms of mediation in helping shape human actions, then we will be driven to consider a middle ground or permanent negotiation between human voluntarism and technological determinism. Neither human action is the expression of free will, independent of its technological infrastructure, nor will the artifacts fully determine the outcome of human actions. The media carry not only action programs that "seek to be learned" but also some degree of flexibility to translations in actual learning circumstances. Sometimes the learning focus is diverted away from what the designer intended to be the object of the learning activity and re-centered on learning about the artifact itself. In a sense, the media become the message.

IT and the organization of learning activities may be aligned or not. That is really circumstantial and teleological. The myth of IT alignment is generally persuasive. In general, we are prone to think that IT artifacts should always be perfectly aligned with desired performance. Yet, we can identify situations where and when alignment is not only difficult but also undesirable. Misalignment can be creative and a transient necessity, for instance, when the learning goal is the mastering of the technological instrument itself. In general, an instrument favors certain organizational patterns of behavior to the detriment of others and, to that extent, it can be made to play a significant role in learning these patterns. IT can also act as a trigger for change by making the learners question the enforced organization patterns. In learning by playing with interactive models it seems important that the IT artifact be designed to reify the desired learning goals, although this seems quite a tricky business, as the designer may be unaware of significant other actors influencing the learners' context. There is also the associated, but quite different, matter of whether the IT is aligned with the social structure inherent or intended within the context of the learning community, and whether that is purposeful or left to chance.

Models as languages, and their use, are expressions of intersubjective understandings. If we want to pursue the goal of emancipation through the development of e-learning contexts, then we have to find ways for the diverse actors, developers, and users of technology to materially express their views and build their own relationships with the media and the learning process. For that, we think of the underlying learning models as expressions of intersubjective understandings: the common ground that enables the collective constitution of meanings and interpretations. For the development of learning experiences it seems necessary to develop models that adequately convey notions about learning motives, goals and paths, influencing actor-networks, roles and organization, interaction patterns and protocols, as well as specific representations relevant within each learning domain. This view of models remains largely a challenge, as currently the previous sharing of technical languages by learners and facilitators is still a requirement. Can a learner influence and benefit from sharing an explicit model of the learning experience or of his or her own learning path? That is still very much dependent on the barriers between disciplinary traditions. General models of the learning experience still retain a fundamental bias, as they are typically developed from the master's viewpoint of the subject matter idiosyncrasies while considering a generalized learner. Considering each learner's point of view in the course of his or her own learning experience in the design for e-learning is a significant challenge, which pertains to questions relating to the understanding of the individual's development process.

Processes Principles

When we proposed the context engineering framework we thought of it as a possible mapping of the action oriented problems when explicitly dwelling between context and media. We do not propose the framework of movements as an algorithm for performing development. In fact, although we think that an immediate instantiation of the framework is possible with currently known techniques, it could easily drift toward a more conventional and deterministic view of prescriptive methods. We think that we do best to recognize the adaptation that goes on in real-life situations. Practitioners may use the CE framework for guidance to think about where they are and what they have done at a moment in development and consider what next move they wish to take to further their development goals contingently. The viewpoints that follow may be understood differently by (a) someone attempting to collaboratively design learning media, (b) someone managing an ongoing e-learning experience, or (c) someone orienting himself or herself though a learning experience while explicitly managing his or her contextual worldview of that experience.

CE proposes no a priori process, but favors a contingent view of development as flux and improvisation. Thinking about e-learning as a complex phenomenon, the result could be understood as an emergence and, either as developers or as managers of the learning experience, our actions only attempt to influence what emergence we would like. As designers of learning media, we attempt not the design of emergence (the learning event in the person) but of what we guess to be its underlying conditions, and this is one main reason why we talk about engineering the context. Of course, from the point of view of someone preparing or organizing an e-learning experience, there is still a place for planning and for managing the resources to be mobilized during actual enactment of the learning situation, as part of modeling the experience.

We should model to make the intersubjective constructions explicit and debatable. (Some would say interobjective—that is a question of basic philosophical stance we will not pursue here.) We think of models as expressions of past, present, or future realities, as currently accessible referents to absent social localities, as shrink-wrapped versions of the "real phenomena," but as yet possessing or representing the relevant relationships and dynamics we wish to acknowledge and deal with. When built on top of shared languages, models enable the construction of intersubjective, explicit, and debatable understandings, which in turn enable user or participant requirements construction and alignment, whatever our positioning in development may be. In managing learning experiences it seems important to adequately communicate the goals and means, so that the learner may play a proactive part in the pursuit if those goals and in the mobilization of the means (e.g., as in learning contracts).

Build early to make the mediators experimentable and the process participative. Interpreting our own experience as developers of IS artifacts, we identified several situations where the early availability of prototypes for the mediators enabled a fast enactment of the context under development and the effective expression by interested actors of their interests and tacit knowledge (Polanyi, 1974) that escaped previous conversations. In these conversations with actual artifacts and procedures, on a microcosm that legitimates more active speech on the part of learners, we uncovered relationships (and actor-networks) that were dormant or unspoken, thus enabling user requirements to be more effectively expressed. Although arguably a difficult situation to achieve and reproduce in developing media for e-learning contexts, it seems particularly important to enact learning situations and reflect on the actual learning taking place and why.

Practitioner's toolbox: collect compatible contextual techniques as instruments to perform the movements and let the context choose them. If we think of the movements as related development problems, we can research and collect useful instruments in the context of these movements. As these movements are related, so are their outcomes and so must be the techniques chosen. At some time or other the learners could become not only participants but also practitioners of their own development, as they acquire the instrumental languages involved and develop new ways to exploit the media at the service of the learning goals. This can easily be witnessed with personal productivity tools. As practitioners, we usually let the situation select the instruments, and not the other way around. While managing an e-learning situation, a choice of techniques and associated media must be made that best fits the goals and learning strategies in that situation, depending on time frames, blend of mediated and presence-based events, availability of learning object resources, range of synchronous and asynchronous modalities, previous development backgrounds or trajectories, social relations between learners, teaming opportunities, and so forth.

Evaluate transformations, not just artifacts. This is possibly the biggest challenge. If we can think of development as a way to achieve transformations, some of these via computational artifacts, and if we can find a way to value these transformations in relation to what they enable further, then we will have more reasons to rethink development beyond technical artifacts. If we consider the value associated with learning to perform some activity or use some technology and the new developments paths that open before us, and that can motivate other transformations, then we are led to think of development and managing learning not only in relation to a fixed performance reference but also on an individual basis, as each learner traverses his or her zone of proximal development. This means managing learning from a learner's viewpoint, which in turn calls for mobilizing learning media, including human resources, from that viewpoint. To what extent this is feasible with the current pressure for a reductionist view of e-learning as economic delivery of content remains largely unknown.

Conclusions

The authors presented a view of the problems related to the role of context in learning and development, individual and organizational, influenced by readings in anthropology, activity theory, and actor-network theory, and of how they relate to the problems of developing e-learning experiences. Next, they briefly presented the context engineering approach to ISD as a framework to think and organize development of virtual contexts for e-learning. This approach proposed to achieve a critical understanding of development as a sociotechnical phenomenon within a cultural and historical envelope, to provide a framework of development problems focused on the relation between a model of context and its mediators, and to use contextuality as the key to performing emancipatory movements while operating on sociotechnical networks as mediators. The authors then attempted to translate fundamental ideas and guiding principles of the approach to the development of virtual learning contexts, elaborating on some of the learning and development issues that arise.

References

Akrich, M. (1992). The de-scription of technical objects. In W. Bijker & J. Law (Eds.), *Shaping technology/building society: Studies on sociotechnical change.* Cambridge, MA: MIT Press.

Alexander, C. W. (1964). *Notes on the synthesis of form.* Harvard: Harvard University Press.

Almeida, A., & Roque, L. (2000, July 3-5). *Simpler, better, faster, cheaper, contextual: Requirements analysis for a new methodological approach to information systems development.* Paper presented at the Proceedings of the 8th European Conference on Information Systems, Vienna, Austria.

Almeida, A., & Roque, L. (2002, April 3-6). Some reflections on IS development as operator of organisational change - A perspective based on activity theory and expansive learning. Paper presented at the *Proceedings of International Conference on Enterprise Information Systems,* Ciudad Real, Spain.

Callon, M. (1991). Techno-economic networks and irreversibility. In J. Law (Ed.), *A sociology of monsters. Essays on power, technology and domination* (pp. 132-164). London: Routledge.

Dilley, R. (1999). *The problem of context.* Oxford: Berghahn Books.

Duranti, A., & Goodwin, C. (1992). *Rethinking context: Language as an interactive phenomenon.* Cambridge: Cambridge University Press.

Engeström, Y. (1987). *Learning by expanding: An activity-theoretical approach to developmental research.* Helsinki: Orienta-Konsultit Oy.

Engeström, Y. (1999). Innovative learning in work teams: Analyzing cycles of knowledge creation in practice. In Y. Engeström, R. Miettinen, & R. L. Punamäki (Eds.), *Perspectives on activity theory.* Cambridge: Cambridge University Press.

Figueiredo, A. D. (2000, June). Web-based learning—Largely beyond content (Keynote address). In F. Restivo & L. Ribeiro (Eds.), *Proceedings of the European Conference on Web-Based Learning Environment* (ISBN 972-752-035-9, pp. 85-88). Porto, Portugal: FEUP Editions.

Gumperz, J. (1992). Contextualization and understanding. In A. Duranti & C. Goodwin (Eds.), *Rethinking context: Language as an interactive phenomenon*. Cambridge: Cambridge University Press.

Hirscheim, R., Klein, H., & Lyytinen, K. (1995). *Information systems development and data modeling—Conceptual and philosophical foundations*. Cambridge: Cambridge University Press.

Iivary, J., Hirscheim, R., & Klein, H. (1998, June). A paradigmatic analysis contrasting information systems development approaches and methodologies. *Information Systems Research, 9*(2), 164-193.

Iivary, J., Hirscheim, R., & Klein, H. (2001, June 27-29). Towards more professional information systems development: ISD as knowledge work. Paper presented at the *Proceedings of the 9th European Conference on Information Systems,* Bled, Slovenia.

Iivary, J., & Lyytinen, K. (1999). Research on information systems development in Scandinavia: Unity in plurality. In W. L. Currie & R. D. Galliers (Eds.), *Rethinking management information systems—An interdisciplinary perspective* (pp. 57-102). Oxford, NY: Oxford UniversityPress.

Latour, B. (1991). Technology is society made durable. In J. Law (Ed.), *A sociology of monsters: Essays on power, technology and domination.* London: Routledge.

Latour, B. (1999a). On recalling ANT. In J. Law & J. Hassard (Eds.), *Actor network theory and after.* Oxford: Blackwell.

Latour, B. (1999b). *Pandora's hope: Essays on the reality of science studies.* Boston: Harvard University Press.

Parolini, C. (1999). *The value net: A tool for competitive strategy.* Chichester: Wiley.

Polanyi, M. J. (1974). *Personal knowledge: Towards a post-critical philosophy.* Chicago: University of Chicago Press.

Roque, L. (2002, August). Teaching and learning engineering design through active socio-technical contexting. Paper presented at the *Proceedings of International Conference on Engineering Education,* Manchester, UK.

Roque, L., Almeida A., & Figueiredo A. D. (2004, June 14-16). Context engineering: An IS development research agenda. Paper presented at the *Proceedings of the 12th European Conference on Information Systems,* Turku, Finland.

Schön, D. (1983). *The reflective practitioner: How professionals think in action.* New York: Basic Books.

Sharfstein, B. A. (1989). *The dilemma of context.* New York University Press.

Vygotsky, L. S. (1986). *Thought and language* (revised by A. Kozulin). Cambridge, MA: MIT Press.

Chapter IV

The Role of Context When Implementing Learning Environments:
Some Key Issues

Bernard Blandin, Cesi-Online, France

Abstract

This chapter presents some outcomes of current research on the role of context when implementing learning environments. It first sets the theoretical and empirical scene of current research on learning, which leads to the conclusion that there is a general agreement on the fact that context influences learning activities. Secondly, the chapter shows how theories of learning materialize and give form to the physical and organizational structure of educational and training institutions. Then, it analyses why institutional praxis applying a given theory of learning may conflict with the implementation of new learning environments. Finally, it provides some sociological guidelines to facilitate the implementation of a new learning paradigm within an organization. With this chapter, the author intends to promote the use of sociology to better understand what is at stake when implementing new learning environments.

Introduction

This chapter is rooted in sociology, and more precisely in the type of sociology that considers that what is called "social" is build through interactions between human beings and between human beings and their environment, including objects (Blandin, 2002b). As a consequence, most human activities—including learning—have to be taken as "situated," and this is why I consider that the context in which an activity takes place is never neutral and plays a role in the achievement of this activity.

The substrate of this chapter is what is called, in France, "learning systems engineering," that is, a methodological approach to designing and managing learning environments and learning situations "taking into account as many variables as possible in order to plan and create an efficient system of action" involving all the stakeholders (Pain, 2003). The question to which the chapter intends to provide some answers is the following: How to produce and implement efficient learning environments taking into account what we know from existing theories?

Answering this question will lead us to better understand the crucial role of context when implementing learning environments: learning environments can neither be designed nor be implemented without taking the organizational context into account, and adapting it in order to fit the learning environment, because context affects several variables of the learning environment, as we will see.

In order to demonstrate this, the chapter is divided into five sections. The first section will establish the theoretical background by investigating modern theories of learning, and showing that they converge toward the evidence that learning is a "situated activity." It sets the theoretical scene and leads to the conclusion that for all current approaches, learning appears as an activity that is context dependant, and some elements of the context appear to have significant impact on learning.

The second section will confront the theoretical background to empirical researches or studies on different learning environments, putting the emphasis on the importance of context on the efficiency of learning situations. It reinforces the conclusions of section 1 with empirical evidences, thus contributing to point out the importance and role of context in the learning process and to understand the influence of contextual issues on learning.

On the basis of these findings, the third section will propose a heuristic model to design new learning environments, which takes context into account, because several variables are context dependant. It is a tentative articulation of two levels (learning situations and the management of learning environments), pointing out the fact that context also includes organizational aspects. This articulation emerges from an empirical model describing the "pillars" on which to build successful implementations of self-directed learning within an organization, and which provides a general framework to design and implement learning environments, including e-learning environments.

The fact that organizational aspects are involved means that any actual implementation of new learning environments within an organization will be confronted with the issue of organizational change. The fourth section explains why this is so and addresses implementation issues. It intends to show that the success of the implementation of a new learning environment is conditioned by change or adaptations of its organizational context.

The fifth section proposes to consider the implementation of new learning environments as an innovation process and summarizes findings from different sociological approaches of innovation that can help design and implement new learning environments. It contributes to enrich the proposed framework by suggesting pragmatic guidelines for a successful development of new learning environments, including organizational learning or knowledge management.

Finally, the conclusion highlights the fact that a sociological standpoint, that is, a standpoint from a discipline that is too rarely concerned with objects such as new learning environments, is necessary to understand the role of context and to successfully design and implement new learning environments.

Theoretical Background

I do not intend to give a full course in learning theories,[1] but a brief reminding of the concepts inspiring contemporaneous thinking is necessary to establish the theoretical background of this chapter.

The first author who pointed out the fact that knowledge results from and is involved in interactions between a human being and his or her environment was, no doubt, John Dewey, in his seminal article "The Reflex Arc Concept in Psychology" (1896). Dewey developed, in this article, a theory in which active manipulation of the environment is necessarily involved in the process of learning. This was further expanded in a number of his writings on education.

In Europe, the ancestor of modern theories of learning was, certainly, Jean Piaget. His general theoretical framework called "genetic epistemology" was targeted to understand how knowledge developed in human organisms. The concept of cognitive structure is central to his theory: cognitive structures are patterns of physical action (schemas) or mental action (concepts) that underlie specific acts of intelligence (Piaget, 1947, 1949). They evolve during the whole lifetime, but the main steps of their development correspond to stages of child development. Cognitive structures change through the processes of adaptation: assimilation and accommodation. Assimilation involves the interpretation of events in terms of existing cognitive structure, whereas accommodation refers to changing the cognitive structure to make sense of the environment. For Piaget, cognitive development consists of a constant effort to adapt to the environment in terms of assimilation and accommodation. For Piaget, learning is, no doubt, a constructive process, since cognitive structures not only are progressively built through different stages during the development phase but also continuously evolve during the whole life, in order to literally "embody" new knowledge, new know-how, or new behaviors as responses to changes in the environment. In other words, learning is provoked by transformations of the context in which someone lives and acts and results from adaptation to the new context.

A second ancestor of modern theories of learning is Lev S. Vygotsky. The major theme of his theoretical framework is that social interaction plays a fundamental role in the development of cognition (Vygotsky, 1962, 1978). He also developed the idea that the potential for cognitive development is limited to a certain cognitive span, which he calls the "zone of proximal development." Furthermore, development, even in the zone of proximal development, depends on full social interaction. As stated by Piaget in his annex to the first English translation of Thought and Language (Vygotsky, 1962), they agree on a number of issues, and in particular on the fact that building cognitive structures depends on "operations" resulting from confrontations either with surrounding objects or with people within the environment, though Vygotsky puts more emphasis on social aspects. Nevertheless, in his approach the context has, again, an influence on the learning process. These theories have been further developed by Jerome S. Bruner. A major theme in Bruner's theoretical framework is that learning is an active process in which learners construct new ideas or concepts on the basis of their current and their past knowledge. The learner selects and transforms information, constructs hypotheses, and makes decisions, relying on cognitive structures to do so. Cognitive structures (i.e., schema, mental models) provide meaning and organization to experiences and allow the individual to "go beyond the information given." In his more recent work, Bruner (1986, 1990, 1996) has expanded his theoretical framework to encompass the social and cultural aspects of learning: our cognitive structures are framed and shaped by our culture, by the "symbolic works" produced by anyone, and by the "worlds" produced by artists. The context, this time in a very broad sense (physical, social, and cultural), influences learning.

Piaget's successors at the University of Geneva try to measure the impact of social relations on learning, through experimentations involving objects and different configurations of group learning: groups of peers, children at different cognitive stages, children and adults. They have found that these configurations have an impact on learning, which confirms and further develops Vygotsky's findings: learning in groups is more efficient than learning alone, small discrepancies in cognitive stages benefit the less advanced learner, social roles have an impact, and so forth. This lead to the theory of "socio-cognitive conflict" as a tentative explanation of these results (Doise & Mugny, 1981): a learning situation is more efficient when the results of an activity conflict with the interpretation provided by the existing cognitive structures, and when this conflict can be resolved through discussion with others, that is, when the accommodation process is forced by the learning situation and steered by some participants. Again, in this theory, social context appears to play a major role in the learning process.

Based on a completely different approach, and rooted in the behaviorist paradigm, though encompassing cognitive aspects, the social learning theory of Bandura emphasizes the importance of observing and modeling the behaviors, attitudes, and emotional reactions of others. It explains human behavior in terms of continuous reciprocal interaction between cognitive, behavioral, and environmental influences (Bandura, 1971). Again, in this theory, the learning process appears to be heavily dependant on the context in which it takes place.

Initiated by Lucy Suchman's research on man-machine communication (1987), the "situated cognition" paradigm led to several works on "situated learning," assuming that if, in general, cognition and knowledge are situated, the acquisition of knowledge might also be situated. In other words, it might depend on the activity, the context, and the culture in which it occurs. Among these, Jean Lave and Etienne Wenger's observations of different cases of apprenticeship (Yucatec midwives, Vai and Gola tailors, U.S. Navy quartermasters, meat-cutters, and nondrinking alcoholics in Alcoholics Anonymous) led them to the conclusions that learning should not be seen only as the acquisition of knowledge by individuals but rather as a process of social participation, and that the nature of the situation impacts significantly on this process (Lave & Wenger, 1991).

Other researchers have further developed the theory of situated learning. Brown, Collins, and Duguid (1989) emphasize the idea of cognitive apprenticeship and of "enculturation": just as the meaning of words is partly inherited from their context of use,[2] either conceptual or practical knowledge inherits from the community in which it has been learned. Thus, ways of doing, uses, and meaning are dependent on the context in which they have been learned and bear its characteristics.

All the theories of learning explored so far consider that learning is context dependant. A recent article reinforces this point by exploring how various cultural aspects impact on learning to such an extent that it is possible to consider also the existence of "cultures of learning" to name different ways of learning according to different "social worlds" (Blandin, 2003b). Many findings of these theories are now confirmed by the functional imagery of the brain: Piaget's accommodation process corresponds in fact to the reorganization of neural maps; emotion and cognition cannot be separated, which means that elements of context having emotional resonance for the learner impact the learning situation; imitation has a biological basis since the discovery of the "mirror neurons" phenomenon; and so forth.[3]

Admitting that most of the learning activity is informal (Carré & Charbonnier, 2003; Pain, 1989; Wenger, 1998), arguments in favor of "situated cognition" are acceptable, and so is, as well, the role played by the context of learning in informal learning situations. But even in formal learning situations, the theories of learning that I have presented earlier consider that several elements of the context, such as the physical environment, the social configurations, the culture of the community in which a learning situation takes place, have an influence on and impact the learning activity. So, we should find a confirmation in field researches, and this is the objective of the next section.

Findings from Empirical Surveys

The successors of Piaget have done a lot of field research in schools, and I have presented earlier their major findings in social psychology: the role of "socio-cognitive conflict" in learning. Others results of these researches can be quoted, such as "social marking," which account for the fact that the social role of a participant in a learning situation impacts the results of learning (Perret-Clermont, 1979).

A wide range of researches have been done around the uses of information and communication technologies (ICT) in education. To survey the results of all these researches would have been quite impossible for this chapter if this job had not already been achieved recently by a team funded by the French Ministry of Education, which wanted to provide an overview of the results of researches on ICT in education. This meta-research surveyed the results of about 1,400 research works worldwide on the use of ICT for learning at school level (Legros & Crinon, 2002). I will briefly present this report and comment on its conclusions.

Research analyzed in this publication belong to various disciplines: cognitive psychology, social psychology, sociology, communication theories, semantics, and even didactics of disciplines like mathematics or languages, which make all of the works related to the subject quite difficult to identify. Two categories of research appear: research based on experimentations, aiming to measure the impact of a given set of parameters on learning (generally, quantitative research); and research aiming to understand, through observations and interviews, what happens when ICT is used in schools in ordinary learning situations (generally, qualitative researches).

The researches surveyed by this team cover a wide range of topics. I have identified two categories of topics surveyed: forms and situations of uses of ICT for learning "in general," stemming from disciplines such as cognitive sciences or communication sciences; and the impact of ICT when acquiring a particular knowledge or skill, driven by disciplines such as didactics of languages and didactics of sciences (mathematics, physics, life sciences, etc.).

Research of the first category measure the impact of different media (texts, images, sound) on learning and the effect of their combination ("multimodality") and of sensorial immersion (or "virtual reality"). Works can be found on the impact of situations of use of ICT (learner alone or in collaboration with others), on effectiveness of ICT according to the type of learner's activity (search for information, problem solving, etc.), or on different combinations of situations and activities (collaborative problem solving, etc.).

Research of the second category has an interest in similar topics, but applied to a particular context of knowledge or skill building: communicating with others, reading and understanding texts, producing texts, learning a second language, and building representations of the world (and in particular scientific concepts) are the five domains that are covered by the research surveyed.

Taking into account the diversity of research methodologies, fields, and topics, the authors of the report are quite circumspect about tentative generalizations of their results and suggest that there is still a need to intensify research in this field to develop cross-disciplinary cooperation and to reinforce the relations between researchers and practitioners. Nonetheless, in spite of this circumspection, it seems to me that two general statements can be drawn from their synthesis:

- If there is a real effect of ICT on learning, it appears when, and only when, the tools are embedded by the teacher within relevant learning situations.
- To generalize such effect implies to develop a culture of ICT among teachers and to help them transform their practices. This can only be done if there is an institutional context favorable to such a transformation.

These general conclusions confirm that context plays a part at two levels: at the level of the learning situation and at the level of the learning institution. Two validated results among those presented in the report illustrate the role of context in the learning situation level.

- A large quantity of data confirm that collaborative learning is more effective than learning alone. Thus, the most effective ways of using ICT appear to be those that are associated with active and collaborative learning environments, that is, those that generate learners' commitment to a collaborative work aiming to produce knowledge, to create common shared meaning, and to build knowledge together.
- Using a computer to acquire skills in the field of written communication is effective only when it allows "multiauthor writing", that is, when it is used for collaborative works stressing the instrumental dimension of writing; for example, when collective writing supports knowledge building while communicating with others through the production of documents or databases, when building Web sites, and so forth. Such learning situations are effective

because they allow the development of meta-cognitive abilities related to the regulation of the collaborative activities: elicitation of aims and methodologies, production of project reports, and so forth.

The research directed by Legros & Crinon (2002) confirms, from an empirical viewpoint, the conclusions drawn from the theoretical background analysis in section 1 on the importance of the context ("situatedness," integration into an activity framework, implementation of social activities, etc.) at the learning situation level. As a conclusion, it also points out the need to consider the institutional context as a key factor for success, stressing the fact that "good practices" in the use of ICT for learning at school, as they appear from the survey, require a favorable institutional context to be implemented and that, in particular, space and time constraints should be made more flexible.

Time and space constraints are not, however, the only factors preventing the use of ICT in schools. Another factor that has been pointed out by the authors, though they have not derived any consequences, is that learning with ICT is effective only in active and collaborative (i.e., constructivist or socio-constructivist) learning environments, which are, currently, not the majority. And to implement such environments means a change of paradigm (Kuhn, 1962), which is not so easy, because it implies to change not only the practices but also elements constituting professional identities (roles, values, etc.). I will come back to this issue in the beginning of section 4. But before that, we need to have a look at what we know about the use of ICT in training within companies.

The number of research studies on how people learn in companies is smaller than the number of those focusing on schools. I have already mentioned Jean Lave and Etienne Wenger's work on communities of practice and "apprenticeship" through "peripheral legitimate participation" (Lave & Wenger, 1991; Wenger 1998). A recent research associating six (French and multinational) companies shows that most "professional" learning is informal and occurs during working situations, such as collaborative problem solving, designing new products and services, and so forth (Carré & Charbonnier, 2003). However, to the best of my knowledge, there are not many works on formal learning environments in companies, as though it was taken for granted that there is nothing more to discover in this field! Or would that be because learning is becoming so strategic an activity that no one feels the need to investigate this field any longer?

Nonetheless, as in schools, introduction of ICT in companies training practices should reveal some variables impacting on learning effectiveness. But there are few research studies on that topic—at least publicly available—despite the fact that huge amounts of money were invested some years ago in e-learning projects, and that some of these e-learning projects appeared to be big failures. In order to understand why, a survey sponsored by the American Society for Training and Development (ASTD), conducted by Eliot Masie, intended to determine the conditions for successfully implementing an e-learning environment (Masie, 2001). It confirms the crucial importance of contextual—and in particular organizational and managerial—factors.

The main results of this survey, investigating the reasons why e-learning projects failed, are as follows.

- In order to be accepted within a company, e-learning should be advertised and promoted, like any new service within the company, because "e-learning" does not mean anything for most of the people. Fostering championship, proposing contests and awards, is a good way to raise rapidly awareness of management and of employees.

- In order to be accepted, e-learning sessions should be completed during working hours, and support (tutoring) should be provided during the whole working time.

- In order for e-learning to be accepted, it is necessary to create an "e-learning culture" within the company. This conclusion can read as follows: learning should be considered as important instead of as a waste of time, and spending time to learn with a computer during working time should be considered as a "normal" activity.

- In order to be accepted, and to confirm the importance given to learning and therefore to acquiring knowledge and skills, learning should be recognized, and provision of incentives such as peer recognition and career advance should be attached to the completion of given learning paths.

This clearly means that, to successfully implement e-learning environments, organizational context and the way it fosters and supports employees' motivation plays the main part. To some extent, successfully implementing e-learning means to be able to create a "culture of learning" (Brown et al., 1989) and the organizational context in which this "culture of learning" could be deployed. Again, depending on the company, this could imply a change of paradigm, the current "managerial paradigm" as well as of the current "training paradigm."

Both theory and empirical research emphasize the importance of context for the effectiveness of learning environments. Context appears to affect the learning environment at two levels.

- *The learning situation:* At this level, the factors that play a role are the learning activities, the tools and means used, and the participants involved and their relations.

- *The institutional surrounding and its organization:* At this level, the factors that play a role are the "culture of learning" (i.e. the learning paradigm in use), motivators and management policies, support activities, and the organization of time and space for learning.

A Heuristic Model to Conceive Learning Environments

As expressed in Legros and Crinon's compilation of research studies on the use of ICT in schools (Legros & Crinon, 2002), learning environments based on ICT or using ICT are effective if and only if they are rooted in constructivist or socio-constructivist paradigms. This empirical conclusion meets the standpoint expressed by many researchers, such as Brandt (1998), Brown et al. (1989), Depover, De Lièvre, Deschryver, Lamm, Quintin, and Strebelle (1998), Jonassen (1991, 1994), Jonassen and Rohrer-Murphy (1999), and Koper (2000).

Thus, there seems to exist wide agreement in that the use of constructivist or socio-constructivist paradigms to design learning environments for schools and for initial education makes them more suitable for learning. Such learning environments need to be activity driven, to take into account the learners' initial level and learning style, and to embed collaborative activities planned to provoke and resolve socio-cognitive and other collaborative activities to develop meta-cognitive abilities. So, it seems that we have the recipe and the ingredients to produce effective learning situations for schools and initial education and to control the factors that might affect it. Once agreed on that, there are, nonetheless, some practical issues remaining: If we design it, will we be allowed to build it? And if we are allowed to build it, will we get staff and administrative support to run it? Finally, if we can answer yes to both, will the learners come? All these questions highlight the fact that a good educational paradigm does not tell anything about the organizational, cultural, and economical context in which it is implemented. If a good educational paradigm is necessary to conceive effective learning environments, it does not appear sufficient to guarantee their implementation.

Now, let us consider adult learning. Though constructivism encompasses all the ages of life, we know that for adults the development stages are supposed to be over and that learning, for them, relies on an essential component that is not present at the beginning of life and that is supposed to result from a fully accomplished development process: self-direction (Knowles, 1973). Since Knowles's pioneering work (1975), a lot of research on self-directed learning has been achieved, providing complementary results on both sides of the Atlantic.[4] Self-directed learning does not necessarily require formal learning situations, though they are not systematically discarded. But if an adult opts for formal learning, the learning environment supporting self-directed learning should meet some particular requirements. Philippe Carré (1992) has proposed and empirically validated such requirements; for example, through the practice of a network of more than 800 learning resource centers in France, which has been dedicated to adult learning for almost 20 years: the "Ateliers de pédagogie personnalisée (APP)" network (Carré, 2003).

According to Carré (2003), the "pillars" that support a self-directed learning environment are the following.

- The learners must have a learning project; that is, they know what they wish to learn, and they are motivated to achieve their project.

- A contract is established between the learner and the learning environment, stipulating when, where, how, through which steps, with which support, under which conditions, and so forth, the learner achieves his or her learning project.

- A methodological support is provided, because self-directed learning implies a capacity for self-study[5] together with meta-cognitive abilities, which have to be developed if not already acquired.

- A mentor or a coach facilitates learning and supports the learning process whenever required.

- An open, flexible learning environment allows the learner to learn when and where he or she prefers or is available for learning activities.

- Alternating individual and collective sequences is required, because collaborative learning is necessary to anchor what has been learned and to develop meta-cognitive abilities.

- Three levels of accompaniment are needed: individual tutoring, group progress monitoring, and institutional facilitation to organize personalized learning paths, schedules, and rhythms.

Learning environments based on these seven pillars are fully compatible with socio-constructivist learning environments, since they require the implementation of features that are necessary to develop such environments. In addition, they require what a socio-constructivist approach cannot guarantee: that the institutional context be adequate! This is, indeed, a very weak point of cognitive or psychological or pedagogical approaches to learning: they only consider the learning situation level, but not the institutional surroundings, which might lead to the design of wonderful learning environments that will never be implemented, because the institutional context will not permit it, for various reasons:

- According to their contracts, teachers have to teach, and no time is allocated for side-activities like tutoring or accompanying an individual learner's path.

- Administrative staff is not ready either to manage real-time flows of registration and prior learning assessment or to deal with flexible schedules and opening hours.

- Nobody has allocated time to assess prior learning, prescribe an individual learning path, and establish consequently a contract.

- Premises or equipment, or both, available do not allow individual learning sequences.

- Normal opening hours do not allow many people to learn out of their working hours.

- The cost for accommodating individual learners in an educational institution delivering classroom learning is too high.

The "seven pillars" approach requires that we address pedagogical issues and organizational issues simultaneously. It provides a heuristic model that appears to be appropriate for the design of socio-constructivist as well as self-directed learning environments, because it takes into account both levels: learning situations and their institutional surroundings. But a sociological approach is needed if the implementation phase has to be "engineered" and managed. This is the raison d'être of the next section.

Implementation Issues

When I give my course "Learning Processes and Learning Paradigms" to young teachers or trainers in vocational training, I always give them the following exercise: after having presented and discussed the main paradigms, the conception of mind they embed, the type of pedagogy and of learning situations they induce, and so forth, each of them has to invent a short learning situation on an easy topic picked up at random, prepare it, and play it for 5 minutes, their colleagues playing the learners' role. They have only one specific constraint: they must design their situation in accordance with one given "learning paradigm" (Blandin, 2003a) (Socrates' maieutics, Aristotelian objectivism, behaviorism, constructivism). They have 1 hour to prepare, and, in case they do not know the topic they have drawn, documentation about it is provided. They have rough material (paper, pens, cardboard) available to build learning material; they can also use a computer to produce texts or images; they can move tables and chairs; and so forth. The result is always the same, whatever the paradigm they are supposed to implement is: they go to the blackboard, write the title of the lesson, and then start to teach, sometimes with images or objects they have built with cardboard or with slides made on the computer. Even if the paradigm they were asked to implement was "constructivism," they go to the blackboard and teach. And when I ask, "Do you think that what you are presenting is a 'constructivist' learning situation?" everybody answers, "No . . . but it is easier to do so, because we are used to it . . . you told us that we have 5 minutes . . . if we use constructivism, it will be too long. . ."

This exercise reveals that a "habit," or, in other words, a know-how that has been embodied and appears as tacit knowledge and skills, can prevail over a more accurate but not so far instrumentalized knowledge that has just been learned, or that does not seem to comply with time or space constraints. And this is a sort of contradiction any new paradigm or tool has to deal with. Using a new paradigm or a new tool results from a several-steps process: discovery; building a first representation; considering the object, enriching its representation, learning about the object, considering potential uses, learning how to use it, and building schemas of use;

starting to use the object, mastering some uses, and so forth (Blandin, 2002b). To achieve such a process, favorable conditions and a lot of effort sustained by motivation are needed. If conditions are not favorable, if for example the first representation is unpleasant, or if no potential use appears or motivation is low, particularly when it is necessary to learn about the object or to learn how to use it, the process might be interrupted and the new paradigm or the new tool will never be "in use."

On the other hand, the constraints that are attached to any educational system, such as the curriculum leading to a qualification, the time allocated to each part of it, and the organization of the classroom space and its equipment, determine what Simmel (1908) called the "form" of the educational relation, which tends to become an acknowledged standard for the educational institutions, taken for granted as "best practices" and reproduced as such. This form, once established, materializes into an organization, which tends to resist to any further change (Alter, 2000). Each learning paradigm produces different forms of the educational relation, which are literally "embodied" into different types of organizations, producing different "formal learning systems," as named by Blandin (2002a): for example, Aristotelian objectivism is embodied into Comenius' amphitheater-and-curriculum model or its reduced version known as the "classroom" (or its virtual implementations), whereas constructivism is embodied into an open space facilitating the achievement of individual learning projects by providing easy access to various kinds of resources, as is a "learning resource center" (or its virtual implementations). The educational relations associated with these formal learning systems are different and can be described as follows: Teacher-who-knows-and-transfers-knowledge/Learner-who-receives-and-records-knowledge within the Aristotelian objectivist paradigm, and Learner-who-builds-knowledge/Mentor-who-helps-learner-to-build-knowledge within the constructivist paradigm. These two examples of different organizations and of different types of educational relation—beyond the different roles of the teacher/trainer/tutor/mentor confirm the hypothesis that the learning paradigms might be associated with and characterize different "social worlds" (Blandin, 2002a, 2003b).

Thus, a "culture of learning" (Brown et al., 1989) is at the same time embodied within human beings under the form of learning or teaching habits and preferences, and within educational institutions, in which they shape premises, activities, and organization. This explains why context necessarily impacts on learning environments: a learning environment is shaped not only by those who conceive it but also by the physical and organizational structures in which it is implemented, which appear as a set of constraints for the design (facilities and equipments available within the institution or for the learners, possible investment, etc.).

Generally individuals working in educational institutions share the same "culture of learning," which is also the one that frames the institution itself. In other words, ideally, the institution and its staff belong to a single "social world." But it may happen that this is not the case: individuals might try to implement other learning paradigms than the one that is generally in use in their institution. In such a case, the forms that shape the activities, the premises, and the organization conflict with the new practices if they simply do not impede their implementation: for example, implementing a learning resource center in a classroom-based institution requires investments and transformations that cannot be done without the agreement of management. Conversely, the institution may have decided to move toward the implementation of a new learning paradigm in order to adapt to a new demand for example, individualization of learning paths—and this implementation may appear to be difficult because the staff is not prepared to change their habits. These are typical issues relating to innovation and organizational change. As a consequence, the shift of paradigm that is required to build efficient self-directed learning environments or learning environments using ICT appears to be similar to a cultural "conversion" of teachers and trainers, and at the same time requires organizational change in the education and training institutions. Thus, implementing new learning environments can easily compare with situations of innovation within other types of organizations, and therefore, sociology of change and sociology of innovation can be useful to understand what is at stake, and how such situations can be successfully managed.

I make the hypothesis that many difficulties pointed out in the "renewal" of education process emerge from the fact that educational institutions are not considered as "organizations" similar to the other organizations, and that lessons learned from the sociology of organizations or sociology of innovation are not considered as applicable to education and training. In disagreement with this, my opinion is that some of these lessons are applicable, as I will show in the next section.

Some Understanding Provided by Sociological Approaches

Within the scope of this chapter, it is not possible to cover all sociological approaches which might be applicable to education and training and from which lessons can be learned. Kerr (1996) presents a vast panorama of sociological approaches used to understand several aspects of technologies in education: sociology of organizations, sociology of groups and classes, sociology of social movements, with a presentation of the main issues and controversies, together with a discussion of sociological methods applicable. I will focus more on approaches addressing innovation issues in order to identify guidelines that can be applied to the implementation of new learning environments, considered as an innovation within an educational organization. The sociological mainstream that will be explored hereafter is sociology of innovation.

Sociology of innovation encompasses several standpoints, elaborated from several recognized meanings of the word "innovation." Five approaches of innovation can be considered (Alter, 2002b), which are summarized as follows: (1) Innovation appears as risk taking, which raises the question of the rationality of the decision, that is, "Why take risks?" (socioeconomical theories). (2) It can also be considered as a result of organizational learning, and the associated question is "How an organization learns?" (theories of organizational learning). (3) A third way to consider innovation is as a collective action, which breaks established rules and which raises the question "How organizational rules are established and negotiated?" (theories of joint regulation). (4) It is also considered through the question of actors, which can be phrased as "Who innovates and where do they come from?" which further raises the questions of identities and interactions of social worlds (theories of sociotechnical networks, or psychosociological theories of influence). (5) Finally, innovation can be considered as a social process based on the emergence of new paradigms or of new forms of rationality, which produces capacities of adaptation and anticipation while generating conflicts between actors or institutions, or both. This approach raises the questions of the dynamics of this process and of its control (theories of "ordinary innovation").

Socioeconomical theories considering innovation in products were initiated by the Austrian economist Joseph A. Schumpeter in the beginning of the 20th century. For him, the innovation process is launched by "outsiders" who are taking risks; then, if the type of product appears to be able to generate profits, imitators invest widely in similar products, and many related secondary innovations burst out. Then, the newly established rules and market positions slow down the innovation process (Schumpeter, 1934).

The dissemination of an innovation within a given population, as described by the psycho-sociological theories of influence (Katz & Lazarsfeld, 1955), though these researches are not rooted in the same discipline, appears to follow the same steps: "pioneers" start to use the innovative product; then, informed and incited by the media, and the message being relayed by communities, "imitators" follow; and finally, the reluctant population adopts the product as well, which marks the end of the process. These two phenomena can be represented by the same diagram, the "S curve" (or Quetelet logistic function).

Both these approaches can be criticized, because the processes they describe are presented as mechanical, and also because there are plenty of inventions that do not follow successfully the "S curve" and fail to appear as an innovation.[6] Furthermore, it does not explain what makes the difference between a successful innovation and a dropout invention. Nonetheless, the lesson that can be drawn from this approach is that, when successful, the innovation changes the rules of the socioeconomical or organizational game, and to succeed in changing actual rules supposes that at one particular moment of the process, when the imitators come in, social norms change (Alter, 2002a). And this leads to a central question: how do social norms evolve?

Another set of approaches, theories of organizational learning, tries to provide answers to this question. Argyris and Schön (1978) first addressed the issue of "organizational learning." They noticed that the rules and the "norms" of an organization, such as those written in official documents, job descriptions, and so forth, are frequently transgressed, and that there is always a gap between actual practices (theories "in use") and what they are supposed to be according to rules and norms (theories "espoused"). Innovation is made possible because there is such a gap, and, in that way, innovation always appears, at the beginning, as a transgression of norms and established rules (Alter, 2000, 2002a). But, according to Argyris and Schön (1978), the organization considered from a rationalistic viewpoint cannot tolerate too large a discrepancy between theories "in use" and theories "espoused," and in order to fill this gap it has to evolve so as to map the rules and the "images" of the organization onto the real practices. A learning organization is an organization that is able to self-adapt continuously to changes in practices when they are provoked by changes in the environment.[7] Learning, for an organization, is a "double loop" process. The first loop allows the employees to adapt to changes in their environment by learning individually in order to become more efficient according to the actual rules. If the process stops there ("single loop learning"), the organization might be more efficient in a given context but does not evolve with the context. This is why the learning organization has to go a step further ("double loop learning"): it also has to change its rules and norms to adapt to the environment through negotiations at the executive level (Argyris & Schön, 1978). Thus, learning, for an organization, is equivalent to changing its rules, and negotiation makes it possible. This is an important lesson from this approach, which is also confirmed by the "theory of joint regulation."

Coming from socioeconomics researches, this theory, as developed by Reynaud (1989), leads to similar conclusions: an organization is ruled by "formal rules" as well as by "tacit rules," agreed on by the working communities. The organization can work and produce only because there is a "space for freedom" between the strict application of formal rules and the implementation of tacit rules, and this space for freedom, or this "maneuvering margin," is negotiated. Not only innovation but also the daily operations within an organization appear to depend on the existence of such a space for maneuvering. Changing the rules, be they tacit or formal, appears as a result of a "collective learning" process. These approaches give a first answer to the question on how organizational rules and norms evolve: they generally evolve informally in order to make the practices efficient enough to achieve the prescribed work and to overcome potential dysfunctions of the prescribed organization. But when the gap between real work and prescribed work is too large, adjustments of the organization are needed, which can only be resolved through negotiation, either to prevent a crisis or to solve it.

Further findings on organizational learning and on how people learn within an organization have been provided by the works, already quoted, on situated cognition and communities of practice (Lave & Wenger, 1991; Wenger, 1998): the rules and norms of a "community of practice," that is, of a group of practitioners within an organization, are learned informally as a social mechanism of integration within the community. This might amend the organizational learning theory as follows: the "single loop learning" level does not involve only individuals but also communities of practitioners, which makes it more coherent with the joint regulation theory and clearly establishes the "double loop learning" as a negotiation of rules and norms between communities of practitioners and the institution, in order to bridge the gap between actual practices within the community and formal institutional rules.

Up to now, the approaches described provide some hints to understand how to address innovation issues within an organization, but do not help to devise a proactive attitude toward innovation from the management side, which is what is, in my opinion, actually missing to facilitate implementation of new learning environments in educational or training institutions. This is where theories of sociotechnical networks can help. These theories emerge from the works done in laboratories in the late 1980s to understand "science in progress" through the observation of daily life (Callon, 1988; Callon & Latour, 1990). They develop an interesting concept: any research or innovative project has to create a network of parties interested in the results of the project around the objects and equipment required to implement the project. This appears as a sine qua non condition to its viability. This network is called a *sociotechnical network* and is the form in which the project is embodied. To bring the project to reality, the network has to give birth to institutional forms materializing its structure and organization (committees, formal associations, titles within the project organization), its decisions (minutes of the meeting, publications, press releases, Web sites), and so forth. This process is called *investing in forms* (Callon, 1988). The result is the creation of communities, habits, documents, information, and so forth, which testify for the project life and for its inscription in a given local, political, professional, scientific, or technical environment.

Any innovation project has to process in that way in order to inform, gather, associate, and motivate followers beyond the pioneering period. The important lesson from this approach is that any project starts in someone's mind and ends with concrete achievements in the real world. The path from the promoter's mind to the implementation in the world is mile-stoned with many "investments in forms," which progressively inscribe the project in the real world, associate people committed to the project achievement, allow to raise money for its completion, and so forth. The wider and more solid the network, the more successful the project is. And this seems to be a general rule, which can be used as a heuristic for innovation project management.

The fifth approach listed in the beginning of this section, the theory of ordinary innovation, at the same time allows both to enrich and to limit the application of such a heuristic: it reminds us that the innovation process, at least under its organizational aspects, can be understood as transgressing rules of an organization in order to be more efficient or to develop new activities. This is becoming at the same time a very common process in current organizations, which are more and more complex and demanding, and a reflexive process, which makes the actors more and more competent in choosing their cognitive, affective, and relational investment toward the organization they are working in (Alter, 2002a). In other terms, their commitment to innovation decided elsewhere will certainly become more and more subject to negotiation.

Since educational or training institutions are all different and evolve in different contexts, the proposed heuristic will lead to specific implementation of new learning environments in each case, and change will have to be managed according to the specificity of the case. Nonetheless, some "best practices" can be drawn from the evaluation of successful projects, such as the following:

- to carefully analyze the context and evaluate the actors' standpoints concerning the project;
- to associate all concerned actors and stakeholders since the very beginning of the project, both at decision level and operational level;
- to make sure that there is a shared vision of the project among actors and stakeholders, which results from negotiation with all actors and stakeholders;
- to make sure that this vision is not betrayed during the implementation phase by carefully writing content-related, technical, and organizational specifications;
- to create organizational structures and rules that provide legitimacy to the project (steering committee, technical committee, organizational chart, agreements and contracts, etc.);
- to look for consensus and to formalize in writing all decisions (in form of "resolutions" or "requests" agreed on during meetings between the participants),
- to carefully monitor each phase of the project, and to regulate relations between actors and stakeholders during the whole project life; and
- to regularly communicate information about the project life and to publicize project events and achievements.

Such practices appear to be necessary to successfully implement a new learning environment, but they are certainly not sufficient: in other words, they should not be taken for the recipe that guarantees in any case to successfully implement e-learning within an organization.

Conclusion

In this chapter, we have seen that modern learning theories consider learning as situated, which means that the context in which learning environments are implemented plays a part in their efficiency. Furthermore, it appeared that organizational context in which learning environments are implemented also conditioned the way they are considered by learners.

I have then demonstrated that even if learning environments are well designed, according to the best practices of "learning systems engineering," and optimized according to learning theories, their successful implementation requires conditions that are dependent both on organizational issues and favorable consideration from the organization in which they are implemented. Not only from a managerial but also a cultural viewpoint, the "culture of learning" of the organization must be appropriate to the type of learning environment that is implemented.

When such conditions are not fulfilled, implementing new learning environments has to be considered as an innovation process, and the findings of sociology of innovation can be helpful to manage such a project. In other words, learning systems engineering does not mean only designing learning systems or learning environments, but also modeling the context in which they will be implemented and managing a project aiming to achieve the favorable conditions for this implementation.

Learning systems engineering, in fact, has to be understood as building a sociotechnical network favorable to a given learning environment, taking into account the organization in which it will be implemented, its rules and norms, and all the actors that might be involved at one stage or another of the project life and with whom negotiation will be necessary: this appears to be the only way to cater for a tentative implementation of a new paradigm within education and training institutions.

Endnotes

[1]   A good overview is given at http://tip.psychology.org/. It presents short notices on 50 theories of learning and their practical issues. In order to avoid what would resemble paraphrasing, this section borrows some synthetic wording from this site.

[2]   Linguistics calls such a property "indexicality."

[3]   A good and easy-to-read synthesis is the work of Jeannerod (2002).

[4]   Basic books on self-directed learning are those by Long (1995) for America and Carré (1992) for Europe.

[5]   Which does not mean that self-study is the only learning situation in such environments (see pillar 6).

[6]   See, for example in the field of media, the interesting initiative of the "dead media project," which tries to identify all the invented media that never succeed on the market (Jennings, 2001).

[7]   The idea comes from "cybernetics," which is part of the theoretical background of Argyris and Schön's (1978) book.

References

Alter, N. (2000). *L'innovation ordinaire*. Paris: Presses Universitaires de France.

Alter, N. (2002a). L'innovation: un processus collectif ambigu. In N. Alter (Ed.), *Les logiques de l'innovation. Approche pluridisciplinaire* (pp. 15-40). Paris: Éditions la Découverte.

Alter, N. (Ed.). (2002b). *Les logiques de l'innovation. Approche pluridisciplinaire*. Paris: Éditions la Découverte.

Argyris, C., & Schön, D. (1978). *Organizational learning: A theory of action perspective*. Reading, MA: Addison Wesley.

Bandura, A. (1971). *Social learning theory*. General Learning Press.

Blandin, B. (2002a). Les mondes sociaux de la formation. In Les TIC au service des nouveaux dispositifs de formation. *Education Permanente, 152*(2002-3), 199-211.

Blandin, B. (2002b). *La construction du social par les objets*. Paris: Presses Universitaires de France.

Blandin, B. (2003a). Usability evaluation of online learning programmes. A sociological standpoint. In C. Ghaoui (Ed.), *Usability evaluation of online learning programmes* (pp. 313-330). Hershey, PA: Idea Group Inc.

Blandin, B. (2003b). Localization of software and learning material for SMEs: How is it possible? In G. Attwell (Ed.), *Exploring models and partnership for e-learning in SMEs*. Bangor, UK: Knownet. Retrieved September 15, 2003, from http://www.theknownet.com/ict_smes_seminars/papers/blandin.html

Brandt, R. (1998). *Powerful learning*. Retrieved February 24, 2003, from the ASCD Web site: http://www.ascd.org/publications/books/1998brandt/1998brandttoc.html

Brown, J. S., Collins, A., & Duguid, S. (1989). Situated cognition and the culture of learning. *Educational Researcher, 18*(1), 32-42.

Bruner, J. (1986). *Actual minds, possible worlds*. Cambridge, MA: Harvard University Press.

Bruner, J. (1990). *Acts of meaning*. Cambridge, MA: Harvard University Press.

Bruner, J. (1996). *The culture of education*. Cambridge, MA: Harvard University Press.

Callon, M. (Ed.). (1988). *La science et ses réseaux. Genèse et circulation des faits scientifiques*. Paris: Éditions La Découverte.

Callon, M., & Latour, B. (1990). *La science telle qu'elle se fait*. Paris: Éditions La Découverte.

Carré, P. (1992). *L'autoformation dans la formation professionnelle*. Paris: La Documentation Française.

Carré, P. (2003). L'autoformation accompagnée en APP ou les sept piliers revisités. In P. Carré, & M. Tetart (Eds.), *Les ateliers de pédagogie personnalisée, ou l'autoformation accompagnée en actes* (pp. 125-148). Paris: L'Harmattan.

Carré, P., & Charbonnier, O. (Eds.). (2003). *Les apprentissages professionnels informels*. Paris: L'Harmattan.

Depover, C., De Lièvre, B., Deschryver, N., Lamm, A., Quintin, J.J., & Strebelle, A. (1998). *Un modèle d'apprentissage à distance basé sur le partage des connaissances*. Retrieved February 21, 2003, from http://www.umh.ac.be/ute/articles/pdf/981_113.pdf

Dewey, J. (1896). The reflex arc concept in psychology. In J. Boydston (Ed.), *The collected works of John Dewey* (Vol. 5, pp. 96-110). Carbondale: Southern Illinois University Press.

Doise, W., & Mugny, G. (1981). *Le développement social de l'intelligence*. Paris: InterEditions.

Jeannerod, M. (2002). *Le cerveau intime*. Paris: Éditions Odile Jacob.

Jennings, T. (2001). *Dead media project: Working notes arranged by category*. Retrieved August 25, 2001, from http://www.deadmedia.org/notes/index-cat.html

Jonassen, D.H. (1991). Objectivism vs constructivism: Do we need a new paradigm? *Educational Technology Research and Development, 39*(3), 5-14.

Jonassen, D. H. (1994). *Technology as cognitive tools: Learners as designers (IT Forum. Paper 1)*. Retrieved February 24, 2003, from http://it.coe.uga.edu/itforum/paper1/paper1.html

Jonassen, D. H., & Rohrer-Murphy, L. (1999). Activity theory as a framework for designing constructivist learning environments. *Educational Technology Research and Development, 47*(1), 61-79.

Katz, E., & Lazarsfeld, P. F. (1955). *Personal influence. The part played by the people in the flow of mass communication*. Glencoe: Free Press.

Kerr, S. T. (1996). Towards a sociology of educational technology. In D. H. Jonassen (Ed.), *A handbook of research for educational communications and technology*. New York: Macmillan. Retrieved February 25, 2003, from http://faculty.washington.edu/stkerr/ETHB04.html

Knowles, M. (1973). *The adult learner: A neglected species*. Houston, TX: Gulf Publishing.

Knowles, M. (1975). *Self-directed learning: A guide for learners and teachers*. New York: Association Press.

Koper, R. (2000). *From change to renewal: Educational technology foundation of electronic environments*. Open Universiteit Nederland. Retrieved November 21, 2003, from http://eml.ou.nl/introduction/articles.htm

Kuhn, T. S. (1962). *The structure of scientific revolutions.* Chicago: University of Chicago Press.

Latour, B. (1989). *La science en action.* Paris: Éditions La Découverte.

Lave, J., & Wenger, E. (1991). *Situated learning: Legitimate peripheral participation.* Cambridge, MA: Cambridge University Press.

Legros, D., & Crinon, J. (2002). *Psychologie des apprentissages et multimédia.* Paris: Armand Colin.

Long, H. (Ed.). (1995). *New dimensions in self-directed learning.* Norman, OK: University of Oklahoma.

Masie, E. (2001). *E-learning: If we build it, will they come?* Alexandria, VA: American Society for Training and Development.

Pain, A. (1989). *Education informelle. Les effets formateurs dans le quotidien.* Paris: L'Harmattan.

Pain, A. (2003). *L'ingénierie de formation.* Etat des lieux. Paris: L'Harmattan.

Perret-Clermont, A. N. (1979). *La construction de l'intelligence dans l'interaction sociale.* Berne: Peter Lang.

Piaget, J. (1947). *La psychologie de l'intelligence.* Paris: Max Leclerc et Cie.

Piaget, J. (1949). *Introduction à l'épistémologie génétique* (Vol. 2). Paris: Presses Universitaires de France.

Reynaud, J. D. (1989). *Les règles du jeu. L'action collective et la régulation sociale.* Paris: Armand Colin.

Schumpeter, J. A. (1934). *The theory of economic development: An inquiry into profits, capital, credit, interest, and the business cycle.* Cambridge, MA: Harvard University Press.

Simmel, G. (1908). *Soziologie.* Leipzig: Duncker & Humblot.

Suchman, L. A. (1987). *Plans and situated actions: The problem of human machine communication.* Cambridge, MA: Cambridge University Press.

Vygotsky, L. S. (1962). *Thought and language.* Cambridge, MA: MIT Press.

Vygotsky, L. S. (1978). *Mind in society: The development of higher psychological processes.* Cambridge, MA: MIT Press.

Wenger, E. (1998). *Communities of practice: Learning, meaning and identity.* Cambridge, MA: Cambridge University Press.

Chapter V

Space as a Learning Context:
The Role of Dwelling in the Development of Academic Reflection

Ellen Christiansen, Aalborg University, Denmark

Adult learners are not blank slates; they don't have funnels in their heads; they have little patience for being treated as "don't knows." . . . New users are always learning computer methods in the context of specific preexisting goals and expectations.

(Carroll, 1990)

Abstract

The concept of "dwelling" is offered as a foundation for learning and for understanding the role of space in educational settings. This chapter is a first attempt to connect the concept of dwelling, perceived as power over space in the phenomenological sense, with the concept of meta-learning as researched in experimental psychology, in distributed cognition, and in experiential learning, all fields sharing the idea that for learning to become self-regulated individual experiences should be acknowledged, some freedom of choice should be offered, and change should be stimulated. Examples of learning environments with a dwelling quality are presented together with a list of behavioral patterns trating the role of space. In this way the chapter shows education managers how to take the quality of dwelling into account in evaluating and designing contexts of learning.

Introduction: Reason Needs to Dwell

The global demand on lifelong learning is challenging the pedagogy of academic education, from the credit system to the architecture of the learning environment. Times are changing, and institutionalized ways of working are no longer automatically accepted and taken for granted on the global market of education, where students are becoming customers. The idea of using information and communication technology (ICT) in university teaching was initially to help overcome space and time constraints: students could be taught at a distance as if they were almost present at campus lectures. Now ICT is also used in on-campus teaching, out of interest in optimizing teaching resources and learning outcome. Many concerns are raised and researched regarding this development. Going virtual is assumed to have implications for the outcome of teaching, the pedagogy, the content, the teacher-student communication, the economy, and the workload on teachers and students. All these elements are supposed to undergo some kind of change—but space, although fundamental, is not much considered, apart from the assumption that physical is somehow different from virtual. In this chapter, this distinction is bracketed because of a deeper concern regarding space: the need for reason to dwell.

Reason needs a "dwelling." By extending university teaching to virtual settings and making content available to more students, the access to the academic way of learning—through reasoning and arguing—is diminished, not because of the virtuality per se (letters have over the centuries proven to be an excellent medium of academic reflection) but because of a potential lack of dwelling. Therefore, managers of learning in virtual settings have to be aware of how to create dwelling in virtual settings and mixed mode learning environments.

Reason is a power of Nature, says Whitehead. In his treatise "The Function of Reason," he describes reason as follows:

> *History discloses two main tendencies in the course of events. One tendency is exemplified in the slow decay of physical nature. With stealthy inevitableness, there is degradation of energy. The sources of activity sink downward and downward. Their very matter wastes. The other tendency is exemplified by the yearly renewal of nature in the spring, and by the upward course of biological evolution. In these pages I consider Reason in its relation to these contrasted aspects of history. Reason is the self-discipline of the originative element in history. Apart from the operations of Reason, this element is anarchic. (Whitehead, 1929/1958, introductory*

*illus*What Whitehead is alluding to may not be what Foucault (1972) meant in his "Archeology of Knowledge," some 33 years later, with his term the evolution of mentalities, where he writes that:

> *it can be given a philosophical status in the recollection of the Logos or the teleology of reason; lastly, it can be purified in the problematic of a trace, which, prior to all speech, is the opening of inscription, the gap of deferred time, it is always the historico-transcendental theme that is reinvested. A theme whose enunciative analysis tries to free itself. In order to restore statements to their pure dispersion. . . . In order to rediscover their occurrence as an event. Perhaps we should speak of "neutrality" rather than exteriority; but even this word implies rather too easily a suspension of belief, an effacement or a "placing in parenthesis" of all position of existence, whereas it is a question of rediscovering that outside in which, in their relative rarity, in their incomplete proximity, in their deployed space, enunciative events are distributed. (p. 121)*

Here, I take the liberty to use the above quotations to illustrate my opening point: reason needs dwelling. What these scholars definitely have in common is the ability to establish an argument by means of words, intelligible and deep, but quite difficult to grasp from the outside. You have to go to "the inside" to get to grips with statements of this complexity. And the statements themselves are full of pointers to the spatial dimension of understanding. We give meaning to our experience by means of words, but at first we have to do something. Experiential educationalists, like Dewey, have elaborated their theories of learning around this axiom. And action takes place in time and space. Always. ICT introduces, however, a temptation to go from an experiential to a transfer-oriented, out-of-context, "anytime, anywhere" understanding of the educational activities. But teaching and learning were always to some extent separated in time and space. Teaching was always to some extent monologistic. The shift from being on campus to being "all over the place" may have impact beyond shift in mode of communication, on to the spatial texture that is the ground of communication, and into which humans, by the recurrence of behavior, weave rhythms, routes, and habitual encounters—in short *locales* to use Strauss's (1993) term. Locales are what make you discover the occurrence of an event, as Foucault (1972) just explained. Locales are what make you know that you have been doing something. The experience of locales prepares you to "undergo the consequences," as Dewey would say. Locales add meaning by allowing you to name the event, and thereby to learn. By depraving students of locales we may jeopardize their sense of home—or dwelling, as Paul Tillich (1989) called it. And, thereby, the prophetic warning of Joseph Weizenbaum (1976/1984) about the risk that computer power will take over human reason gets a deeper meaning, referring to the risk that students are no longer able to reason. Because they no longer have a place to go and do so because what Pirsig (1974/1984), in another prophetic warning, called "the church of Reason," the university has been not closed but spread out so widely that reason has become homeless.

In this chapter, I am going to describe the place where students can go to come to grips with expressions as these (i.e., of Whitehead, 1929/1958, and Foucault, 1972) and suggest ways in which managers of educational technology implementation can act to ensure that such places exist in the world of ICT-based university education.

The Notion of "Dwelling"

If experience is the key to learning, a phenomenological approach to understanding the locus of learning is appropriate. The phenomenologist Paul Tillich (1989) has analyzed space as a phenomenon, conceiving it to be power over space, which I take to have the implication that learning is dependent on the learner to feel a sense of dwelling. To conceive space as power over space is the result of philosophical abstraction, whereas dwelling, according to Tillich, designates concrete living reality, defined by power over space. Dwelling is the first and most immediate relation humans have to space at all (Tillich, 1989). In creating a dwelling we create our space, and only by starting out from our space we can trust further from space at large to infinite space. Tillich makes the observation that three conditions must be met for a space to turn into a dwelling for someone.

First, dwelling is coexistence, living next to one another. "The power of creating space," Tillich (1989) says, "has in this sphere the character of filling space, impenetrability, existence in itself and the warding off of every other thing, hardness and opposition, or being over against one another. In the space-filling power of a wall of rocks one can see the power of entities at this stage. The impenetrability and hardness of every wall of a house testifies to the same being" (p. 82).

Second, in addition to filling out and unfolding, there is movement. Cast out of mother's womb we take into our head a distant space toward which we are heading and trust forward toward spaces that are not immediately adjacent. At the same time, however, a counterpole is developed, a longing for our own nest and cave, a drive to return to the enclosing, sustaining space. Movement causes simultaneously a strive outward toward the unknown and inward toward the well known. In these forms—space in which to be contained and which to fill out, and routes out into the unknown and back to the "cave"—humans create dwellings in the physical world and in our inner, private world, too.

Third, on top of this, humans have the ability to break away through every spatial limit and create infinite space in accord with the power of our being. "The human mode of creating space for oneself is that of breaking through every finite boundary" (Tillich, 1989, p. 83). This external transcending is connected with an internal transcending: we never stop with the given but press beyond to further achievement. We project and configure, and reconfigure. This way, humans live in multiple worlds. Tillich concludes that creating a dwelling is the way humans come into being: dwelling is where I can be, where I can depart from and return to, where I can store trophies as tokens of my voyage, and where I can rest and dream of worlds different from the one I am in now.

Subscribing to this idea makes dwelling or "my space" crucial for learning. For learning to happen we must experience recurrence or redundancy as well as transcendence or breakthrough, and, first and foremost, we must feel included, contained, and as the persons we are.

We learn by building on what is there, and we build by noticing difference. A difference that makes a difference to someone in a system is a learning item, and the learning items are connected in patterns by presence, and these patterns scaffold the learning of whatever content is to be learned (Bateson, 2000). This is, in fact, also the essence of "situated learning" (Lave & Wenger, 1991), a position also emphasizing the learner's need of a point of orientation, a point from where to take power over space, and *somewhere to place experience*. That is dwelling. And as demonstrated in the theory of situated learning, collective experiences, too, have dwelling as a precondition: recognizing *your* place as different presupposes a notion of *my* place, as does the creation of a place as *our* place. Taking power over space presuppose an experience of *my* place, of dwelling.

In sum, dwelling is the sense that

1.   My being is contained and included as is, *because* my life world de facto includes me as the person I am.

2.   I feel curious and I long for home, and these longings map out a path for me to follow, *because* by means of maps my life world tempts me to explore it and offers me somewhere to bring tokens of my adventure.

3.   I am projecting and arranging a space of my own, *because* my life world is plastic enough to allow me to do so.

Inclusiveness, mapping out routes for going out and coming back, and transformability are the qualities through which power over space can be described in a phenomenological sense, and dwelling is the metaphor for the experience of these qualities.

"Classroom" and "Workshop" as Dwelling: Examples

In order for the notion of dwelling to become more concrete, let us look at a couple of examples.

The concept of "classroom" has a long history in children's education, and so has the concept of "workshop" in adult apprenticeship learning. Jean Lave (1988) has, in her research on cultural-historical contexts of learning, studied these two types of settings, first the workshop apprenticeship learning of tailors in Monrovia, Liberia, and later "burn-out-learning" in U.S. high school classrooms. These studies have laid out the foundation for the theory of situated learning, which she published in collaboration with Etienne Wenger in 1991 giving rise to the concepts of "community of practice" and "legitimate peripheral participation." Being ethnographers, Lave and Wenger (1991) do pay attention to the physical layout of the learning environment, but as the backdrop of social interaction. In this chapter, to illuminate the concepts of inclusiveness, mapping, and transformability, the layout of the physical space is taken as the figure and the social interaction as the ground. Both examples are personal experiences, reflected through the lens of Tillich's (1989) analysis of dwelling, but also inspired by Logan's account of how to create inclusiveness among sixth graders in public schools in San Francisco (1997) and personal conversation with Sara Kuhn about her and Donald Schön's pedagogical ideas of design lofts at MIT (see also Winograd, 1996).

The Classroom Example

In 1995 my 12-year-old daughter was to start school in sixth grade at a Palo Alto Middle School. Her teacher was Ms. Roxen. In this middle school the teachers had classrooms and kids would wander from class to class during the day, as opposed to what happens in Denmark, where it is the teachers who do the walking. My point here is that it does not seem to be ownership to physical space as such that determines "the dwelling quality." Whenever there was a parent arrangement at school, our daughter would drag us to Ms. Roxen's classroom to show us stuff. There were always new layouts and new arrangements, of her personal desk, of the

Figure 1.   Dwelling as power over space

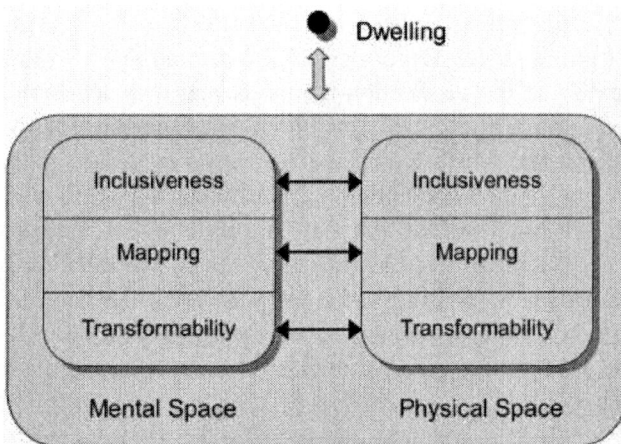

reading corner, and of the exhibitions on the walls. And she would tell us about the purpose and history of each part of the classroom, explaining what rules of behavior applied to each. There would be stuff from Ms. Roxen's other students, too, a source of inspiration, and a challenge to show respect.

Ms. Roxen worked in the following way. Two weeks before school began we received a note from Ms. Roxen asking us to write an essay telling all we found important about our child, the coming sixth grader. And before school began we received a welcome letter saying how much she appreciated the information she had received. I almost cried out of relief that my precious child was so warmly welcomed, and my words about her so well understood. After the first day in school our daughter came home and told that her teacher, Ms. Roxen, was just great but that she had the weirdest interest of all: she loved pigs! Ms. Roxen had a rag pig on her desk and, at home, in her garden, she had a real living pig as a pet. And Ms. Roxen had told them to bring pictures of their favorite animal on the next day, and that they could store it in their desk. And on it went, the children putting up pictures of stuff that mattered to them, from home as well as from their school projects. The message of mutual engagement and of persons both having a school life and a life beside school was clear: in the classroom both teacher and students put out what was important to them and to their work. They were of more than eight different nationalities, and colors, in my daughter's class. Quite a few were new to the U.S. school system, and, from what we could tell from listening to their conversation, Ms. Roxen's classroom was really their anchor in school, offering a feeling of safety and belonging. Interpreting the many changes this room underwent during one year, they also sensed that they could project and they could change. As far as I can tell, Ms. Roxen's classroom was a true dwelling in the life of learning for these sixth graders.

The Workshop Example

The layout of a workshop is primarily defined by the craft and the production that takes place there. Apprenticeship learning is a spin-off, a side dish, something you may as well get going since the youngsters are around anyway, and the maintenance of the quality of the production demands that they learn the tricks of the trade. This way of conveying craftsmanship has prevailed for thousands of years. And when the academic world undertook education of architects and designers, they found that laying out the teaching space as workshops might be a good idea, even though here the teaching and learning, not the product per se, is the heart of the matter. ICT design, however, is mostly taught in a traditional university setting with impersonal lecture halls as the basic teaching location; hence in this case an extra effort is required should the learning environment of the ICT design students become a dwelling. I have, in close collaboration with my colleague Arne Kjær, for three consecutive years, experimented with bringing dwelling into a university course in design of human-computer interaction (Christiansen, in press) by applying the workshop concept and mixing virtual and physical space.

Before we met, the students received a letter asking them to bring a description of their personal design experiences and a picture, which they were asked to post on the cubicle partitions while introducing themselves at the group tables on the very first day. These descriptions would stay but gradually be overlaid with project descriptions, project plans, items collected from the design universe, and so forth. At the end of the semester, the cubicle walls carried the history not only of the students' prior design experience but also of what happened during the course. The students formed groups around a theme of production, something they wanted to build, so each group was a workshop of their own, while at the same time being part of one big workshop: the design course. We hosted around 50 students on 200 m^2 of left-over library space for teaching, for group work, and for workshops and exhibitions throughout a semester, and the groups maintained for the same period of time a Web site where they posted whatever they wanted, in addition to a portfolio of the groups' work on their assignments. The Web site reflected other aspects of the work in the groups, but it created an easy access for the students to each other's workshop and to one's own workshop without having to meet physically all the time. In all three years, this design course received positive evaluation from the students, especially for its organization, and you could tell that every year the students would be arriving with still higher expectations. The layout of both the physical and virtual space had the quality of letting each student be visible in their own way, within the context of the common map laid out by the teachers, and with support to do things differently and rearrange the layout as they were going along. In the papers from the following year of their studies, the students referred to the design course as something similar to dwelling, with sentences like "It was where all the things we had learnt in the first two years came together and we understood the bigger picture, and why we had to learn the curricula of the first two years."

Window and Mirror: Requirements for Space to Serve as Dwelling

Designers operate by taking forms apart into elements and materials and systematically consider which element is best expressed in what material. To do so, they need a goal, a vision of what problem is to be solved by their design. To serve this purpose, the phenomenological approach to space must relate to the goal of university teaching: the development of self-regulated learners and researchers. Hence, a definition of self-regulated learning will have to merge with the notion of space as power over space. According to Deci and Ryan's (1985) model of self-determined and non-self-determined behavior, motivation to learn is at the outset non-self-determined. Depending on information input, the environment, and the personal need structure, physiologically and in memory, the learner will develop a state of self-determination where the motivation is coming from within, because the externally enforced motives have been internalized. The input from the environment must be right and, therefore, "external regulation" is the most interesting state in the five-state development in styles of regulation described by Deci and Ryan (nonregulation, external regulation, introjected regulation, regulation through identifications, integrated regulations). External regulation is going from experiencing initiating events as pressure to perform accordingly and not experiencing a real sense of choice, to gradually getting more to grips with the control oneself. Of most importance at this stage is the feedback from the environment. It should be characterized by:

- choice so that the learner experiences self-determination,
- guidance for performance, and
- acknowledgment of feelings.

(Ryan & Deci, 2000)

All of these have relevance for the design of space and for the requirements coming from the phenomenological analysis in this chapter: experience of inclusiveness (acknowledgement of feelings), mapping (guidance), and transformability (choice).

There seems to be sufficient congruency between the phenomenological analysis of space as power over space and the social-psychological analysis of the development of self-determination to infer that, to support self-regulated learning, space has to be laid out in a way so that the learner feels included, guided, and able to transform.

The designer will have to consider how to make the initiating events and the controlling feedback leave the student with choices, how to provide effectance-relevant information vis-à-vis performance, and how to make mixed feelings acknowledged by the environment with space as the material. All of which illustrates that the important divide with respect to space in educational settings is not between virtual and physical but between empowering and disempowering settings. It takes, however, a combined design and pedagogical effort to make this happen, with design as the planning and projecting part and pedagogy as the realization. In all cases of allocating space, virtually and physically, course designers need to be aware of the ways that support the students in making for themselves a dwelling out of the space allocated. If schools, when at first meeting the students and during the course of teaching, fail to leave room for the students' experiences, the students will deutero-learn that their experience does not count as a contribution. This is the silent teaching of not allocating space for dwellings. But, on the other hand, of course, in order to invoke curiosity schools *should* send the message to the students that the school has something entirely new to offer. They should proudly present the treasure of academic knowledge and of reason. So how can designers meet both goals?

In a recent book, *Windows and Mirrors* (Bolter & Gromala, 2003), an artist designer and a historian theorist of digital technology show how digital art may reawaken an awareness of contexts by reflecting the context of the viewer while sending whatever message the artwork is (also) sending. The idea is not new. In fact, these authors refer to Plato and his cave allegory. But it has, it seems, to be repeated frequently: we look into a mirror, also, when we think we look through a window, and when we see ourselves in the mirror we also see our context and thereby we can broaden and deepen our knowledge about ourselves.

This idea of designing educational setting to be both mirror and window seems a good way of implementing the idea of dwelling. As a practical example of how it can be done, I can refer to the design and use of space in a mixed mode master study program at Aalborg University called "Master of ICT and Learning" (http://www.hum.aau.dk/mil/) (MIL; see Sorensen, 1999a, 1999b). This Web document says that students will:

> *learn to understand and use theories and work methods related to ICT; develop and integrate ICT-based learning processes; participate in experimental and user-oriented development of ICT-based learning processes; analyze, test and evaluate and critically appraise ICT-based learning processes; and analyze and understand the consequences of ICT-based learning systems.*

The studies of MIL begin with a weekend seminar, where the students come together physically on campus for lectures and team-building sessions, since pedagogically the study program is founded on the paradigm of problem- and project-based learning. The students are introduced to the university library and bookstore and other facilities. They have their picture taken, and these pictures and the bio-sketches are posted on the course Web, thereby creating for each student a presence within the community. The on-campus lectures are given in an auditorium and taped, so that the students are able to (re)watch them as streaming video on their desktop at home. For the students working from home the course Web is a continuation of the spatial layout of the physical university space, in this case supplemented by a content management system, "Virtual-U" (http://www.virtual-u.org/), which has a university campus as its guiding metaphor. The students will get access to written material through online library facilities and a specially designed online facility presenting itself in the metaphor of a "metro." For supervision and peer discussion the students go to a virtual classroom or a virtual team room.

The design of the MIL course does in all initiating events and the controlling feedback leave the student with choices, provides effectance-relevant information vis-à-vis performance, and leaves room for mixed feelings to be acknowledged by the environment. And it does so by offering personalization of shared workspaces and maps for tours and detours in the landscape of knowledge presented, and by encouraging and supporting critique and reflection through the availability of mentors. But, first and foremost, the study program is remarkable being designed by its teachers, a group of experienced educational scholars who teach what they preach (Dirckinck-Holmfeld & Fibiger, 2002), thereby maintaining a good fit between form and context, ensuring that the deutero-learning matches the content.

What Managers Can Do to Support the Development of Self-Regulated Learners by Means of Space Design

The grand old man of systemic management theory, Harold Leavitt (1972), maintained that "everything triggers everything else," meaning that among the constituting elements of an organization (task, structure, technology, people) whatever element you start messing with, the others will inevitably change some way or the other. In the context of managing education with the goal of supporting students in becoming self-regulated learners and researchers, the management of space will have implications for the management of tasks, technologies, and people as well.

If dwelling is given priority in space design, the teaching *task* becomes a task of presenting material and guiding the students in their formulation of research problems, by means of route maps, and couching and stimulating the students while leaving "home" and welcoming them when they return with trophies from their voyage. The demands on *technology* become heavy with respect to flexibility and tailorability, and, accordingly, also in demands on support staff. The demands on *people* will be that the teachers, students, and supporters become collaborators. The manager will have to deal with four forces, preferable maybe one at a time, knowing that they all influence each other, both at the conscious level, where design and political discussions take place, and at the unconscious level, where culture and value systems operate and where—keeping the garbage can metaphor in mind (Cohen, March, & Olsen, 1972)—accidental coincidences of co-presence have enormous, unplanned effects. Given this situation of management, control is not possible, only guidance. And to inform the managerial guiding activity with respect to the design of space as power over space for students and teachers in collaboration, checkpoints are necessary. In Figure 2, checkpoints are inserted in the model of space as power over space presented in Figure 1.

Conclusion

Reason, the self-discipline of the originative element in history and the grail that all true researchers are looking for, product and process in one, is inevitably related to space. Therefore, space deserves attention from educators who seek to give students the best possible support for their development into self-regulated and self-determining researchers. The chapter has presented the metaphor of dwelling as a way of conceptualizing space with regard to design of physical and virtual learning environments as part of a way of supporting self-regulated learning. Dwelling has been conceptualized through a phenomenological approach as power over space: power to be, power to move, and power to transcend. This phenomenological conception has been related to Deci and Ryan's (1985) summary of findings in experimental psychology, showing that self-regulation is brought about by letting learners have a choice and a sense of self-regulation or self-movement and acknowledging mixed feelings. The importance of this was further related to Bateson's (2000) argument that deutero-learning is the key to learning, which is ultimately why educators should give priority to space design, because space design expresses and mirrors the deutero-learning. In relation to this theoretical framework, a list of focus points was presented as a practical help to managers of education when considering whether actual learning environments are meeting the requirements of a dwelling. All of this needs to be further researched in order to determine to what extent these suggestions are consistent with the overall paradigm of experiential learning. Further empirical studies to further establish how people arrange material and use the infrastructure of academic life, intentionally or unintentionally; how students come across useful information, just in the process of interacting socially and physically within departments and scientific laboratories, at conferences, and so forth; and how these serendipitous encounters are a product of proximity, either electronically or physically.

Why? Because at a moment in history where companies worldwide try hard to become learning organizations and facilitate knowledge creation among employees, time should be ripe, also at the universities, to fully acknowledge the insights gained from research in experiential learning. Dewey saw "the undergoing of consequences" as where the development happens. Bateson (2000) would say that "the undergoing" is where habits are formed, where the deutero-learning happens. The journey of learning should be the destination of education, and the point of departure should be each student having a dwelling of his or her own to take off

Figure 2. Check of mirror and window qualities of a learning space

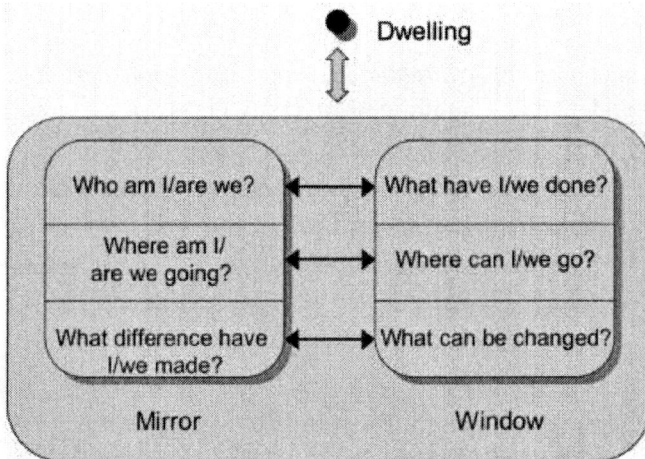

from. Recently, the knowledge management discourse presented by Nonaka and Takeuchi (1995) has brought the idea of experiential learning (back) to the workplace, or to the human resources departments at least. Researchers, for example those within the International Society of the Learning Sciences (ISLS) community (http://www.isls.org/index.html), seek to bring the ideas of experiential learning in sync with the ideas of how to use ICT in support of this. But the issue of space seems also somewhat overlooked here.

References

Bateson, G. (2000). *Steps to an ecology of mind.* Chicago: University of Chicago Press.

Bolter, J. D., & Gromala, D. (2003). *Windows and mirrors. Interaction design, digital art, and the myth of transparency.* Cambridge, MA: MIT Press.

Carroll, J. M. (1990). *The Nurnberg Funnel.* Cambridge MA: MIT Press.

Christiansen, E. (2004). Educated by design - learning by doing - outline of a HCI-didactics. *ITcon, 9*, 209-217 (Special Issue ICT Supported Learning in Architecture and Civil Engineering). Retrieved from http://www.itcon.org/2004/

Cohen, M. D., March, J. G., & Olsen, J. P. (1972). A garbage can model of organizational choice. *Administrative Science Quarterly, 17*(1), 1-25.

Deci, E. L., & Ryan, R. M. (1985). *Intrinsic motivation and self-determination in human behavior.* New York: Plenum.

Dirckinck-Holmfeld, L., & Fibiger, B. (Eds.). (2002). *Learning in virtual environments.* Copenhagen: Samfundslitteratur.

Foucault, M. (1972). *The archaeology of knowledge and the discourse on language.* New York: Pantheon Books.

Lave, J. (1988). *Cognition in practice.* Cambridge, UK: Cambridge University Press.

Lave, J., & Wenger, E. (1991). *Situated learning: Legitimate peripheral participation.* Cambridge, UK: Cambridge University Press.

Leavitt, H. J. (1972). *The volatile organization: Everything triggers everything else. Managerial psychology: An introduction to individuals, pairs, and groups in organizations* (3rd ed.). Chicago: University of Chicago Press.

Logan, J. (1997). *Teaching stories.* New York: Kodansha International.

Nonaka, I., & Takeuchi, H. (1995). *The knowledge creating company.* New York: Oxford University Press.

Pirsig, R. M. (1984). *Zen and the art of motorcycle maintenance. An inquiry into values.* New York: Bantam Books. (Original work published 1974.)

Ryan, R. M., & Deci, E. L. (2000). Self-determination theory and the facilitation of intrinsic motivation, social development, and well-being. *American Psychologist, 55*(January), 68-78.

Sorensen, E. K. (1999a, March). *Collaborative learning in virtual contexts: Representation, reflection and didactic change.* Paper presented at the International Conference on Technology in Education-99 (ICTE99), Edinburgh.

Sorensen, E. K. (1999b). *Intellectual amplification through reflection and didactic change in distributed collaborative learning.* Paper presented at the Computer Support for Collaborative Learning (CSCL), Stanford University, Palo Alto, CA.

Strauss, A. (1993). *Continual permutations of action.* New York: Aldine De Gruyter.

Tillich, P. (1989). Dwelling, space, and time. In J. Dillenberger & J. Dillenberger (Eds.), *On art and architecture* (pp. 81-85). New York: Crossroad.

Weizenbaum, J. (1984). *Computer power and human reason. From judgment to calculation.* New York: Pelican. (Original work published 1976.)

Whitehead, A. N. (1958). *The function of reason.* Beacon Press Books. (Original work published 1929.)

Winograd, T. (Ed.). (1996). *Bringing design to software.* Reading, MA: Addison-Weshley.

Chapter VI

The Dynamics of Online Collaboration:
Team Task, Team Development, Peer Relationship, and Communication Media

Ke Zhang, Texas Tech University, United States

Xun Ge, University of Oklahoma, United States

Abstract

This chapter aims to help readers build a solid understanding of the complex dynamics of online collaborative learning from multiple perspectives, and thus become more capable to utilize different instructional strategies to achieve productive online collaboration. On the basis of extensive review and integration of research from multiple disciplines, the authors discuss the dynamics of online collaborative learning from four aspects: team task, team development, member relationship, and communication media, with one section designated to each of them. The sections each comprise presentation of the issue, theoretical frameworks, suggested strategies, and how it relates to other aspect(s), as applicable. The chapter concludes with implications for practice in online collaborative learning and future research for managing learning in virtual collaborative environments. This chapter is considered a valuable artifact to guide practice and research in online collaborative learning in various settings.

Introduction

Research indicates that small groups facilitate learning as compared to individual learning (e.g., Bruffee, 1999; Johnson, Johnson, & Stanne, 1985) and that peer group work has significant impacts on varied learning outcomes in both face-to-face and online learning environments (e.g., Bruffee, 1999; Harasim, 1990; Scardamalia & Bereiter, 1996; Uribe, Klein, & Sullivan, 2003). As a new learning method, however, online collaboration does not happen automatically, nor does it simply make learning easier. Instead, it may be challenging for learners in many ways (Bonk & King, 1998; Zhang, 2001; Zhang & Harkness, 2002). Being very different from traditional learning through face-to-face communication, misunderstanding and miscommunication are more likely to happen and are also less detectable in an online environment. In addition, online communication technology is relatively new as an educational tool, and so learners may experience a learning curve with the technology as well as with the learning method. Zhang and Ge's research (2004) shows that as a two-fold innovation, online collaborative learning challenges learners with the new methods of learning and the technologies it involves.

Research and instructional efforts have been made to deal with challenges faced by students and instructors in online learning environments and to facilitate successful online collaboration (e.g., Bonk & King, 1998; Clark & Mayer, 2003; Harasim, 1990; Kaye, 1991). Recently, Zhang (2003, 2004), Zhang and Carr-Chellman (2001), and Zhang and Peck (2003) conducted a series of studies investigating the effects of externally structured and moderated peer interactions in online collaborative learning. These studies support the past research on the effectiveness of structuring group work for productive group interactions in face-to-face learning environments (see Webb & Palincsar's review, 1996). Further, using a naturalistic research approach, Zhang and Carr-Chellman (2001) also explored issues surrounding online collaboration. Four issues emerged from the study as the major themes: team task, team development (or interaction pattern for short-term collaborative groups), peer relationship, and communication media. These themes appeared to be the critical issues that may determine the success of online collaborative learning.

The purpose of this chapter is to develop a deeper understanding of the dynamics of online collaborative learning from the four perspectives, supported by theoretical frameworks and empirical research from related disciplines. Online collaboration is relatively a new pedagogy, and thus it is interdisciplinary by nature. In addition to the field of education, many other fields, such as communication, psychology, organization and management, and information science, have developed rich resources of literature regarding team collaboration, team facilitation, media behaviors, groupware, and social informatics. Instead of looking at online collaborative learning from any single perspective in isolation, this chapter attempts to further bridge literature from varied fields to detangle the complex dynamics of online collaborative learning. We believe that this conceptual approach adds significant value to the previous literature on online collaborative learning, and thus it will be instrumental for future empirical studies and practices in this regard.

In this chapter, each of the four issues is specifically discussed in a separate section. The team task section is concerned with task types and complexity with regard to their cognitive demands for collaboration and requirements for media. The team development section discusses possible challenges that may be encountered during different stages of team development. The relationship section addresses the impacts of peer relationships on team development and performance. The media section examines the selection and use of appropriate media for different tasks and at different team development stages. Each section comprises presentation of the issue, theoretical frameworks, and suggested strategies. The chapter concludes with implications for practice in online collaborative learning and future research on managing learning in virtual collaborative environments. The dynamics of online collaborative learning is conceptualized in Figure 1, which graphically represents the interrelationship of the four aspects and indicates the need for using various strategies to facilitate online collaboration. Although the four perspectives are discussed in separate sections, we must emphasize that online learning is a complex, dynamic process with all the four perspectives interrelated. We strongly recommend that research on and practice with online collaborative learning be approached from all the four aspects in order to gain a deeper understanding of the dynamics.

Team Tasks

The ultimate goal of collaborative learning is quality performance or product, or both. Thus team task is the core in the dynamics of the collaborative learning process. It is important to understand the nature of team tasks, their cognitive demands for collaboration, and their requirements for media use and selection. In this section, we examine team tasks from the following dimensions: task type, complexity, and its relation with communication media.

Types of Tasks

The understanding of tasks can help us to facilitate online collaborative learning effectively. Team tasks can be categorized into discussion, problem solving, decision making, and production (Kabanoff & O'Brien, 1979), just to mention a few. Discussion tasks emphasize the process or evaluation, not necessarily the actual production (Kabanoff & O'Brien, 1979). These tasks require high level of critical thinking skills and distributed cognition from all members (Hara, Bonk, & Angeli, 2000; Henri, 1991). As the ultimate goal for group discussion is to construct knowledge and to produce "the fruit of the collective endeavor" (Henri, p. 118), exchanging views, negotiating meaning, challenging each other's critical thinking, and evaluating different ideas are critical in the process of group discussion.

Problem solving is more action oriented than discussion (Kabanoff & O'Brien, 1979), particularly when the problem is authentic and ill defined. In order to arrive at sound solutions, individuals often need to collaborate to define the problem, identify relevant factors and constraints, propose strategies, and test solutions. Authentic problem-solving tasks represent a meaningful challenge and provide an enabling context for meaning making in the collaborative learning environment (Hannafin, Land, & Oliver, 1999; Jonassen, 1999). Kumpulainen and Kaartinen (2000) found that open-ended problem-solving tasks encouraged collaborative and intensive task-engagement and exploratory activities, including reasoning and problem posing and solving.

Figure 1. A graphical conceptualization of the dynamics of online collaborative learning and strategies for managing virtual collaborative teams

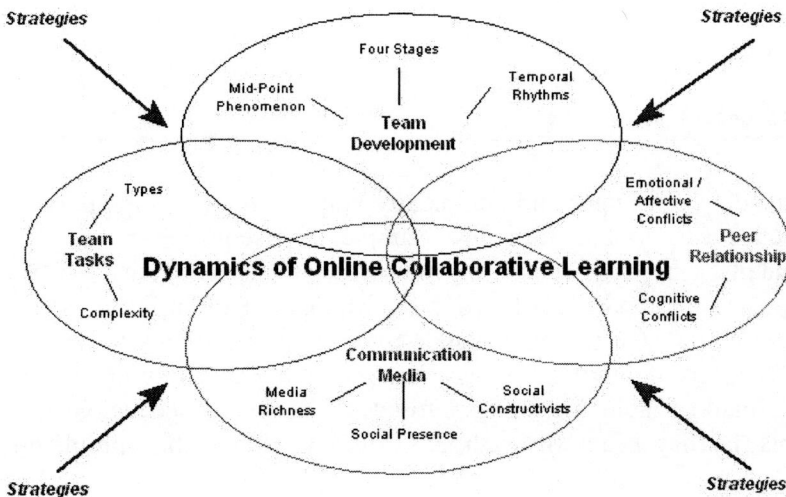

In both decision-making and problem-solving tasks, it is critical to guide students to seek explanations, elaborate thinking, challenge and counter-challenge one another, make justifications, and reach consensus (Derry & DuRussel, 1999). It is particularly important that participants make their thinking and strategies visible to their peers and engage in task-focused argumentation and reasoning, instead of personal remarks, in the course of problem solving (Diezmann & Watters, 2001).

Production-type tasks are performance based. The success of such tasks depends on how team efforts are organized (Kabanoff & O'Brien, 1979). Kabanoff and O'Brien found that when information was shared, initial collaboration among group members enhanced performance; whereas, when each person had complete information, absence of collaborative planning enhanced performance.

Complexity of Tasks

Task complexity is another dimension of team task that either supports or inhibits team collaboration. Research shows that collaboration happens when a task is sufficiently challenging and learners are more likely to be actively engaged in collaborations (Diezmann & Watters, 2001). Chizhik (2001) found that variable-answer tasks, for which there were no correct answers, encouraged more collaboration while single-answer tasks might lead to the domination of a single person over the group. Diezmann and Watters's (2001) study indicated that collaboration was preferred only when the task was sufficiently difficult and challenging; whereas when the task was relatively easy, the students preferred minimal interaction with others and were independently successful on easy tasks. They concluded that when tasks were appropriately challenging, collaboration had cognitive, metacognitive, and affective benefits for students.

Tasks and Media

Understanding task types and complexity helps us to select appropriate media for effective team collaboration. For example, tasks requiring groups to generate ideas and plans may require only the transmission of specific ideas, and thus may find the use of computer-mediated system best fit (Hollingshead, McGrath, & O'Connor, 1993). On the other hand, tasks requiring groups to negotiate and resolve conflicts of views or interests may require the transmission of maximally rich information, including values, attitudes, emotions, expectations, and commitments (Hollingshead, McGrath, & O'Connor, 1993). Thus, problem-solving and decision-making tasks require rich information, including additional redundant cues as found in face-to-face communication. Our recent study, which examined the collaborative efforts of undergraduate students in solving an authentic problem in special education, shows that when students were engaged in ill-defined collaborative problem solving, they were unsatisfied with the limited selection of the online communication tools (e.g., the group bulletin board). Rather, they attempted to seek additional or alternative media (e.g., email, chat, or phone) to provide prompt feedback or response to their peers. More discussion on media is presented later in this chapter.

Suggestions for Task Selection and Structuring

In order to facilitate online collaborative learning successfully, it is important to consider the type and the complexity of a task and develop appropriate guidance and strategies accordingly. Providing guidelines to students can be helpful to engage students in various types of tasks of different complexity. For example, guidelines for online discussion should prompt students to ask questions, provide explanations, make clarifications, negotiate meanings, share experience, make inferences, and make justifications. Guidelines for problem-solving tasks should guide students to engage in cognitive and metacognitive processes of problem solving, such as representing the problem, developing solutions, constructing arguments, and monitoring and evaluating. Guidelines for decision-making tasks should direct students' interactions in areas of negotiating meanings, reaching consensus, and making justifications.

Past research (e.g. Johnson et al., 1985, 1986; also see Webb & Palincsar's review, 1996) revealed that structuring tasks through providing instructional strategies or requirements helped to monitor peer interaction process, ensure high-level reasoning and inquiry, and encourage collaborative knowledge construction. The recent study by Hara, Bonk, and Angeli (2000) indicated that providing structure to online collaboration helped students to produce cognitively deep and interactive messages and challenged them to use metacognitive strategies. Zhang (2003, 2004) and Zhang and Peck (2003) found that online collaborative learning, when well structured and moderated, as compared with peer controlled, helped achieve better reasoning in well-structured problem-solving tasks (Zhang & Peck, 2003) and better performance in both well-structured and ill-structured problem-solving tasks (Zhang, 2003, 2004). In addition, the learners reported that they were more likely to use an optional online collaborative tool for future group tasks (Zhang & Peck, 2003). Zhang and Carr-Chellman's (2001) study illustrated that structuring and moderating efforts enhanced peer online discourse by promoting more intense, and multidirectional, interactive collaboration as compared with nonmoderated groups, in which more fragmental reasoning and fewer interactions were found.

Modeling and question prompting are some of the strategies that have been empirically proven effective in promoting reasoning and higher-order thinking (e.g., King, 1992, 1994; Palincsar, 1986; Palincsar & Brown, 1984). Palincsar and Brown (1984) used the strategy of reciprocal teaching to model question-asking on the reading comprehension tasks. King's studies focused on mediating peer interactions by teaching students to generate thought-provoking questions and elaborate their thinking. These studies indicated the effectiveness of peer-generated questions in supporting meaningful knowledge construction. Ge and Land (2003) recently found that groups that were provided with question prompts during ill-structured problem solving performed significantly better than those without such support. Therefore, we argue that the strategies described earlier can also be effectively transferred to the online learning environment. For example, posing questions in online discussion helps to initiate discussions, prompt students to think critically and make in-depth inquiries, direct students' attention to some important issues, and encourage active interactions (e.g. Ge & Mansell, 2003). Modeling problem-solving processes using templates can also help students to go through the major steps of problem solving (e.g. Uribe et al., 2003).

Team Development

As online collaboration proceeds, learners face different challenges and issues at different stages of the team development process. Understanding team development enables us to interpret the changing group dynamics and online discourse from another perspective. Such understanding may help instructors to better facilitate online collaborative learning. This section provides a close examination of different stages of team development, followed by suggestions for moderating team development.

Stages of Team Development

Tuckman's (1965) four-stage team development theory is most well known in the field and is applied widely in team facilitation and management in research and practice (Guzzo & Dickson, 1996; Guzzo & Shea, 1992; Schwarz, 1994). According to Tuckman (1965), team growth is a sequential and developmental process, including four stages in the following order: forming, storming, norming, and performing. Each stage is characterized by two major dimensions: the task-related issues and peer relationship growth.

Through the four varied stages, a team faces different issues related to the team task and member relationships. In general, at the forming stage, members tend to be polite and preserved, but not trusting with one another. Typical team behaviors at the forming stage are testing other members and getting oriented with the team task. At this stage, members are uncertain about their roles in the team.

At the storming stage, team members start to communicate more about their feelings and thoughts; they get to know one another better and typically obtain more information on the team task as well. As more communication and collaboration happen, however, arguments, conflicts, and disagreements are typical at this stage. Leadership is often challenged, and the team requires more clarifications on individuals' roles and responsibilities. Excessive storming leads to anxiety and tension, whereas suppressed storming leads to resentment and repeated and unhealthy conflicts.

After the storming stage, the team will have obtained shared understandings and thus will establish norms regarding team procedure, relationship, and team performance. In this norming stage, the team shows more cooperation and cohesion as a united whole, with joint efforts and shared understandings.

Finally when reaching the performing stage, the team will work with openness, trust, and flexibility and become able to perform as a unity. At this stage, members assume their varied roles, encourage cooperation and collaboration, and develop more interdependency. Teams now are able to focus their energy on the tasks and function efficiently as a whole.

An important addition to the traditional four-stage development theory is Gersick's (1988) finding of the transitional point of the team development process. In the study on work groups, Gersick found that time, associated with the changing context, had significant impacts on team dynamics and team performance. The study showed that teams experienced a drastic transition at the midpoint of the time frame, and the awareness of the deadline significantly changed the team dynamics. Zhang's (2004) research with about 80 undergraduate learning groups found the same phenomenon; that is, dramatic changes occurred at the midpoint of time during the online collaborative problem-solving process. The needs for moderation also changed accordingly. During the first half of the time frame the needs for moderation were mainly about motivation and scheduling. In the second half, however, the groups became more conscious about the timetable and made more aggressive progress toward the tasks. Thus for the second half of the timeframe, the needs for moderations concerned the team task itself (e.g., problem-solving strategies) more than the team process (e.g., communication strategies or motivational messages; Zhang, 2004). Being aware of the possible different needs for moderation associated with time, the instructor can be better prepared for the role of a moderator for online collaborative groups.

Similarly, in their research on global virtual teams, Maznevski and Chudoba (2000) found that effective teams demonstrated temporal rhythms in the collaborative process. Thus timely moderations in accordance with the temporal rhythms may help improve the effectiveness of group collaboration.

Team Development in Online Collaborative Learning

Zhang and Carr-Chellman's (2001) research indicated that the team development during online collaborative problem solving centered on leadership building and buy-in. They also found that groups receiving external moderation established team norms at an earlier time, whereas peer-controlled groups either did not build norms at all or did it much later. With the absence or delay of norm building, the groups experienced more relationship problems associated with lack of mutual respect, support, or encouragement. As a result, these teams conducted less interactive collaboration on the team task. Zhang (2003) also found that groups that had worked out a team contract achieved better performance in both well-structured and ill-structured problem-solving tasks through online collaboration. Zhang (2004) also found that groups receiving external moderations were able not only to employ group and problem-solving strategies but also to model the external moderations and provide internal moderating efforts. The moderation efforts led to better utilization of problem-solving strategies and more effective communication during the ill-structured problem-solving process (Zhang, 2004). The team-generated contract, or team discussions on such a contract, also became a structuring protocol for the groups to use as a guide for their collaborative problem solving (Zhang, 2004). Thus a team contract, or the collaborative contracting efforts, may serve as a macrostrategy for groups to handle teamwork. In the practice of peer collaboration, online or in person, team contract can be a strong, powerful strategy to help the teams build shared understanding of teamwork and collaboration, and thus help to smooth the collaboration process.

Suggestions for Moderating Team Development

Theoretically, teams must resolve all the issues and challenges they face in order to move on to the next stage; and no stage can be skipped (Tuckman, 1965). In practice, however, teams often try to jump from initial forming to final performing stage. It is common that teams avoid or suppress conflicts and minimize personal relationship building with the hope to focus all the energy on the task itself. Thus, it is strongly recommended that a person with certain authority from outside of the team play the role of a facilitator or moderator. Such a role should encourage and help the team to address issues they face at the current stage. It is also suggested that during the forming stage, assistance should be provided to make leadership clear in order to help the team deal with both the task and relationship issues (Tuckman, 1965; Schawrz, 1994). Substantial information is also critical at this stage for groups to get oriented with the team task. The norming process, as well as the norms built through joint efforts, will help groups to stay focused on task, maintain a positive dynamic, and thus work more effectively. During the storming stage, it is critical to let the conflicts surface out and let the team resolve them with joint efforts. The understanding of the midpoint phenomenon and the temporal rhythm of online groups will provide instructors with different, timely moderations as needed and hence help improve the effectiveness of group collaboration.

Peer Relationship

Relationship is one of the two dominant themes throughout the team development process (e.g., Guzzo & Dickson, 1996; Guzzo & Shea, 1992; Tuckman, 1965; Weiss & Cropanzano, 1996). It also emerged as one of the major themes in the online discourse of undergraduate groups in Zhang and Carr-Chellman's (2001) study. Past research (i.e., Jehn, 1997; Thompson, 2000) indicated that relationship-related issues, such as emotional conflicts, had different impacts on team development and performance and thus needed to be addressed differently from cognitive conflicts or task-related issues.

Emotional or Affective Conflicts vs. Cognitive Conflicts

Researchers and practitioners have long believed that affective factors are important in teamwork. They argue that people come to work as a whole, with all the affective factors as part of the individual, and thus affective and cognitive factors both influence task performance and team dynamics (e.g. Guzzo & Shea, 1992; Zajonc, 1984). For example, at the storming stage, the team developmental task is about control and power. Conflicts are typical at this stage, yet conflict suppression is not uncommon. These conflicts are either emotional (also referred to as affective, or A-type conflict) or cognitive (also referred to as C-type conflict). Emotional conflicts are personal and defensive (Thompson, 2000). Researchers believe that cognitive conflicts are productive and beneficial for teams (Thompson, 2000), whereas emotional conflicts threaten team development and reduce decision quality, understanding, commitment, and affective acceptance (Jehn, 1997).

In a review of literature on computer-assisted teams, Hollingshead and McGrath (1995) found that teams mediated by information and communication technology (ICT) had less interactions and information exchanges and that they took longer time on tasks as compared with face-to-face teams. They also found that in terms of resolving conflicts, the ICT-mediated teams were not as good as face-to-face teams. Therefore, it is particularly important, yet challenging, to understand the relationship-related issues and be better able to resolve affective conflicts in an online collaborative environment.

Suggestions for Building Healthy Team Relationship

To deal with emotional conflicts, which are harder to be detected, expressed, and addressed in a virtual environment, Thompson (2000) suggested utilizing an open forum to transform emotional conflicts into cognitive conflicts. Timely response to emotional conflicts helps to create internal comfort, motivate participation, stabilize personal and professional relations, and improve team effectiveness (Bocialetti, 1988).

It is difficult to establish trust among people who are only connected through ICT. For this reason, it is highly recommended for virtual teams to arrange one or more initial, face-to-face meetings, if possible at all (Mittleman, Briggs, & Nunamaker, 2000). In cases where face-to-face meetings are unavailable, initial contacts can be made through the use of rich media, which are capable of conveying both verbal and nonverbal communication cues as well as social presence (refer to the media section for detailed discussion). Mittleman et al. (2000) also suggested using an informal break for online team meetings when all parties can share casual talks and social jokes with the assistance of ICT. Another useful strategy, as found by Zhang and Carr-Chellman (2001), is to promote some small social talks and encourage members to greet each other in a positive tone.

Communication Media

Online collaborative teams face many challenges due to the lack of face-to-face communications or shared social context. The fading or blurry physical, temporal, and psychological boundaries make it difficult for online teams to establish a team identity or sense, which is critical for effective team performance. Appropriate selection and utilization of communication media may help learners better overcome some of the difficulties. With a variety of information and communication technologies, it is very vital yet difficult to select and utilize appropriate media for different tasks and at different team development stages. Thus media research provides another lens to look into the dynamics of online collaboration.

Rational Media Theories

Media richness and social presence theories are the most well-accepted rational theories that explain media choices and media behaviors. Media richness theory (Daft & Lengel, 1984) measures the richness of media in terms of the capacity for immediate feedback, multiple cues, natural language, and personal focus on voice tone and inflection. Media have varied capacities to reduce ambiguity and thus facilitate mutual understanding (Daft & Lengel, 1984). Richer medium facilitates more accurate and meaningful transmission and exchange of ideas. However, as discussed earlier, tasks of different types and complexity have different requirements for information richness in order to achieve maximal group performance. Some tasks require more information and richer medium than others for the best team performance.

Social presence theory (Short, Williams, & Christie, 1976) studies media in terms of the degree to which they are perceived to convey the presence of a communication party. The quantity of social presence is how much one believes another party is present. In communication, the psychological distance among communicating parties is referred to as immediacy (Wiener & Mehrabian, 1968). Thus there are two forms of immediacy: technological immediacy and social immediacy. Technological immediacy is inherent, whereas social immediacy can be changed (Heilbronn & Libby, 1973). Heilbronn and Libby state that the maximum amount of exchanged information ensures technological immediacy, and social immediacy is conveyed through communications with verbal or nonverbal cues. Walther (1996, 1997) suggests that ICT is also able to convey social information, just as face-to-face communications, but with lower transfer rate. Walther has also found that ICT mediated groups have greater social discussion, depth, and intimacy than face-to-face groups.

In a review of social presence theory and studies on ICT-mediated communication, Gunawardena (1995) concluded that immediacy enhanced social presence, which in turn enhanced interactions. As related to online collaborative learning, it indicates that the online teams, with assistance from the instructor or an external moderator, should promote the use of media that better convey the notion of social presence in order to increase interactions among the members.

Social Constructivist Theories

Social constructivists (e.g. Fulk, 1993; Fulk, Schmitz, & Steinfield, 1990) believe that both media perception and media behaviors are socially constructed and that media choices may not necessarily follow precisely the rational choice theories, such as the media richness theory (Daft & Lengel, 1984) and the social presence theory (Fulk et al., 1990). Many studies (e.g. Hinds & Kiesler, 1996; Zack & McKenney, 1996) confirm that communication is a function of the context, setting, and timing rather than the characteristics of the media. These studies can help us understand learners' media choices and media behaviors in educational settings. In our experiences as instructional designers, instructors, and researchers, we have observed that learners either do not always use the communication tools made available to them within the online learning environment or use these tools differently from the original intention. For instance, they tend to choose a medium that is already popular among the members (Zhang, 2004) even though the courseware has the same or even a better medium for the same purpose. The social constructivist theories help us understand such a phenomenon and shed light on media selections in our design efforts of a collaborative learning environment.

In addition to rational understanding of media, as media richness and social presence theory suggest, the instructional designers should also investigate the social contexts in terms of media perception and utilization and integrate such understandings into the design of an online collaborative learning environment. Practically, the online collaborative environment should provide communication media that are already well accepted and widely utilized by the learners, rather than develop a new medium for the same purpose. For example, if all members have been using certain instant messenger software, then the better solution would be to integrate this messenger rather than select or develop another similar tool.

Media and Team Development

Teams at different stages of development face different issues and problems, which generate different needs for social presence and richness of media. For example, at the forming stage, during which the major task is information seeking, the richer the medium is, the more information input members can detect and process. In addition, the more social presence is perceived, the more likely and easier it is to establish trust. Similarly, at the storming stage, when conflicts occur frequently, there is a strong need for social presence to address these conflicts, especially affective conflicts. Face-to-face is identified as the richest medium (Daft & Lengel, 1984) and also the best medium to convey social presence (Short et al., 1976). Mazinevski and Chudoba's (2000) findings about the temporal rhythms, which were highlighted with intense face-to-face meetings for effective global virtual teams, also support the theoretical needs for rich media and social presence to accomplish complex team tasks. Therefore, face-to-face communications and other media that convey rich information and social presence are strongly recommended to facilitate trust building and information seeking, as well as for addressing emotional conflicts.

In their review, Guzzo and Shea (1992) found that almost all studies on group collaboration had reflected an underlying input-process-output model. All the qualities that each member brought to the team were inputs, such as expertise, personality, and strength. The inputs were then processed through group interactions and activities, such as information exchange, cooperation, collaboration, and taking leadership role, which were later transformed into output of the teamwork. For online collaborative teams, all the input identification and processing are expected to happen with the assistance of ICT. Yet it can be very difficult for online collaborative teams to detect or benefit much from some of these inputs, such as personality. The relatively less knowledge about those inputs may delay the progress of team development, especially in the forming and storming stage, and for conflict-resolving and complex problem-solving tasks.

Media richness theory and social presence theory enlighten the understanding of rational choice of media. Social constructivist theories help to understand media behaviors, which are not always consistent with the rational theories. These theories enable instructors and instructional designers to understand why some medium works better than the others at a certain stage, and such knowledge enables the instructors to better provide facilitation and moderation as needed.

Suggestions for Media Selection

Instructors can help learners make rational media choice on the basis of their needs at different stages and for different purposes and tasks. At the same time, instructors and instructional designers should understand the social contexts of the teams in order to understand, predict, and facilitate their media behaviors accordingly. In addition, Schwartz (1994) suggested that teams should work out a team contract through collaborative efforts and have discussions on media choice for the team in varied situations. Such efforts will help online collaborative teams to establish positive personal and professional relationships and thus improve performance and effectiveness (Bocialetti, 1988; Zhang, 2004).

Conclusion

In this chapter, we have presented a conceptual model for understanding online collaborative learning from four aspects: team tasks, team development, peer relationships, and communication media. The model serves to guide research and practice related to online collaborative learning. For instance, the model provides researchers new insights to examine online collaborative learning and additional ways to analyze collaborative discourse. The model is also intended to direct instructors and instructional designers to design and moderate online collaborative learning activities with reference to the four aspects. The specific suggestions at the end of each section also have a practical value for instructors, facilitators, instructional designers, collaborative groups, and others who are interested in online collaborative learning.

To further improve the conceptual model in the future, it would be worth pursuing to map out the interrelationships among the four aspects through empirical studies. Drawing upon the essence of research from different disciplines and applying it to the field of education, specifically distance education or e-learning, we consider this chapter a valuable artifact contributing to the growing research on online collaborative learning.

References

Bocialetti, G. (1988). Teams and the management of emotion. In W. B. Reddy (Ed.), *Team building: Blueprints for productivity and satisfaction* (pp. 62-71). VA: NTL Institute.

Bonk, C. J., & King, K. S. (Eds.). (1998). *Electronic collaborators: Learner-centered technologies for literacy, apprenticeship, and discourse*. Mahwah, NJ: Erlbaum.

Bruffee, K. (1999). *Collaborative learning: Higher education, interdependence, and the authority of knowledge* (2nd ed.). Baltimore: Johns Hopkins University Press.

Chizhik, A. W. (2001). Equity and status in group collaboration: Learning through explanation depends on task characteristics. *Social Psychology of Education, 5*, 179-200.

Clark, R. C., & Mayer, R. E. (2003). Learning together on the Web. In R. C. Clark & R. E. Mayer (Eds.), *E-learning and the science of instruction: Proven guidelines for consumers and designers of multimedia learning* (pp. 197-223). San Francisco: Wiley.

Daft, R. L., & Lengel, R. H. (1984). Information richness: A new approach to managerial information processing and organization design. In B. Straw & L. Cummings (Eds), *Research in organizational behavior* (Vol. 6, pp. 191-233). Greenwich, CT: JAI Press.

Derry, S. J., & DuRussel, L. A. (1999, July). *Assessing knowledge construction processes in online learning communities.* Paper presented at the Annual Meeting of the International Society for Artificial Intelligence in Education, Lemans France. (ERIC Document Reproduction Service No. ED446897)

Diezmann, C. M., & Watters, J. J. (2001). The collaboration of mathematically gifted students on challenging tasks. *Journal for the Education of the Gifted, 25*(1), 7-31.

Fulk, J. (1993). Social construction of communication technology. *Academy of Management Journal, 36*(5), 921-950.

Fulk, J., Schmitz, J., & Steinfield, C. W. (1990). A social influence model of tech-nology use. In J. Fulk & C. Steinfield (Eds.), *Organizations and communica-tions technology* (pp. 117-140). Newbury Park, CA: Sage.

Ge, X., & Land, S. M. (2003). Scaffolding students' problem-solving processes in an ill-structured task using question prompts and peer interactions. *Educa-tional Technology Research and Development, 51*(1), 21-38.

Ge, X., & Mansell, R. A. (2003, April). *Content analysis of knowledge construc-tion in an instructor-led online discussion.* Paper discussion at the Annual Convention of American Educational Research Association, Chicago, IL.

Gersick, C. J. (1988). Time and transition in work teams: Toward a new model of group development. *Academy of Management Journal, 31*(1), 9-41.

Gunawardena, C. N. (1995). Social presence theory and implications for interac-tion collaborative learning in computer conferences. *International Journal of Educational Telecommunications, 1*(2/3), 147-166.

Guzzo, R. A., & Dickson, M. W. (1996). Team in organizations: Recent research on performance and effectiveness. *Annual Review of Psychology, 47,* 307-338.

Guzzo, R. A., & Shea, G. P. (1992). Group performance and intergroup relations in organizations. In M. D. Dunette & L. M. Hough (Eds.), *Handbook of indus-trial and organizational psychology* (2nd ed., Vol. 3, pp. 269-313). Palo Alto, CA: Consulting Psychologist Press.

Hannafin, M., Land, S., & Oliver, K. (1999). Open learning environments: Founda-tions, methods, and models. In C. M. Reigeluth (Ed.), *Instructional-design the-ories and models: A new paradigm of instructional theory* (Vol. 2, pp. 115-140). Mahwah, NJ: Erlbaum.

Hara, N., Bonk, C. J., & Angeli, C. (2000). Content analysis of online discussion in an applied educational psychology course. *Instructional Science, 28*(2), 115-152.

Harasim, L. (1990). Online education: An environment for collaboration and intel-lectual amplification. In L. Harasim (Ed.), *Online education: Perspectives on a new environment* (pp. 39-64). New York: Praeger.

Heilbronn, M., & Libby, W. L. (1973). *Comparative effects of technological and social immediacy upon performance and perceptions during a two-person game.* Paper presented at the Annual Convention of the American Psycholog-ical Association, Montreal.

Henri, F. (1991). Computer conferencing and content analysis. In A. R. Kaye (Ed.), *Collaborative learning through computer conferencing* (pp. 117-136). New York: Spring-Verlag.

Hinds, P., & Kiesler, S. (1996). Communication across boundaries: Work, struc-ture, and use of communication technologies in a large organization. *Organi-zation Science, 6*(4), 373-393.

Hollingshead, A. G., & McGrath, J. E. (1995). Computer-assisted groups: A critical review of the empirical research. In R. A. Guzzo, E. Salas, et al. (Eds.), *Team effectiveness and decision making in organizations* (pp.46-78). San Francisco: Jossey-Bass.

Hollingshead, A. G., McGrath, J. E., & O'Connor, K. M. (1993). Group task performance and communication technology: A longitudinal study of computer-mediated versus face-to-face work groups. *Small Group Research, 24*(3), 307-333.

Jehn, K. (1997). A qualitative analysis of conflict types and dimensions in organizational groups. *Administrative Science Quarterly, 42*, 530-557.

Johnson, R. T., Johnson, D. W., & Stanne, M. B. (1985). Effects of cooperative, competitive, and individualistic goal structures on computer-assisted instruction. *Journal of Educational Psychology, 77*(6), 668-677.

Johnson, R. T., Johnson, D. W., & Stanne, M. B. (1986). Comparison of computer-assisted cooperative, competitive, and individualistic learning. *American Educational Research Journal, 23*(3), 382-392.

Jonassen, D. (1999). Designing constructivist learning environments. In C. M. Reigeluth (Ed.), *Instructional-design theories and models: A new paradigm of instructional theory* (Vol. 2, pp. 215-239). Mahwah, NJ: Erlbaum.

Kabanoff, B., & O'Brien, G. E. (1979). The effects of task type and cooperation upon group products and performance. *Organizational Behavior and Human Performance, 23*, 63-181.

Kaye, A. R. (Ed.). (1991). *Collaborative learning through computer conferencing*. New York: Spring-Verlag.

King, A. (1992). Facilitating elaborative learning through guided student-generated questioning. *Educational Psychologist, 27*(1), 111-126.

King, A. (1994). Guiding knowledge construction in the classroom: Effects of teaching children how to question and how to explain. *American Educational Research Journal, 31*(2), 338-368.

Kumpulainen, K., & Kaartinen, S. (2000). Situational mechanisms of peer group interaction in collaborative meaning-making: Processes and conditions for learning. *European Journal of Psychology of Education, 15*(4), 431-454.

Maznevski, M. L., & Chudoba, K. M. (2000). Bridging space over time: Global virtual team dynamics and effectiveness. *Organization Science, 11*(5), 473-492.

Mittleman, D. D., Briggs, R. O., & Nunamaker Jr., J. F. (2000). Best practice in facilitating virtual meetings: Some notes from initial experience. *Group Facilitation: A Research and Applications Journal, 2*, 5-14.

Palincsar, A. S. (1986). The role of dialogue in providing scaffolded instruction.

Educational Psychologist, 21(1/2), 73-98.

Palincsar, A. S., & Brown, A. L. (1984). Reciprocal teaching of comprehension-fostering and comprehension-monitoring activities. *Cognition and Instruction, 1,* 117-175.

Scardamalia, M., & Bereiter, C. (1996). Computer support for knowledge-building communities. In T. Koschmann (Ed.), *CSCL: Theory and practice of an emerging paradigm* (pp. 249-268). Mahwah, NJ: Erlbaum.

Schwarz, R. (1994). *The skilled facilitator.* San Francisco: Jossey Bass.

Short, J., Williams, E., & Christie, B. (1976). *The social psychology of telecommunications.* London: Wiley.

Thompson, L. (2000). *Conflicts in teams: Leveraging differences to create opportunity. Making the team: A guide for managers.* Englewood Cliffs, NJ: Prentice Hall.

Tuckman, B. W. (1965). Developmental sequence in small groups. *Psychological Bulletin, 63*(6), 384-399.

Uribe, D., Klein, J. D., & Sullivan, H. (2003). The effect of computer-mediated collaborative learning on solving ill-defined problems. *Educational Technology Research and Development, 51*(1), 5-19.

Walther, J. B.(1996). Computer-mediated communication: Impersonal, interpersonal, and hyperpersonal interaction. *Communication Research, 23,* 1-43.

Walther, J. B. (1997). Group and interpersonal effects in international computer-mediated collaboration. *Human Communication Research, 23*(2), 342-369.

Webb, N. M., & Palincsar, A. S. (1996). Group processes in the classroom. In D. C. Berliner & R. C. Calfee (Eds.), *Handbook of educational psychology* (pp. 841-873). New York: Macmillan.

Weiss, H. M., & Cropanzano, R. (1996). Affective events theory: A theoretical discussion of the structure, causes and consequences of affective experiences at work. *Research in Organizational Behavior, 18,* 1-74.

Wiener, M., & Mehrabian, A. (1968). *Language within language: Immediacy, a channel in verbal communication.* New York: Appleton-Century-Crofts.

Zack, M. H., & McKenney, J. L. (1996). Social context and interaction in ongoing computer supported management groups. *Organization Science, 64*(4), 394-422.

Zajonc, R. B. (1984). On the primacy of affect. *American Psychologist, 29,* 117-123.

Zhang, K. (2001, June). Promoting peer online collaborative learning. *Educational Technology 2001 Proceedings,* Arlington, VA.

Zhang, K. (2003, April). *Effects of two types of online collaboration (peer-controlled vs. externally-structured-and-moderated) on group problem solving (well-*

structured and ill-structured). Paper presented at the Annual Meeting of the American Educational Research Association, Chicago, IL.

Zhang, K. (2004). *Effects of peer-controlled or externally structured and moderated online collaboration on group problem solving processes and related individual attitudes in well-structured and ill-structured small group problem solving in a hybrid course.* Unpublished doctoral dissertation, Pennsylvania State University.

Zhang, K., & Carr-Chellman, A. A. (2001). Peer online discourse analysis. *Proceedings of the 24th Annual Meeting of the Association for Educational Communications and Technology, 2.* (ERIC Document Reproduction Service No. ED470141)

Zhang, K., & Ge, X. (2004, October). *Online collaborative learning in hybrid courses: Comparative case studies across time and domains.* Paper presented at the Annual Meeting of the Association for Educational Communications and Technology, Chicago.

Zhang, K., & Harkness, W. L. (2002). Groups going online in a large class: Critical reflections. *Journal of Interactive Instructional Development, 14*(3), 14-18.

Zhang, K., & Peck, K. L. (2003). The effects of peer-controlled or moderated online collaboration on group problem solving and related attitudes. *Canadian Journal of Learning and Technology, 29*(3), 93-112.

Chapter VII

Designing for Unique Online Learning Contexts:
The Alignment of Purpose, Audience, and Form of Interactivity

Mark Schofield, Edge Hill College of Higher Education, United Kingdom

Andrew Sackville, Edge Hill College of Higher Education, United Kingdom

John Davey, Edge Hill College of Higher Education, United Kingdom

Abstract

This chapter argues that more attention needs to be given to problematizing design at the level of purpose, audience, and form of online interactions and to seeking alignment of these components. It derives from experiences of conceptualization, design, and delivery processes. Some online students are more active than others; some groups respond to a series of planned activities and online tasks while others do not, and in some cases patterns of interactivity develop that are not planned and designed for. We propose that the design of online programs is not a simple, but a skilled and complex, phenomenon with a large number of independent and inter-dependent variables. We present our ideas in three sections and use the allusion of a bespoke tailor customizing a jacket for a client. These sections comprise the "jacket," "the body," and the skilled task of tailoring the jacket to fit the body, which represents the process of designing for unique online contexts.

Introduction

The foundations of this chapter began in 1998 when we started to use a virtual learning environment (VLE) to deliver online learning opportunities to a range of students. These were on a variety of programs at different levels, both on-campus and at a distance. As embryonic online learning designers, we sought ideas in a wide range of literature about online learning and eagerly read case studies about how other tutors had developed practice. As educationalists, we were concerned to use pedagogic concepts, models, and insights that we had already developed and incorporated into face-to-face teaching. We found many useful lists of dos and don'ts and collections of suggestions for "how you could. . .," many of which tended to focus on the technological rather than the pedagogical aspects of online learning. Attempts in the literature to conceptualize the pedagogic design process were few and far between, and we had difficulty in connecting those that existed with the unique contexts presented to our practice.

On developing design and delivery of online learning, we became more interested in and concerned with aspects of *interactivity*, that is, the interactions between people and with online media. We noted that some online students were more active than others. Some groups responded to series of planned activities and online tasks; others did not. In some cases patterns of interactivity developed that we had not planned and deliberately designed for (Sackville & Schofield, 2001). This led us to examine interactivity in more detail to recognize that the design of online programs was not a simple, a skilled and complex, task with a large number of independent and interdependent variables that needed to be considered when attempting to design for interactivity.

This chapter is essentially generic, as it represents our distillation of general principles, guiding ideas, and broader conceptual issues, which may be adopted, adapted, and developed by the reader. We present our latest version of a conceptual model that we have been, and still are, developing. It seeks to capture the complexity of planning for online learning. We argue that more attention needs to be given to problematizing design at the level of purpose, audience, and form. That is, we need context-related interactivity analysis in our designing—that is, alignment of the interactivity with the proposed purpose and notion of the audience (see Figure 1). The model derives from our immersion in the conceptualization, design, and delivery processes. As such, we have undertaken much reflection and post facto problematizing. Immersion as a condition for learning and development has itself been reported (Bickmore-Brand, 1995; Schofield, 2000). It sug-

Figure 1. Model of bespoke tailoring

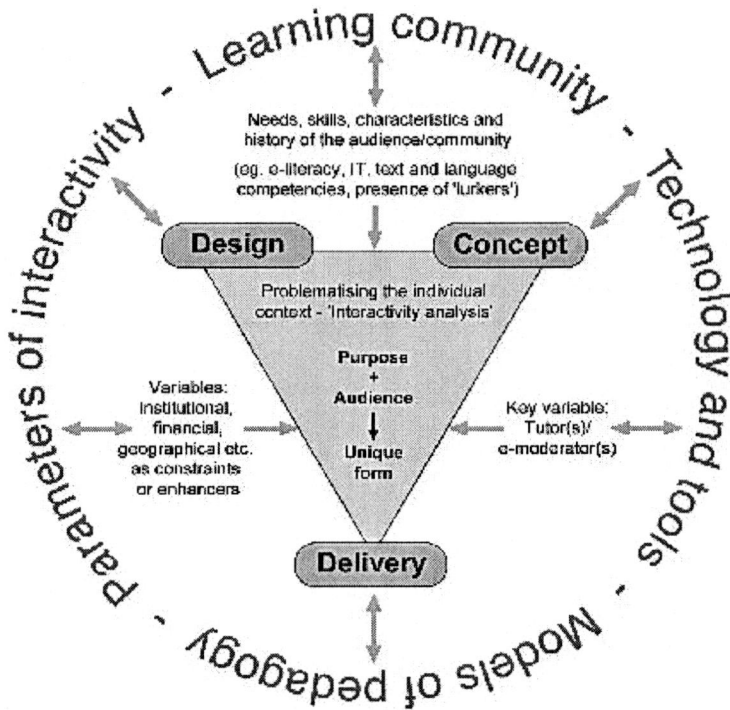

gests the efficacy of having specific experiences as a prelude to reflection, learning, and formulating new concepts and approaches. The model presented here developed as a consequence of reflection upon our immersion in practice of design for, delivery of, and participation in online learning.

Our ideas are presented in three sections by using the metaphor of a bespoke tailor, making a jacket for a client to fit the body, and subsequent tailoring and adjustment that needs to be undertaken. The "jacket" surrounds the online learning program or experience. We identify a number of "off the peg" features of designing for online learning and suggest that these embrace the current technology and range of tools available, models of pedagogy, parameters of interactivity, and conceptions of a learning community.

We suggest that the body fits inside the jacket and comprises the conceptualization, design, and delivery of the online learning experience. Bodies can gain or lose weight, and so eventually they come to fit the jacket. But this is often a slow process. Similarly a body may become sick and regain health. As such, online learning programs may change as they are delivered. They are dynamic, organic, and not static.

Finally we have the skilled task of tailoring the jacket to fit the body. We suggest that discussion of "purpose," "audience," and "form of interactivity" becomes crucial. This "interactivity analysis," as we have called it, enables the production of a uniquely fitting jacket. It also leaves us with the possibility of altering the jacket if the body shape changes. In conceptual terms this is affiliated to constructive alignment of outcomes, pedagogy, and assessment (Biggs, 1999).

The model of bespoke tailoring, in designing for effective online learning, is presented diagrammatically in Figure 1.

The "Jacket"

We propose four elements of the "jacket" within which our conceptual design model sits: (a) technology and tools, (b) models of pedagogy, (c) parameters of interactivity, and (d) learning community.

Technology and Tools

In the authors' specific context, development of design for online learning was accelerated by certain features that adoption of a VLE offers. These included

- a single site that combined both information and communication tools
- emancipatory features that reduce the limiting factors of time and geographic location of learners
- the opportunity to convene groups in cyberspace, and the potential for interaction and community development
- the opportunity to instigate "communities of practice" (Lave & Wenger, 1991)
- the potential to extend face-to-face activities or "replicate" them using communications tools
- perceived ease of use of the VLEs communications and operating tools by tutors and students

Increased use of the Internet by students or participants and changing demands on patterns of study complemented the decisions to adapt a VLE to support online learning development.

Technology is constantly changing. We wished to move away from purely text-based tools in order to solicit the other senses—visual, auditory, and kinaesthetic. We do not subscribe to using technology just for its own sake. It needs to be harnessed for pedagogic purposes.

The skilled tailor is aware of changes in fashion (changing technologies), but he or she also listens to the client (the students and the tutors). This consultation takes place before making the garment, during its assembly, and often later when appropriate alterations are required. Hence the birth of the bespoke tailoring metaphor.

Models of Pedagogy

The intention here is not to undertake a detailed epistemological analysis of learning via VLEs, but to share ideas and challenges that led, and will lead, us to design in a particular way. However, it is appropriate to consider the social constructivist backdrop to much of our ongoing work in this area at Edge Hill.

There has been extensive literature on constructivism (e.g., Cripps & McGilchrist, 1999; Fox, 1997; Jarvis, Holford, & Griffin, 1998; Noddings, 1990; Von Glasersfeld, 1987). The version of social constructivism that provides the basis for our work is characterized by a metaphor of people in conversation, as such, socially constructing and sharing a version of the world as they experience it. Jarvis et al. (1998) elaborate this notion of social constructivism, triggering consideration of alignment to be made between this theoretical stance and the design and delivery within interactive VLEs: "A central (constructivist) method is 'real talk' which includes discourse and exploration, talking and listening, questions, argument, speculation, and sharing, but in which domination is replaced by reciprocity and co-operation" (Jarvis et al., 1998, p. 73).

Constructivism has a fundamental core component, which is that understanding and knowledge are actively constructed within the individual as a result of the activation of the senses (in this context, as a product of online interaction). This involves dynamic processing of sensory information and schematic assembly within the brain of an individual (see Desforge's analysis of information processing in Fox, 1997, p. 20 et seq.). It involves testing ideas and thoughts against prior knowledge and experience and integrating the new knowledge or understanding with pre-existing intellectual constructs. Online, these processes may be supported by language interchanges; hence the emphasis on social constructivism.

The metaphor of conversation resonates with the domain of interactivity, which we will define here as that communication which may exist between people, with information or media supplied to or generated by members of a group. It may be helpful to consider that if interactivity is desirable in learners' experiences, how might one design for its inclusion in VLEs or to remove barriers to its occurrence? How might one engage learners in individual and joint construction of knowledge, supported by social-dialectic interchange? Teachers in (higher) education may be forgiven for suggesting that this focus is indeed an ongoing challenge in traditional face-to-face teaching. Hence it is worthy of analysis in order to explore challenges facing those employing VLEs as a learning tool or who are considering doing so.

Figure 2. Relationship between learning, interactivity, learning community, and the conditions underpinning our social constructivist notion of online learning

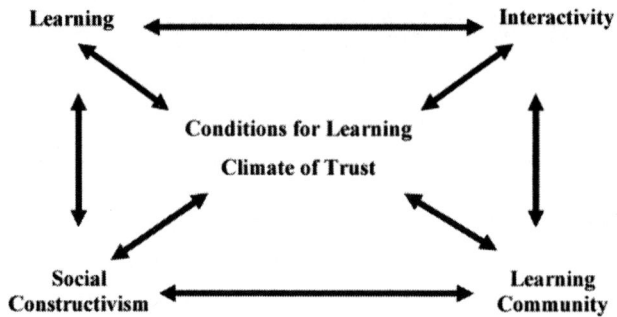

It is indeed a particular challenge to understand and engineer a climate and conditions both in traditional terrestrial settings and within a VLE for the development of a learning community, amid the variety of locations, types of learners, and available technology and tools.

Figure 2 offers a relationship between learning, interactivity, learning community, and the conditions underpinning our social constructivist notion of online learning.

The figure illustrates our proposal that communities may develop as a consequence of interactivity and that interactivity is a consequence of community. It reflects the notion of the potential for the emergence of communities of practice considered by Wenger (1998).

The conditions and climate for such social constructivist learning are dependent on instructional design, are vital, and rely on many variables. These include both those in the "jacket" and the human variables of tutors' design and e-mentoring capabilities, and the unique context and nature of the learners or participants in the "body."

Our current subscription to social constructivism raises the issue of the operations of the tutor in the conceptualization, design, and delivery phases. We are alerted to Forsyth's dilemma, which proposes that "the nature of the internet technology seems to lead to a confusion among the education and training fraternity. One view of the internet is that it is a technology to deliver information. A more considered view is that access to the internet as a technology and a delivery tool needs to be considered after the educational methodology is determined" (Forsyth, 2001, p. 6).

This alerts us to the importance of problematizing the VLE, its association with the purpose and audience, and hence the alignment that is inherent in our model.

The model still envisages a crucial role for the tutor (tailor) in the educational process. It would be possible for us just to provide free-floating materials and thread in cyberspace and allow our learners to produce any clothes they wanted—trousers, skirts, suits, hats; and, yes, there can be models of pedagogy which allow for that. But we would argue that for these free-floating materials to be valuable in constructing new knowledge, the learner or participant must have some ideas about how to access them and have cognitive frameworks onto which they can be grafted to make meaning or artifacts for their own wardrobe of learning. We see the tutor as providing a basic set of patterns, which learners can adapt for their own use. The learners (customers) can be supported and guided in the assembly of learning though freedom, choice, and recognition of differential need may emerge as key design maxims.

Parameters of Interactivity

Interactivity has been conceptualized as a "universal good," and judgments of quality have often been made about online courses in terms of the volume of interactions that have been recorded (Sackville, 2002). Although we started our online design careers with a similar aim, we quickly became aware that there were different forms of interactivity taking place and that there were sophisticated parameters of interactivity we needed to take account of in tailoring our online programs.

The first three forms of interactivity we used were identified by Moore (1989). These were

- Learner – Content/ information/ learning materials
- Learner – Tutor
- Learner – Learner

Even these apparently straightforward parameters are far more complex, and each can be analyzed in terms of whether the interactivity is synchronous or asynchronous; whether it is in the private or the public arena; whether it is dealing with one-to-one interactivity, one-to-many interactivity, small group interactivity, many-to-many interactivity, and so forth, as elaborated in Paulsen's seminal work (1995).

Through our practice, we then added further three major forms of interactivity:

- Learner – Technology and complex multimedia
- Participants (learners/tutors) – The professional community they belong or aspire to belong to
- Intrapersonal interactivity – Self-reflection and meta-cognition elicited by presence in an online experience

Figure 3. Identifying the parameters of desired interactivity: A planning grid for alignment of purpose, audience, and form

Size of Interactivity (Audience) / Type of Interactivity (Purpose)	One to One	Small Group (Tutorial)	Whole Group	Inter-Community (within or across VLEs)
Learner(s) ⟶ Technology				
Learner(s) ⟶ Content/ Multimedia				
Learner(s) ⟷ Tutor(s)				
Learner(s) ⟷ Learner(s)				
Participants ⟷ Professional Community				

The designer has a responsibility to ensure that potential learners can use their learning technology effectively, whether it is how to critically read a conventional in-print book or how to use a VLE in cyberspace. Similarly, as much of our design work relates to providing learning opportunities for members and potential members of a number of professions (e.g., teachers, nurses, doctors, dentists.), we had to ensure that links were being made and maintained into the larger professional learning community around the world. All subscribe to the efficacy of learning in a reflective mode.

We are continuing to work on identifying other parameters of interactivity, since we would argue that there is a need for a clear framework, to allow interactivity analysis when tailoring learning activities and e-moderation tasks to the unique purpose of a particular audience in cyberspace. Figure 3 indicates some of the parameters of interactivity we may design to achieve and provides a practical, problematizing tool for use when looking at designing for online interactions. Our experience is that the tool's structure creates a focus for dialogue and debate around the particular unique context and learners or audience. The conversations may be between designers and stakeholders, such as university teachers, learning technologists, employers, and online learners. As such, it further exemplifies the bespoke tailoring metaphor as a process of achieving alignment and thus enhancing quality.

When a particular form of interactivity is desired, it should be possible to suggest online activities that might be able to encourage and support such interactivity (Bonk & Reynolds, 1997; Palloff & Pratt, 1999). If parameters are elucidated, then the designer and tutor can select those appropriate to align forms of interactivity with the unique purpose and audience at the center of the problematization proposed within the model presented in Figure 3.

Learning Community

Wenger (1998) has exerted a good deal of influence in developing the concept of a learning community. He has suggested that communities involve the mutual engagement of participants, a commitment to joint enterprise, and a shared repertoire of approaches or techniques (p. 73).

There have been a number of attempts to analyze the development and support of learning communities online. The Online Tutoring Skills Project (OTiS) report (2001) recognized that we can "pull" (extend invitations to join a community), "push" (build in requirements that learners participate in a community), and "avoid" (ensure our designed community is not antagonizing potential members; p 3.11).

In planning for a "learning community" (online or face-to-face) the instructional designer may need to answer, or at least recognize, a number of key questions:

- Is the community pre-existing, and what is its history?
- How will the community be convened?
- By community do we mean a large group, or subsets within a large group?
- If the latter, what will the interrelationship of the subsets be?
- How may the community be developed and by whom?
- How may the community be supported and support itself?
- What may the role(s) of tutor and students or participants be?
- What may the needs be as the community changes and develops?
- How may reconsideration of the above questions reapply as community changes and develops?

After such analysis, how may these facets be aligned, and subsequently re-aligned, with the use of tools and planning of opportunities for interactivity?

Reflection on Practice, Experience, and Research

Before we started designing our first program, we had a rudimentary conception of the technology and tools we would be using, the model of pedagogy that would underlie our design, the patterns of interactivity we wanted to incorporate in our programs, and the ultimate aim of developing a learning community for our students. But on moving forward with the design process and becoming immersed in online learning, we developed and refined our understanding of these concepts and identified other issues that we needed to take on board. This section briefly identifies some of the challenges we met in design and also some of the unexpected issues that arose in our experience, many of which emerge as desirable design maxims.

Within a four-year part-time undergraduate program using a VLE we noted

- a mixing of social and academic/professional aspects of interaction and the participants' vehemence in wanting to keep these elements of interaction combined;
- cross-group communications within a large multi-cohort VLE where groups of students studied on different courses. There were many instances of unplanned peer support, mentoring, and guidance of both an academic and a social nature across different year cohorts within the same VLE;
- informal technical support from students and cross-year group "peer" tutoring;
- students or participants reporting a "sense of early belonging" in new courses of study where a blended delivery mode prevailed. Value appeared to be added to the student experience by incorporating a VLE;
- organic growth of resources within the VLE—students taking ownership and specifying new hyperlinks and learning objects;
- the benefit of the involvement of central campus student support services personnel in enhancing links with a distal satellite campus;
- the potential to create a communications conduit for the completion of quality assurance and enhancement communications loops; and
- emergence of a "social and academic cohort club" metaphor.

Several of these features were also noticed in a contrasting one-year postgraduate certificate for busy health service professionals, which was delivered primarily via a VLE with very limited face-to-face contact. This program also identified

- a concern among participants about colleagues who were not joining in with the online discussion or completing the online activities;

- a readiness on the part of learners to "police" their stray members, that is, those who were missing and those who sped ahead of the group. Both support and discontent was expressed;

- a greater degree of reflection on material and more engagement in challenging existing ideas than the tutor had experienced in similar face-to-face groups; and

- the expression of ideas online by those who were silent in face-to-face groups and the curbing of the excesses of those participants who were perceived by peers and tutors to be dominating and loquacious in face-to-face situations.

Research was completed on these "patterns of interaction," although some of the existing research methods and tools were not always effective in capturing all the nuances of the interactivity that was occurring (for a fuller exposition of this, see Sackville, 2002).

Interestingly, different types of e-learners were identified: the "express-train," the "slow starter," the "model student," the "fast-starter/slowing down," and the "witness learner." The program team who identified these types of learners redesigned aspects of their online program to encourage more "model learners" and to curtail the numbers of what were perceived by the tutors as "less desirable" typologies. For example, "three-week time envelopes" for the completion of online activities were incorporated into the calendar of the program, online contributions were recognized within the summative assessment scheme, and so forth. Initial evidence suggests that this redesign strategy has been largely successful, although on occasions at a cost—the encouragement of more reflective communications and the loss of the initial spontaneity of keen participants engaging in more frequent if less reflective debate. We have included this example to demonstrate the continuing development of our model of online design and pedagogy. It also illustrates the complexity of interactions that are worthy of analysis both during and after delivery. Finally it raises the question of how far we can design for some of these "unexpected" features of interaction and, indeed, asks if those features are desirable anyway. As such, we suggest that the alignment of purpose, audience, and form of interactivity should be an ongoing and dynamic phenomenon in instructional design.

The appearance of apparent "lurkers" (online but not overtly participating) has focused our attention on both the pedagogy in the "jacket" and the uniqueness of the "body" within. "Lurkers" we believe is a pejorative and contestable idea. The emergence of "witness learners" as a term is more considered and related to an understanding of social constructivist pedagogies. As such, a challenge is presented to designers for acceptance of such behavior, or systematic or instrumental inclusion via activities and assessment processes. The justification of witness learners in a social constructivist model is one of permissiveness, predicated on a notion of a learner taking from the text, media, and conversational artifacts and pursuing self-constructions. These are still related social interactions and events, though value judgments may be brought to bear on the types of individual commitment to interaction. This may compare with rights we give learners in face-to-face situations to listen and follow the interactions of others without actively conversing. This does not preclude their engagement and subsequent constructions. Issues may be raised in relation to agreements with learners or participants, the ethics of inclusivity, and pedagogic design for conditions and environments that are welcoming and matched to individuals' preferences and needs.

At the conception of a curriculum, how far can we deliberately design for such issues? This leads us to focus more closely on the "body" within the "jacket."

In designing online opportunities we recognized phases of initial conceptualization and initial design for a program. But both of these facets have been altered and amended in the light of our experience of delivery. The relationship between conceptualization, design, and delivery is not a simple linear relationship. It is a dynamic relationship, which is constantly changing to suit a particular context. To continue our metaphor, a tailor has to assess the needs and status of the client so that the jacket's materials and pre-existing patterns can be selected. It involves "bespoking the fit," making the jacket fit the body in the first instance, then making subsequent amendments and alterations. A second fitting or some re-tailoring is needed as the VLE continues in operation.

We suggest the need to problematize, at the level of purpose, audience and forms of interactivity so the VLE-experience may be pursued with sharper focus and the art of bespoke tailoring be exercised. It is a dynamic and formative process and should be ongoing during the life of such an online experience.

Helping the Jacket Fit the Body or Helping the Body Fit the Jacket?

The body does not just float around freely within the jacket. As you tailor the jacket to fit the body, other variables come into play. These are the nips and tucks of tailoring that help the jacket to fit the body.

We have identified and started to analyze some of these:

- Quality of tutors or e-moderators as a key variable
- Needs, skills, characteristics, and history of the audience
- Other variables—institutional, financial, geographical, cultural

These can be constraints or enhancements in the design process, stimulating realignments and sometimes compromises as to purpose and form of interactivity.

Tutors and E-Moderators

Younie (2001) has identified a cognitive flexible literacy:

> *To develop a cognitively flexible literacy is to prepare individuals for living and working with ICTs in lifelong learning contexts. The critical intellectual abilities needed for higher order thinking are reasoning, abstraction, analysis, evaluation, and problem solving. Learning with ICTs provides opportunities to develop these skills within a supportive environment of interaction and collaboration with peers and guidance of the teacher. Encouraging interpersonal development engenders the ability to communicate in a variety of ways with others, which is needed to sustain cognitive flexible literacy. This enables learners to adapt to changing novel situations and new information, which requires the spontaneous restructuring of a learner's knowledge. (Younie, 2001, p. 215)*

This raises a challenge to developing communication skills and interpersonal consciousnesses, and assumptions may prevail about the status of these in learners and VLE tutors. Such online "text-literacy" emerges as a vital consideration. It extends to the continuing professional development of tutors and e-moderators. Loveless, de Voogd, and Bohlin (2001), having worked with cross-disciplinary MA students in conceptualizing the role of improving teaching through ICT use, suggest the following emerging dimensions to the tutor role:

- A manager of collaborative teaching and learning
- A director-actor (supporting teaching with technology)
- A facilitator (of interactivity and learning community)
- A designer (involved in team approaches)

(p. 72)

A sensitive question is posed here. Have we accomplished this to a confident level of scholarship in face-to-face teaching? To transfer teaching and teachers to VLEs without previous consideration of the complexities of online interactivity may be in itself problematical, but avoidable via professional development. Additionally, as a community is convened and nurtured in cyberspace, how may its nature change in time, and how will the tutor detect change in the audience (and possibly purpose) and subsequently be contingent in the e-moderation process, thus reorienting interactivity?

Wood and Wood (1996) refer to the notion of the *contingent teacher* in an online environment as one who can judge when to intervene and when to withdraw from online interactions between learners. Although contingency is desirable, these authors recognize that—even with the prerequisite skills and knowledge of this approach, teaching expertise and history—adhering to it and achieving it with consistency is extremely difficult. Contingency raises challenges both to virtual and face-to-face teachers. However their dimensions of the role offer a helpful framework for VLE tutors to attempt to articulate their craft. Given this elaboration of contingency, how may these components manifest? What tools and professional development may necessarily underpin them? What maxims and guidance may need to be articulated to facilitate awareness of contingent teaching in a VLE? When to steer a group or withdraw and allow space for interaction are sophisticated judgments in any form of teaching.

Needs, Skills, Characteristics, and History of the Audience

Blanket Coverage or Bespoke Tailoring?

It is important to consider the geographical location and the context of participants prior to establishing a VLE community. To what extent is the community new or pre-existing? What is their technological expertise, and what is their immediate access to technology? Are these adequate to support operation of the VLE proposed? These factors may be different for a group of newly convened part-time students, for a group of established clinicians in the northern United Kingdom, for a group of distal students in rural Africa, or for a group of learners involved in an amalgam of VLE and face-to-face experiences. It may be helpful to consider the following. What may be needed by participants in terms of

1.   information,
2.   skills,
3.   understanding, and
4.   technology?

Therefore:

- How might one ascertain this intelligence (1-4 above) at the design stages?
- How might differential support and provision be achieved if necessary?
- Will induction be a static "pre-course" provision or ongoing and online?
- Will it be text-manual driven or supported by facilities such as telephone and video conferencing?

- How may an induction experience be linked to our understanding of strategies for initiating and sustaining the positive features of a VLE community alluded to earlier?

- What may be the balance between investment in induction and support and the sequestration of revenue for provision of online programs? How may this look different for a six-week or a one-year course? Are there ethical boundaries to consider?

- What mutual understandings and expectations (between tutors, students, and finance providers) may be important to offer initially and sequentially during the VLE experience?

In our experience there is a growing commitment to the strength, when possible, of having face-to-face contact as a key feature of induction and inoculation of the community dimension. This can be for technical training; activities aimed at sharing ideas and anxieties; sharing approaches and mutual expectations and purposes; and negotiating or imposing netiquette protocols. It can be used for signaling the dynamic nature of community to a VLE group and the tutors' need to be contingent and responsively.

Other Variables

We have included this section in our analysis since we are aware that both tutors and audience do not exist in an ideal or ultimately predictable environment. The context in which the design takes place and the online learning occurs is shaped and influenced by a number of national, institutional, and subject policies and expectations. In short, design for online learning cannot be divorced from the socioeconomical realities of the specific location of designers.

These challenges may include an expectation that

- you will easily deliver "made to measure" quality within an "off the peg software" production line, with consequent financial savings. Online learning is not necessarily a cheap and easy solution to growth in student numbers;

- skilled face-to-face teachers can transfer their skills to the online environment with minimum difficulty;

- many patterns can be used by the bespoke tailor in different garments (the "learning objects" approach—which appears to be gathering momentum!);

- you will keep conventional assessment methods with which professional bodies are often most comfortable;

- you will keep static learning outcomes in the design no matter how the composition of your audience differs or evolves. This is a wider issue about the support for rigid program specifications by such bodies as the Quality Assurance Agency in the United Kingdom.

These other variables do have an impact on the design process and tend to operate as constraints on the design opportunities that face the bespoke tailor. Off-the peg courses and solutions are often perceived as an easier and cheaper option, and skilled bespoke tailors may face the possibility of redundancy in tight financial situations, and their replacement by technologists may be a lamentable aspect of the future.

Conclusion

This chapter has deliberately raised a number of questions and has sought to illustrate the complexity of a number of apparently "straightforward" aspects of the design process. It could be argued that if every one of the issues raised in this chapter were considered afresh by every designer, the jackets (online learning opportunities) might never be finished. This is not necessarily the case. We have argued that design tools and patterns can be developed to assist the tailor or designer in making and fitting the jacket, although many of these remain in the heads of the existing bespoke tailors and need to be publicized in "pattern books." Ironically, a danger existing in this is that some new designers then simply take the patterns and make their jackets, without considering the skills of tailoring that we have emphasized in this chapter. Patterns, like recipes, are often linear and all too easy to follow, as a chef reflecting on an unsuccessful soufflé will report.

The fragility of static design principles may lead to lower quality when surface features of the "jacket" predominate and less attention is given to problematizing at the level of purpose and audience and interactivity analysis. Thus, it is proposed that the complexity of planning for learning and interactivity online means that design and delivery should be predicated on problematization of the type presented in the model here.

References

Bickmore-Brand, J. (1995). *Stepping out: Literacy, language and learning.* Perth: Department of Education, University of Western Australia.

Biggs, J. B. (1996). Enhancing teaching through constructive alignment. *Higher Education,* (32), 347-364.

Biggs, J. B. (1999). *What the student does: Teaching for quality learning in universities.* Buckingham: Open University Press.

Bonk, C., & Reynolds, T. (1997). Learner-centered Web instruction for higher order thinking, teamwork, and apprenticeship. In B. H. Kahn (Ed.), *Web-based instruction*. NJ: Educational Technology.

Cambourne, B. (1988). *The whole story: Natural language and the acquisition of literacy in the classroom*. Auckland: Ashton Scholastic.

Cripps, C., & McGilchrist, B. (1999). Primary school learners. In P. Mortimore(Ed.), *Understanding pedagogy and its impact on learning*. London: Chapman.

Forsyth, I. (2001). *Teaching and learning materials and the Internet* (3rd ed.). London: Kogan Page.

Fox, R. (1997). *Perspectives on constructivism*. Exeter: School of Education, University of Exeter.

Jarvis, P., Holford, J., & Griffin, C. (1998). *The theory and practice of learning*. London: Kogan Page.

Lave, J., & Wenger, E. (1991). *Situated learning: Legitimate peripheral participation*. Cambridge: Cambridge University Press.

Loveless, A., de Voogd, G. L., & Bohlin, R. M. (2001). Something old, something new. Is pedagogy affected by ICT? In A. Loveless & V. Ellis (Eds.), *ICT, pedagogy and the curriculum* (pp. 68-84). London: Routledge.

Moore, M. (1989). Three types of interaction. *American Journal of Distance Education, 3*(2), 1-6.

Noddings, N. (1990). Constructivism in mathematics education. In R. B. Davis, C. A. Maher, & N. Noddings (Eds.), *Constructivist views on the teaching and learning of mathematics*. Reston, VA: National Council of Teachers of Mathematics.

Online Tutoring Skills. (2001). Building an online community. In C. Higginson (Ed.), *Online tutoring e-book*. [n.p.]: Online Tutoring Skills Project.

Palloff, R., & Pratt, K. (1999). *Building learning communities in cyberspace*. San Francisco: Jossey Bass.

Paulsen, M. F. (1995). *The online report on pedagogical techniques for computer-mediated communication*. Available at http://nettskolen.com/forskning/19/cmcped.html

Sackville, A. (2002, March 26). *Designing for interaction*. Paper presented at the Third International Conference—Networked Learning, University of Sheffield, England.

Sackville, A., & Schofield, M. (2001). *Whoops! We've got a learning community*. ILT Conference presentation. Retrieved June 7, 2004, from http://www.edge-hill.ac.uk/tld/tldstaff/sackvila.htm

Schofield, M. (2000). *Constructivism: Building blocks for induction into undergraduate study*. ILT Conference paper. Retrieved June 7, 2004, from http://www.edgehill.ac.uk/tld/tldstaff/docs/constructivism.pdf

Von Glasersfeld, E. (1987). *The construction of knowledge contribution to conceptual semantics*. Seaside, CA: Intersystems.

Wenger, E. (1998). *Communities of practice.* Cambridge: Cambridge University Press.

Wood, D., & Wood, H. (1996). Vygotsky, tutoring and learning. *Oxford Review of Education, 22*(1), 5-16.

Younie, S. (2001). Developing a cognitive flexible literacy - From industrial society to the information age. In M. Leask (Ed.), *Issues in teaching using ICT* (pp. 206-222). London: Routledge.

Chapter VIII

Communities as Context Providers for Web-Based Learning

Ana Paula Afonso, Universidade de Coimbra, Portugal

Abstract

This chapter addresses the use of communities as a context-creating approach for the management of learning in virtual settings. It stresses the lack of consensus around the concept of community, its recent deployment in the educational domain, and the extent to which the educational use of virtual settings has neglected the construction of appropriate learning contexts. On the other hand, it points to the existence of a large body of knowledge from areas such as organizational learning, actor-network theory, sociology, constructivism, and learning communities that may help overcome the limitations of Web-based learning as it is currently put into practice. The theory covered will offer a better understanding of the relationships between different concepts and trends and of learning communities as entirely new tools for contextual approaches to the management of learning in virtual settings.

Introduction

On a recent trip to New Zealand, while wandering through the bookshelves of one of the bookshops at Heathrow airport, I bumped into a book titled *The 13¹/₂ Lives of Captain Bluebear* (Moers, 1999), a novel that made the remaining 27 hours of flight not only bearable but, indeed, very amusing! In spite of its good share of craziness and delightful entertainment, it is quite an enlightening and pedagogical book. It speaks of life, fear, hope, dreams, nightmares, frustration, friendship, loneliness, learning, collaboration, and community, apart from the crazy adventures of the sweet Bluebear. Its 703 pages go through the lives and adventures of the Bluebear in the fantastic lands of old Zamonia. There is a lesson to be learned from each life, but I would like to tell you about the life of the Bluebear in the Demarara Desert.

While falling into a black hole from his past adventure, the Bluebear literally lands on a sugar-made desert named the Demerara Desert. When he wakes up, he realizes he has been found by the Muggs, a nomadic tribe roaming in the desert in search of a place called "Anagrom Ataf." The Muggs invite him to follow them, and since the Bluebear has nowhere else to go, he agrees; this is how his adventure on the Demerara Desert begins.

The Muggs were put together by chance. They pursue their own ideals of freedom, leisure, and independence, and they easily accept newcomers regardless of status, wealth, or gender, as long as rules are respected. The admission of newcomers is quite informal and unbureaucratic—just dressing a dark blue robe, calling out "Anagrom Ataf," and trotting along with the caravan through the desert. The community of the Muggs was, thus, one of outcasts and dropouts that came together chasing the vision of Anagrom Ataf. They almost never quarreled and, like every other community, they had rules to be respected. But these were not common rules: they were found in a drifting bottle, made sense to no one else but the Muggs, and became their code of conduct.

The Muggs had a mission in life to which they were committed: finding, trapping, and occupying the city named Anagrom Ataf. The sole dream of finding this city was the vision that kept the Muggs roaming the desert.

When the Muggs and the Bluebear finally found Anagrom Ataf, they had to capture and occupy it. And though the facts said it was an impossible thing to do, with lateral thinking, collaborative work, joint effort, involvement and commitment, they managed to capture the city by fusing it with the desert floor through molten sugar. Occupation was the next step and it was an easy one. However, some problems started to show up. Trapped within the walls of a city, even if it was a mirage city, the Muggs did not know what to do; the only thing they knew how to do was roaming the desert. Conflicts became unavoidable and the chosen leader—the Bluebear—had to negotiate a solution. New rules were created, and a new mission was established. The Muggs were now sent to roam in search of "Esidarap Sloof."

The Muggs were on the move again. The Bluebear abandoned the community and resumed his lonely journey toward the next adventure in quest of his identity and place of belonging.

This is a story about bonds, about how people gather together around a common goal, and about how they commit to it and get involved with other people, sharing individual identities and building on a collective history. This is a story about community.

Communities: A Deconstructivist Approach

Communities: In Search of Identity

The complexity of the term *identity* comes from the articulation of different and, apparently, contradictory elements (e.g., individual vs. social, stability vs. change). This reflects on the difficulty of finding a consensus definition.

Following the tradition of symbolic interactionism, the concept of identity had a central role in the early 20th century and kept being discussed up to the present studies of the relationships between groups and about social behavior (Anderson, 1991; Bellah, 1997; Estanque, 2000; Jacques, 1998).

Identity is related to subjectivity, to the image we have of ourselves. But identity is, simultaneously, a public and relational phenomenon, embracing all walks of life. It might be said that we have as many identities as social categories, social groups, or social networks we belong to, though one of these identities tends to rule over our conscience and behavior. Genov (1997) considers that the "multiple identities of modern individuals are formed and maintained because of their participation in functionally defined formal organizations and in community like associations" (p. 419).

Under this perspective, it is plausible to understand personal identity as being simultaneously a social identity, or "psycho-social identity" (Neto, 1985), that expresses the interrelation between personal identity (individual attributes) and social identity (attributes denoting the belonging to social groups or categories).

The concept of identity thus encloses the paradox of the duality "equality vs. difference," since it stands for a set of characteristics that makes the individual unique but, at the same time, similar and close to a specific social group. Furthermore, identity seems to be a process of deconstruction and reconstruction of personal projects and life paths that calls upon relational elements and interacts with other previously structured identities.

According to Jacques (1998), the modes and alternatives of our identity, in both its cognitive and affective dimensions, develop from social and cultural context of belonging. Thus, identity results from the "articulation of the identity assumed by the socio-cultural context, the active action of the individual and the social relationships in which the individual is involved" (p. 314).

Along this line, some authors (Estanque, 2000; Giddens, 1991) find it pertinent to relate identity to the process of identity search. Taking into account the variety of identification processes of today's societies, it becomes difficult to think of solid and unified identities. Instead, we are dealing with simplified and fragmented identities.

As a substantive dimension of the sociocultural reality, identity faces the influence of social and symbolic factors of diverse origins that have translated into the current trends of identity fragmentation, or structuring, in more complex societies. Thus, in an approach that emphasizes the constructionist, symbolic, and interactive dimensions of reality and subjectivity, the construction of identity emerges under the shape of imagined communities (Estanque, 2000).

Communities: Imagined and Fragmented

Most of the classical authors in sociology—Comte, Marx, Durkheim, Weber— have dealt with the concept of *community* without rigorously defining it, though it has most frequently been conceived around the idea of collective action and in the framework of the industrialization of western societies (Estanque, 2000).

Thus, neither sociology nor psychology has been able to come forward with a satisfactory and unanimous definition for either identity or community.

In this context, Anderson (1991) suggests that both community and identity are cultural artifacts that "become 'modular', capable of being transplanted, with varying degrees of self-consciousness, to a great variety of social terrains" (p. 14). Thus, discussing the subject of nationalism, the author argues that it is quite difficult to define either of the terms *nation, nationality*, or *nationalism* but, yet, the phenomenon has existed and exists. Reporting its origins to the end of the 18th century, Anderson (1991) conceives the nation as imagined. This vision of the nation as imagined triggers considerations of self, identity, and collectivity, and it means, for the author, that the nation is also a limited and sovereign community. Thus, he claims that it is a cultural artifact of some kind that can only be fully understood in regard to its historical origin and changing meanings.

The sovereignty of a nation relates to the moment of history in which the concept arose, when the legitimacy of dynastic realms was being destroyed by enlightenment and revolution. It is limited, because all nations have boundaries, even if elastic, beyond which another nation rises. And a nation is a community, because it has always been conceived as a deep fraternity, a horizontal comradeship that makes it possible for people to be willing to die for this imagined artifact. Thus, there is a projection of individual diversity onto a collective history.

Finally, communities are all imagined because "the members of even the smallest nation will never know most of their fellow members . . ., yet in the minds of each lives the image of their communion" (Anderson, 1991, p. 15). Communities distinguish themselves by the style in which they are imagined, that is, by the representational systems a group of people, encircled by a territorial boundary, uses to create a dominant mode of belonging.

The possibility of imagining the nation as a broad community has its historical origins in the disappearance of three major axiomatic cultural conceptions: sacredness of language, dynastic power, and homogeneity of time (Anderson, 1991). The sacredness of language means the belief that a particular language or group of signs was part of the ontological truth and provided unique access to that same truth (e.g., Christendom). Classical communities, such as religious ones, were linked by sacred languages, often written but orally dead. Through these languages, the conception of the world transmitted by the dominant religion was shared by virtually anyone. However, with the discoveries and the exploration of the non-European world, the cultural and geographical horizons widened up and the conception of the world changed. Thus, the fall of sacredness of certain languages led to the decline of the corresponding "religious" communities, which slowly became territorial, plural, and fragmented.

The dynastic realms reported to political systems according to which society was organized around, and under, rulers that were considered as having a divine character. But the decline of both languages and dynastic realms was not the single origin of imagined communities. The modes of understanding the world were also changing.

The idea of a simultaneous past and future in an immediate present, with no separation between past and present, led to the idea of time as a homogeneous line in which cosmology and history were essentially identical and where simultaneity was transverse, marked by temporal coincidence, and measured by the calendar. This vision of a homogeneous time supported the idea of nation conceived as a solid community where every actor was unaware but confident in the steady and simultaneous activity of his or her fellows.

Moreover, the decline of these axiomatic conceptions, along with economic, social, and scientific changes, and the development of rapid and effective communications have created a gap between cosmology and history, thus creating the need for new forms of connecting people. The conception of horizontal and time-transversal communities thus gained terrain, and the challenges and representations posed by the conceptions of identity and of imagined communities in current societies required the creation of new forms of collective life.

Communities: Retrospective and Definitions

Humans have always been social animals, living and working in groups that later evolved into communities.

The term *community* has been broadly and diversely used both in scientific and popular languages. The systematic use of the term has been made by sociologists, to whom a community is a special type of social group. A social group is a group of people that establish a network of relationships through interaction and communication, ruled by common norms and shared values and interests, and aiming at a common goal (Silvio, 1999). These common and shared interests, norms, and values provide the group with a unique identity around which the members congregate, and this distinguishes the group from its surrounding context.

These social groups differ from social categories and social conglomerates, since the latter are groups of people that have common characteristics (e.g., gender, age) but do not necessarily develop and sustain internal relationships. The affective element becomes a key issue in community development, providing a sense of belonging that lets the group members identify with the cultural values and norms.

In agreement with this, classical authors like Tönnies (1887/1963) placed community in opposition to society. On one end, there was the *gemeinschaft* or "community," involving three fundamental issues: memory, family, and the sense of belonging to a place. Community had an affective and relational motivation and an organic nature, being ruled by union, uses, and religion. On the other end, there was the *geselschaft* or "society," a product of modernity. Society had an objective motivation and mechanic nature; being ruled by conventions, law, and public opinion, it was based on complex social relationships and embraced the nation, the state, and the world (Estanque, 2000; Recuero, 2002).

Though not in opposition to Tönnies (1887/1963) on this dichotomy between community and society, Weber (1987, 1989) and Durkheim (Aldus, 1995) had considered that community and society were not necessarily two opposing extremes, but rather concepts that complemented each other, since most of the social relationships have both a communitarian and a social character. Thus, both concepts are considered to have the characteristics of social groups.

Clearly departing from Tönnies's (1887/1963) conceptions and drawing on the proposals of Dewey and Durkheim, Bellah (1997) argues that in a community there is involvement, time, and consensus through the continuous negotiation of the meaning of shared values and goals. Indeed, Bellah (1997) considers that in a community agreeing and disagreeing elements coexist concerning the meaning of shared values and of the supposed-to-be objectives for the common good. Aldrich (1999) claims that "communities emerge not only from forces that generate new organizations and populations, but also from new commensalistic and symbiotic relations between populations" (p. 310). By this he means that, in a community, processes of competition and cooperation coexist that sort populations into different niches.

From the previous topics, we realize that sociologists have thought of communities as social groups in the form of relational networks based on face-to-face relationships, intrinsically connected to the idea of a physical space and time (Estanque, 2000).

Though the space-time framework is still a relevant level of analysis, the advance of information and communication technology (ICT) and the rise of the digital economy and of a knowledge society has questioned the supremacy of a physical space for the development of community. Within the current context of globalization, the community's dependence on a territorial basement or physical space has no longer the same importance or meaning. Moreover, in the modern age, the detachment of the concept of community from the one proposed by Tönnies (1887/1963) and the decline of Anderson's (1991) axiomatic conceptions led to the fragmentation and detachment of communities borders. The classical concept of community as a family or small unit, intrinsically connected to a physical space seen as an aggregation enabler, has become senseless. Several authors (Anderson, 1991; Beamish, 1995; Estanque, 2000; Palácios, 1998; Silvio, 1999) now consider that physical proximity is not the single or the most important issue in community development. However, "as seen in this broader perspective, social life has been and always will be marked by the existence and influence of community" (Genov, 1997, p. 418).

Currently, the concept of community varies according to the context and, also, its deployment is broader and more varied nowadays. Furthermore, we agree with Aldrich (1999) in his claim that "a definition should also preserve evolutionary theory's emphasis on a future that is constructed rather than designed. Communities emerge from relationships between units that involve competition, cooperation, dominance, and symbiotic interdependence, rather than coming into being according to plan" (p. 300).

Furthermore, communities have transcended the geographical borders and are based in specialized, contextual, and global relationships. People no longer relate to each other in a total and integral way, but within specific contexts and objectives and, though this is not really a new phenomenon, ICT has accelerated and facilitated this transposition, thus creating the possibility of new forms of sociability and community (Wellman & Gulia, 1999).

Communities: A (Socio)Constructivist Approach

Communities: New Forms and Concepts

In the current transition from modernity to postmodernity, moving from the ideals of nationality to those of the imagination, we witness the reinvention of the concept and forms of community.

Maffesoli (1996) considers that the increasing globalization of society enables the development of microgroups with communitarian ideals. Moreover, he believes that the classical concept of community, characterized by a feeling of belonging, territoriality, the belief in honesty of relationships, and the existence of a collective project and own language, will be replaced by the idea of a neotribalism, according to which communities emerge from people's need of joining other people with common interests.

At present, communities do not exist outside the structural conditionings of social formations, thus belonging to community networks. The realization of community means the existence of processes under construction aspiring to a new form of collective identity (Estanque, 2000).

In this sense, and drawing on Santos (1995), the communities of the present may fall within the amoeba-communities paradigm, in opposition to the more traditional fortress-communities paradigm. The latter is characterized by exclusive communities, which are very hierarchical internally and which base internal identification on external closure. On the contrary, amoeba-communities are permeable, searching for intercultural comparison, with an identity that is always multiple, unfinished, and undergoing a process of ongoing identification.

These neo-communities would be characterized by their ephemeral nature, changing composition, local inscription, and uses (Maffesoli, 1996). Furthermore, with the development of Web technology, it did not take too long for the transposition of this social phenomenon to migrate to the Web.

On the basis of Anderson's (1991) concept of imagined community, discussed earlier, we might say that the Web represents the technological-symbolic support for the emergence of a transnational imagined-virtual community, thus forming a "meta-imagined community, a reflexive (re)interpretation of the 19th-century nationalism" (Brabazon, 2001, p. 2). By representing a worldwide connected network, the Web enables the sustainability of existing forms of sociability while it catalyzes the creation of new forms and structures of sociability.

These forms and structures of sociability converge into the creation, not just of a segmented community but also of multiple decentralized and fragmented communities that share the same imagined transnational space. These virtual communities—which might be real communities, pseudo-communities, or a new form of community—emerge as an answer to the increasing need of community-like aggregations that followed the disintegration of the 19th-century traditional communities (Rheingold, 1996).

When we speak of these new communities, the issue of space reappears. If, in the more classical definitions, territorial grounding appeared as a key element in the development of communities, this same question arises nowadays but with new contours. Indeed, we may argue that nowadays the space of community involves the "social relations gathered together around the production and reproduction of physical and symbolic territories and communitarian identities and identifications" (Santos, 1995, p. 420).

After the materialization of modern age, postmodernity carries with it a process of dematerialization of physical space and time, a process where real time slowly extinguishes physical space. So, where do these communities settle and develop?

In the attempt to answer this question, Jones (1997) proposes the concept of *virtual settlement* as a place in cyberspace that is symbolically delimited by a topic of interest, where the majority of the group's interaction takes place, and to which a community is linked. This is a common public space in which a variety of actors exist and where a minimum level of sustained association takes place. The virtual settlement provides community with a sense of place, of locus, in cyberspace.

This leads to another concept, in the attempt to answer the question of where new communities settle and develop: cyberspace. Cyberspace is the frontier for which society redefined the concepts of space and time, of natural and artificial, and of real and virtual, being connected to archaic, imagined, and symbolic structures of all societal life (Lemos, n.d.). Thus, cyberspace is, simultaneously, the space where we are in a virtual environment and the network of computers all over the world, thus representing a real identity, though not a physical one.

In convergence with the concept of imagined communities (Anderson, 1991), cyberspace may be understood as a transnational, imagined, and mediating space, a sort of "<<non-place>>, and <<utopia>> where we must rethink the sensorial meaning of our civilization based on digital, collective and immediate information" (Lemos, n.d., p. 2). Furthermore, cyberspace becomes a metasocial mediator, a post-tribal and imagined space where ICT enhances truth and sharing.

Cyberspace represents a place of passage, a symbolic mediating space through which individuals fully integrate in social life. Connecting to cyberspace represents the passage "from an isolated social marked by an autonomous individual to the tribal and digital collective" (Lemos, n.d., p. 5).

With a decentralized structure, multiple and differentiated connections, and an anarchic and wide reproduction, cyberspace allows the creation and development of virtual communities as complex and self-organized systems. These communities can be understood as entities with permeable borders, a unified core and a petering periphery, as cultural formations where the bidirectional link of determination and membership produces and reproduces the community's living tissue (Bauman, 1995).

In this context, a more constructionist approach to the idea of community makes sense, since collective action carries symbolic dimensions crucial for the understanding of the construction and reconstruction process of individual and collective identity (Estanque, 2000).

Communities: Virtual Communities

Against the predictions of the more pessimistic, the threat of dehumanization through computer networks not only did not come true but, instead, gave rise to an interesting sociological phenomenon: computer networks are, indeed, being used to connect people to other people. Originally restricted to the elite, computer networks are now widespread and the target of public interest and popular culture. They have allowed the creation of different social forms and spaces, where people meet, gather, and interact. The ability to support social interaction seems to be the key feature of our connection to cyberspace, where complex collective projects sustain and support many-to-many interactions around a wide range of subjects, missions, and forms. The social places and interactions people create in cyberspace are "more complicated than can be captured in one-sided utopian or dystopian terms" (Kollock & Smith, 1999, p. 4).

The virtual communities differ from some real communities in features such as their permeable borders, the anonymity of online interactions, and the possibility of high social diversity among their members (Kollock and Smith, 1999; Smith, 1999). Furthermore, virtual communities differ from real communities in the way their members perceive their relationships as based on shared interests rather than on shared social features; their ties are geographically dispersed and specialized in content (Wellman & Gulia, 1999).

However, taking into account over half a century of sociological research on communities and the previously discussed concept of community, now conceptualized in terms of social networks, we can say that virtual communities do meet any definition of community, even in the more traditional sense (Estanque, 2000; Recuero, 2002; Silvio, 1999; Wellman & Gulia, 1999).

According to Preece and Maloney-Krichmar (2003), virtual communities are neither specifically designed nor emergent. They result from the interaction and mutual influence of the technological and social dimensions. A virtual community may be envisioned as a process or as a system that develops and evolves along time in order to achieve a life cycle rich in knowledge and rewarding to the community members. As they come together, they develop a culture that enhances the shared construction of knowledge.

In the last decade, to a large extent because of the digital economy, the term *virtual community* has gained the status of a buzzword and, much as in face-to-face communities, there is no consensus on a definition for it. As it became a multidisciplinary domain of knowledge and practice, several disciplinary definitions of virtual community have arisen in the past decade, covering both sociological and more technological perspectives that point to different elements, attributes, and features.

Rheingold (1993), who is credited as the creator of the term *virtual community*, defines a virtual community as a social group that emerges from the network when a considerable number of people establish public discussion long and intensively enough to create networks of personal relations in cyberspace. In its essence, a virtual community might be understood as a group of people who interact through computer-based means long enough to create and organize social relations in a virtual settlement (Recuero, 2002). As put by Silvio (1999), a virtual community is a set of dynamic networks for interaction; or, even, as proposed by Kim (2000), just a community that exists on cyberspace rather than in the physical world.

Since Rheingold's (1993) definition, a lot has been said and written about virtual communities, and though the term is quite easy to understand, it seems slippery to define (Preece, 2000). However, from the definitions suggested by several authors (Bonk & Wisher, 2000; Kim, 2000; Kollock & Smith, 1999; Preece, 2000; Preece & Maloney-Krichmar, 2003; Recuero, 2002; Rheingold, 1993; Silvio, 1999; Wellman & Gulia, 1999), we have come to a definition of virtual community that might be general enough to be applicable to different communitarian spaces:

> *A virtual community is a circumscribed group of people that act and interact in cyberspace in a shared, meaningful, and negotiated context, for a stable period of time, while driven by common goals and guided by common norms and values.*

Though there is no consensus in the definition of virtual community, it is possible to capture some key features that major authors in the domain have identified (Bonk & Wisher, 2000; Fischer, 2002; Hirschi, 2001; Kim, 2000; Lave & Wenger, 1991; Preece, 2000; Preece & Maloney-Krichmar, 2003; Recuero, 2002; Silvio, 1999; Kollock & Smith, 1999; Wellman & Gulia, 1999; Wenger, 1998a; cf. Table 1).

As we engage in a community, our knowledge and vision of the world are influenced by this community. Knowledge exists in individuals but also in socially negotiating minds, in the discourse among the individuals, in the relationships that

Table 1. Elements of communities

Elements	Description
Autonomy	It means responsibility for self -directed learning and self -management of time. Members are able to select the activities suitable for the achievement of the goals, to define goals according to their needs and to redefine goa ls according to contingency.
Belief	It refers to consent and agreement about value systems, artifacts, institutions and people. It means trust, conviction and persuasion.
Belonging	It means enculturation, sharing values. It includes: bonds, affection, im age of "us", common history, rituals, symbols, a vision, orientation for the future, legitimate peripheral participation.
Boundary Objects	It means the structuring elements around which the community negotiates meanings. These elements are used to communi cate and coordinate the perspectives of several actors. They externalize the knowledge created the community and have similar meaning along the several frontiers of individual knowledge. They allow different knowledge systems to interact while providing sh ared and meaningful references.
Collaboration	It means a way of collectively exploring a certain domain and of enjoying the roles needed to complete a given task. It promotes the social creation of knowledge through social interaction. The joint work of e very community member toward common goals, partnerships, co -evolution and co -learning.
Commitment	It refers to agreement and engagement, obligations and responsibilities. It involves time and effort in action and requires support and equal participation i n social activities.
Connection	It refers to our interest by other people, it determines our acceptance of social norms and the development of a social conscience. It includes: association, alliances and relationships.
History	It means the creation of a collective history through the collection of events that link the members of the community to a common culture.
Identity	It represents both a public and a relational phenomenon. A shared identity represents a set of subjective values that create a collec tive identity around a common project.
Integration	It means the interdependence of practices, it involves the reciprocity of practices or the total participation in the community.
Involvement	It refers to the responsibility for and engagement in the act ivities that carry the community's interests.
Interaction	Based on shared and negotiated meanings, it involves the reflected exchange of ideas, resources and connections, and systems of influence
Knowledge Creation	It means a change of values, norms, str ategies and assumptions, a new or renewed theory of action, the emergence of a new culture and the promotion of systemic changes.
Learning	It refers to the process of a development of human characteristics. It is, to a large extent, a social activity supp orted by knowledge construction through social interaction.
Mutuality	It means the reciprocity and horizontal organization of relations. It involves: collaborative and interactive tasks, symbiosis, interdependence, and peripherality.
Plurality	It refers to the diversity and multiplicity of knowledge, resources, ideas and relations in the group. It means unity through diversity.
Practice	It is a response to design. It includes: shared entrepreneurship and repertoires, mutual engagement and responsibility, interpretation, styles, artifacts, actions and relationships.
Property	It refers to all that belongs to us and that we can freely deploy; individual and collective patrimony.
Rituals	It involves organization systems, cults, initiation, passage and patte rns.
Sharing	It means having the same understanding and meaning, and/or, the equal use of and participation in resources and knowledge.
Asymmetry of Knowledge	It means that if no single individual or group of non -individuals holds all the relevant knowledge in a specific domain, problem solving tasks require the proactive participation of every actor in the network.
Social Creativity	It emerges from communities as a result of the collaborative constructions of artifacts and knowledge, by exploring and so lving new perspectives of a certain task. It results from the interaction of the individual with the surrounding context and other individuals, and its major challenges are that of capturing the knowledge created in communities.
Technology	It supports soc ial interaction and collective work. It is not an end but a means toward community creation.
Time	It means the longevity of relationships.
Values	It refers to principles, rules, axioms, and systems.

bind them, in the artifacts that they have created and use, and in the theories, methods, and models they have used to produce them (Jonassen, 2000). Thus, knowledge and learning are distributed among the culture and history of their existence and the communities they engage in, being mediated by the tools they use and gaining meaning through boundary objects (cf. Figure 1).

Figure 1. Elements of community

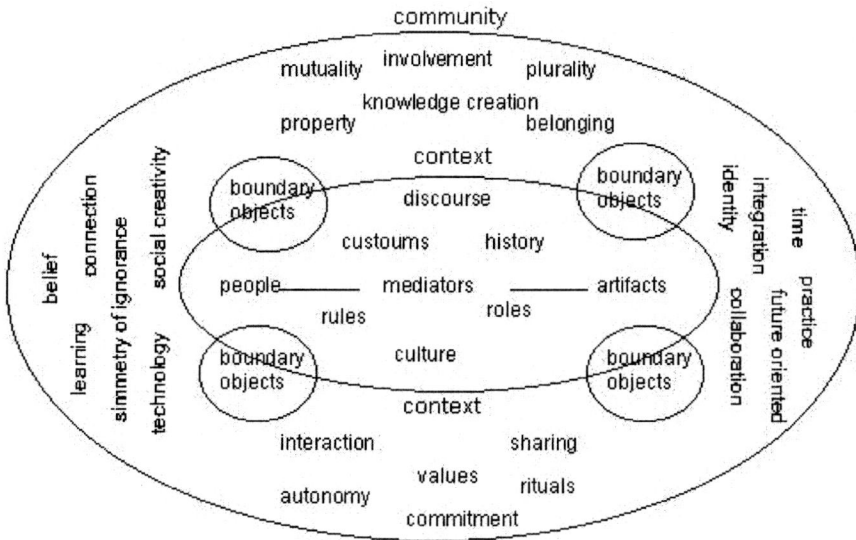

Through legitimate peripheral participation (Lave & Wenger, 1991), we absorb part of the integral culture of the community, while this same culture is also affected by all the members of the community. As we engage in communities, our knowledge, values, and beliefs are influenced by these same communities, and so is our individual and collective identity.

The biggest challenge of these virtual environments becomes that of being able to build context-rich virtual communities where individual and collective learning takes place, and where the learners take responsibility not just for their individual learning but also for the collaborative construction of spaces of belonging where collective knowledge develops (Afonso & Figueiredo, 2000).

Communities: Practice and Learning Communities

While institutions face the challenges of the knowledge society and the digital economy, an emerging organizational form is changing the institutionalized structures of knowledge creation and dissemination. We refer to learning and practice communities that not only have changed the organizational scenery but are also complementing all previously existing forms of knowledge creation and organizational learning.

According to Wenger, McDermott, and Snyder (2000), a community of practice consists of "groups of people informally bound together by shared expertise and passion for a joint enterprise" (p. 139). They are, in general, groups of people, geographically dispersed and acquainted, bound together by a common goal and a shared understanding of their mission and corresponding rules.

A learning community is similar to a group of people sharing the same interest and goal: learning.

Communities of practice and learning communities are hard to define due to their organic, spontaneous and informal nature (Wenger, 1998a). They both represent self-organized groups, with a self-selected membership (that requires cultivation) and where members learn together. Hence, considering that, ultimately, the main goal of a community of practice is learning through collaboration, we think of communities of practice as integrating learning communities.

People create communities of practice all the time and for several reasons. In these communities, people share knowledge and experiences in creative ways that foster new approaches to problems and to learning itself. Hence, communities are showing to be a privileged context for the acquisition and social creation of knowledge.

These communities have been around for centuries, taking different forms and names at various times (Gongla & Rizzuto, 2001). Though the development of theory can be traced back to the work of social constructivist authors (Afonso, 2000), the changes in society's values systems of the last century and the development of decentralized resources encouraged by ICT has brought a new perspective to the issue: "Technological innovations are the most visible fomenters of change, but abrupt change in norms and values, or in laws and regulations, can also create a new set of core organizations around which populations, and then communities, form" (Aldrich, 1999, p. 311).

Departing from a vision of learning that views the engagement in social practices as the main process of knowledge construction, we consider the communities people build and engage in, along their lives, as basic units of analysis of the process of knowledge construction.

This supports the view that individuals learn when engaged in communities in which knowledge is built through interaction (within collaborative activities of both social exchange and self-discovery), discourse, and consensus. These communities are an important alternative to traditional learning and organizational contexts, and, being supported by ICT, they have become more tangible today than they were a decade ago. They represent intellectual, social, cultural, and psychological environments that facilitate and support learning, while promoting interaction, collaboration, and the development of a sense of belonging in their members.

In this way, communities emerge as alternatives to traditional learning environments and as decentralized groups of people that become self-organized into functional and stable teams with the aim of scaffolding each other in the development of constructive learning activities. With the group as the core unit of these communities, shared identities are constructed, and so is the social context that supports this sharing (Brown, Collins, & Duguid, 1989).

These communities provide different ways of learning through collaborative activities. Indeed, collaboration may be considered as the keystone of communities in learning, as it promotes the social construction of knowledge through social interaction. This collaborative working mode is based on a reflexive dialogue that develops around specific "elocutions" dedicated to particular interests of the interacting individuals and results from the collective inquiry promoted by the community. We may thus say that the major goal of developing and managing learning communities includes the development, through collaborative practices, of timeless propositions that represent knowledge objects and the enhancement of the ability to apply knowledge in distinct contexts.

Furthermore, learning communities seem to provide a common learning infrastructure focusing on the relational nature of human cognition and the crucial role of context in promoting the development of horizontal and transversal competencies and the social construction of knowledge.

According to Wenger (1998b), these communities act independently, trying to cope and fulfill the member's and the context's needs, thus leading to a wide variability in the way they look, talk, and organize, and making them different from any other learning group.

We enculturate into different communities all the time, but the issues and problems we deal with originate from, are defined by, and are solved within the constraints of the activity we are pursuing and of the context in which it has emerged. So, following what has been said earlier in this chapter, we can only explain cognitive activity and, therefore, learning in relation to its context.

Within the social-constructivist assumptions that emphasize the role of context and discourse in learning, this is a fundamental issue for the development of communities, which stresses the role of psychological tools and discourse as mediators of interaction and learning. This mediating role taken by psychological tools and discourse generates transformative communication, spawned through interaction, that lets the community promote contextual learning as well as learning activities that suit the community's goals and interests.

If we accept that virtual settings are entirely new tools for the creation of communities and that psychological tools deeply influence the sense we make of the world (Cole & Werscht, n. d.; Vygotsky, 1978; Wasson, 1996), it is crucial to recognize the need for a new perspective on the creation of learning contexts (Afonso & Figueiredo, 2000).

Communities: A Contextual Approach

Communities: Context Creation Through Activity and Social Interaction

For the more cognitivistic tradition, knowledge can be owned and transferred, and, hence, learning becomes a matter of delivering and receiving. The dominant paradigm is that of transmission, and ICT are seen as pipelines that carry information/knowledge/learning faster than any other medium to a greater amount of learners. In opposition to this paradigm, we value and embrace the community paradigm.

The community paradigm is described by the social learning theory proposed by Lave and Wenger (Lave & Wenger, 1991; Wenger, 1998a; Wenger et al., 2002), centered on the concept of community of practice, "which offers a rich framework for modeling learning, creating and sharing knowledge as social processes" (Putz & Arnold, 2001, p. 184).

The analysis of mainstream learning theories reveals that most of the approaches to explain learning neglect its social and contextual character (Afonso, 2000; Lave & Wenger, 1991; Wenger, 1998a). In the community paradigm, learning is conceived as legitimate peripheral participation within a community in which "the mastery of knowledge and skill requires newcomers to move toward full participation in the socio-cultural practices of a community" (Lave & Wenger, 1991, p. 29). Participation in a cultural practice is considered as an epistemological characteristic of learning (Putz & Arnold, 2001).

This vision of learning as occurring to people that act as practitioners leads to a vision of learning communities as providing the contextual frameworks, shared by all their members, that scaffold learning activities and social and intellectual interaction while promoting the social construction of knowledge through collective learning.

This agrees with the constructivist postulates claiming that in the absence of a relevant context, learning is much less meaningful. Indeed, meaningful and effective learning requires contextually based and rich environments that are meaningful to the learners (Jonassen, n. d.). It is, thus, no longer possible to neglect the role of context in any attempt at building learning communities.

Learning Contexts

What is context? For Erikson and Schultz (1976, in Griffin, 1993), "context description simply put, is an attempt to say 'what is going on here'" (p. 121). How-

Table 2. Context approaches

APPROACH	CONTEXT
Activity	• Activity is an interpretative plan to understand human action in full. • Introduces the idea of the ubiquity of mediation in human action. • Provides the framework of analysis of the role of mediators, competences, social relations, norms and work organization.
Social Network	• Emphasizes the interdependence among the distinct social actors. • Allows the analysis of the socio-technical contexts in the perspective that technology influences the relations of power among the actors and those among the actors and the environment. • The socio-technical network is considered the context itself.
Media (of integration)	• Context is an instantaneous culture that shapes and is shaped by the individual. • Intervention plan in the construction of relations through intervention on the media that supports it. • Operates in the space of relation among the actors that constitute the context.

ever, there is no consensus about the definition or about what to focus on in the study of context. If we agree with Griffin et al. (1993) who write that "descriptions of context, too, are sensitive to the contexts with which they are mutually constitutive" (p. 122), we have to recognize that context is a dynamic, fluid, and complex entity that emerges from the actions of, and interactions between, community members, that is, the context participants. Context is, in itself, a choice and a human creation (Roque & Almeida, n. d.; Roque, Almeida, & Figueiredo, 2004).

Within this lack of consensus, the concept of context may be approached from, at least, three perspectives (Roque & Almeida, n. d.; Roque et al., 2004): context as activity, context as social network, and context as media of integration (cf. Table 2). Though a deeper explanation of these perspectives is beyond the scope of this chapter, we may say that they complement each other in emphasizing the pluralistic nature of context and they contribute to a better understanding of the relation between context and learning.

Pluralistic perspectives of context may be traced back to the cultural models and social representation theories. Cultural models stress that our ideas become our property, being "part of one's sense of self and sense of place, cherished and held dear in spite of changes in the world's fashion" (Roque & Almeida, n. d.; Roque, Almeida & Figueiredo, 2004, p. 163), thus suggesting that the adoption of a particular perspective is a matter of identity and of belonging to a group or culture. The analysis of social representations brings to evidence that context is not defined by an external reality imposed on the individual, but, rather, in terms of the representation the individual has of the world and of his or her role in the social structure of the community of belonging.

In the past decades, researchers began to draw attention to the relation between perception, cognition, and context; perception was considered to be situated, since it consists of obtaining information from the active relation between the individual and the environment (Butterworth, 1992). Schmeck (1988) stresses that the learning context is perceived even before a behavioral change takes place, and he emphasizes the existence of a relationship between current experiences and the patterns of previous experience. According to Butterworth (1992), "perception presupposes context in deriving meaning from experience" (p. 3) and "provides the public frame of reference within which socially shared acts of communication occur and it may be the first contextual determinant on which other contexts are founded" (Butterworth, 1992, p. 8).

Drawing on these conceptions, socio-constructivism considers the learning context as crucial and develops the idea of contextual or situated learning, which takes into account the situational character of actions within an articulated network of sociocultural meanings. The learner takes an active role in the activities that are of particular relevance for learning, which occurs within a culture similar to that of the context of future deployment.

In this sense, no learning activity is really de-contextualized if we take into consideration that the construction of meaning is a social process and that the success of learning relates to the acquisition and development of a contextual framework as a reference for problem solving and task performance. Hence, learning and cognition are more a matter of re-contextualization than of de-contextualization.

Table 3. Strategies for the promotion of knowledge-building communities

STRATEGY	MAIN FEATURES	EXAMPLES OF ACTIVITIES	CONCRETE ACTIVITY
ACTION	• Involves the collaborative construction of knowledge. • Strong engagement of learners in the learning process. • Higher levels of learner control. • Emphasis on the process of learning itself.	Case studies Role playing Simulations	Each case is a case
INTERACTION	• Promotes debate and idea exchange. • Calls for higher order cognitive competencies. • Requires alternative visions and reflection mechanisms. • Transfers the locus of control to the learner.	Brainstorming Forums Narratives	Committees Inquiry
PRESENTATION	• Suited to attract interest to a topic, stimulate controversy and structured presentation of subjects. • Significant control by the learner. • Strengthens the ability to manage time, information flow and resources in collaborative environments.	Symposia Demonstrations	Presentation-Question

Learning Activities

Beyond these general considerations, the concept of context remains unanalyzed, in spite of the fact that it is generally accepted as an implicit conception in the development of learning activities. Broadly, context represents everything individuals find as relevant to perform a certain task and make sense of it, that is, "they create a meaningful context for an activity, and the context they create consists of whatever knowledge they invoke to make sense of the task situation" (Mercer, 1992, p. 32). In a certain context, individuals may evoke an adequate action scheme from their previous social experience and specific cultural contexts, meaning that "everyday reasoning is generally based on types of culturally specific knowledge, whose representation is evoked by the appropriate context" (Butterworth, 1992, p. 7). Moreover, culture transmits general lines of action that translate into certain activities, which associate to other contexts and other responsibilities: "contexts can coexist in such a way that individuals may participate simultaneously in several culturally constrained modes of knowing" (Butterwoth, 1992, p. 7).

The conception of a connection between contextual conditionings and knowledge creation toward a perspective in which cognition and learning are understood as situated in a physical and social context, and are rarely de-contextualized, is begin-

Table 4. Some examples of context creating Web-based activities

ACTIVITY	DESCRIPTION
Each case is a case	• Engages multiple learners in the selection of case studies. • Involves the teacher in scaffolding the process. • Creates teams for the solution. • Creates a repository of cases for the future.
Committees	• Assigns to small groups the responsibility to act on behalf of the large group, with the aim of solving a complex common problem. • Five teams are organized with different tasks. • The groups end up producing a final web document that is discussed. • Creates a repository of solutions for the future.
Inquiry	• Brings into play the principles of question posing. • Themes are proposed for discussion; the learners study the themes and split into the 'inquiring group' (asks questions) and the 'inquired group' (answers questions). • A final web document with questions and answers is created. • A repository of questions and answers is created.
Presentation-Question	• Reproduces a symposium where 2 to 5 recognized experts are asked to produce presentations on a number of topics and to answer questions raised by the learners for a period of time. • Learners organize into teams that synthesize the presentations, stress their most relevant points and reinterpret then in light of the answers received to the questions. • The resulting synthesis is put up on a web page repository.

Table 5. Dimensions of learning

Dimensions	Characteristics
Participation / Reification	• Participation is a source of identity, a social experience involving all kinds of relations, an active process that shapes experience and communities.
	• Reification is the process of giving form to our experience by turning an abstract idea into a concrete object or artifact, where form becomes a focus for the negotiation of meaning.
	• They represent unity in their duality.
	• They represent an interacting duality where both are necessary for negotiation of meaning.
	• They assume different forms and degrees.
Design / Emergency	• Design is a structuring element, sort of a boundary object functioning as a communication artifact around which communities can negotiate their contribution, position and alignment.
	• Emergency represents the ability to negotiate meanings.
	• Practice is a response to design.
	• The structure of identity and the structure of practice are both emergent.
	• The challenge is enabling the design to include emergency and make it an opportunity.
Locality / Globality	• Locality represents the more immediate focus of the learning design.
	• Globality represents a much broader scope of the learning design.
	• Learning design requires connections among localities in their constitution of the global.
	• Practice must combine different kinds of knowledgeability.
Identification / Negotiability	• Identification represents the contribution of the individual to the learning design.
	• Negotiability is inherent to the conception of the learning design; the learning framework is negotiable in practice.
	• Design creates identities and also requires power to influence the negotiation of meaning; it shapes communities and economies of meaning.
	• Design creates fields of identification and negotiability, orients the practices and identities of those involved to various forms of participation and non-participation.

ning to gain strength. This perspective of learning as situated upholds that the study, comprehension, and conception of learning must take into account content, activities, and context as integral parts of learning.

Every activity is, then, situated, in the sense that no activity may exist independently from the way in which it is contextualized by the actors: "the perception of task describes a relation between context and student experience" (Ramsden, 1988, p. 162)

To illustrate the creation of learning contexts in virtual settings we will take learning activities as condensed examples of context creating environments and propose some models for the management of learning in virtual environments, based on three complementing categories of learning strategies: interaction, action, and presentation strategies (cf. Table 3) (Afonso, 2000; Afonso, 2001a, 2001b; Figueiredo,

Table 6. Modes of belonging: facilities and resources

Components	Concept	Facilities	Resources
Engagement	• Provides the context for learning. • Supports community building, emergent knowledgeability and social energy.	• Mutuality (interactional, joint tasks, peripherality). • Competence (initiative, knowledgeability, accountability, tools). • Continuity (reificative memory, participative memory).	Shared histories Relationships Interactions Practices
Imagination	• For learning to encompass and deal with a broader context.	• Orientation (location in: space, time, meaning, power). • Reflection (breaks in rhythm, models and patterns, sabbaticals and conversations). • Exploration (opportunities and tools for experimenting, creating alternative scenarios, play and simulation).	Images of: possibilities, the world, the past/future, ourselves
Alignment	• Connecting learning to broader enterprises.	• Convergence (common interests, vision, shared understanding, values and principles). • Coordination (standard methods, communication, boundary, feedback). • Jurisdiction (policies, mediation, conflict resolution, distribution of authority).	Discourses Coordinated enterprises Complexity Styles Compliance

Afonso, & Cunha, 2002). The use of these strategies is illustrated through a variety of concrete Web-based learning activities[1] that might promote the creation and development of contexts for collective learning (cf. Table 4).

Developing from the postulates of socio-constructivism and situated learning, where learning is perceived as a social process and a situated activity, the main feature of the proposed framework is maintaining that individuals engage in learning communities looking for participation in their social practices (Afonso, 2000) while focusing on the crucial relationships between incoming and existing members and on the existing interactions between knowledge, artifacts, practice, and activities.

The design of learning contexts thus involves the analysis of multiple dimensions of learning. For Wenger (1998a), the design of learning involves four major dimensions, which he describes as dualities, each involving different tradeoffs and challenges: participation/reification, design/emergence, locality/globality, and identification/negotiability (cf. Table 5).

These proposed dimensions, through their components, define the learning architecture, which combines modes of belonging in support of learning communities.

One of the functions of design is to provide facilities for these modes of belonging: engagement, imagination, and alignment (cf. Table 6).

The challenge underlying the project of learning contexts is that of achieving a balanced combination of all the dimensions and components of the learning architecture, where the need for a dimension cannot be fulfilled at the expense of the others. Furthermore, a framework for the design of learning contexts is needed to provide a deeper understanding of how a specific design serves the different requirements of the learning architecture of a learning community.

Communities: Why, What For, and Why Not?

The transformation that has been taking place in society has been inducing deep changes in all paths of life. In this context of deep and fast changes, ICT are raising great interest in the educational domain, because of their potential to make educational activity less dependant on time and space constraints. Hopefully, this could allow educational institutions to redirect their attention from teaching to learning, from teacher to learner, and from content to context.

Though most of the times educational technologies do not correspond to the normative expectations of institutions, the complex social interactions, and behavioral patterns that define educational institutions, as we know them, we might not be able to answer adequately to the current educational challenge if we do not integrate ICT in education in an effective way.

The decentralized development of information resources promoted by ICT represents an interesting development for continuous education, training and education in general, and this is having a great impact in our conceptions of teaching, learning, time, space, and community.

We witness the virtualization of space, but, still, we follow the traditional human imperative of socialization, which has been leading us to venture in this virtual space with the aim of getting involved with others in virtual communities. We may argue that these communities might not be real communities, because they mainly exist outside the geopolitical borders that we have been drawing on maps for centuries. However, could not it be plausible to consider the communities we know as being, generally, virtual?

As we have discussed earlier, communities might be considered as imagined (Anderson, 1991), since they are not really based on physical contact but on a communion supported by the common values and interests of their members, which is strengthened by common symbols and a feeling of belonging and sharing.

The increasing interest in virtual communities is partially due to the fact that we may find in them a sort of collective goods, in the shape of social capital, knowledge capital, and communion. Social capital refers to the network of relationships that develop and strengthen through virtual communities; knowledge capital refers to a set of intellectual resources created and constructed through interaction in virtual communities; and communion means a sense of belonging and a feeling of empathy that is developed by and between the members of a virtual community.

Among these general virtual communities, virtual learning communities bloomed. In this context of development of virtual learning communities, networks of people and resources for learning-related purposes have been gaining shape and strength.

In a paradigm of learning as a social process of knowledge creation, through interaction and constructive activities, virtual learning communities might become an intellectual environment (representing an endless source of information, able to fulfill the individual's cognitive needs), a social environment (providing opportunities for the construction of a transactional space for collaborative learning), and a cultural environment (gathering distinct cultural experiences and encouraging changes in the dominant discourse and culture). Hence, virtual learning communities facilitate and support learning by promoting interaction, collaboration, and a sense of belonging.

These communities provide interaction opportunities that seem to be richer than those provided by traditional learning contexts, providing a common learning infrastructure and stressing the relational nature of human cognition and the importance of context in learning. Individuals learn when engaged in communities in which knowledge is built through interaction and discourse in the context of collaborative activities.

The development and exploration of Web-based learning supported by virtual learning communities opens up new opportunities for learning and triggers changes at the pedagogical level. The change to the community paradigm, with the development of new educational architectures and cultures, becomes even more complex with the need of the actors to master the technology and redefine their roles in the educational scene. More than technologists, all the educational actors must also become experts in the management of complex social interactions and in the scaffolding of individual and collective learning.

Virtual learning communities might represent an important alternative to more traditional teaching-learning contexts, having ICT as their technological support and making them more viable today than in the past.

In a time "where the technology allows a concept to take shape, and the interplay between technology and theory will likely continue in the years to come" (Wilson & Ryder, n. d.), ICT have brought with them the Herculean challenge of building new learning environments that facilitate and promote the existence of constructive spaces for collective learning.

That is, perhaps, the turning point for the emergence of new paradigms in learning.

Conclusions

If, until a decade ago, the technology of cellulose had provided the transmission and diffusion of knowledge, the technology of silicon goes further beyond the dissemination of the patrimony of human knowledge. By introducing different nuances in the conceptions of time and space, which have been enriched and virtually enlarged, it triggers the urgent need of rethinking academic institutions, teaching, and learning.

Learning is no longer an exclusive territory of academic institutions, and it makes sense to speak of networked learning. The idea of a network is a pillar for the construction of platforms for the community paradigm in learning. With the social construction of knowledge and collaborative learning at its core, this paradigm re-conceptualizes and reorganizes learning toward learning communities.

This migration to learning communities is not an easy one, but it is quite plausible if we take into account the frequent enculturation of individuals in communities of practice, where they learn in (pro)active and collaborative ways within diversified and complex contexts. Context gains a new dimension in this educational scenario. It is through context that the individual gives meaning to content, structures its experiences, and interacts with its equals in the construction of knowledge.

A first step toward such a change requires the perception of the importance of translating this paradigm into more effective and meaningful pedagogical practices. A next step would be the attempt to build a model for the management of learning in virtual settings supported by contextualized collaborative learning and by learner-centric activities, capable of promoting the individual's cognitive development and interpersonal skills, as well as the social construction of knowledge.

It may be possible to walk toward a systemic conception of learning in which the educational actor network—from the learner to the context—reflects not only a learning architecture but, mainly, a learning culture.

In this chapter, we have tried to stress the lack of consensus around the concept of community and its recent deployment in the educational domain and how the educational use of virtual settings has neglected, if not ignored, the construction of the learning context.

We have also worked to show the existence of a large and solid body of knowledge from areas as diverse as learning theories, sociology, socio-constructivism, and communities of practice that, when put together and articulated in their potentialities and valued in their similarities, may provide useful insights to overcome the limitations of many online learning experiences.

Finally, we believe that learning communities are entirely new tools for a contextual approach to the management of learning in virtual settings.

Acknowledgments

This chapter was written with the support of the Portuguese Foundation for Science and Technology under PhD scholarship SFRH/BD/3289/2000. The author would also like to express her recognition to António Dias Figueiredo and Elísio Estanque for their most useful and enriching comments to this chapter.

Endnote

[1]   A full description of these activities is beyond the scope and extension of this chapter. If interested, please read Afonso (2000) or get in touch with the author for further details.

References

Afonso, A. P. (2000). *Models for the management of learning in virtual environments* (in Portuguese). M.Sc. thesis, Coimbra: Faculty of Psychology and Educational Sciences of the University of Coimbra.

Afonso, A. P. (2001a). Comunidades de aprendizagem: um modelo para a gestão da aprendizagem. In P. Dias & C. Freitas (Eds.), *Proceedings of the II International Conference on Information and Communication Technologies in Education / Desafios 2001–Challenges 2001* (pp. 427-432). Braga: Universidade do Minho.

Afonso, A. P. (2001b). Models for the management of knowledge in educational sites. In M. Khosrowpour (Ed.), *Proceedings of the 2001 International Resources Management Association / Managing Information Technology in a Global Economy* (pp. 1195-1196). Hershey, PA: Idea Group.

Afonso, A. P., & Figueiredo, A. D. (2000). Web-based learning and the role of context. In Kinshuk et al. (Eds.), *Proceedings International Workshop on Advanced Learning Technologies 2000* (pp. 270-271). Los Alamitos, CA: IEEE.

Aldrich, H. E. (1999). *Organizations evolving.* London: Sage.

Aldus, J. (1995). O intercâmbio entre Durkheim e Tönnies quanto à natureza das relações sociais. In O. Miranda (Ed.), *Para ler Ferdinand Tönnies*. São Paulo: Edusp.

Anderson, B. (1991). *Imagined Communities: Reflections on the origin and spread of nationalism.* New York: Verso.

Bauman, Z. (1995). Searching for a centre that holds. In M. Featherstone, S. Lash, & R. Robertson(Eds.), *Global modernities* (pp. 140-153). London: Sage.

Beamish, A. (1995). *Communities on-line: A study of community-based computer networks.* Unpublished master's thesis, MIT Retrieved October 6, 1998, from http://alberti.mit.edut/arch/4.207/anneb/thesis/toc.html

Bellah, R. (1997). The necessity of opportunity and community in a good society. *International Sociology, 12*(4), 387-393.

Bonk, C. J., & Wisher, R. A. (2000). *Applying collaborative and e-learning tools to military distance learning: A research framework.* Alexandria, CA: U.S. Army Institute for the Behavioral and Social Sciences. Retrieved May 21, 2004, from http://carbon.cudenver.edu/~mryder/dlc.html

Brabazon, T. (2001). How imagined are virtual communities? *Mots Pluriels, 18.* Retrieved December 9, 2004, from http://www.arts.uwa.edu.au/MotsPluriels/MP1801tb2.html

Brown, J., Collins, A., & Duguid P. (1989). Situated cognition and the culture of learning. *Educational Researcher, 18*(1), 32-42. Available at http://www.sociallifeofinformation.com/Other_Writings.htm

Butterworth, G. (1992). Context and cognition in models of cognitive growth. In P. Light & G. Butterworth (Eds.), *Context and cognition: Ways of learning and knowing* (pp. 1-14). New York: Harvester Wheatsheaf.

Cole, M., & Werscht, J. (n.d.). *Beyond the individual-social antinomy in discussion on Piaget and Vygotsky.* Retrieved May 20, 2000, from http://www.massey.ac.nz/~Alock/virtual/colevyg.htm

Estanque, E. (2000). *Entre a Fábrica e a Comunidade: Subjectividades e práticas de classe no operariado do calçado* (pp. 40-57). Porto: Afrontamento.

Figueiredo, A. D., Afonso, A. P., & Cunha, P. R. (2002). Learning and education: Beyond the age of delivery. In UMIST (Eds.), *Proceedings of the International Conference on Engineering Education–ICEE2002* (CD). Manchester, UK: UMIST.

Fischer, G. (2002, December). *Social creativity and meta-design as foundations for learning communities.* Tutorial of the International Conference on Computers in Education–ICCE2002–IEEE, Auckland, NZ. (distributed copy)

Genov, N. B. (1997). Four global trends: Rise and limitations. *International Sociology, 12*(4), 409-428.

Giddens, A. (1991). *Modernity and self-identity: Self and society in the later modern age.* Cambridge: Polity Press.

Gongla, P., & Rizzuto, C. R. (2001). Evolving communities of practice: IBM Global Services experience. *IBM Systems Journal, 40*(4), 842-862.

Griffin, P., Belyaeva, A., Soldatova, G., & the Velikhov-Hamburg Collective. (1993). Creating and reconstituting contexts for educational interactions, including a computer program. In A. Forman, N. Minick, & C. A. Stone (Eds.), *Contexts for learning: Sociocultural dynamics in children's development* (pp. 120-152). Oxford: Oxford University Press.

Hirschi, T. (2001). *Causes of delinquency.* New Brunswick, NJ: Transaction.

Jacques, M. G. (1998). As dimensões cognitivas e afectivas da identidade. *Psicologia, Educação e Cultura, 2*(2), 309-321.

Jonassen, D. H. (2000). Preface. In D. H. Jonassen & S. M. Land (Eds.), *Theoretical foundations of learning environments* (pp. 3-9). NJ: Erlbaum.

Jonassen, D. H., Mayes, T., & McAleese, R. (n. d.). A manifesto for a constructivist approach to technology in higher education. In T. Duffy, D. Jonassen, & J. Lowyck (Eds.), *Designing learning environments.* Heidelberg, FRG: Springer-Verlag. Retrieved September 25, 2004, from http://apu.gcal.ac.uk/clti/TMPaper11.html

Jones, Q. (1997). Virtual-communities, virtual settlements & cyber-archeology— A theoretical outline. *Journal of Computer Mediated Communication, 3*(3). Retrieved from http://www.ascusc.org/jcmc/vol3/issue3/jones.html

Kim, A. J. (2000). *Community building on the Web—Secret strategies for successful online communities.* Berkley, CA: Peachpit Press.

Kollock, P., & Smith, M. (1999). Communities in cyberspace. In M. Smith & P. Kollock (Eds.), *Communities in cyberspace* (pp. 3-25). London: Routledge.

Lave, J., & Wenger, E. (1991). *Situated learning: Legitimate peripheral participation.* Cambridge: Cambridge University Press.

Lemos, A. (n. d.). *As estruturas antropológicas do cyberespaço.* Retrieved November 11, 2003, from www.facom.ufba.br/pesq/cyber/lemos/estcy1.html

Maffesoli, M. (1996). *The time of tribes: Decline of individualism in mass society (Theory, culture and society).* Thousand Oaks, CA: Sage.

Mercer, N. (1992). Culture, context and the construction of knowledge in the classroom. In P. Light & G. Butterworth (Eds.), *Context and cognition ways of learning and knowing* (pp. 28-46). New York: Harvester Wheatsheaf.

Moers, W. (1999). *The 13$^1/_2$ lives of Captain Bluebear—A novel.* London: Vintage.

Neto, F. (1985). Identidades Migratórias. *Psiquiatria Clínica, 6*(2), 113-128.

Palácios, M. (1998). *Cotidiano e sociabilidade no cyberespaço: apontamentos para discussão.* Retrieved from September 25, 2004, from http://facom/ufba/br/pesq/cyber/palacios/cotiadiano.html

Preece, J. (2000). *Online communities–Designing usability, supporting sociability.* Chichester: Wiley.

Preece, J., & Maloney-Krichmar, D. (2003). Online communities. In J. Jacko & A. Sears (Eds.), *Handbook of human-computer interaction* (pp. 596-620). Mahwah, NJ: Erlbaum.

Putz, P., & Arnold, P. (2001). Communities of practice: Guidelines for the design of online seminars in higher education. *Education, Communication & Information, 1*(2), 181-195.

Ramsden, P. (1988). Context and strategy: situational influences on learning. In R. Schmeck (Ed.), *Learning strategies and learning styles* (pp. 159-184). New York: Plenum.

Recuero, R. C. (2002). *Comunidades virtuais–Uma abordagem teórica.* Retrieved September 20, 2004, from http://www.bocc.ubi.pt

Rheingold, H. (1993). *The virtual community: Homesteading on the electronic frontier.* New York: Adison-Wesley.

Rheingold, H. (1996). *A comunidade virtual.* Lisboa: Gradiva.

Roque, L., & Almeida, A. (n. d.). *Engenharia do Contexto: um modelo de intervenção sócio-técnica.* (Distributed copy)

Roque, L., Almeida, A., & Figueiredo, A. D. (2004). Context engineering: an IS development research agenda. Leino et al. (Eds.), *Proceedings of the European Conference on Information Systems, ECIS 2004* [CD]. Turku, Finland: ECIS.

Santos, B. S. (1995). *Toward a new common sense: Law, science and politics in the paradigmatic transition.* New York: Routledge.

Schmeck, R. (1988). An introduction to strategies and styles of learning. In R. Schmeck (Ed.), *Learning strategies and learning styles.* New York: Plenum Press.

Silvio, J. (1999). *Las comunidades virtuales como conductores del aprendizaje permanente.* Retrieved November 6, 2002, from http://funredes.org/mistica/xastellano/ciberoteca/participantes/docuparti/esp_doc_31.html

Smith, M. (1999). Invisible crowds in cyberspace: Mapping the social structure of the Usenet. In M. Smith & P. Kollock (Eds.), *Communities in cyberspace* (pp. 195-219). London: Routledge.

Tönnies, F. (1963). *Community and society* (Gemeinschaft und Gesellschaft). New York: Harper Torchbooks. (Original work published 1887)

Vygotsky, L. (1978). *Mind in society: The development of higher psychological processes.* Cambridge, MA: Harvard University Press.

Wasson, B. (1996). *Instructional planning and contemporary theories of learning: Is it self-contradiction?* Retrieved May 20, 2000, from http://www.ifi.nib.no/staff/barbara/papers/Euroaied96.html

Weber, M. (1987). *Conceitos básicos de Sociologia.* São Paulo: Editora Moraes.

Weber, M. (1989). Classe, status e partido. In M. Braga da Cruz (Ed.), *Teorias Sociológicas: Vol. 1. Os fundadores e os clássicos* (3rd ed., pp. 737-749). Lisboa: Fundação Calouste Gulbenkian.

Wellman, B., & Gulia, M. (1999). Virtual communities as communities: Net surfers don't ride alone. In M. Smith & P. Kollock (Eds.), *Communities in cyberspace* (pp. 167-194). London: Routledge.

Wenger, E. (1998a). *Communities of practice–Learning, meaning, and identity.* Cambridge: Cambridge University Press.

Wenger, E. (1998b). Communities of practice: Learning as a social system. *Systems Thinker, 9*(5), 2-3.

Wenger, E., McDermott, R., & Snyder, W. M. (2002). *Cultivating communities of practice: A guide to managing knowledge.* Boston: Harvard University Press.

Wilson, B., & Ryder, M. (n. d.). *Dynamic learning communities: An alternative to designed instructional systems.* Retrieved May 21, 2004, from http://carbon.cudenver.edu/~mryder/dlc.html

Chapter IX

Activity Theory and Context:
An Understanding of the Development of Constructivist Instructional Design Models

Laura G. Farres, Douglas College, Canada

Colla J. MacDonald, University of Ottawa, Canada

Abstract

Constructivist instructional design (ID) models have emerged with more frequency within e-learning. These models offer guiding principles congruent with constructivist approaches to teaching and learning. Although constructivist ID models share common principles, each model also offers a unique approach to e-learning based on its context of development. Consequently, certain models will also be more authentic and meaningful for a particular situation depending on their compatibility to that particular context. If that context can be understood, then direction can be given as to the best application for the model. This chapter introduces activity theory (AT) as a lens from which to understand the context of constructivist

ID model development in e-learning. It argues that AT provides a suitable frame-work for naturalistic inquiry within complex settings and establishes a language from which a better comparison of context can occur.

Introduction

The trend for e-learning instructional design (ID) models is shifting to include more constructivist perspectives that offer guiding principles congruent with constructivist approaches to teaching and learning. This trend is perhaps related to the number of experts recommending constructivism as the optimal approach for e-learning (Hill, 1997; Jonassen, 1994; Jonassen, Peck, & Wilson, 1999; Relan & Gillani, 1997). Willis (2000) suggests that one of the major strengths of constructivist approaches to ID is that each constructivist ID model is unique and reflects a different angle of approach to e-learning based on its context of development. He recommends that this diversity between models be recognized by moving away from the tendency to view one ID model as "THE way to think about design" (Willis, 2000, p. 5). His recommendation suggests that there is value in distinguishing between constructivist models and in determining their authenticity as a tool for ID within different e-learning contexts. The goal of this chapter is to present a conceptual framework that will allow for the examination of constructivist ID model development with the aim of identifying the unique contribution to the field of constructivist ID that the model makes.

The emphasis on context is unique to constructivist ID models in e-learning, but not to the field of education in general. Numerous studies within education suggest that context influences educational process. For example, Boud and Walker (1998) recommended that teachers create a microcontext within the classroom to overcome barriers to reflective practice that may be present in the dominant context. Turner, Meyer, Cox, Logan, DiCintio, and Thomas (1998) found that in classrooms where the students were highly engaged in activity, the teachers negotiated understanding, supported intrinsic motivation, and allowed students to take more responsibility for their learning. Perry (1998) demonstrated that context factors such as specific tasks within the classroom and evaluation practices facilitated self-regulated learning with young children. Further, a number of other researchers have highlighted the influence of context on such aspects as learning and motivation (Ames, 1992; Blumenfield, 1992), instructional practices (Feiman-Nemser & Floden, 1986), classroom climate (Turner & Meyer, 2000), and leadership (Gronn & Ribbins, 1996).

The challenge with many of the studies examining context is that there is no common language or framework for comparative analysis. Context becomes a description that is situationally bound and limited as a comparator to other contexts. Different studies are apt to offer different expressions of context, especially if there remains no conceptual framework to guide the descriptions. Agreeably, context is a complex and dynamic issue that is difficult to narrow down. However, as more and more participatory-type methodologies are adopted to examine everyday practice in education and in e-learning, the need to compare and generalize research findings to further the field will only increase (Nardi, 1996). Nardi suggests that a common vocabulary will set the stage for developing a comparative framework or taxonomy that will allow for "cumulative research results."

Recently, *activity theory* or AT (Engeström, 1987, 1993; Leont'ev, 1974; 1981; 1989; Nardi, 1996) has emerged as a contributing lens from which to examine context within e-learning settings (Issroff & Scanlon, 2002; Jonassen, 2000; Nardi, 1996). Activity theory is concerned with the relationship between consciousness and activity and is composed of subject, object, and community and the elements that mediate these interactions (i.e., tools, rules, and roles); see Figure 1. Activity theory suggests that context relates directly to the activity itself. Nardi (1996) summarizes the AT perspective on context:

> *What takes place in an activity system composed of object, actions, and operations, is the context. Context is constituted through the enactment of an activity involving people and artifacts. Context is not an outer container or shell inside which people behave in certain ways. People consciously and deliberately create contexts (activities) in part through their own objects; hence context is not just "out there". (Nardi, 1996, p. 76)*

Indeed, Nardi goes on to suggest that AT is a more viable framework for understanding e-learning contexts than both situated action and distributed cognition perspectives, because AT gives primary agency to the subject in the activity. That is, people are not viewed simply as nodes in a system but rather as the driving force of the system. Their motives, actions, and operations guided by the varying conditions within the activity system are the impetus guiding transformation of the object of the activity. The theory is an attractive conceptual framework for the field of education in general and also as a framework from which to understand the context of development for constructivist ID models in e-learning.

Constructivist ID models often emerge through a complex and ill-defined process in which a number of experts with competencies in various areas collaborate in the activity of developing a framework from which instructional design is guided. Various elements will mediate the object of the activity, such as computer programs, experience of designers, roles within the team, time lines, and outcome expectations of the designers and the community at large. Each model will be unique based on the activity system from which it emerges. Consequently, certain models will also be more authentic and meaningful for a particular situation depending on their compatibility to that particular context. Context gives meaning to actions and objects and is integrated within the activity; objects and actions cannot be separated from the context from which they emerge (Jonassen, 2002). Therefore an understanding of the development of construc-

Figure 1. Activity theory

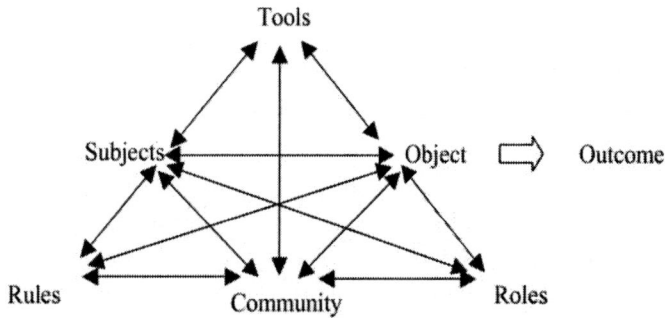

tivist ID models needs to be integrated within the context, and AT offers a viable framework in this regard.

The goal of this chapter is to use AT as a framework to explore the uniqueness of constructivist ID models. First, the tenets of AT will be presented. Second, we will present a framework grounded in AT from which to examine context within the development of constructivist ID models. Finally, we will apply the framework and examine two constructivist ID models within e-learning.

Activity Theory

Activity theory is offered as a lens through which to understand the link between consciousness and activity. Jonassen (2000) described four main assumptions underlying AT. The first assumption is that consciousness and activity are inter-dependent. This perspective draws on Vygotskian theory of cognition (Vygotsky, 1978), where higher mental functions appear twice and on two planes. Activities include individual interaction with the objective environment (i.e., social plane—between people) and then with the mental processes embedded within those actions (i.e., psychological plane—within individual). The second assumption is intentionality. All actions and behaviors are intentional or goal directed. The goals, however, are contingent on the context of the intended activity and can be constrained or enabled by various elements or conditions within the activity system. The third assumption is mediated action. Higher cognitive functioning within an activity system is mediated by tools (technical tools) and signs (mental processes). These elements mediate action by how they are used and integrated into social practice. The final assumption is historicity. Activities evolve over time within a culture, and attention needs to be paid to the evolution of the activities over time.

In AT (Engeström, 1987, 1993; Leont'ev, 1974, 1981, 1989; Nardi, 1996) the central unit of analysis is the activity, which is composed of a subject, an object, actions, and operations (see Figure 1). A subject is a person or a group of people participating in the activity. The object (or objective) relates to the intention of the activity as determined by the subject. It gives the activity its purpose and direction. Actions are conscious, goal-directed processes that must be carried out in order to achieve the objective. Operations relate to how the actions are carried out. They are routinized procedures that become automatic the more they are undertaken.

This relationship between subject and object is not direct but rather mediated by several factors including tools or instruments, community, rules, and division of labor (see Figure 1). The subjects or actors are the perspective from which the activity is grounded and from which the objects evolve or are transformed. Objects can be physical, such as raw materials, or mental, such as conceptual understandings or problems. Tools are the elements that the subjects use to transform the object. Again, they can be technical, such as computers, or mental, such as theories. Community within an activity system relates to those individuals or subgroups that play some role in the transformation of the object. These communities are defined by the mediating factors of division of labor (roles) and rules. Division of labor can be distributed hierarchically or equally across members of the community depending on the division of status and power. Finally, all systems have formal, informal, or technical customs, values, or rule structures that govern and, in some cases, restrict practice while guiding and defining relationships among community members.

The context is the whole activity system, which includes the subjects and objects along with the mediating factors. Therefore, AT as a lens for analysis moves beyond simply viewing the context as a container or situationally embedded space to viewing it, rather, as a unified system with subject, object, and tools integrated as a whole (Engeström, 1993). It is the analysis and description of this entire system in action that precipitates an understanding of the subjects' actions, the impact these actions have on the transformation of the object, and the awareness of the various components mediating this transformation. As such, analysis is bound to descriptions of the creative process occurring for the subjects of the system and an identification of the contradictions that emerge as a process of the activity.

Leont'ev (1974) and Engeström (1987, 1993) contended that activity systems are characterized by primary and secondary contradictions. The contradictions are tensions or imbalances that can occur within one element of the system (primary contradictions; e.g., the subjects) or between various elements of the system (secondary contradictions; e.g., subjects and tools). The contradictions manifest themselves as problems that need to be addressed within the system. As such, these contradictions drive the system to change and develop so that these disturbances can be accommodated.

The use of AT is increasing in the field of education and technology as it provides a framework for naturalistic inquiry within complex settings (Nardi, 1996). Peal and Wilson (2001) suggested that AT is a perspective that can inform practice within e-learning and promote understanding of what is happening and how it is happening in relation to the participants within the activity system. Jonassen (2002) summarizes the implications of using AT as an alternative lens that captures the context and the community in a more complex and integrated fashion. "It focuses on the activities, the social and contextual relationships among the collaborators in those activities, the goals and intentions of those activities, and the objects or outcomes of those activities" (p. 51).

Activity Theory as a Framework for Examining Constructivist ID Model Development

Engeström (1993) suggested that AT is not a methodology and, as such, does not offer "ready-made techniques and procedures" for research. He recommended using AT in research as a conceptual tool that researchers can operationalize based on "the specific nature of the object under scrutiny" (p. 97). Figure 2 is our attempt to operationalize an activity system in the context of the development of constructivist ID models. The object of the activity systems will be to create a constructivist ID model to guide practice. This objective will lead to purposeful actions such as discussions, social negotiation, and concept mapping and operations such as writing, drawing, and researching aimed at achieving the goal set out. The subjects will be the individuals who are involved in the development of the constructivist ID model. The number of subjects, along with their backgrounds and experiences, will vary from activity system to activity system, as will their individual social interactions and mental processes within the activity itself. Community will include those involved in the transformation of the model, whether directly or indirectly. This list might include students, other faculty, the institutions, technical or financial partners, and stakeholders.

Inextricably linked with each of these elements are tools, rules, and roles. Tools can be such things as computers, research papers, conferences, reflections, and discussions. Rules can include such elements as guidelines for interactions, course requirements, and needs of intended audience. Finally, roles can include researcher, student, writer, leader, and audience. Tools, rules, and roles will mediate between the various components of the activity system such as between subjects and objects, subjects and communities, and object and community. The tools selected will depend on the subjects within the activity system and overall object of the activity. Tools, rules, and roles will serve a critical role in the final model presentation.

Contradictions within the activity system may also provide some insight into the development of the constructivist ID model. As mentioned previously, con-

traditions are resistances, dilemmas, or conflicts that get in the way of achieving the intended goal. These contradictions place conditions on the activity system that may force actions to be modified in order to continue to work toward
the object. Contradictions may occur within one element of the system, such as
between the subjects. For example, two subjects may have different experiences
with e-learning and therefore advocate for different approaches or selection of
tools. Contradictions can also emerge from the interaction between the various
components of the system, such as between the subjects and the community. For
example, the community may have a vested interest in the way an object transforms. If the transformation is not occurring in the desired direction, then the
community may pose restrictions or place different conditions on the system
that affect the process of the activity.

Finally, the outcome within the activity system will be the final product of the
activity, the constructivist ID model. Its depiction, purpose, and guiding properties
to instructional designers will reflect its process of development. As a result, certain models may be more suited to particular contexts.

To help guide the analysis of the development of constructivist of ID models through
an AT lens, a series of questions are presented (see Figure 3) related to key compo-

Figure 2. Examining constructivist ID models through activity theory

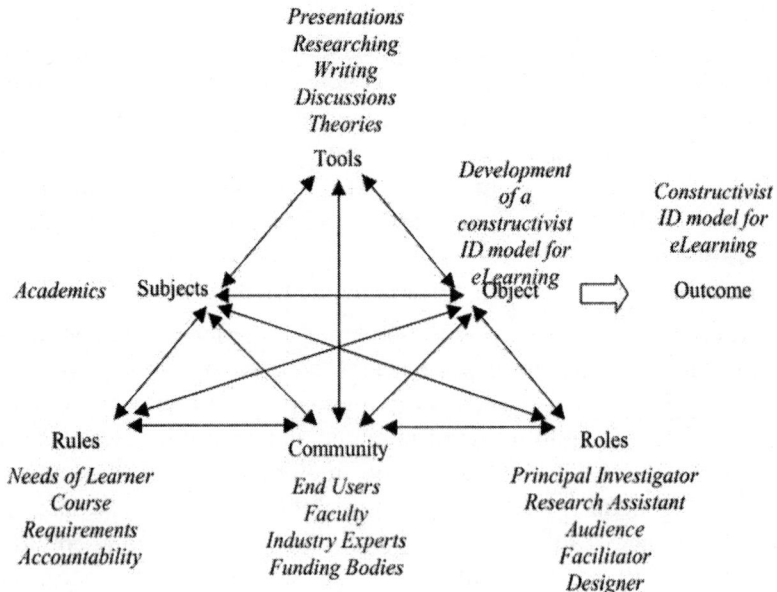

nents of the system. The questions are not presented as a comprehensive list but rather as a starting point for the analysis. The goal now is to apply the framework to examine its utility as a means to highlight the uniqueness of constructivist ID models.

Applying the Framework

Two constructivist ID models, Layers of Negotiation (Cennamo, Abell, & Chung, 1996) and Demand Driven Learning Model or DDLM (MacDonald, Stodel, Farres, Breithaupt, & Gabriel, 2001), are used to demonstrate the utility of the AT framework. We recognize that in presenting these examples we are doing so only from our understanding of the material presented in the papers related to the specific models. We offer these examples here cautiously and with an acknowledgment that proper analysis of process needs to occur from within the activity system (Jonassen, 2002).

Figure 4 highlights the activity system for the development of the Layers of Negotiation Model (Cennamo et al., 1996). The Layers of Negotiation Model emerged out of the concern regarding the use of traditional ID models to design learning materials for constructivist environments. Cennamo et al. argued that materials should be aligned with the learning environment for which they are intended. As such, the materials for constructivist environments should be developed through a process that adheres to the same philosophical underpinnings as constructivism. The object of their activity was to propose an approach to designing materials consistent with constructivist ideas based on their experience of designing a set of case-based interactive video disks for a constructivist learning environment.

The subjects in the activity system were Cennamo et al. (1996). The team consisted of two methods course instructors, one graduate assistant, one science content specialist, and one instructional designer. The community was composed of the students and teachers within the teacher education program, the Department of Education Computing and Instructional Development, and Purdue University.

Social negotiation was a central tool in mediating the process of the activity, as was the process of the members actually designing the case-based interactive videos. Members negotiated a shared perspective in approach to designing the learning materials and in developing the model. Reflection, articulation, and questioning skills were valuable tools in this process. Additional tools were members' previous experiences in their own classes, their beliefs about the teaching and learning process, and their understanding of the content area involved. This examination was ongoing with various points being revisited several times, adding depth and complexity with each layer of negotiation.

Figure 3. Questions guiding examination of constructivist ID model development

Subjects

> Who is directly and indirectly involved in model development?
>
> What are the backgrounds and expertise of the developers of the model?
>
> What are the roles and responsibilities of these individuals within model development?
>
> Who are the stakeholders and end users and what is their role?
>
> Is model development intended as a team or individual project?
>
> How did individuals in model development influence outcome?
>
> What rules are governing actions?

Tools

> What tools are mediating action? Consider mental and technical.
>
> Is there a guiding theoretical framework?
>
> Is there a preference for tool selection?

Objects

> What is the intended use of the model?
>
> Why is there a need to develop the model?
>
> What type of learning does the model support?
>
> How did the model evolve through the process?
>
> How does the model guide practice?
>
> What context is best suited for application of the model?

Contradictions

> Have any challenges arisen through the activity system?
>
> How do challenges impact the activity system and the object?

Social negotiation also played a central role in determining roles and responsibilities through the activity.

The community was indirectly involved in the process of model development through their participation in the product design process. They reviewed material and provided feedback regarding the product. Cennamo et al. (1996)

pointed out that end-user perspective on versions of the product is vital to the process as they are representative of others who will use the material. However, they also suggested that clients may have difficulty envisioning the final product in comparison to experienced designers and therefore their roles will be more limited.

Social negotiation between members appeared as the only contradiction influencing the object. The awareness of ongoing negotiation of shared meaning and perspective as more and more detail became available seemed to lead to the conception of the spiral or layered approach to design.

The outcome of the activity system is a nonlinear model and is depicted as a spiral where the process of ID can move repeatedly through four stages: analysis, design, development, and evaluation (see Figure 5). As more information becomes available, the questions of design can be re-addressed, adding more detail through the spiraling process. The model appears quite simple as a diagram, and therefore one could imagine it being applied in a number of different settings. The model provides general guidance within constructivist ID. It appears that the model best supports an ID process related to the production of e-learning materials for use within the classroom or traditional face-to-face settings.

Figure 6 highlights the activity system for the development of the Demand Driven

Figure 4. Example of Layers of Negotiation Model (Cennamo et al., 1996) development as an activity system

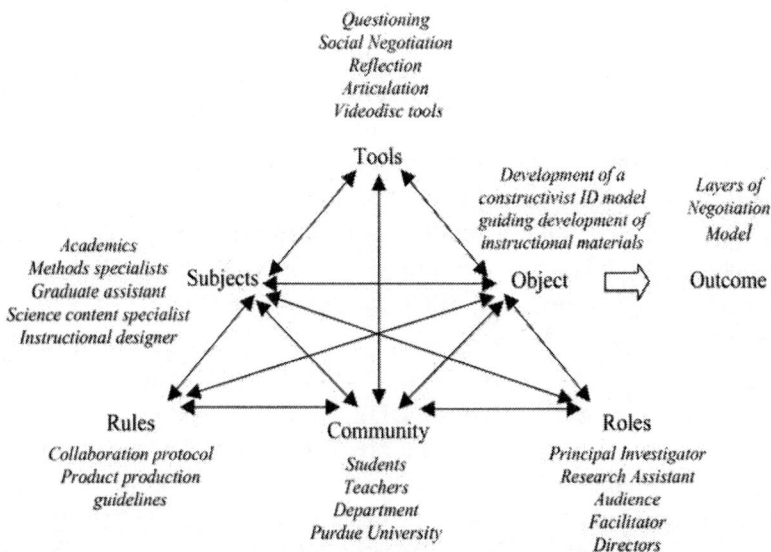

Learning Model, or DDLM (MacDonald et al., 2001). The DDLM emerged from dissatisfaction with the quality of ID models guiding practice within adult education. The object was to design a model to specifically address the needs of working adults and the needs of industry. Furthermore, the object was to provide a model not only to guide the design process but also for the structure the process of development and delivery of an e-learning course.

The DDLM was developed through a collaborative process between the subjects (academics) and the community (industry). The five academics had strong foundations in curriculum design, evaluation methods, e-learning, and educational psychology. The community included a sampling of the most influential and innovative North American stakeholders in online technology and the education field (i.e., Nortel Networks, Alcatel, Lucent Technologies, Cisco Systems, Arthur D. Little Business School, Learnsoft Corporation, Lucent Corporation, and KGMP Consulting Services).

Numerous tools mediated the process of the activity, such as discussions, social negotiation, writing, researching, and presentations. The academic team conceptualized the initial framework of the DDLM. This framework emerged from an extensive review of the literature in distance education. The team was influenced by several researchers who suggested that there is a need to be more responsive to consumer demands within higher education (Daniel, 1996; Duderstadt, 1999; MacDonald & Gabriel, 1998; MacDonald et al., 2001; McElhinney & Nasseh, 1999; Palloff & Pratt, 2001) and that unique features of e-learning, such as cost effectiveness, convenience, and flexibility, are attractive options for the nontraditional learner such as the working adult. Additionally, the model design team saw a need to develop a model that was driven by sound pedagogical principles. They noted that the literature provides lists of attributes that are being used to define successful e-learning events but that these lists do not provide a fully functional model that educators can use to build or assess effective e-learning programs. Their conclusion was that effective e-learning delivery requires a commitment to planning the learning experience and a need to produce a blueprint to guide development, evaluate success, and guide improvement. Therefore their goal was to move beyond a pure ID model and to develop a model that addressed design, delivery, and evaluation of e-learning. Numerous discussions and revisions to the model occurred at this stage. Their objective was to develop a draft model related to high-quality standards emerging from the literature and present this model to stakeholders.

The community or industry experts were presented with a draft describing the DDLM. The research team modified the DDLM on the basis of appraisals from these stakeholders. Specifically, two main areas warranted further attention and modification. First, inconsistencies were questioned related to the placement of constructivist theoretical variables and program outcomes within the same model. Second, an apparent overlap among the four variables in the framework was identified. Steps used to resolve these issues included additional searches of

Figure 5. Layers of negotiation model (Cennamo et al., 1996)

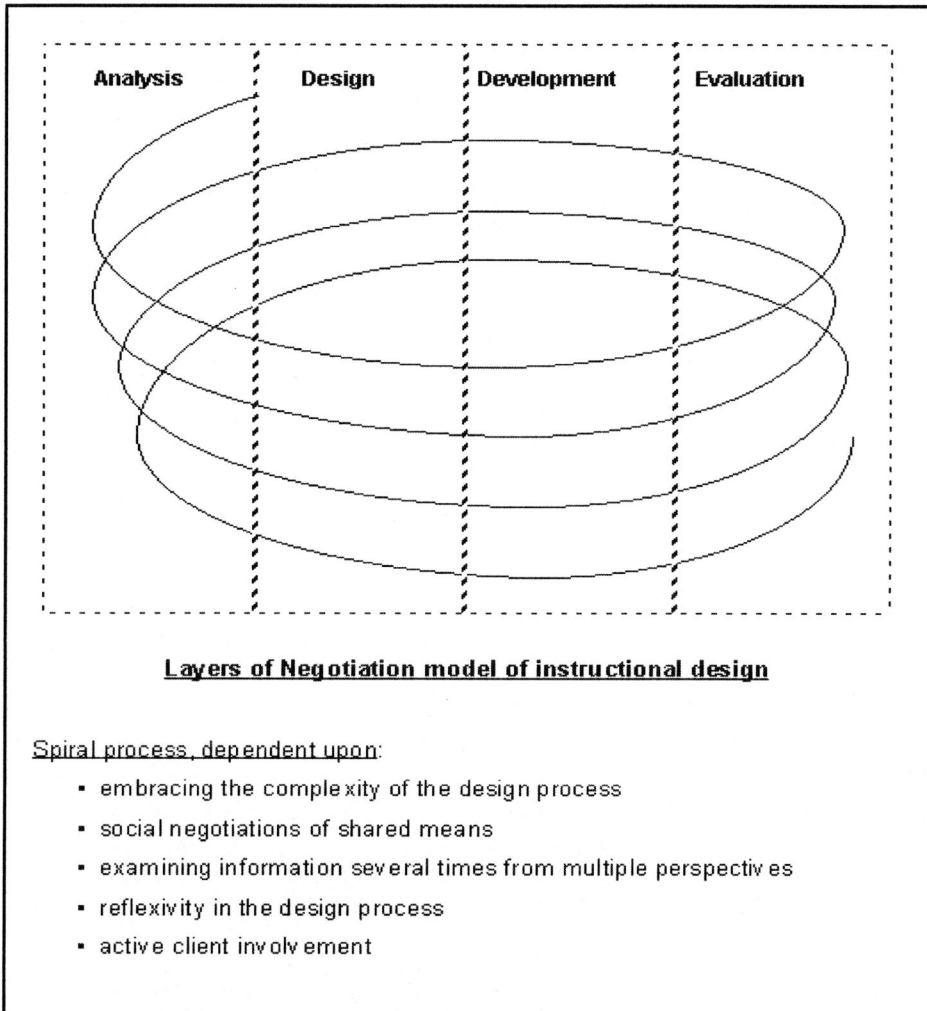

| Analysis | Design | Development | Evaluation |

Layers of Negotiation model of instructional design

Spiral process, dependent upon:

- embracing the complexity of the design process
- social negotiations of shared means
- examining information several times from multiple perspectives
- reflexivity in the design process
- active client involvement

the literature and the construction of a formal description of the theoretical and empirical work forming the foundation for the original DDLM. In this process, a decision was made by the team to adapt the DDLM and to revise definitions of the categories.

The subject-community interaction described previously is a good example of a contradiction mediating the activity system. The academic team presented their

Figure 6. Example of Demand Driven Learning Model (MacDonald et al., 2001) as an activity system

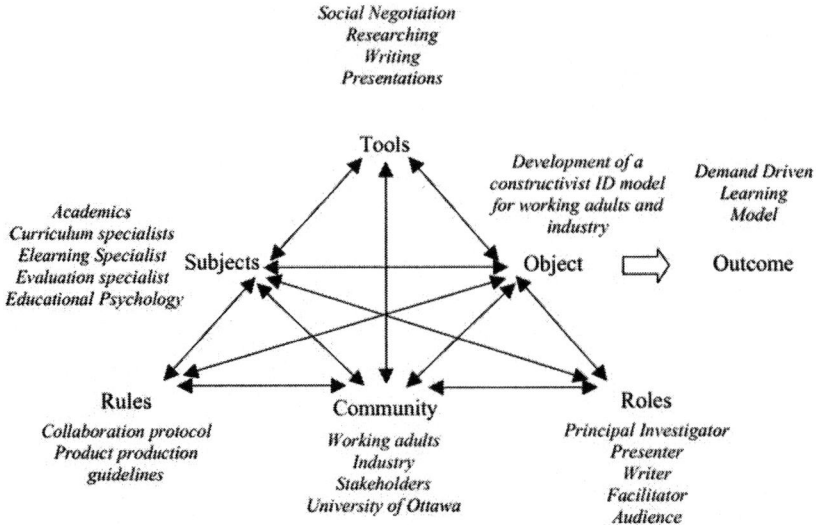

conception of the model, in which the industry experts provided feedback that required resolution on the part of the academic team.

The outcome of the activity system is DDLM. It is defined by five main components: the quality standard of superior structure; three consumer demands of content, delivery, and service; and learner outcomes. Further, it is framed within frequent opportunities for ongoing adaptation, improvement, and evaluation. Superior structure can be viewed as a standard of high quality attained only by e-learning programs that adequately address learner needs, learner motivation, the learning environment, program goals, pedagogical strategies, learner evaluation, and learner convenience. The elements of superior structure are required to meet consumer demands for comprehensive, authentic or industry-driven, and researched content; usable, interactive, and appropriate tool-based delivery; and resource-rich, supportive, accessible, and responsive service. Learner outcomes will be optimized as a result (MacDonald et al., 2001).

The DDLM is presented as a linear model with a distinct starting point at the bottom of the structure. A small, thin rectangular bar containing the term superior structure supports a larger and thicker rectangle with an upright triangle positioned within it. The triangle is divided into four sections. The bottom three sections of the triangle contain the three elements of content, delivery, and service. The upper portion or point of the triangle contains the outcome section. Surrounding the triangle and contained within the larger rectangle are the terms *ongoing program evaluation and continual adaptation and improvement* (see Figure 7).

The model is comprehensive as a diagram and it provides specific guidance for e-learning programs for adult learners. It provides design teams with a model for developing practical tools and open and flexible learning environments. It appears to be the model that best supports an ID process related to the production of e-learning courses for working adults.

Conclusions

The goal of this chapter was to present a conceptual framework that would allow for the examination of constructivist ID model development with the aim of identifying the unique contribution to the field that the model made. Activity theory was presented as the conceptual lens for the analysis. This theory provided a common language from which to describe the transformation of the objects, as well as a lens from which to examine the similarities and uniqueness of the two models.

The Layers of Negotiation Model and the Demand Driven Learning Model share some features common to constructivist models (Willis, 2000). First, both models highlight recursive practices in ID. The components of the models are reciprocal and interrelated rather than separate and mutually exclusive. Second, the models support reflective practices in ID. Reflective practices entail ongoing problem framing, implementation and improvisation, and an understanding of the context in which the professional work is done. Finally, both models encourage participative practices. Participative practices involve frequent opportunities for observation, input, discussion, and collaboration among all individuals involved in ID context.

The uniqueness of the two models was also highlighted. First, the DDLM was developed for a specific purpose (the design, delivery, and evaluation of e-learning courses) and for a specific population (working adults). As such, the model is best suited for application in these contexts. It provides specific categories to address when developing the e-learning event, and it provides significant guidance to first-time designers. In contrast, the Layers of Negotiation Model emerged as a framework from which to develop constructivist materials from constructivist learning environments. Although specific in purpose, the presentation of the model is more general and it could be applied to a number of contexts both for the development of constructivist materials and constructivist learning environments. It may pose some challenges to novice designers as the process assumes expertise both in content area and in design protocol.

For constructivist models, Willis (2000) suggests that "the best we can do . . . is to provide guidance, not specific rules that invariably apply to certain types of sit-

Figure 7. Demand Driven Learning Model (MacDonald et al., 2001)

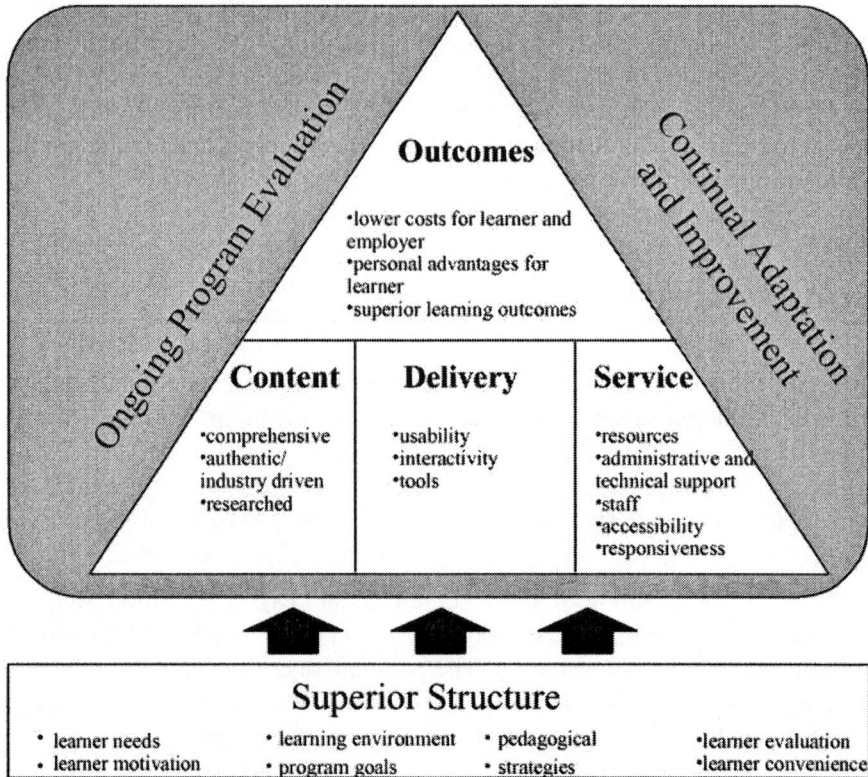

Outcomes
•lower costs for learner and employer
•personal advantages for learner
•superior learning outcomes

Content
•comprehensive
•authentic/ industry driven
•researched

Delivery
•usability
•interactivity
•tools

Service
•resources
•administrative and technical support
•staff
•accessibility
•responsiveness

Ongoing Program Evaluation

Continual Adaptation and Improvement

Superior Structure
• learner needs
• learner motivation
• learning environment
• program goals
• pedagogical
• strategies
•learner evaluation
•learner convenience

uations" (p. 8). However, we contend that perhaps the role of the models is not just about guidance from a global and generalized standpoint but rather about guidance within a specific context. As more constructivist ID models emerge in the field of e-learning, it will be necessary to provide a framework or taxonomy to identify the utility of the models for different contexts and also identify the gaps where new constructivist models might be developed to offer new and unique approaches.

Activity theory presents itself as a framework from which to ground future research in the area. Nardi (1996) suggests that AT in comparison to traditional research approaches is a tool for describing issues of context and practice that helps provide perspective on both individual and social levels. We believe that this framework offers a starting point for examining the context and constructivist ID models in e-learning, one that can be expanded upon. We also hope that the framework will spark discussion around the issue of context and the appeal to develop a more common language in order to move toward more "cumulative research results."

References

Ames, C. (1992). Classrooms: Goals, structures, and student motivation. *Journal of Educational Psychology, 84,* 261-271.

Blumenfeld, P. C. (1992). Classroom learning and motivation: Clarifying and expanding goal theory. *Journal of Educational Psychology, 84,* 272-281.

Boud, D., & Walker, D. (1998). Promoting reflection in professional courses: The challenge of context. *Studies in Higher Education, 23*(2), 191-207.

Cennamo, K., Abell. S., & Chung, M. (1996). A layers of negotiation model for designing constructivist learning materials. *Educational Technology, 36*(4), 39-48.

Daniel, J. S. (1996). *Mega-universities and knowledge media: Technology strategies for higher education.* London: Kogan Page.

Duderstadt, J. J. (1999). *Dancing with the devil.* San Francisco: Jossey-Bass.

Engeström, Y. (1987). *Learning by expanding.* Helsinki: Orenta-konsultit.

Engeström, Y. (1993). Developmental studies of work as a testbench of activity theory: The case of primary care medical practice. In S. Chaiklin & J. Lave (Eds.), *Understanding practice: Perspectives on activity and context* (pp. 64-103). Cambridge, MA: Cambridge University Press.

Feiman-Nemser, S., & Floden, R. E. (1986). The cultures of teaching. In M. C. Wittrock (Ed.), *Handbook of research on teaching* (pp. 505-526). New York: Macmillan.

Gronn, P., & Ribbins, P. (1996). Leaders in context: Postpositivist approaches to understanding educational leadership. *Educational Administration Quarterly, 32*(3), 452-474.

Hill, J. R. (1997). Distance learning environments via the world wide web. In B. H. Khan(Ed.), *Web-based instruction* (pp. 75-80). Englewood Cliffs, NJ: Educational Technology.

Issroff, K., & Scanlon, E. (2002). Using technology in higher education: An activity theory perspective. *Journal of Computer Assisted Learning, 18,* 77-83.

Jonassen, D. H. (1994). Thinking technology: Toward a constructivist design model. *Educational Technology, 34*(4), 34-37.

Jonassen, D. H. (1997). Instructional design models for well-structured and ill-structured problem-solving learning outcomes. *Educational Technology Research and Development, 45*(1), 65-94.

Jonassen, D. H. (2000). Revisiting activity theory as a framework for designing student-centered learning environments. In D. H. Jonassen & S. M. Land (Eds.), *Theoretical foundations of learning environments* (pp. 89-121). Mahwah, NJ: Erlbaum.

Jonassen, D. H. (2002). Learning as activity. *Educational Technology, 42*(2), 45-51.

Jonassen, D. H., Peck, K. L., & Wilson, B. G. (1999). *Learning with technology: A constructivist perspective*. Upper Saddle River, NJ: Prentice Hall.

Leont'ev, A. (1974). The problem of activity in psychology. *Soviet Psychology, 13*(2), 4-33.

Leont'ev, A. (1981). *Problems of the development of mind.* Moscow: Progress.

Leont'ev, A. (1989). The problem of activity in the history of Soviet psychology. *Soviet Psychology, 27*(1), 22-39.

MacDonald, C. J., Breithaupt, K., Stodel, E.J., Farres, L.G., & Gabriel, M. A. (2002). The demand-driven learning model: Testing a framework for Web-based learning. *International Journal of Testing, 2*(1), 35-61.

MacDonald, C. J., & Gabriel, M. A. (1998). Toward a partnership model for Web-based learning. *Internet and Higher Education, 1*(3), 203-216.

MacDonald, C. J., Stodel, E., Farres, L., Breithaupt, K., & Gabriel, M. A. (2001). The demand driven learning model: A framework for Web-based learning. *Internet and Higher Education, 1*(4), 9-30.

McElhinney, J. H., & Nasseh, B. (1999). Technical and pedagogical challenges faced by faculty and students in computer-based distance education in higher education in Indiana. *Journal of Educational Technology Systems, 27*(4), 349-359.

Nardi, B. (Ed.). (1996). *Context and consciousness: Activity theory and human-computer interaction*. Boston: MIT Press.

Palloff, R. M., & Pratt, K. (2001). *Lessons from the cyberspace classroom: The realities of online teaching.* San Francisco: Jossey-Bass.

Peal, D., & Wilson, B. (2001). Activity theory and Web-based training. In B. Khan (Ed.), *Web-based training* (pp. 147-153). Englewood Cliffs, NJ: Educational Technology.

Perry, N. E. (1998). Young children's self-regulated learning and contexts that support it. *Journal of Educational Psychology, 4*, 715-729.

Relan, A., & Gillani, B. B. (1997). Web-based instruction and the traditional classroom: Similarities and differences. In B. H. Khan (Ed.), *Web-based instruction* (pp. 41-46). Englewood Cliffs, NJ: Educational Technology.

Savery, J., & Duffy, T. (1996). Problem-based learning: An instructional model and its constructivist framework. In B. Wilson (Ed.), *Constructivist learning environments: Case studies in instructional design.* Englewood Cliffs, NJ: Educational Technology.

Turner, J. C., & Meyer, D. K. (2000). Studying and understanding instructional contexts of classrooms: Using our past to forge our future. *Educational Psychologist, 35*, 69-86.

Turner, J. C., Meyer, D. K., Cox, K. E., Logan, C., DiCintio, M., & Thomas, C. T. (1998). Creating contexts for involvement in mathematics. *Journal of Educational Psychology, 4*, 730-745.

Vygotsky, L. (1978). *Mind in society: The development of higher psychological processes.* Cambridge, MA: Cambridge University Press.

Willis, J. (2000). The maturing of constructivist instructional design: Some basic principles that can guide practice. *Educational Technology, 40*(1), 5-16.

Chapter X

The Distance from Isolation:
Why Communities are the Logical Conclusion in E-Learning

Martin Weller, Institute of Educational Technology, Open University,
United Kingdom

Abstract

This chapter argues that the Internet is built around key technology design features of openness, robustness, and decentralization. These design features have transformed into social features, which are embodied within the cultural values of the Internet. By examining applications that have become popular on the net, the importance of these values is demonstrated. If e-learning is considered as a subset of Internet activity, then the types of approaches that will be popular and meaningful for students will be those that appeal to these three core values. An examination of online communities reveals that these approaches are indeed in keeping with these values and provide a valuable learning experience. The community can be seen as a natural conclusion in e-learning driven by the expectations of a generation of learners who have been enculturated into the values of the Internet.

Introduction

One way of looking at the values of the Internet is to ask what social values it seems to champion. This might cover questions such as the following:

- What are the social norms expected of behavior when you join an online community?
- How are you expected to communicate?
- What is unacceptable behavior?
- What sorts of topics generate online debate?
- What does the online community perceive as threats to its core values?
- Is there such a thing as one set of values for the Internet?
- What sort of technologies take off online and why?
- How do people actually use the different technologies in everyday life?

The answer to all such questions lies in the essence of the Internet and what it was created for—namely communication, and in particular robust, decentralized, and open communication. Although these were *technological* features of the Internet design, they also became *social* features of the system as the Internet took off. A comparison of these two aspects of the Internet (i.e., its technological and social features) reveals how each of these three key features (viz. robustness, openness, and decentralization) is realized. In terms of robustness, the Internet was designed as a distributed system that could survive attack, failure, or sabotage of any particular part and still function as a meaningful communication system. In order to do this it had to be a network system, with no centralized control. This is fundamental to all that follows. Having opted for a decentralized system, this means that there need to be many different connections, with no single node being more important than any other. This is realized through the network of Internet routers, where if one is down, then information will simply find an alternative route. An open system follows from the decentralized approach, because if the system is to have no central control, then it is necessarily open, so that any compatible computer can hook up onto it and allow communication to continue.

If we view the Internet in terms of social features and communication, these three key characteristics are evident again. Robustness is seen through the ability to communicate from different locations, using a variety of devices. It is also evidenced through the failure of governments or commerce to really control the Internet and what is discussed on it. The decentralized nature of the Internet is key to this—no one body or organization owns or controls the Internet. Every server or Web site is potentially as significant as any other one. This makes the Internet an obviously open and democratic place. Anyone can publish, and debate is not governed or censored. In many ways, the Internet acts like a living organism, driven by these social values. As John Gilmore famously observed, "The Internet interprets censorship as damage and routes around it." As well as making a strong case against censorship, what Gilmore's quote indicates is that the social behavior of the Internet mimics the technological behavior.

This provides an insight into the social values of the net and answers to the questions above. In short, the values of the Internet are based around the sanctity of communication. Anything that appeals to these three key features of the net, namely openness, decentralization, and robustness, is likely to take off online. Anything that threatens or impinges on these is likely to cause concern and debate (I am speaking about the open Internet here; different values might apply regarding Internet use within an organization, although often it is the conflict between these two cultures that causes difficulties). This perspective on all Internet developments, but especially those in e-learning, provides a useful means of not only predicting what developments might be successful but also analyzing why certain technologies or approaches have been successful or unsuccessful. Using this approach to examine the potential of communities offers a fresh perspective on their likely uptake.

This chapter explores this hypothesis in detail by examining some successful developments on the Internet. Each of these is examined in light of the three fundamental social characteristics outlined earlier. This analysis demonstrates the validity of the hypothesis. The educational motivation for adopting a community-based approach is then set out. These two areas combine to suggest that communities are a natural endpoint in e-learning, since they meet the three social characteristics and there are powerful pedagogical advantages for their adoption. Some of the issues in realizing e-learning communities are then addressed.

Successful Developments

Napster

Napster (the music sharing system) was something of an Internet phenomenon. Between 1999 and 2002 the software gained some 80 million registered users, led to a number of similar programs being developed (e.g., Gnutella, Kazaa), changed the manner in which people viewed the Internet, and caused great concern in the music industry. The software allowed users to swap MP3 music files between themselves. This led to the rise of peer-to-peer computing, which bypasses central servers.

The reasons behind Napster's success are varied; for example, it focused on an activity that was always popular (sharing music) and opened this up to the global scale of the Internet. Similarly, it appealed to an audience that was keen to adopt new technology and had a strong interest in the area of music.

But if we look at our three key features, then Napster can be seen as appealing directly to these. It was open in that anyone could download the software and start sharing files. Indeed its very openness was the reason the music industry eventually shut it down through legal action. It was decentralized, in fact more decentralized than previous usage of the Internet. Napster was the pioneer of peer-to-peer (P2P) computing, and the rise of this may well be Napster's main legacy. Purists claim that Napster was not strictly peer-to-peer since it retained a central database, but it demonstrated several key features of P2P computing. Firstly, it was operated by users installing client software on their computer. Secondly, they could then exchange files directly with each other, without the need for going through a central server. Lastly, it led to the creation of new communities, with many Napster users communicating with each other, swapping files, passing on recommendations, exchanging views, and so on. This community was outside normal controls and moderation precisely because it was peer-to-peer. This bypassing of normal regulation is one of the main issues (both for advocates and detractors) surrounding P2P computing. The central database mentioned earlier did prove to be something of an Achilles' heel for Napster, as the legal case focused on this as an item that should be opened up. So, in this respect, Napster was not decentralized enough and this in itself demonstrates the validity of the initial Internet design.

Napster was also robust in that it could not be shut down easily. Only legal action against the founding company succeeded, but by this time there were many imitators, such as Gnutella, as well as the facility to swap files through instant messaging clients.

Blogging

Web logs, or blogs, have become the fastest growing use of the Internet over the past year or so. Blood (2000) differentiates between two types of blog. The first type is the journal, which acts as an online diary and contains thoughts, opinions, reflections, and so forth. This is usually personal, giving an account of the individual's life. The second type is the filter-style blog, where the blogger posts links to other Web content (be it obscure or mainstream), with a commentary on this. This second type is probably of more interest and value to the reader. As Blood puts it,

A filter-style weblog provides many advantages to its readers. It reveals glimpses of an unimagined web to those who have no time to surf. An intelligent human being filters through the mass of information packaged daily for our consumption and picks out the interesting, the important, the overlooked, and the unexpected. This human being may provide additional information to that which corporate media provides, expose the fallacy of an argument, perhaps reveal an inaccurate detail. Because the weblog editor can comment freely on what she finds, one week of reading will reveal to you her personal biases, making her a predictable source. This further enables us to turn a critical eye to both the information and comments she provides. Her irreverent attitude challenges the veracity of the "facts" presented each day by authorities.

Blogcount.com estimates there are approximately 2.4 to 2.9 million active blogs as of June 2003. Although an impressive figure for a new phenomenon, Jupiter Research indicates this is only 2% of the online community (Greenspan, 2003).

The development of easy-to-use tools, such as Blogger.com, Radio Userland, and MoveableType, has meant that users can easy publish diaries from any location. They can allow comments on each of their postings, thus creating debate around issues of importance to a particular set of individuals. Communities of bloggers have grown up, linking and commenting on one another's postings. There are also community blogs, such as MetaFilter, which anyone can post to and discuss issues.

Blogs are a technologically simple development, yet they have been seized upon by the Internet community. If we examine these in the light of the three main features, the reasons for this popularity are demonstrated.

Firstly, they greatly increase the degree of openness by allowing simple "push-button" publishing. There is no need to design Web pages or upload these—the users can choose from a variety of design templates and then simply type their text into a box and click on "publish." This democratizes the net further, making it open to a large portion of the population.

Next is the feature of decentralization. Part of the popularity of blogs is that they can be updated from anywhere and thus take advantage of the Internet's global pervasiveness. For example, at conferences with wireless networks, many people in the audience will be uploading comments on the current presentation to their blog as the presentation is in process. For example, Lisa Guernsey (2003) gives this example:

> *Some people who have experienced the phenomenon cite a speech given last year at a computer industry conference by Joe Nacchio, former chief executive of the telecommunications company Qwest. As he gave his presentation, two bloggers—Dan Gillmor, a columnist for The San Jose Mercury News, and Doc Searls, senior editor for The Linux Journal—were posting notes about him to their Weblogs, which were simultaneously being read by many people in the audience.*
>
> *Both included a link forwarded by a reader in Florida to a stock filing report indicating that Mr. Nacchio had recently made millions of dollars from selling his company's stock, although he complained in his speech*

about the tough economy. "No sympathy here," Mr. Gillmor wrote.

"When Dan blogged that, the tenor of the room changed," Mr. Doctorow said. Mr. Nacchio, he said, "stopped getting softball questions and he started getting hardball questions."

Decentralization is therefore an important aspect in the popularity of blogs. The third feature, robustness, can be seen in two main ways. The first is simply the robustness offered by the Internet itself. As a means of keeping a public diary or commentary, the Internet has few rivals. However, what is more interesting is the community aspect of blogging. When the Internet was still relatively new and with far fewer users, the most popular application (apart from e-mail) was that of newsgroups. In these, like-minded individuals could discuss anything from rare diseases to conspiracy theories. Although they are still popular, the newsgroups have suffered from the rise in popularity of the Internet. Many are now unusable because they are populated almost entirely by spam messages or users who are deliberately provoking angry responses (known as *trolling*) or prolonged debates between a few users. Put in terms of the Internet design, the newsgroups are not robust enough to this type of attack. Thus, much of the informed debate that used to be found in newsgroups now takes place in blogs. As mentioned, bloggers will often post comments on other bloggers' postings, thus creating a distributed debate. Because these are owned by the individual user, they are much less susceptible to the kind of attack that has crippled newsgroups. Similarly, the comment function can be used by trollers, but as each comment link is a separate page, it is more difficult for them to be corrupted by spam.

Open Source

The open source model of software production is based around a community of developers who contribute pieces of code, fixes, and improvements to an ongoing software project, for example an operating system. The software code is then regularly updated to incorporate contributions that have been deemed useful by the community. Several important software products have come out of the open source approach, including the operating system Linux and the Web server software Apache. These are not merely "hobbyist" applications, but robust systems that are widely used in industry.

Much of the open source community is driven by strong philosophical beliefs in the importance of freely available, nonproprietary software. This is often portrayed as an anti-Microsoft approach, in that Microsoft personifies the opposite approach to open source—that of proprietary development. In Microsoft's case, the software is developed by programmers working for a company, and the software is owned by that company. There are two basic tenets to the open source philosophy: that robust, complex software is best developed by a community of developers; and that only by keeping the source code open can this be achieved.

There are several key principles to the open source model. First, the code is freely available. Second, the contributors provide their services for free. Third, changes to the code are decreed by perhaps one person or a committee, but they usually arise out of acceptance by the community as a whole.

The open source model thus directly relates to the three main characteristics of Internet success. It is open, in that it is nonproprietary and anyone can contribute. As Raymond (2003) puts it,

> *Most software is fragile and buggy because most programs are too com-plicated for a human brain to understand all at once. When you can't rea-son correctly about the guts of a program, you can't be sure it's correct, and you can't fix it if it's broken. It follows that the way to make robust programs is to make their internals easy for human beings to reason about. There are two main ways to do that: transparency and simplicity.*

Open source is decentralized, in that the software consists of small modules, which can be adapted by anyone, rather than the software being a single large piece of code, developed by a closed team. It is, crucially, robust, and this is one of the main arguments of the proponents of the open source approach. Because the software is open, it can be updated regularly, and because it is developed by a community of developers the knowledge base is spread wider, leading to software that is arguably more robust than proprietary products.

The Educational Motivation for Communities

There has been some research examining the development of online communities, particularly among learners. For example, Brown (2001) suggests that there are three levels of community:

- *Online friends and acquaintances:* Individuals communicate with other students who they get on with or with whom they share interests.

- *Community conferment:* This is when students felt a degree of membership to the community of learners. This is gained through participation in threaded, thoughtful discussion.

- *Camaraderie:* This was the highest level of community, involving signifi-cant levels of commitment and involvement. It is usually achieved through prolonged association, for example, when students have studied more than one course together, and often extends beyond the time frame of the current course.

In their study, several students reported that they did not feel part of a community, however, which demonstrates that a community cannot be forced upon individuals. As Brown states, "Community did not happen unless the participants wanted it to happen."

The temporal element is interesting, since it may (although not necessarily) be in conflict with other trends in e-learning, such as just-in-time delivery, personalized content, and learning objects. Rheingold (1993, p. 5), one of the gurus of Internet community, similarly stresses the importance prolonged discussion plays in the formation of community. He defines a virtual community as "social aggregations that emerge from the [Internet] when enough people carry on those public discussions long enough, with sufficient human feeling, to form webs of personal relationships in cyberspace."

The case for community and viewing learning as a social activity has been made powerfully by Lave and Wenger (1991), Wenger (1998), and Brown, Collins, and Duguid (1989) among others. The notion of a "community of practice" has gained much credence, whereby individuals learn by participating in a real-context community. This particular approach has proven popular with large corporations, which see it as the next step in a knowledge management process. By facilitating experts to form a community, they share knowledge and improve their own performance, and the knowledge is elicited for future employees. For example, Gongla and Rizzuto (2001) detail the development of 60 "knowledge network communities" in IBM that covered the various countries in which they have a presence and the numerous roles within the organization.

There is therefore a good literature about the benefits of a community (be it virtual or real) in the learning process, but being pedagogically sound is not in itself sufficient for these to be adopted on a large scale. The traditional approach to teaching, embodied in the face-to-face lecture, has a good deal of inertia and is supported by an existing framework that is realized through assessment and accreditation strategies, administration, financial structures, physical buildings, and so forth. There is also, currently, an expectation from students that this is the form their education will, and should, take. For community-based approaches to become widespread in education and training, there needs to be a market pull for such learning experiences, and this is what we will look at next.

Learning Communities as a Natural Endpoint

Given the reservations, seen earlier, regarding the uptake of online communities as a widespread approach in education, we shall now look at reasons why these reservations may be overcome. If we return to the original three features that determine the success of a technology or service on the Internet, we can analyze e-learning communities in the light of these.

The first of these characteristics is openness. E-learning communities are necessarily open in that all individuals are encouraged to contribute, and the ethics of collaborative activity usually dictate that all contributions are valid. However, in order to prevent them from becoming subject to the same sort of disturbance and attacks that newsgroups have suffered, there may need to be a degree of control over this openness. For example, most universities have a code of conduct for online behavior, breaches of which can result in the individual being set to read-only status or banned altogether. Similarly, access to communities may be limited to individuals within an organization, or on a particular course.

The key aspect of openness, though, is that an online community is open to the flow of material. In many ways, the approach of traditional education has been analogous to that of established broadcast media. The educator and educational establishment were seen as the holders of knowledge, which was then imparted to the students at the discretion of the organization. Just as the Internet challenges this power relationship with news media, so it challenges it within education. Students can find out a great deal of information online, they can discuss issues with a wide variety of people, and, significantly, they have an expectation to feel involved in the whole process—that is, for the process and dialogue to be open. Educators still have an important role in helping students frame their thoughts and arguments and in constructing information they find online within a meaningful framework, but it is a different role from any they might have been engaged in. This brings us on to the second characteristic: decentralization.

Decentralization is fundamental to the difference between a community approach and traditional approaches, including those adopted by many e-learning providers. Much of the current e-learning material is based around an instructivist pedagogy and is firmly rooted in the belief that "content is king." This is seen with the use of video lectures, high-quality animations, lecture notes, and so forth. There has been a good deal of interest in constructivist approaches to online learning, and indeed some (e.g. Beaty, Hodgson, Mann, & McConnell , 2002) suggest that e-learning should always be constructivist in approach. As suggested earlier, there is considerable resistance to this change in power relationships within education. Many perceive it as a threat to their status or power. Currently, there is not a sufficient demand from students for this view to be seriously challenged. However, as the "net generation" enter higher education, they will come with an expectancy of discussing subjects in detail, seeking alternative views, and challenging authority. The traditional "lecturer knows all" approach will simply not satisfy such an audience.

These will be students who have grown up using software such as Napster and keeping blogs and whose cultural experience has been largely influenced by the culture of the net, including the sort of values espoused by the open source approach. They will have come to view "the network as the organizational form of our age," as Castells (2002) argues. He proposes that the Internet can enable networks to compete against the traditional centralized models of control in terms of effective realization of goals while retaining their advantages of adaptability and flexibility. The emergence of the network as the most effective organizational model is, he suggests, the result of three convergent factors:

1.   changes in the economic climate that have seen the globalization of business and a demand for flexibility in management,

2.   the social values of individual freedom and freedom of communication, and

3.   advances in technology, particularly the Internet and related computing.

The essence of the network society is that of decentralization. The next generation of adult learners will be from a culture of decentralization and so will resist models of education that are based on a centralized model.

The last characteristic is robustness. The open source model is again a good analogy here. This is a working model of how knowledge is best created by a community, to the mutual benefit of all. And the resultant knowledge (in this case embodied in a piece of software code, and also realized through improved programming practice throughout the community) is robust in a variety of situations. E-learning communities may be robust in a number of ways: they can lead to a robust understanding of a topic that does not fade the day after the exam has been sat, as knowledge is created through activity and in context; they are robust to different individual approaches and preferences as individuals contribute different resources; they are robust to changes in content, since the most up-to-date content is shared by individuals, rather than being reliant upon one individual to keep abreast of all developments.

E-learning communities therefore satisfy all three of the characteristics that have been identified as determinants of successful Internet applications. This, combined with their benefits from a pedagogical perspective, suggests that, almost regardless of the efforts of educators to promote or resist them, they will become a key feature in educational practice. This is no surprise; in many ways we have come full circle. The Internet was designed fundamentally as a communication medium and as Fernback and Thompson (n.d.) state, "The structural process that is associated with community is communication." So communities seem a natural product of the Internet, and particularly so in e-learning.

Realizing E-Learning Communities

So how might e-learning communities be realized, or encouraged? It is important to appreciate from the outset that one needs a broad definition of a community, and how one is realized. In e-learning, the tendency is to think of a community being built up over time through asynchronous text-based forums. Although this is certainly an important instantiation of the online community, it is not the only one. Indeed, there may be multiple modes of communication existing within an online community.

Gongla and Rizzuto (2001, p. 845) propose a five-stage model of community evolution:

1.   Potential stage, when the community is starting to form

2.   Building stage, when the community begins to coalesce and define itself

3.   Engaged stage, when the community operates with a defined and shared purpose

4.   Active stage, when the community reflects and analyzes its own purpose and value

5.   Adaptive stage, when the community may expand into new environments and adapts to external conditions

At each stage, they identify three key factors: "There is a pattern to how the communities evolved and the pattern is influenced by a dynamic balance of people, process, and technology elements" (Gongla & Rizzuto, 2001). These three factors can be used as the key ingredients in the development of a learning community.

Firstly, if we look at the people element of the triangle, there needs to be an appropriate set of users. This means learners who are at least willing (but preferably enthusiastic) to engage with the technology and to interact. A community is only as successful as its members make it; so if you have a reluctant group, who have private reasons for not wanting the community to succeed, then the community will not develop. However, as I argued earlier, it is likely that increasingly learners will come to education with an expectation of learning in exactly this way. Perhaps more problematic is having the right input from educators. Again, they need to be willing and enthusiastic, but importantly, they need to adopt new pedagogies.

The next element in the triangle is process. In e-learning terms, this can be said to refer to the pedagogy and the accompanying support structures. From a pedagogical perspective, communities need to form around dialogue, and so approaches that promote this will be successful. An obvious contender here is to include collaborative or cooperative tasks (which help foster the "community conferment" level in Brown's analysis). Communities can also form around discussion of content, and so content that suggests or promotes dialogue is important (as are educators who foster it). Similarly, activity-based approaches that give students a common experience and ability to share resources can foster community.

Such approaches need to be supported and recognized by the surrounding framework also. For example, assessment regulations need to be able to accommodate methods that will recognize more than just the formal exam. Similarly, there needs to be support for the range of technologies used and for these to be incorporated into the pedagogy of the course.

This brings us to the last element in this triumvirate of seeding factors: technology. Easy-to-use asynchronous tools, with affordances for dialogue, are usually seen as the sine qua non of an online community. Although this may be true, there is some suggestion that synchronous "events" are important in establishing a sense of communal identity. For example, Haythornthwaite, Kazmer, and Robins (2000) claim that, "synchronous communication, particularly during the live lecture times, contributes much more to community building than asynchronous communication." Technologies such as expert Webcasts with a subsequent synchronous exchange may therefore be important components in creating a community, even if they only represent a small percentage of the overall course content. Any technologies that promote communication will be useful. For example, a community of bloggers may form within a set of learners, as they share their experience of studying. Similarly, students will make increasing use of tools such as instant messaging, so they can be alerted when one of their friends or someone from the same course comes online. This could be incorporated into Web material, so that a learner could see who was studying this particular material at that time and engage in a discussion around it. Many of these tools create a community, which is "outside" of the one that might be recognized or moderated by formal education, but they all constitute a facet of the overall community.

Conclusions

The Internet was constructed around three design principles: robustness, decentralization, and openness. As usage of the Internet developed these design principles became social characteristics of the Internet. Successful Internet developments usually display all three of these characteristics. This has been demonstrated through an analysis of three such developments: Napster, blogging, and open source software.

There are strong educational motivations for communities in e-learning, as has been evidenced by much of the current focus on communities of practice. E-learning communities also satisfy the three major characteristics of successful Internet developments: they are robust, decentralized, and open. When a development has a strong motivation and it meets these three characteristics, then it is likely to become an adopted approach through the actions of users and participants, regardless of whether it is formally encouraged or not.

The challenge now facing educators is how to accommodate the potential of new technologies and the sophisticated communication strategies of a new generation of learners into formal structures. If a solution to this can be found, then the learning community will become the norm, and we will have found, in the words of Phillip Larkin, a "unique distance from isolation."

References

Beaty, E., Hodgson, V., Mann, S., & McConnell, D. (2002, March 26). *Working towards e-quality in networked e-learning in higher education: A manifesto statement for debate.* Presented at Understanding the Implications of Networked Learning for Higher Education Seminar series, University of Sheffield, Sheffield, UK.

Blood, R. (2000). *Weblogs: A history and perspective.* Retrieved October 3, 2003, from http://www.rebeccablood.net/essays/weblog_history.html

Brown, J. S., Collins, A., & Duguid, P. (1989). Situated cognition and the culture of learning. *Educational Researcher, 18,* 32-42.

Brown, R. (2001). The process of community-building in distance learning classes. *Journal of Asynchronous Learning Networks, 5*(2). Retrieved October 5, 2003, from http://www.aln.org/publications/jaln/v5n2/index.asp

Castells, M. (2002). *The Internet galaxy: Reflections on the Internet, business, and society.* New York: Oxford University Press.

Fernback, J., & Thompson, B. (n.d.). *Virtual communities: Abort, retry, failure?* Retrieved October 2, 2003, from http://www.well.com/user/hlr/texts/VCcivil.html

Gongla, P., & Rizzuto, C. (2001). Evolving communities of practice: IBM global services experience. *IBM Systems Journal, 40*(4), 842-862.

Greenspan, R. (2003, July 23). Blogging by numbers. *Big Picture.* Retrieved September 26, 2003, from http://cyberatlas.Internet.com/big_picture/applications/article/0,1301_2238831,00.html

Guernsey, L. (2003, July 24). In the lecture hall, a geek chorus. *New York Times.* Retrieved October 3, 2003, from http://www.nytimes.com/2003/07/24/technology/circuits/24mess.html?ex=1060315200&en=98dc374912ea9fda&ei=5070

Haythornthwaite, C., Kazmer, M., & Robins, J. (2000). Community development among distance learners: Temporal and technological dimensions. *Journal of Computer-Mediated Communication, 6*(1). Retrieved September 3, 2003, from http://www.ascusc.org/jcmc/vol6/issue1/haythornthwaite.html

Lave, J., & Wenger, E. (1991). *Situated learning: Legitimate peripheral participation.* Cambridge: Cambridge University Press.

Raymond, E. S. (2003). *The art of Unix programming.* Retrieved October 3, 2003, from http://catb.org/~esr/writings/taoup/html/

Rheingold, H. (1993). *The virtual community: Homesteading on the electronic frontier.* New York: Addison-Wesley.

Wenger, E. (1998). *Communities of practice: Learning, meaning, and identity.* New York: Cambridge University Press.

SECTION II

EXPERIENCES

Chapter XI

Narrative:
Designing for Context in Virtual Settings

Patricia Arnold, Helmut Schmidt Universität, Germany

John D. Smith, Learning Alliances, United States

Beverly Trayner, Escola Superior de Ciências Empresariais, Instituto Politécnico de Setúbal, Portugal

Abstract

In this chapter we consider the role played by narrative in negotiating and revealing contexts: we explore how narrative can help make more visible the contexts of individuals as well as of the evolving community in virtual settings. We use the narrative genre to "walk the talk" of a research story that highlights three stories of learning in virtual settings. Our set of cascading stories includes both designed learning settings and settings that arose through the interactions of members in a self-organizing community. In exploring how narrative potentially fosters meaning making and helps uncover contexts we draw mostly on Bruner's work on narrative and on situated theories of learning. In our research quest we aim to deepen our understanding of the intricate relation between narrative, context, and learning. To inform our design practice we summarize the "moral" of our story, transferring our insights into some initial guidelines for designing virtual settings for learning.

Once Upon a Time There Were Virtual Settings . . .

Information and communication technologies (ICTs) increasingly represent new settings for learning. These technologies can bring geographically dispersed groups together via e-mail, Web conferencing, chat, blogging, and yet-to-be-developed media. Virtual learning settings differ in a number of ways from face-to-face settings; they connect people with more diverse biographies and from more varied cultural backgrounds than was previously possible, offering more flexibility as to when and where people participate. While many courses in virtual settings now begin with personal introductions or participant résumés to help identify fellow learners, this may not be sufficient for a learning process that values exploring and reflecting on shared and different personal histories, worldviews, and future trajectories. This is where our exploration of the use of *narrative* for designing for context begins and to which we will return later.

Looking at virtual settings from another angle we observe both increased transparency and more opaqueness. By means of automatic archiving of synchronous or asynchronous text messages, virtual settings represent a more transparent environment than a traditional classroom. In contrast to a face-to-face setting, participants' contributions and discussions can be recorded, shared, and reflected on in ways other than intrusive and costly video or audio recording. However, at the same time, virtual settings also risk becoming somewhat opaque: computer-mediated communication renders communication "thinner." For example, participants' non-verbal cues and gestures are not easily conveyed in a written text message. Cues provided by facial expressions, gesture, or intonations are missing. When people begin to interact in virtual settings there is no visible context for the *here* and *now*. Space and time dimensions become more ambiguous, as do the contexts of fellow participants. Again, we claim that narrative may be able to help us.

So let us start with a personal story as it begins right here: we three, authors, researchers, and practitioners involved in virtual settings for learning, met precisely within these new virtual learning settings. Living and working thousands of kilometers apart, in three different time zones and three different contexts, we met initially through a course on communities of practice offered as an online workshop to an international audience. Beverly and Patricia have been alumni of the workshop; both are carrying out ongoing research on learning in virtual settings. John has been one of the designers of the workshop, researching some of its dynamics to improve his design practice. This has led us to our current connection through a virtual discussion space: John's watch in Oregon (United States) is showing 1 p.m., Beverly's in Setúbal (Portugal) shows 9 p.m., and Patricia's in Hamburg (Germany) says that it is 10 p.m. as we log on to our space and meet for our telephone conference.

As well as our common interest in *communities of practice*, a term coined by Jean Lave and Etienne Wenger in 1991, we are drawn to each other in a shared desire to design for learning in virtual settings. All three of us distance ourselves from what we call "e-learning hype," whereby public and private institutions alike seem to use the computer as a convenient storage space or distribution channel for content enriched with multimedia. We are joined by a conviction that this virtual setting is a socially constructed space where participants' practice sets the stage for learning, a far cry from being a space for transmitting course materials and setting tasks or activities.

In fact the question that has intrigued us most centers on *context*—context in the conception of learning as a culturally and historically situated activity as put forward by Jean Lave (1996, p. 30), whose work we jointly draw on. Although contexts in virtual settings may be harder to share, they are no less crucial for learning. This suggests to us that we should be designing for learning in virtual settings in ways that participants' past, present, and emerging contexts can be revealed and negotiated. In other words, if our practices in these new virtual locations are to support learning, it seems appropriate to explore the relationship between contexts and virtual settings in greater detail. In particular, we ask ourselves, *How do we reveal and negotiate understanding of contexts in virtual settings?* If we can find effective and powerful ways of doing this and are able to translate them into design guidelines for learning in virtual settings, our joint research journey may improve our diverse design practices regardless of what time each of our watches is showing.

A previous study by two of us, Arnold and Smith (2003), set us on a trail: a comparison of three virtual learning settings that pointed to narrative as an important way of revealing and negotiating contexts in virtual settings. So we looked around and reviewed some of the writings about narrative, learning, and new virtual settings. For the relationship between *narrative* and *learning*, we immediately thought of Jerome Bruner. He has been hailed as the architect of the cognitive revolution in psychology and his studies and writing illustrate how stories structure our lives. Bruner (1990) talks about narrative thought as an expression of someone's experience of the world through their own eyes. Bruner (1986) explores the difference between expository writing and narrative.

The first time we came across *narrative in the realm of learning in virtual settings* was in respect to the problem of providing orientation in Web-based training courses and preventing cognitive overload in hypertextual structures. Open university course designers experimented with the use of narrative in this way (Laurillard, 1998; Weller, 2000). Martin Weller (who provides another research story in Chapter 10 of this same book) used novels to provide a coherent structure for the Web-based training material in a computing course. In Weller's case students were asked to read two set textbooks parallel to following course activities. The textbooks "were both chosen because they operated at the level of narrative. They were readable accounts of the development of the personal computer and the Internet respectively" (Weller, 2000, p. 5).

The second "encounter" with narrative and learning in virtual settings concerned interface design and navigation concepts: Laurel, Oren, and Don (1992) elaborated on the use of a narrative interface-metaphor, using dramaturgic effects to fully "immerse" learners in the material as in computer games. A reduced element of this approach is often found in "guides," small figures that help the learner through a computer-based training, popping up and explaining or introducing a new topic.

Lisa Neals' article in 2001 was the third meeting with digital story-telling. Neals' focus is on the act of *digital storytelling* as it changes from the improvised, oral tradition to a way of digital recording that has to come to terms with the constraints of asynchronous technologies and the "lack of spontaneity and the tendency to sanitize stories when capturing them as text, audio, or video" (p. 1). So while there already exists a body of research on narrative, learning, and virtual settings that provides valuable insights we can draw on, there is no research story so far that focusses on *revealing and negotiating contexts in virtual settings by means of narrative*. This is the point of departure for our research story in this chapter, or rather for a set of cascading stories that represents our quest to explore narrative as meaning-making activity in virtual settings, and thus supporting learning.

Our set of stories is structured as follows: having explained what triggered our joint research effort in the first section we offer a second story that situates our research story within existing theories of learning and narrative in detail in the second section. Here we will clarify the concepts of context, narrative, identity, and practice that we have used so far without explanation with the aim of enticing you further into our research endeavor. We also present ideas of other protagonists in research on learning to help frame our own research questions more precisely. Then in the third section we share with you the methodology we employed to ground our main narrative in data. Our subplots, or central set of stories, follow in the fourth section. In this section each one of us refers to a particular case with which we have been involved. Although none of these cases was designed explicitly to include narrative or storytelling, our case stories show that narrative in diverse forms and genres played a significant role in each one. Our analytical stories of the three cases, or our readings of the stories, explore different genres of narrative that appear to help make contexts more visible to participants.

What is the moral of our research story as a combination of all these stories? Is there a happy ending? Our conclusions in the fifth section will transfer our findings into some guidelines for designing for learning by using narrative and suggest areas for future research so we can all live happily ever after.

So We Prepare Our Action

We begin this section with a warning story, reminding ourselves that talking of context has previously led us into trouble. In a presentation by two of the authors titled "Adding Connectivity and Losing Context with ICT" (Arnold & Smith, 2003) an irate member of the audience, whose background was in cultural studies, insisted that it was impossible to "lose context." With that in mind she was unable to "see the sense" of the rest of the presentation and her interventions left us dejected. The lesson we took from this was to heed our own caution that words carry different meanings in different discourse communities and we considered it wise, before we go on, to explicitly define how we will be using the concepts of context, narrative, identity, and practice in a learning setting.

Situational Contexts

Seth Chaiklin and Jean Lave's (1993) elaboration on context is a key issue in situated theories of learning. Context is of crucial importance but defined and used quite differently in disciplines ranging from applied linguistics to computer science, cultural studies, and psychology. The Latin root of the word (*contextus*) refers to the weaving together of words and the giving of coherence. We extend this theme of weaving to include those interrelated conditions in which learning takes place, including temporal conditions of the past, present, and future. In line with the work on situated learning, we also include the conditions of identity and social practice that will be discussed later.

In taking up the subject of context we appreciate the distinction between macrocontexts of wider sociocultural influences, including the sociocultural, political, and economic contexts, and the microcontext related to situational and social aspects of group practices. Both these contexts interact and influence each other to varying degrees and together constitute a greater ecology of learning. Although we acknowledge that microcontext needs to be understood in terms of the macrocontext, our focus in this chapter will be more specifically on microcontext or to "the events that are going on around when people speak (and write)" (Halliday, 1991, in Johns, 1997, p. 5).

At the same time we should point out that those events going on around us do not refer just to the immediate concrete surroundings, but are "historically constituted concrete relations within and between situations" (Lave, 1997, p. 18). Moreover, even in the micro sense of the word, context is by no means a "static container." Context is the social world of a person, a tightly interwoven human activity and a social practice.

So our area for study in this chapter is the virtual setting, looking both for ways to "bring in," or reveal, participants' locally situated microcontexts to the learning arena and ways to design for negotiating new and ongoing collective context(s).

Narrative Genres and Storytelling as a Form of Meaning Making

Once there was a man who was widely known for his research on thought, perception, memory, and language. In the 1960s he was an advisor on education to the U.S. president and is, to this day, a major writer and influence in education. His name is Jerome Bruner. In the 1980s Bruner became increasingly interested in the nature of narrative both as a mode of thought and as text. In his work he refers to narrative as being expressed in "the subjunctive mode," which kindles our imagination about *what is possible* in the world and not just *what is*. He tells us how the subjunctive helps us imagine how the world supports or prevents certain projects and how characters in a story make sense of the world and of themselves. This sense making involves emotions and intentions and draws upon the context as understood by the characters, both individually and collectively.

Elaborate distinctions have previously been made between narratives and stories, but we have found it more useful in our reflection to ignore these distinctions and use "first-person accounts of experience" (Riessman, 1993, p. 17) as a summary definition of both. In particular we want to frame narrative as a form of meaning making where human beings engage in symbolic activities to construct and make sense "not only of the world, but of themselves" (Bruner, 1990, p. 2). Additionally, we share Brown's description of stories as carrying the "smallest portable context" (Kahan, 2003) and Daniel's analysis (2002) of storytelling as a "protocol for exchanging experience."

Narrative has been referred to as a "homely" or familiar genre (Miller, 1984) recognizable across generations and cultures. For Brown, Collins, and Duguid (1989) knowledge of (past) contexts and their genres is a sort of situated cognition that makes the narrative transferable to other, comparable contexts. People often remember and order their memories or careers as a series of narrative chronicles or a series of stories marked by significant events. "Old-timers" often recount their stories so as to pass on cultural heritage or good practice. Accounts of leaders and personalities help maintain a sense of collective identity. Tales of incompetence warn against making mistakes. How-to accounts become part of the repertoire for solving ongoing problems. Canonical stories serve as summaries of collective experience, representing a standard of the larger community of practice. Narrative genre, like other familiar genres, something that "defines, organizes and finally communicates social reality" (Bhatia, 1993, p. 18).

Current social constructivist perspectives on learning emphasize the importance of communicating through negotiating meaning (cf. Rogoff, 1990; Greeno, 1989;

Resnick, 1991). Wenger (1998) highlights especially the importance of imagination in this process of negotiation: "Stories . . . can be appropriated easily because they allow us to enter the events, the characters, and their plights by calling upon our imagination" (p. 203). As a result of the way stories involve us in producing the meanings of those events, "they can be integrated into our identities and remembered as personal experience" (p. 204). Furthermore, "it is this ability to enable negotiability through imagination that makes stories, parables, and fables powerful communication devices" (p. 204). Stories thus become an important tool for imagining the identity of others and also an important element of negotiating our identity in practice. In other words, they form part of our learning trajectory.

It was these temporal notions of narrative and identity that led us to consider how past, present, and future contexts might be woven into the practices of online learning environments. We asked ourselves how narrative as shared meaning making could help in the process of revealing and negotiating these contexts. Also we asked ourselves if the notion of the subjunctive was something that helps bring in participants' worlds and the sense they make of those worlds to the online setting. We were challenged by Bruner's discussion in which he contrasts traditional academic genre and a narrative approach, which traffics in "human possibilities, rather than in settled certainties" (Bruner, 1986, p. 26). This resonates with the use of narrative and stories in qualitative research methods (e.g., Coffey & Atkinson, 1996) and it was this that challenged us to write an academic paper that might traffic in those human possibilities. And so it was that narrative began to emerge in our conversations as a design element for learning and practice in virtual settings.

Identity in Learning and Narrative

Much has been written about socially situated identities (Castells,1997; Foucault, 1980; Gee 2000-2001) with identity as a key component in Vygotskian derived sociocultural theories of learning. Learning as the creation of an identity is the basis of Lave and Wenger's theory of situated learning (1991), with the importance of identity creation further developed by Wenger in 1998. He states, "We accumulate skills and information, not in the abstract as ends in themselves, but in the service of an identity. It is in that formation of an identity that learning can become a source of meaningfulness and of personal and social energy" (p. 215). This idea of a trajectory of identity is taken up by Gee who proposes that learning "requires taking on a new identity and forming bridges from one's old identities to the new one" (Gee, 2003, p. 51).

Narrative and identity have long been partners in literature and more recently in sociocultural theories of narrative: "narrative's natural connections to personal identity are made apparent" (Gover, 1996). Gover also points out that identity is a socially constructed enterprise where "narrative language practices, in particular the pragmatic functions of storytelling, constitute the ongoing construction of personal identities in their social, cultural, and historical contexts."

Practice and Identity for Learning in Communities of Practice

The connection between present, past, and future in narrative also resonated with Wenger's notion of "identity in practice" (1998). Wenger affirms the temporal nature of identity and proposes that identity, a key concept in social constructivist views of learning, is being constantly renegotiated in our learning trajectory. As Bruner talks of narrative, so Wenger talks of identity: "As trajectories, our identities incorporate the past and the future in the very process of negotiating the present" (p. 155). What is more, Wenger refers in his notes to the linguist Charlotte Linde who "views identity as a narrative, a life story that is cast in terms of cultural systems of coherence and that is constantly and interactively reconstructed in the telling" (Linde, 1993, in Wenger, 1998, p. 282).

Wenger claims that an individual's identity and the social practice of the community are profoundly connected (Wenger, 1998), and in our chapter we take up Lave and Wenger's concept of community of practice as a way of viewing learning and identity as situated social practice. This means conceptualizing learning as participation in ongoing social practice, moving from legitimate peripheral participation to full participation in a given community of practice. Learning in this broad sense can be understood as "part of the subject's moving, changing participation across multiple contexts of their daily lives" (Lave 1997, p. 123). The connection between situated learning and narrative is notable in Lave and Wenger's argument that rests in no small measure on the narratives they provide, where five cases make sense of the learning in five different communities of practice (Lave and Wenger, 1991, pp. 59-87).

Thus the analytical dimensions we use for learning are those of community, domain, and practice as first put forward by Wenger (1998) and developed by Wenger, McDermott, and Snyder in 2002. The three fundamental and interrelated elements of a community of practice are a *domain* of knowledge defining a set of issues; a *community* of people who care about this domain; and the shared *practice*(s) that they are developing to be effective in their domain (Wenger et al., 2002, p. 27). All three elements are developed in parallel in a community of practice and it is the interaction between them that makes for a healthy community that fosters learning. In designing for context we need to look at narrative in all three elements: domain, community, and practice for learning *and* the interaction between them. In fact this interaction between these three elements helps *prevent* us from seeing context as something static when learning is taking place. We will use these three elements to organize our insights when we tell the moral of our story in the fifth section.

How Did We Proceed

In this section we briefly describe the three cases of virtual settings for learning and explore the role of stories. It is important to point out that none of these learning situations was designed deliberately to *test* storytelling as an element of design for virtual learning settings. On the contrary, they are an *ex post* analysis of the role that stories played in three diverse learning situations. Two of these settings were designed specifically according to community of practice principles, whereas the third evolved as a self-organized students' grassroots initiative, which shows the characteristics of a community of practice. In all three cases, which we refer to as our stories, storytelling is an integral (if tacit) part of the community's practice and is intertwined with the learning that takes place.

Essentially our stories are of three learning situations that we offer as sense-making snapshots that traffic in human possibilities rather than de facto design wisdom. Our accounts of the cases contain a number of subplots that we do not attempt to explore, highlighting only some of the features of each. Different and complementary aspects of the learning in these virtual settings have been treated elsewhere (for online workshop cf. Arnold & Smith, 2003; Smith & Coenders, 2002; Trayner, 2003; for online class cf. Putz & Arnold, 2001; for students' network cf. Arnold, 2003). We intended both to ground our analysis in our participation in the settings as designers, participants, and researchers and to suggest a

Table 1. Summary of the stories: Their characters, location, genre, and author information

The story	A student's network	An online class	An online workshop
Characters	Part-time students	Working professionals	Full time students
Location	Self-organized community within a special distance education degree program	University class offered for credit toward a degree	Training offer from CPsquare with no official "credit"
Narrative genres	*"How-to"* accounts of problems in practice and their solutions.	Canonical stories that help situate the domain.	Chronicles of experience and sharing of values in community.
Authors engaged as	Researcher	Guest expert	Researcher / facilitator

retrospective analysis of the archived written messages. Where personal stories of participants are used we obtained permission from the "story protagonists" for the data in this analysis.

Three Stories We Want to Share with You

Patricia's Story about the Students' Network

This is a story about a self-organized community. Members negotiate and reveal context of their practice with their "how-to" accounts of problems and their solutions.

I became interested in students' self-organizing collaborative practice as part of my research on computer-supported collaborative learning. It was here that I met "virtually" distance learning students who had set up an online community structure in 1995 using basic Internet tools. The students run and administer the technological infrastructure and the discussion space independently from the distance education provider. The network is an ongoing community that also organizes regional, informal face-to-face-meetings with a membership of between 500 and 800 students.

The primary community space is a listserv. A Web-based discussion forum, data repository, and individual Web pages supplement it. Access to resources and communication spaces is not restricted; Web sites are accessible to the public, as is a subscription to the listserv. In addition to students who are enrolled in the program, those who are considering starting the program subscribe to the listserv. Previously enrolled students stay registered to keep in touch—and researchers like me use the resources.

Students' stories within the network are *personal stories* about how they are going about their learning and how they organize themselves and their studies. Most of the how-to stories are "short stories" focusing on one aspect of their learning activities. Sometimes students also share long, detailed personal accounts reflecting their personal trajectory as a distance learner, particularly focusing on "crossroad" decisions once they have obtained their degree. How-to stories then move to "how I did it" stories. Students tell their personal story most of the time in response to a question: How do I plan the sequence of studying? How do I work through a manuscript? How do I negotiate with an employer about reducing workload? How do I prepare for an exam? How do I select a topic for a thesis? One question often triggers various individual and diverse stories from different students in response.

Example

Triggering Question: Dear FESA1-People,

As I just started my studies, I don't have much time to talk with other students. I would be interested to know what advice you have about working on the yel-

low scripts. Do you take notes separately as you study or just comment in the scripts themselves? How do you handle the control questions at the end of the script: do you answer them without looking things up in the script or do you regard it as helpful to go frequently back into the script while answering?

Answering Story: (4 hours later) Hi Michael,

FESA has produced a little booklet for methods of studying: Learning more easily— Learning methods for FESA-students. You can order it in T.

I always have a student paper block next to the script when I am studying (that is, if I find time to study, moaning!) In the script I emphasize important keywords with a text marker. Sometimes I add marginal comments like R for REMEMBER or ? for No idea. Read again LATER. I try to answer control questions at the end of the script just in my head. If I get the feeling that I just have a feeling of answering it, I try to write the answer down in precise words. At this point I clearly realize gaps in my actual understanding. . .

Retelling the Story from an Analytical Perspective

The students' how-to stories are prompted mostly by questions of other students. This way the "audience" is actively asking for storytelling as sharing personal experience in a narrative form. Sometimes students also share their particular how-to story without prompting. The practice of sharing these stories among one another is so deeply embedded in the community over time that a "triggering question" is not necessarily needed. "Applause" to a story by expressing appreciation for getting this sort of personal advice generates a generalized prompting. Students assume that their stories will be helpful for fellow students.

The genre of how-to stories is so established in this community that students elaborate their story only as much as needed both when asking for stories and when telling them. The general setting is mostly sketched out in a few comments and with some abbreviations. Both comments and abbreviations are meaningful to other students as they are enrolled in the same program and share a similar situation as a distance learner with a tight "time budget." The listserv conveys other small contextual cues such as an automatic date-time stamp. Students react to these "contextual markers" by indicating that they find comfort in seeing that somebody works the same odd hours as they do or even bothers to share their story with you at that time of the night!

In the story above there is a reference to a booklet by the distance education provider. In which ways does this how-to story complement the official booklets? Learning methods described by a fellow student with the same time constraints, in a personal story, seems to help situate and give credibility to the method. As in storytelling, in general there is room for identification and "subjunctivising": an imagined learning method can be the start of trying out a new one.

Where is the gain for the storyteller here? On one level the storytellers' actions become visible and provoke a reaction, even getting criticized. A participant's learning trajectory becomes visible in his or her transition from being someone who is primarily asking for other people's stories to becoming a person with stories to tell and share. Reflecting on this transition can reinforce a sense of achievement and an awareness of having learned. Moreover, sharing individual and organizational contexts in practice helps contextualize learning methods. Suggested methods are perceived quite differently from an official booklet, whose authors remain invisible. In each telling of the how-to stories we also see the ongoing (re)construction of identity, which we discussed earlier as being important for successful learning.

How do how-to stories help to reveal and negotiate context? How-to stories particularly bring in participants' present context, both at an individual level and for the community as such. The how-to genre easily extends to the community's practice as well: How do we want to design our community space? Which procedures do we adopt to collectively prepare for exams? The stories help make procedures, routines, and new tools visible and open for discussion.

We move now to John's story. It is a different one and is told in a different style. In it we see how stories can both reveal educational practice and address domain issues.

John's Story of an Online Class

This story is about an online class in which canonical stories help situate the knowledge domain.

In the fall of 2002, Peter Putz, a researcher in knowledge management, invited me to be a guest speaker in his online class about knowledge management at the University of Linz. Peter and I had first met in an online workshop on communities of practice and then again at a four-day dialog organized by alumni from the workshop in Setúbal, Portugal. So we already shared some online and face-to-face experiences, common interests in the intersection of information and communication technologies, and communities of practice perspective on learning. Following Peter's advice I log on to the online class Web site to familiarize myself with the software and previous class conversations to help me get a sense of the style, the people, and the class conversations. In reading the online discussions I find that Brigitte Jordan, an anthropologist based in California and Costa Rica with whom I once corresponded, has been a guest speaker on this course a few weeks before me.

What follows is my description and interpretation of this event after a careful rereading of the postings in one of the class discussions that took place during that time with Brigitte Jordan as guest speaker. The class was held on BSCW, a Web board platform, with several different conversations going on in distinct spaces.

In the event, two students lead a discussion of Lave and Wenger (1991) and have posted an analysis of the book. The students' leadership task involved posing 10 questions or discussion topics and then responding to other students' postings about those questions or topics. I see students conducting a valiant debate (in English as a second language) on the theory of "legitimate peripheral participation," a key concept in a theory of situated learning. In particular the students are discussing what constitutes "proof" of a theory and whether one theory invalidates another.

Although Brigitte Jordan only posted five times during this discussion, most of the conversation in that area of the class and all the stories recounted here revolve around her postings. I have chosen several stories recounted in the discussion of legitimate peripheral participation (LPP), each of which illustrates a different function of storytelling.

Vignette 1

During an abstract discussion about the scope of application of LPP, Brigitte Jordan tells an extended story about the emergence of the theory of legitimate peripheral participation. She describes how and when the theory of LPP evolved and goes on to explain why attention had previously focused on "the transfer problem" in theories of learning. She talks about the work of the individuals involved in the development of the theory were doing at that moment in time.

In telling this story Brigitte appears to be suggesting to the students that theory arises through the development of a specific situation and is adopted through use rather than through argumentation and debate. Implicitly she seems to be calling into question the students' assumptions about proof.

Vignette 2

Brigitte Jordan and Peter Putz make some connections between LPP and ideas about tacit and explicit knowledge as put forward by the writers Nonaka and Takeuchi (1995). In their exchange they establish and situate their connection with each other, with Nonaka and with the students. Their conversation also describes Peter's first contact with the concept of "situated learning," which came about through his professional relationship with Brigitte Jordan and their participation in conversations at the Xerox PARC laboratories where thought leaders such as Ikujiro Nonaka and Steve Denning have presented their work.

Such stories serve to highlight that not only are the content and the ideas important, but so is the "discourse community" where those stories are taking place. The implicit (subjunctivizing) message is that this social network not only includes thought leaders, course teachers, and guests, it also extends to the students in the class.

Vignette 3

Brigitte Jordan joins a discussion about learning in different work situations and a debate about whether learning can coexist with the profit motive in business. Her participation involves telling a story that took place during her fieldwork in the Yucatan. She refers to a midwife who taught her something profound in the distinction between "knowing about" and "knowing how" in her evading of the anthropologist's questions. Brigitte ends this story with a statement that refers to her experience in the Yucatan but that alludes to the "present moment" in the online class on knowledge management: "As I slowly took on various tasks, and not through instruction, I slowly became accepted [thus gaining access to situated knowledge]. The eye-opening lesson for me was that the learning was in the doing, not the talking (as all of my many years of education had tried to tell me)."

Brigitte passes on her message to the students through the moral of her own story.

These three vignettes represent canonical stories about situated learning. In this Internet-based "classroom" the stories all serve to situate the subject under discussion in a specific social and historical context. In addition, by augmenting the context around the concept of legitimate peripheral participation, its development, and its communication, the stories help situate the students in the conversation and dramatize how learning itself is more than a matter of absorbing information or logical debate. What is more, these stories help bring in past contexts of facilitators and other participants, as well as prepare students or participants for future contexts.

In the next story Beverly analyzes the way stories reveal personal values of storytellers in a process of negotiating context with fellow participants.

Beverly's Story about the International Café

This is a story about an international café where participants tell narrative chronicles of their experience. The stories reveal participants' values in the ongoing negotiation of a new collective context.

Following some of my own research I was invited last year to facilitate in "the international café." The location of the café was between two online workshops—both about communities of practice and both with similar design principles, including the use of Web crossing as the software platform. One of these workshops took place in English and the other in Dutch. The workshop that took place in English had participants from different countries, many of whom spoke English as their second language.

The idea of the café was to create a shared space between the Dutch and English workshops where people could explore ideas in a social setting related to language and culture. I worked with a co-facilitator to prepare some ideas for the café, and we got ready for the opening.

The first person to come into the café was Etienne Wenger, a leading writer about communities of practice and one of the organizers of the workshop. To our surprise and alarm he proposed that messages be posted in English, French, Spanish, and Dutch. He invited everyone to translate their own messages if possible (and other people's messages as well) in the hope that each posting would be presented in four languages, a challenge to the dominance of English. Not only would we *talk about* language in the café, but we would *do* language.

The café was open for two weeks, during which time 58 messages were posted, all of which were voluntary translated. This issue of translation kept messages fairly short. The informal nature of the café lent itself to brief narrative chronicles that either brought in someone else's story about dealing with different languages or that described significant personal experiences.

I look at two of these stories to see if and in what ways they brought in participants' context to the virtual setting and how they make sense of the new one. I offer some

Table 2. Summary of the stories - 1

The story	A reading of the story
Subject header: One traveller's perspectives	*This is going to be a story about trajectory. The perspective of "one traveller," avoiding claims of universality, gives a sense of humility. The "path perspective" is alluded to, suggesting that a person is transformed by their path (in this case by travel).*
Ironically,	*I am sufficiently confident to begin with a story that is in opposition to our political purpose here ...* *I have sufficient humility to be inspired by someone who*
an inspiring practice I recently heard about comes from a person who has decided to speak only one language: English.	*practises something quite different than what I might otherwise deem to be politically correct ...*
Some of you may know	*I assume I am talking to people who read a certain type of book ...*
Pico Iyer's writing, which has typically involved extensive travel to many parts of the world.	*This type of book represents middle-class aspirations for travel, where travel symbolises the challenging of preconceptions and a humble search for saving humanity from abstraction and complacent assumptions.*
Pico was born in India of parents who were from different parts of India. Their only common language was English. He lived in England and America in his youth, and for many years now has traveled incessantly, with the exception of a few months in Japan each year.	*I am aware of the post-modern condition where roots and identity are not always clear.* *I am also aware of the many of the more common excuses mono-lingual English speakers offer by way of an apology.*
He has made some attempts to learn other languages, but found that people craved the opportunity to speak English with him. He quickly learned that he had to become a much more skilled, deep and active listener in order to learn in a meaningful way.	*I am someone who knows about the writer and not just his writings ...* *I want to highlight the concepts of deep and active listening and meaningful learning.*
The reason I found this story strangely inspiring, is that it spoke to several rare commodities: respect for others' desires to choose the language in which they want to communicate; silence (time between thoughts; reflection); and humility.	*I relate to and inspired by the values I have just described as being represented by this writer.* *These are the values that I respect and aspire to.*

simple discourse analysis for reading what participants are *doing* in their stories, rather than what they are saying.

My reading of the context revealed by the author of the message takes place in the right column with the story, as it was originally posted in the café, in the left column (Table 2).

At this point it is interesting to contrast this with the information taken from the participant's formal biography, which tells us that "her interests include leadership, individual and organizational learning and transition, knowledge sharing and business intelligence." Although the biographical information presents us with some of the formal information we might like to know about the participant, it is through her brief story that she reveals some of her own grounds for negotiating meaning, interacting and creating an identity of participation in the international café and in the workshop.

We also see this process in a second story from the café (Table 3), which comes from someone whose biography describes her as "a document officer" and who is also "interested in improving accessibility to information by those who really need it." Not only does her story describe her experience, she uses it to echo some of the values of inspiration and humility for learning across languages and sends a message of

Table 3. Summary of the stories - 2

The story	A reading of the story
Subject header: **How do we judge people?**	*I am going to make a criticism in which I include myself as a protagonist. The question: How do you judge people would be an accusing one. Use of "we" puts me in with the accused. My position as accused is said with the confidence and humility of a woman from Nepal who speaks several languages.*
I used to work for the International Centre for Integrated Mountain Development…I spent 6 months as an editor in their publications department. (There were) several highly qualified staff from different countries and cultures.	*The context of my story is a reputable international and cosmopolitan organisation.*
I had to spend hours helping edit research papers and books written by Chinese, Nepali, Indian, European and American staff members.	*I am sufficiently qualified and multi-literate to work on research papers written by people from different countries. I have spent a lot of time doing this.*
Not always an easy task.	*I am alluding to an enormously complex and difficult practice. It requires persistence and patience.*
I realised that people often tend to judge people by their proficiency in using the English Language.	*The highly qualified staff from different countries that I spoke about earlier (and who were proficient in English) were unjustly critical about the content of work written by people whose first language was not English.* *I refer to both proficient and non-English speakers as "people" obscuring the differences between them and to the camp to which I belong.*
Something very easy to do when trying to decipher a document on landslides written by someone whose first language is Chinese.	*I am understanding of the people who were critical.* *I want to point out the significance of mountain research that comes from a Chinese perspective and made accessible to us in English.* *In a positive rather than critical spirit I leave my own position as "unfair critic" obscure.*
But as I struggled with the documents, I also realised how much those people know and that it was I who was ignorant not them. When the end result arrived from the printers, we always felt a sense of achievement at managing to help colleagues say what they knew in a way others would understand.	*A lot of work was, and is, needed to truly hear what someone is saying when they are communicating in a second language. But the end result was, and is, enlightening and humbling.* *The role of editing, which includes interpreting and struggling with meaning, is immensely satisfying. "People" involved in the writing and the editing were (and are) all colleagues. There is no implied hierarchy because of language differences.*
A true effort to work across language barriers."	*I believe in making connections between people of different languages. My history shows that I am committed to working towards that end.*

inclusion and respect for people (including those in this workshop) who may be struggling with language. By opening up her own context in this story, she is suggesting some ground rules for listening to people in the conversations to come.

In conclusion what we see in these stories told in the international café are those of participants weaving aspects of their context into a multilingual social situation in a way that their biographies or their opinions about any given topic might never be able to do. In these two stories the authors bring enough of their own contexts into the conversation to show that they are genuinely involved in opening dialogues across languages and cultures and are prepared to spend time listening, interpreting, and negotiating meaning. Through their stories they are co-constructing the café as a space for careful listening, humility, and learning.

What's the Moral of Our Research Story?

As we think about the power of narrative to support learning in online settings we are reminded of the Wenger's comment: "Learning cannot be designed . . . . Learning happens, design or no design" (1998, p. 225). All the same, our cases indicate that the elements of narrative, identity, and practice could help us in designing for context in a virtual learning setting by making it more visible and open to interpretation and reflection. Our cases show different genres of narrative work in different contexts; no one genre is privileged above all others. Rather, different genres have different objectives and are connected to different primary concerns or phases of a learning community's trajectory, whether in virtual settings or face-to-face.

We present these guidelines as a way of sharing some observations of what we have seen working, rather than prescriptions of what we believe would work for the reader. In particular, we hope that our stories have been subjunctive enough so that your imagination is filled with more possibilities than before. You might read the following comments with a narrative frame in the background: "We have seen such-and-such work well."

As we have tried to model in this chapter, a general rule of thumb is that a facilitator who models storytelling is more effective than one who tells others about the importance of storytelling. What is more, a facilitator who responds positively to stories often proves more effective in stimulating productive stories from participants than one who merely requests that others offer their stories. We propose that storytelling be viewed as a mindset rather than as an activity.

In addition, we propose that the following aspects of storytelling illustrate three important aspects of learning: (1) narratives help connect students or participants to the contexts of the communities and practices in which they aspire to participate; (2) they help create community around the domain and practices of the actual learning setting; and (3) they show how domain is always tethered to a community and to a practice. Again, we organize our thinking around the community, practice, and domain facets of Wenger's model of a community of practice.

Community

- A way of situating participants in their possible future context is telling stories about how participants in a learning event are connected, however peripherally, to an existing community. Stories can act as a kind of social scaffolding that connects newcomers to leaders in the field, with whom they are connected through their teacher or facilitator, and through each other. The stories act as bridges between the actual and possible future identities of participants in the learning setting and the communities to which they may aspire.

- Stories about the ways in which concepts and theories advance through conversations and events situated in particular historic and social contexts can show how personal and institutional contexts are linked, sometimes in a particularly potent fashion. Such stories challenge the notion that a "classroom" is a special location for transmitting decontextualized knowledge; storytelling is shown to be part of the practice of creating new knowledge.

- Stories, whether invited or welcomed, can help reveal the context around people and their actions. In particular, because these stories are recorded, one person's story represents a potential learning resource for another.

- Sharing stories is a way of informally negotiating meaning and creating an identity of participation in the group learning process.

Practice

- Stories that illustrate the practices that students seek to master, such as Jordan's stories of learning "in the field" (although far, far away and a long time ago), are especially important in suggesting the context from which relevant knowledge comes and in which it can be applied. Through understanding the context, people imagine possible locations for transferring and transforming practices rather than merely repeating the words that describe the practices.

- Providing opportunities to unpack the context around the stories that are offered in a learning situation is an opportunity to show how the negotiation of meaning can occur on different levels depending on the interests and intentions of people in the conversation. In particular, making explicit and negotiating different "readings" (or interpretations) of texts (or postings) helps foster individual and collective meaning-making.

- Building reflection on the processes of telling stories and on the narrative genre helps generate a meta-awareness of practice. It is also useful for participants to be able to identify genre moves such as "once upon a time there was a context" ("statement of the problem") or "and the moral of the story is ..." ("conclusions and recommendations").

Domain

- Narratives and warning stories about how "elders" came to learn what they know can be encouraged, for example by inviting "elders" or "guest speakers" into the virtual setting.

- In order to unpack and negotiate local theories of cause and effect and encourage stories that question fundamental assumptions (such as the story about the monolingual Indian travel writer), it is important to allow and allocate enough time for reflection about the stories.

- Canonical stories like case studies bring particular attention to domain issues and are especially linked to future contexts of participants. How-to stories focus rather on participants' present, practical contexts. In the case of the student network, they shift the primary domain of the students from their study domain, such as business informatics, to the domain of "successful distance learning." How-to stories in general can help to situate domain in practice and community.

To extend and refine these guidelines, further research is clearly necessary. In a further step we would like to explore the dynamics of narrative genre, context, and virtual settings with finer granularity. We think it looks promising to explore if and how different technologies in virtual learning settings encourage storytelling. We would also like to explore the multimodal aspects of narrative and identity. As course designers and as designers of our own learning, what are the different modes through which we can shape our stories and actions and through which our stories and actions are shaped?

The research story that we have presented in this chapter sets the ground for these follow-up projects. Extending the scope of investigation by looking at a broader variety of cases as well as exploiting single stories more fully seems to be a viable road to gain further insights and to inform our design practice.

Acknowledgments

We would like to thank Peter Putz for his thoughtful contributions to this chapter. Our thanks also go to colleagues of Ian Glasweg.

Endnote

1   FESA is the name of the organization that provides the distance education program the students are enrolled in. The program offers academic degrees in business administration and business informatics. The name is changed here to make it anonymous.

References

Arnold, P. (2003). *Kooperatives Lernen im Internet. Qualitative Analyse einer Community of Practice im Fernstudium.* Münster: Waxmann.

Arnold, P., & Smith, J. D. (2003). Adding connectivity and losing context with ICT: Contrasting learning situations from a community of practice perspective. In M. Huysman, E. Wenger, & V. Wulf (Eds.), *Communities and technologies. Proceedings of the First International Conference on Communities and Technologies; C&T 2003* (pp. 465-484). Dordrecht: Kluwer Academic.

Bhatia, V.K. (1993). *Analysing genre: Language use in professional settings.* Cambridge: Cambridge University Press.

Brown, J. S., Collins, A., & Duguid, P. (1989). Situated learning and the culture of learning. *Education Researcher, 18*(1), 32-42.

Bruner, J. (1986). *Actual minds, possible worlds.* Harvard: Harvard University Press.

Bruner, J. (1990). *Acts of meaning.* Harvard: Harvard University Press.

Castells, M. (1997). *The power of identity.* MA: Blackwell.

Chaiklin, S., & Lave, J. (1993). *Understanding practice. Perspectives on activity and context.* Cambridge: Cambridge University Press.

Coffey, A., & Atkinson, P. (1996). *Making sense of qualitative data: Complementary research strategies.* Thousand Oaks, CA: Sage.

Daniel, B. (2002). *Building social capital in virtual learning communities.* Research paper at the University of Saskatchewan, Canada (Professional and Theoretical Issues in Educational Technology). Retrieved September 15, 2003, from http://www.usask.ca/education/coursework/802papers/daniel/ index.htm

Foucault, M. (1980). Power/knowledge: Selected interviews and other writings 1972-1977. In C. Gordon, L. Marshall, J. Meplam, K. Soper, & Brighton (Eds.), Sussex: Harvester Press.

Gee, J. P. (2000-2001). Identity as an analytic lens for research in education. *Review of Research in Education, 25,* 99-125.

Gee, J. P. (2003). *What video games have to teach us about learning and literacy.* New York: Palgrave Macmillan.

Gover, M. (1996, October 18-20). *The narrative emergence of identity*. Paper presented at the Fifth International Conference on Narrative, Lexington, KY. Retrieved December 16, 2003, from, http://www.msu.edu/user/govermar/narrate.htm

Greeno, J. (1989). Situations, mental models, and generative knowledge. In D. Klahr & K. Kotovsky (Eds.), *Complex information processing. The impact of Heribert A. Simon* (pp. 285-318). Hillsdale, NY: Erlbaum.

Johns, A. M. (1997). *Text, role and context: Developing academic literacies.* Cambridge: Cambridge University Press

Kahan, S. (2003, February 10). *John Seely Brown interviewed by Seth Kahan.* S. Denning (Ed.). Retrieved June 4, 2004, from http://www.sethkahan.com/Resources_0JohnSeelyBrown.html

Laurel, B., Oren, T., & Don, A. (1992). Media integration and interface-agents. In M. Blattner & R.G. Dannenberg (Eds.), *Multimedia interface design* (pp. 53-64). New York: Addison-Wesley.

Laurillard, D. (1998). Multimedia and the learner's experience of narrative. *Computers & Education, 31,* 229-242.

Lave, J. (1996). The practice of learning. In S. Chaiklin & J. Lave (Eds.), *Understanding practice: Perspectives on activity and context* (pp. 3-32). Cambridge: Cambridge University Press.

Lave, J. (1997). On learning. *Forum kritische Psychologie, 38,* 120-135.

Lave, J., & Wenger, E. (1991). *Situated learning. Legitimate peripheral participation.* Cambridge: Cambridge University Press.

Miller, C. (1984). Genre as social action. *Quarterly Review of Speech, 70,* 151-167.

Neal, L. (2001). Storytelling at a distance. *E-Learn-Magazine*. Retrieved December 16, 2003, from http://elearnmag.org/subpage/sub_page.cfm?section=7&list_item=1&page=1

Nonaka, I., & Takeuchi, H. (1995). *The knowledge-creating company: How japanese companies create the dynamics of innovation.* New York: Oxford University Press.

Putz, P., & Arnold, P. (2001). Communities of practice: Guidelines for the design of online seminars in higher education. *Education, Communication & Information, 1*(2), 181-195.

Resnick, L. (1991). Shared cognition. Thinking as a social practice. In L. Resnick, J. Levine, & S. Teasley (Eds.), *Perspectives on socially shared cognition* (pp. 1-20). Washington, DC: American Psychological Association.

Riessman, C. (1993). *Narrative analysis.* Newbury Park: Sage.

Rogoff, B. (1990). *Apprenticeship in thinking. Cognitive development in social context.* New York: Oxford University Press.

Smith, J. D., & Coenders, M. (2002, October 15-19). E-feedback to reflect legitimate peripheral participation: Towards a redefinition of feedback in online learning environments. *E-Learn 2002 Conference Proceedings*, Montreal, Canada.

Trayner, B. (2003). The international café: A respectful critique. In M. Huysman, E. Wenger, & V. Wulf (Eds.), Communities and technologies. *Proceedings of the First International Conference on Communities and Technologies; C&T 2003* (pp. 407-425). Dordrecht: Kluwer Academic.

Vygotsky, L. S. (1987). *Thought and language* (A. Kouzulin, Ed.). MA: MIT Press.

Weller, M. (2000). The use of narrative to provide a cohesive structure for a Web based computing course. *Journal of Interactive Media in Education, 2000*(1). Retrieved December 16, 2003, from http://www-jime.open.ac.uk/00/1/

Wenger, E. (1998). *Communities of practice. Learning, meaning, and identity.* Cambridge: Cambridge University Press.

Wenger, E., McDermott, R., & Snyder, W. (2002). *Cultivating communities of practice.* Boston: Harvard Business School Press.

Chapter XII

The Voice of the Online Learner

Kathy L. Milhauser, Pepperdine University, United States

Abstract

This chapter examines the role of context in online settings from the perspective of the online learner. The chapter attempts to situate the reader within the context of the online environment studied, using biographical stories of four learners who participated in a cohort graduate program that was held primarily online. The reader will experience the process that all the learners went through as they grappled with their current beliefs, were challenged and stretched technically as well as intellectually, and learned to rely on the context of their shared experience, as well as their local communities, for support and encouragement. The reader will also recognize the transformation these individuals experienced as they let go of some of the pieces of their previous identities in a search for a preferred future. The author suggests that the design of the online program studied was critical to the transformative learning experienced by the individuals studied and hopes to encourage individuals involved in the design of similar programs and environments to think carefully about the powerful potential of socially constructivist design.

Introduction

At the heart of constructivism lies the belief that "meaning is imposed on the world by us, rather than existing in the world independently of us" (Duffy & Jonassen, 1992, p. 3). Embedded in this belief is the realization that the context for learning exists within learners and is not external to them. The power lies in the cumulative effect of the learner's past and present and personal and professional experiences. When provoked by compelling questions and nurtured within a social construct of diverse minds searching for the answers to similar questions, learners can experience deeply transformative learning.

If we can accept that learners are the best designers of their own instruction, then we can design learning environments with instructional integrity at the highest level and facilitate the learning process as they work to build their own meaning collaboratively within that structure.

This type of situated learning may be more readily facilitated within the online environment. When the virtual learning environment is socially constructed with embedded interdependence between learners, connections can be quickly and deeply formed to support, accelerate, and enrich the experiences for all involved—learners and instructors alike.

Literature Review

Dewey (1938) urged us to embed learning in life and not separate it within classroom walls that have no context for the learner. He believed that learning was an essential lifelong process and challenged the belief that once a child had completed learning, he could go on to live a well-prepared adult life.

Bruner reached into the history of cultural psychology as he developed the externalization tenet—a foundation for what we now refer to as *constructionism* (Papert 1993). He refers to the work of Meyerson (1948), a French cultural psychologist who believed that the primary function of cultures was to produce "oeuvres" or "works." Bruner describes minor works produced by small groupings of people that serve to create a sense of "group solidarity" (Bruner, 1996, p. 22).

Greatly influenced by Piaget's (1976) work, Papert (1993) went on to define constructionism by asserting that the "construction that takes place in the head (constructivism) often happens especially felicitously when it is supported by a more public sort in the world" (Papert, 1993, p. 142).

Holmes, Tangey, Fitzgibbon, Savage, and Mehan (2001) wrote of a communal approach to constructivism in which students not only construct their own knowledge as a result of interacting with their environment, but are also actively engaged in the process of constructing knowledge for their learning community (Holmes et al., 2001). Leask and Younie (2001) contrast the work of Vygotsky on social constructivism with the work of Holmes et al. on communal constructivism, concluding that technology provides a potential learning environment that can be especially facilitative of communal constructivist learning.

Thorpe's work on learner support (2002) and the writings of Duffy and Jonassen (1992) and Palloff and Pratt (2003) provide further support for strategically designing online learning environments that support the theories of social constructivism and constructionism and also expand on the role of context in the virtual environment.

Method of Development

This chapter includes a summary of the experiences of several graduates of an online program. These are all adult learners who completed their master's degree in education at an accredited university on the West Coast of the United States via an 85% online delivered program over a period of 13 months. These learners worked in a cohort of 24 students. They were involved in a series of collaborative experiences that required them to reach deeply into their belief systems, their past experiences, and their present personal and professional lives, as well as their own vision of their future, in order to develop meaning as individuals and as a group.

Four short biographical stories that grew out of these learner interviews form the body of this chapter. The reader will experience the process all the learners went through as they grappled with their current beliefs, were challenged and stretched technically as well as intellectually, and learned to rely on the context of their shared experience, as well as their local communities, for support and encouragement. The reader will also recognize the transformation these individuals experienced as they let go of some of the pieces of their previous identities in search for a preferred future. Lastly, the reader will be reintroduced to these learners as they have emerged from the program and have gone forward to provide leadership in the many communities in which they interact.

The chapter will conclude with a recap of the key elements that are essential to transformative online learning environments: social constructivism, metacognition, community development, and learner support, with comments on the design of the learning environment that supports these elements from the designers of the online program studied.

Stories from an Online Learning Community

Story can transport us not only to experiences we have not had, but to insights that cannot be expressed in conventional discourse.

(Carter, 1993, p. 6)

A.—Getting Ready for the Long Haul (Horton & Kohl, 2001)

A. is a corporate training and development specialist and the owner of his own video production company, with clients in the corporate, academic, and public broadcasting industries. He came to online learning with fresh experiences as a parent and professional with the U.S. education system, and some of the challenges and struggles inherent in traditional teaching methods. He had the sense that things could have been easier for his kids in school if he had just had a better understanding of how learning occurs and a firmer grasp of the many factors that affect learner success. He entered the online graduate program with the desire to broaden his knowledge in order to validate some of his assumptions.

I had a pretty good feel for the problems, but had no clear way of expressing solutions. (A., personal interview, November 11, 2003)

A. was pleasantly surprised early on to discover that the online program he had selected was more about communication and learning than it was about technology tools. He reports a quick grasp of the philosophy and strategy of using technology as a medium for learning, and not as an outcome.

Open to having his assumptions challenged, A. discovered that community building could be enabled, and even enhanced, via technology. He was excited to begin experiencing that technology could have an "invigorating community building capacity" (A., 2003).

Unlike many of his classmates, A. tended to play the field and not to become deeply identified with any small group within the learning community. He wanted to experience the networking power of learning online, and he extended this throughout the year to other online and face-to-face communities in which he was involved. He used his online graduate cohort as a laboratory of sorts—coming back for support and validation, and consistently applying his learning to the many other community contexts in his life.

A. reports a dramatic increase in confidence as a result of his experience learning and collaborating online:

> *I'm getting to know more PhDs and the like now that I'm in "the club." I knew the language but I was not at all confident that I could back up my assumptions. So I developed more confidence to enter and engage . . . knowing that I could argue a bit more deeply. (A., 2003)*

A. entered the online program very ready to test his theories and apply new thinking to a fresh direction in his life. He believes that his online learning experience gave him the context and an academic framework for his ideas. He credits the reading, his professors, and the broad perspectives gained by working online with individuals from a variety of professional and academic perspectives to the development of his new vision. He now plans to combine teaching and learning in his video production workplace in a way that "teachers and learners, young and old alike, can work together to formulate solutions" (A., 2003).

An accredited U.S. university is currently considering A.'s proposal to use his video production facility as a learning laboratory for students. If approved and funded, the 5500square foot facility, complete with state-of-art video production equipment, will be converted into a teaching and learning laboratory aimed at servicing the needs of various disciplines within the University. A. hopes to redefine the mission of his business to align with his life goal of promoting community-based learning.

What part did the online learning program play in A.'s journey? He now believes that online community may be the best way to form a legitimate grassroots movement. "How about the net as the pot-bellied stove of the new millennium?" (A., 2003). He knows his vision will not be realized overnight. He knows that community development and social reform efforts take time and he is ready for the long haul.

S.—Bridging Communities

S. manages the education efforts of a Los Angeles museum. She had been at the museum for seven years when she entered the online graduate program. She had previously earned a master's in museum education in 1994, which was primarily an elementary education degree with a concentration in museum studies.

S. believes that her ability to apply what she was learning to the context of her professional experience was a key element in her learning. Contrasting her recent learning experience to her earlier graduate studies, S. reports that her experience this time was completely different. She attributes this to the confidence of a working professional with a context for learning application.

S. had the same expectations as her classmates when entering the online learning program. She expected to learn all about technology and emerge with a mastery of hardware and software that she could apply to make her more marketable.

> *I got a different degree than I thought, but am so much happier with the one we ended up with. It's kind of like the "teach them how to fish" thing. They gave us the tools and now we know where to look and have a starting point. (S., personal interview, November 10, 2003)*

S. encountered a steep technology learning curve and found herself turning to her learning community online for assistance. At first, she was embarrassed at her struggles. Still believing that the intent was to master a full suite of technologies, it became apparent to S. and her classmates that they would have to form alliances and rely on one another in order to be successful. Only much later did S. realize that this was by design, and that the real learning was about the power of collaboration and community, not about technical prowess.

> *I started begging for help doing that first Microworlds project, but didn't internalize it until doing my Agentsheets project (the next Term)." (S., 2003)*

When she did begin to internalize this dynamic, she found she could easily transfer it to her interaction with other online communities.

> *After I went to Museums on the Web in March, I sent an e-mail to a bunch of people whose presentations I watched, and a bunch of them got back to me with really thoughtful answers and suggestions and encouragement . . . and I realized how much I like helping others, so why shouldn't they derive satisfaction as well. (S., 2003)*

Then she took the next step. She had a community of teachers in her online cohort and now access to a community of museum professionals online as well. Why not bring them together?

> *I suddenly had a group of people at my fingertips who knew exactly what I was going through and what I was trying to achieve. (S., 2003)*

S. credits her success to the ability to apply concepts she learned within her online cohort to the context of her professional life. She found the cohort to be very supportive, with an unwavering sense of belief in one another. Still, she discovered the real power of her learning when she was able to turn and apply it within her own field. Bringing the two together is now a dream of hers.

Museum people working with K-12 teachers via the web!" (S., 2003)

S. can now see how the design of the program supported her process. The technical challenges in the beginning of the program caused her to quickly bond with and rely upon her peers. As she grew in confidence, she discovered that she was able to reciprocate by sharing her own skills, experiences, and insights with the community inside the cohort, and eventually outside in her work environment. She now reflects on the increase in her self-confidence since completing her online graduate program. Like A., she now feels competent to speak up at a higher level, both in her workplace and in her professional community. S. recounts a conversation she had recently at an annual science and technology conference. She says that a year ago she would not have even had the courage to approach this person because of his experience and credibility in the field, but now she feels confident to engage, and even argue, at a much higher level.

I guess what I am trying to say is that (the University) churned out another person agitating for change, not content with the current system. A lot of my ideas from over the years gelled. No, I did not think as clearly a year ago. Now I have the language and the resources. (S., 2003)

As a graduate of the online graduate program, S. has committed to staying within the field of science. She believes her next step needs to be developing a niche for herself in the intersection between science and educational technology. She now feels comfortable exploring with software and hardware tools, and she hopes to learn about Geographic Information Systems (GIS) and how to apply handhelds in educational settings. She is ready to branch out of the museum now and believes she has a lot more to offer as a "bridge between teachers and authentic science" (S., 2003).

T.—Transformative Learning Through Struggle

When T. joined the online learning community, she knew she would have an uphill climb when it came to technology. She wanted a program with a foundation in constructivist theory, and she already had some experience with the practical application of constructionism through working with children as a preschool teacher. She had a friend who had introduced her to Seymour Papert, whose work with children had greatly influenced her. Education had always been her love, and she could see how technology could support the work that she wanted to do. The program that she selected seemed to be a good fit for the direction she hoped to take in her future career.

T. had made the decision to make a career change, and gaining her master's degree was a big step along that path. She reports having rebelled against the idea of getting a master's degree since finishing her undergraduate degree 20 years earlier.

Therefore, she entered the program feeling very sober about the challenges that lie ahead for her.

> *I knew that technology was something that I needed to learn a lot about and quickly, just to be able to function in the online format. (T., personal interview, November 22, 2003)*

In the beginning the program was very difficult for T. She had to come to terms with what it would take for her to be successful. The early projects required her to do things such as create a Web page, gain access to synchronous and asynchronous communication tools, and learn a programming language to the level that would allow her to develop an interactive tool. She had the sinking feeling that everyone in the program knew how to do these things except for her.

> *We had not established our community yet so I did not know where to turn. The first month or two was horrible, crying, not knowing if I could make it. (T., 2003)*

At one point in the first few weeks, T. reached a decision point. She considered dropping out of the program, as she could not see how she could do this alone. Instead, she mustered her courage, assessed her resources, and found help in her own local community.

T. believes that this time of difficulty, when she faced the decision about whether or not to quit and then eventually reached out and found help, was defining for her. She believes that her resourcefulness and persistence were the essential qualities that allowed her to continue, and eventually excel, in the online program.

> *Giving up old paradigms and ways of being is not a smooth ride at all, but it is also the most worthwhile journey. (T., 2003)*

After overcoming the technology hurdles, T. began to truly thrive as an online learner. She loved the learning theory she was studying and applying in her daily work at the preschool. She developed deep bonds with other learners, as she shared her struggles and then her successes. She began to hold weekly Lego Robotics club meetings for a group of local children, including her son, and this became the context for the application of her action research. Everyone in the online cohort looked forward to her weekly reports, complete with digital pictures, audio files of the children's voices, and videos of their budding robotics projects. It was hard to believe that this was the same person who had been so intimidated by technology just a few short weeks earlier.

After graduating from the program, T. found the confidence to take the next step on the career path she had envisioned. A few weeks after graduating, she accepted a position as the technology specialist for a children's school in the southeastern United

States. Now she works with over 300 children in grades K-6 as they come through the computer lab each week. She runs the lab, plans all of the activities and technology acquisitions, and helps teachers integrate technology into their curriculum.

T. says she has developed a new appreciation for the hard work that is involved in deep learning. She has rediscovered the importance of understanding the learning style of her students, as well as herself. And she insists she could not have done it without the community (in her online cohort and locally) that supported her and gave her confidence while she was struggling.

R.—Learning Through Failure

R. is a high school teacher who has been teaching a diverse group of high school students for the past seven years. She also teaches at the community college level, primarily in the areas of business computing, Web design, and multimedia tools. Prior to becoming a teacher, she earned a degree in accounting and worked as an auditor.

R. entered the online program with the intention of learning some new technologies to use in her classroom and to add to her technology mastery. She felt good about her skills as a teacher. She had earned her teaching credential and had extensive training in education theory and application. She was not looking for new learning theory or teaching practices when she began the program.

R. reflected on one of the early projects she did with her online cohort. The goal of the project was to create an interactive program that simulated a living thing. There were many technologies to choose from, and the group members were challenged to support and teach one another as they worked through the process. R. remembers the struggle to learn and the breakthrough in her perspective on learner context as a result:

> I remember taking the first class . . . where we created our virtual pet. The light began to come on . . . I get excited when I think about it . . . I was struggling and trying to figure Flash out and becoming more and more frustrated. I decided to change the project to be my dog and I was excited about creating it! I learned that choice is important. Now I offer more choice to my students. (R, personal interview, November 10, 2003)

R. compares her experience to that of her students, who typically want her to "tell them every single detail and when I don't they get very nervous" (R., 2003). She came to realize the power of constructive learning as she worked through the process of de- and then re-constructing what she believes about learning. After this experience, R. reflected on her change in approach. She now coaches her students to understand the value of reflection to the learning process.

Throughout the year, R. continued to learn more about her own self than about new technologies. She remembers being very annoyed at first when the instructors would not tell her exactly what they wanted her to do. Eventually, she found the technology immersion and carefully constructed challenges to be effective in creating an environment of collaboration with her fellow classmates. This not only began to bond the group more closely, but also provided increased reflective opportunities for her.

R. had never enjoyed group projects, preferring throughout her career to work alone. The social constructivist nature of the projects in the online program placed her in a position where she had to support and rely on other learners for the first time, in an intense process of interdependence. For the first time, she was faced with the reason why group work had always been so uncomfortable:

> *What I learned about myself somewhere during the year is that I am actually afraid of failure. It's a lot safer for me to learn privately. Then I can take as long as I need to learn something. This has helped me tremendously in the classroom. I spend a lot of time now helping the kids to feel like the environment is safe. (R., 2003)*

She discovered for the first time that she could learn more by being part of a community than by working alone. She remembers rushing to share discoveries with her online learning group, and finding that others could see things in her work that she could not always see. The depth of the discussions and projects that her learning group had been immersed in online created an environment where they could honestly question one another and challenge one another's viewpoints. R. also believes that the technical challenges early in the program helped the group to form a bond as they struggled to learn together.

R. now feels that she has been given a whole new toolbox full of tools that she can implement in order to increase student learning. She has redefined failure for herself as well as her students, now believing that failure and reflection are acceptable and essential components of the learning process. She uses discussion forums and reflective journaling with her students to discuss their problems and help one another. She now feels that she can help her students see that learning is a natural process that they are driving, rather than one that is imposed on them.

> *I thought that I knew all of the strategies—it was like an awakening! (R., 2003)*

Now a graduate of the program, R. feels that she has learned something that needs to be communicated. In addition to her teaching role, R. now participates at the district level as a facilitator for new business teachers, and in her school's leadership committee. She also mentors new teachers through the Beginning

Teacher Support and Assessment (BTSA) and Pre-Intern Coach programs. She wants to help new teachers explore alternatives to the behaviorist techniques that she learned as she was starting out. She believes that the experience she had as an online learner gave her not only a new way to look at learning, but also the confidence and the context to take this learning forward and apply it in many areas of her life.

Key Design Elements in Transformative Online Learning

Social Constructivism

The initial gathering of the online cohort consisted of a one-week class meeting. The learners gathered from around the world to meet one another for the first time, and they were led through a week of constructivist exercises intended to set the tone for the year to follow.

Without exception, the learners interviewed reported that they expected to come to that first meeting and learn about technologies. They expected a well-designed week of technology training that would prepare them for the year to come. Also without exception, they discovered quickly that this was not the plan.

> *It seemed very unorganized. I wondered what I had gotten myself into. (R., 2003)*

Although there was an overarching goal of technology introduction that framed the week, the learners found that instead of being led from subject to subject, they were faced with significant problems to solve that required them to use all of the resources available in their small groups to be successful. Training in technologies was a very small part of the week, and yet the learners emerged with a sharper awareness of the tools and resources available, as well as a good sense of the strengths and needs within their cohort.

The program designers confirm that the initial weeklong meeting, and ensuing technology projects that followed directly after, were meant to be "a bit of a shock" (Dr. S. Talley, personal interview, November 22, 2003). They find that this helps bond the online learners quickly by placing them in the position of becoming quickly interdependent. The program then transitions into a period of deep theory-based learning, where constructivism, social learning, metacognition, and the power of community collaboration are reinforced through reading and discussion.

Dr. Talley reports that those who initially experience feelings of failure and struggle often get the most value from the experience when they learn to depend on their co-learners. She disagrees with the typical profile of a successful online learner as someone who must be self-motivated in order to succeed in distance learning, believing that the community can provide momentum and sustenance to learners. This community development can then produce an environment where people want to come together, developing a commitment toward one another that keeps them going as a group even when their individual self-motivation is challenged.

In addition to the constructivist experiences, there is also an element of constructionism and a healthy dose of reflective thinking in the online program studied. One project consisted of picking something that the student wanted to learn how to do, and then working through a reflective learning process. One learner described making the connection between learning and creating when she realized she had become so focused on what she wanted to create that she stopped thinking of it as a learning project. She reframed the objective of the experience, focusing on the creation of a meaningful artifact within the context of her personal life. She reported a boost of creative energy and accelerated learning after this reframing.

Metacognition

Bransford defines metacognition as "the ability to monitor one's current level of understanding and decide when it is not adequate" and transfer as "the ability to extend what has been learned in one context to new contexts" (Bransford, Brown, & Cocking, 2000, pp. 47, 51). He asserts that overcontextualization of knowledge can actually reduce transfer and that arranging contrasts can be helpful to aid the learner in viewing information and experiences from a variety of perspectives. When the learners are focused on their processes, they can apply a variety of contexts to what they are learning in a way that transfer of learning is better enabled. Throughout the online program, the learners reported breakthroughs in their thinking when they challenged their previous belief systems, and they turned to their local context to contrast and compare what they were learning with what they were living.

Langer's (1997) work on mindfulness is also significant to the development of context. As the cohort moved through their learning process, they repeatedly experienced the power of being mindful of what was going on within the many contexts of their lives. They moved away from their previous orientation toward outcomes and developed an appreciation for what they commonly referred to as the process. The process of learning became one of primary importance. And through self-reflective journaling and group blogging they became reflective practitioners, learning, discussing, reflecting privately and collectively, and then applying changes to their local environment in order to test new beliefs.

The program was supported by a context of action research (McNiff, Lomax, & Whitehead, 1996), culminating in a project that demonstrated learner success in working through a series of cycles to apply change, research the affect of this change, reflect, and then adjust their practice. The designers of the program assert that the use of action research is an intentional substitution for the traditional master's thesis, and is intended to ground the learning within the student's local context in a way that they not only learn, but also begin to affect change in their environment as they learn.

Community Development

It was extremely explicit in the facilitation of the online program that learners were intended to learn about communities of practice (Wenger, McDermott, & Snyder, 2002) by becoming a community of practice themselves. The program designers report that students coming from traditional education backgrounds typically have belief systems that must be challenged early on, and that unlearning is sometimes a necessary part of the process. They report that the program intentionally avoids excessive structure, but instead is carefully designed to encourage the participants to learn socially. The learners are encouraged to turn to their peers when they struggle—and typically this happens very early on. The group begins to form as they work through the process of identifying individual member strengths and areas for development, and continues as the group strives to achieve mastery of the program content.

As the group dives deeply into the application of learning theory, researching innovative approaches to the integration of technology, they begin to develop the sense that their new community is on the edge of breakthrough thinking. The program designers report that this typically has the effect of creating even deeper bonds as the participants turn outward to their local context to test and apply their learning, and back inward to their online community to collaborate, compare, and provide support for one another.

Learner Support

Lave and Wenger (1991) speak of learning environments where there is "very little observable teaching; the more basic phenomenon is learning" (p. 92). Wenger went on to explore the phenomena of community development. His work toward cultivating communities of practice (Wenger et al., 2002) is a central theme to the development of online learning theory as a community phenomenon. These works describe a community of learners with engagement in and reflection on practice as the central theme, and where community members achieve a state of shared participation.

Wenger et al. (2002) teach that community spaces can be designed to facilitate this development. He encourages development of private, as well as public, spaces to allow for the natural emergence of peripheral participants and intimate, local groupings within the larger community.

In their recently published book, *The Virtual Student,* Palloff and Pratt (2003) refer to an educational process of self-directed learning called *heutagogy* (Hase & Kenyon, 2000). With heutagogy, the focus of the learning is not only on the adult, but is actually constructed by the adult learner. As the adult applies what he is learning to his own personal context, he finds his understanding enhanced by situations within which he constructs meaning.

The concept of adult learners constructing learning as a community has significant implications to the design of the support structures created for online learning. Building on the work of Keegan (1996) and Tait (1995), Thorpe defines *learner support* as "all those elements capable of responding to a known learner or group of learners, before, during and after the learning process" (Thorpe, 2002). This becomes troublesome when applied to constructivist design, as the learner or group of learners cannot always be known and as a matter of fact may change as the transformative learning process occurs. Thorpe emphasizes the role of the online tutor as key to success in constructivist online learning, noting that the profile of successful online facilitators will continue to change as they adapt their strategies to address the needs of the changing learner.

The experiences of the online learners studied for this chapter indicates that the role of the peer is equally essential. Vygotsky believed that learning consists of movement through a zone of proximal development defined by the learner's current knowledge, potential for development, and access to peer support (Wink & Putney, 2002). Within the online cohort, peer-based learning support was a critical and defining element of learner success. The formal tutors or instructors were present but intentionally maintained transparency in order to encourage the learning cohort to provide this peer support. Not only did all members of the cohort find their strengths and learn to share their own skills, but they also learned to be vulnerable and to ask each other for help. This provided a sustainable environment for the group during their months of collaborative learning, but even more significantly it created an environment where success was completely dependent on the ability of the cohort to become self-supporting. It was a powerful, socially constructivist experience that could not have been taught through an instructionist method.

The online learners reported the use of a variety of tools that they came to rely on to support their self-constructed environment. Synchronous chat tools became central to their support structure. The "back channel" became a well-worn term for the chat sessions in the background during times of high stress.

One learner compared the sound of her computer alert as peers logged on and off (door opening and closing) to the sound of a physical door in the classroom of her imagination.

Additionally, the learners interacted in a set of asynchronous newsgroups, where discussions regarding the content of the courses were held in a 24x7x365 flow of group consciousness.

The program designers confirm that the technology used to support the learning community was chosen with an emphasis on collective distributed dialogue, rather than one-to-many instruction. They agree that although many online programs allow for dialogue, it is at most an add-on, and state that with this online program, dialogue between learners and instructors is central to the design.

Simply stated, this group of distance learners did not feel isolated though they were geographically dispersed over thousands of miles. And they did not have the experience of being in a space that was constructed for them so much as in a place constructed by them.

Conclusions

The online learners experienced the sense that they had been set adrift without a tangible, physical environment within which to find context. There was no well-structured course management system within which to find comfort. They had to become very resourceful and very reliant upon one another's strengths in order to be successful. Although almost all experienced frustration, especially early in this process, they eventually reported to have developed not only a deep grasp of the content within the program, but also a variety of new perspectives on their own needs as learners, teachers, community leaders, and social beings.

This leads me to conclude that the key to creating online learning environments is to apply less, and not more, structure in the technology environment. The curriculum designers and online facilitators of the future will need to be adept at creating frameworks and scaffolding for learners without overly architecting the environment in a way that inhibits the group process. They will need to become coaches, providing guidance and shepherding for learners involved in their personal discovery process. They will need to become comfortable in the absence of a well-defined plan and learn to trust that the community of learners will construct for themselves that which is not constructed for them.

Only then can we offer online learning environments that offer more than convenience, knowledge transfer, and application for their learners, but actually set in place a process of lifelong learning and potential for personal and cultural transformation. And only then will we produce evangelists like these online graduates, who are driven to go forward and replicate their community learning experience wherever they go next in life.

References

Bransford, J., Brown, A., & Cocking, R. (2000). *How people learn: Brain, mind, experience, and school.* Washington, DC: National Academy Press.

Bruner, J. (1996). *The culture of education.* Cambridge, MA: Harvard University Press.

Carter, K. (1993). The place of story in research on teaching and teacher education. *Educational Researcher, 22*(1), 5-12.

Dewey, J. (1938). *Experience and education.* Hampshire, UK: Macmillan.

Duffy, T. M., & Jonassen, D. H. (1992). Constructivism: New implications for instructional technology. In T. M. Duffy & D. H. Jonassen (Ed.), *Constructivism and the technology of instruction: A conversation* (pp. 1-16). Hillsdale, NJ : Erlbaum.

Hase, S., & Kenyon, C. (2000). From andragogy to heutagogy. *UltiBASE Articles.* Retrieved April 4, 2002, from http://ultibase.rmit.edu.au/Articles/dec00/hase2.htm

Holmes, B., Tangney, B., Fitzgibbon, A., Savage, T., & Mehan, S. (2001, March). Communal constructivism: Students constructing learning for as well as with others. *Proceedings of the 12th International Conference of the Society for Information Technology and Teacher Education* (pp. 5-10, 3114-3119). Charlottesville, VA, USA.

Horton, M. J., & Kohl, H. (2001). *The long haul, an autobiography.* New York: Teachers College Press.

Keegan, D. (1996). *Foundations of distance education.* London: Routledge.

Knowles, M. (1992). *The adult learner: A neglected species.* Houston, TX: Gulf.

Langer, E. (1997). *The power of mindful learning.* Cambridge, MA: Perseus.

Lave, J., & Wenger, E. (1991). *Situated learning: Legitimate peripheral participation.* Cambridge, MA: Cambridge University Press.

Leask, M., & Younie, S. (2001). Communal constructivist theory: Information and communications technology pedagogy and internationalisation of the curriculum. *Journal of Information Technology for Teacher Education, 10*(1-2), 118-122.

McNiff, J., Lomax, P., & Whitehead, J. (1996). *You and your action research project.* London: Routledge.

Meyerson, I. (1948). *Les Fonctions Psychologiques et les Oeuvres.* Paris: J. Vrin.

Palloff, R. M., & Pratt, K. (2003). *The virtual student: A profile and guide to working with online learners.* CA: Jossey Bass.

Papert, S. (1993). *The children's machine.* New York: Basic Books.

Piaget, J. (1976). *The grasp of consciousness: Action and concept in the young child.* Cambridge, MA: Harvard University Press.

Tait, A. (1995). Student support in open and distance learning. In F. Lockwood (Ed.) , *Open and distance learning today* (pp. 232-241). London: Routledge.

Thorpe, M. (2002). Rethinking learner support: The challenge of collaborative online learning. *Open Learning, 17*(2).

Wenger, E., McDermott, R., & Snyder, W. (2002). *Cultivating communities of practice.* Boston: Harvard Business School Press.

Wink, J., & Putney, L. (2002). *Visions of Vygotsky.* Boston: Allyn & Bacon.

Chapter XIII

Learning Agency in New Learning Environments:
An Australian Case Study of the Influence of Context[1]

Hitendra Pillay, Queensland University of Technology, Australia

John A. Clarke, Queensland University of Technology, Australia

Peter G. Taylor, Bond University, Australia

Abstract

The Bandurian concept of learner agency was originally embedded in a paradigm where behavior, self and environment influenced each other significantly. However, evolution of the concept has focused almost exclusively on individuals as the locus of agency ignoring the potential contribution of context. It is argued that learning environments should be considered truly reciprocal with individuals through mutual and iterative influence by contextual elements and by individual learners. It is postulated that learner agency be broadened to a more inclusive concept of learning agency. This concept is explored empirically with data collected on an e-learning university campus from 125 students about their approaches to learning, perceptions of their learning environments, and episte-mological reflections on themselves as learners. Results indicate that students' behavior cannot be explained by individual characteristics but by the influences of the technology-rich learning environment and peers, suggesting that individu-als' approach to learning arises from mutual interactions between individual and contextual agency.

Introduction

Over the last two decades of the last century, research into student learning in higher education was both extensive and intensive. However, it focused on tradi-tional learning environments[2] (TLEs), tending to provide explanations that not only assumed participation in formal lecturer-dominated or defined on-campus environments but also were based on traditional learning theories. While this research has been going on, higher education has been undergoing an accelerating transformation driven by technological innovations and the emergence of a knowledge-based society. This transformation has seen considerable private and public sector financial investment aimed at developing new learning environ-ments (NLEs). These environments are characterized in this chapter by an increasing reliance on information and communication technologies (ICTs), par-ticularly the use of the Internet, less reliance on traditional face-to-face teaching, and a greater use of peer-based learning tasks.

NLEs can be thought of as lying on the continuum between TLEs that are cam-pus based, and virtual learning environments (VLEs) that support education through the use of technology, namely e-learning. They involve both e-learning and campus-based participation. They also provide an environment that allows exploration of the impact of significant changes in the pedagogical and resource practices associated with TLEs, including the impact of e-learning on student experiences of the environment. In the NLE that informs this chapter, pedagogi-cal practices also explicitly valued community and interaction, and through this, the actual social, cultural, and material context of learning.

Regrettably, the development of VLEs has been based largely on advocacy of the potential in adopting ICTs in the education sector rather than on an empirically-based understanding of its effect on student learning. The aim here is to explore a new way of conceptualizing learning within NLEs that (1) integrates recent views on the role of learners and learning environments in learning that chal-lenge some of the traditional theories and (2) is supported by empirical evidence in the form of a case study. This conceptualization may offer some useful chal-lenges for those who are focused on VLEs, as well as those focusing on NLEs. It uses as a starting point, a concept central to traditional views on learning—learner agency.

Agency: Evolution of a Concept

As with all outcomes of evolution, the concept of learner agency has undergone significant development over time, a journey that draws on preexisting concepts. Bandura (1997) suggests that "people make causal contributions to their own psycho-social functioning through mechanisms of personal agency" (p. 2) and that the most central or pervasive mechanism of agency is the individual's belief in personal efficacy. "Unless people believe they can produce desired effects by their actions, they have little incentive to act. Efficacy belief, therefore, is a major basis of action" (pp. 2-3) and individuals guide their lives by their beliefs of personal efficacy. Bandura (1997) defines perceived self-efficacy as "the beliefs in one's capabilities to organize and execute courses of action required to produce given attainments" (p. 3). Thus, in the social cognitive literature, personal agency is understood to involve a combination of the individual's self-efficacy and their incentive to act; it "refers to the intentional pursuit of a course of action" (Goddard, Sweetland, & Hoy, 2000, p. 688).

Where the focus is on learning situations, personal agency can be referred to as learner agency, conceptualized as a combination of the learners' self-efficacy in working in these learning situations and the learners' desire to become proactive in engaging with the learning process. The later is similar to Krapp's (2002) notion of how the learner values the learning act. Both elements are influenced by learners' beliefs about, and expectations of, learning and the learning environments (Bandura, 1997; Perry, 1970; Pintrich, Smith, Garcia, & McKeachie, 1991).

In social cognitive theory, Bandura (1997) suggests that human agency operates within an interdependent causal structure involving personal factors, the external environment and behavior, a process he refers to as triadic reciprocal causation. "In this transactional view of self and society, internal personal factors in the form of cognitive, affective, and biological events, all operate as interacting determinants that influence one another bidirectionally" (Bandura, 1997, p. 6). In a learning activity then, learning behavior is evidenced by an interdependent causal relationship between learners' beliefs about and expectations of learning and the learning environment, and the learning environment itself. The triad of personal agency, the person's actions, and the proximal environment dynamically interact and this interactive emergent agency arises constantly as the person learns (Bandura, 1989). Further, he suggests that people actively perceive their environments and are influenced by these perceptions.

However, the direction taken by subsequent theorists and researchers in the evolution of the notion of agency has been to focus almost exclusively on the individual as the locus of agency and, if only by default, to ignore the potential and complexity of the environment as a significant contributor. Eccles and Wigfield (2002) for example, in reviewing work on Bandura's social cognitive theory, conclude that researchers have concentrated on the "individuals' efficacy expectations [as] the major determinant of goal setting, activity choice, willingness to expend effort, and persistence" (p. 111). Similarly, the Lent and Lopez (2002) review concluded that "researchers have largely focused on . . . actions performed by (or having consequences for) an individual rather than activities . . . that involve complex social interaction" (p. 257) and further that they have held constant or not considered the potential influence of contributions from the environment (p. 260).

The significant elements of the evolution of the concept of agency, then, despite the potential inherent in Bandura's original theorizing, are

- the centrality of the individual as learner, and
- the limited attention given to the nature and influence of the environment.

Consistent with international trends, Australian higher education is undergoing an accelerating technological transformation (Australian Vice Chancellors' Committee, 1996). With regard to the impact of this change on learning, Bandura (2001) recently noted that "information technologies will be transforming educational systems, . . . transforming how people communicate, educate, [and] relate to each other. . . . These new realities place increasing demands on human agency . . . transforming the nature, reach, speed, and loci of human influence" (p. 15).

The aim here is, with the limitations of the current conception of agency identified above in mind, to explore the notion of learner agency as it manifests itself in an environment that has significant characteristics of a VLE, and which, according to its advocates, has the potential and complexity to significantly influence learning.

An Empirical Examination of Agency: A Case Study

The Setting

The setting is a purpose-built NLE campus of a large Australian University. This setting is unique among the three campuses of that university in that all teaching involves at least a Web-supplemented level of online delivery, one of the significant characteristics of a VLE. It also has a nontraditional "open plan" design for all formal learning spaces and numerous spaces and furniture for informal gatherings. Details of the rationale, design, development, and operation of the campus can be found in Taylor and Blaik (2002).

The Study

Overview

The study drawn on here is a three year longitudinal research project based at that campus, tracking the developmental patterns in students' perceptions of themselves as learners and of their learning environment. Data are collected using written responses to questionnaires (each year) and focus-group interviews (each semester). The project began in 2002 and aspects of the data collected during that year and in 2003 are referred to here. Where possible, data is to be collected from the same students or at least from their cohortpeers as they progress through their degrees in 2003 and 2004. Further details of the study are available elsewhere (Pillay, Clarke, & Taylor, 2003; Taylor, Pillay, & Clarke, 2002, 2003, 2004).

Sample

The sample consists of 125 students from the 2002 intake into the business (n_{B02}=58) and education (n_{E02}=46) degrees and the 2003 education intake (n_{E03}521). While the two cohorts were significantly different with regard to gender due to the dominance of females in the education cohorts (χ^2=16.35, p<.001),[3] they were similar with regard to age (M_{B02}=24.53, M_{E02}=25.54; M_{E03}=25.00, F(2,122)=0.18, ns), the majority of students in all three cohorts were in their first year of university study (n=116; 92.8%) and just over half of each cohort were the first tertiary students in their family (n=69; 55.2%). In the data reported here, the sample is being treated as a whole with no cohort or year-based comparisons made, and the data drawn upon arise from questionnaire and interview data from the 2002 cohorts collected in 2002 and 2003 and questionnaire data from the 2003 cohort collected in 2003.

Data Collection

Students provided responses to three questionnaires measuring their approach to learning, the perceptions of their learning environments, and their epistemological reflections on themselves as learners and influences on their learning, and verbal data in focus group interviews.

The instruments used were as follows:

- A short form of the Study Process Questionnaire (SPQ-S) developed by Fox, McManus, and Winder (2001). The SPQ is a well established and commonly used instrument designed to identify students' approaches to learning (Biggs, 1987). The 18-item Short Form has six subscales, and the second order factor structure preserves the presence of the same three learning approaches (deep, surface, achieving) as the original longer 42-item version (Fox et al., 2001).

• The Perceptions of Learning Environments Questionnaire (PLEQ) developed by Clarke (1995). This semistructured openresponse questionnaire invites students to identify aspects that they perceive help or hinder their learning in specific learning environments that they nominate from a supplied list. The original 1995 list (large and small group lectures, seminars, one-to-one teaching, practical settings on and off campus) was augmented in this study by the addition of "informal or self-directed peer group learning activities," "formal or lecturer-required peer group learning activities," and "Web-based learning environments." A typical response provides a "statement" and a "reason." For example, "In seminars, my learning is helped when the tutor gives practical examples (statement) because it increases my understanding of the concept (reason)."

• The Measures of Epistemological Reflection, or MER (Baxter Magolda, 2001; Baxter Magolda & Porterfield, 1988). This shortessay questionnaire is designed to assess students' epistemological development in terms of six domains: roles of the learner, roles of the teacher, roles of peers, roles of assessment, the nature of knowledge, and the process of decision making.

All three instruments have been used in TLEs in tertiary settings (e.g. Baxter Magolda, 1992; Clarke, 1998; Prosser & Trigwell, 1999).

The focus-group interviews explored such topics as students' expectations of university life, how they have been changed by university experiences, current and future challenges of university life, perceived responsibilities of themselves and their teachers for their learning, and forms and quality of support for their learning.

The Evidence

The Bandurian concept of triadic reciprocal causation among behavior, personal factors, and the environmental context was used here as a framework to assess what were the active influences—the determinants of agency—on behavior. To use this framework, it is necessary to identify the learning behavior and then attempt to explain it in terms of personal or contextual influences, or both. In terms of the data collected, these variables were represented in the data as follows:

Because of the theoretical relationship between learning motives and learning strategies and their centrality to this discussion, a brief overview of these concepts is given here. Approaches to learning were originally conceptualized by Marton and his co-workers (Marton, 1975; Marton & Säljö, 1976) who found that, depending on their intention or motivation, students would use a strategy to suit. Subsequent work, for example, Biggs (1987), Entwistle and Ramsden (1983) and Watkins (1983), firmly established the notion of deep and surface approaches with attendant motives and strategies. Theoretically and empirically, it has been determined that "students have fairly stable sets of motives for . . . learning and each set determines a generic strategy for handling a range of learning tasks. Thus the surface motive and surface strategy comprise the surface approach [and] the deep motive and deep strategy the deep approach" (Biggs and Moore, 1993, p. 311). The association between motive and strategy is exemplified by Prosser and Trigwell's (1999) discussion of the deep and surface approaches. When using the deep approach "students aim to understand ideas and seek meaning. They have an intrinsic interest in the task and . . . adopt strategies that help satisfy their curiosity" (p. 3). When using a surface approach, "students see tasks as external impositions . . . and seek to meet the demands of the task with minimum effort. They adopt strategies that include . . . the reproduction of the essentials [i.e. facts] as accurately as possible, and the rote memorizing of information for assessment purposes rather than for understanding" (p. 3). Prosser and Trigwell (1999) also summarize research that reflects the motive-strategy congruence (pp. 83-107).

Against this theoretical and empirical background, the collected data were explored for evidence of agency to explain the students' behavior in the NLE.

Behavior

As indicated above, the learning behavior available from the data collected is the espoused learning strategies as identified by the SPQ-S. A comparison of surface (SS) and deep (DS) strategies found a significant difference (M_{SS}=2.79, M_{DS}=3.57 t=7.39, p(.001, d=1.05) indicating that the students espouse that they use deep strategies more than surface strategies. These results also indicate that the difference is not only statistically significant but also has a substantial effect size, as measured by Cohen's d. Cohen (1988) provides benchmarks of d50.8 as an indicator of a large effect size and d=0.5 as an indicator of a medium effect size. To find an explanation for this pattern, other collected data were explored to look for any agency residing in the personal or environmental context variables.

Behavior	Espoused learning strategies as identified by the SPQ-S
Personal variables	Espoused learning motives as identified by the SPQ-S
Contextual variables	Perceptions of the learning environment as reported in the PLEQ and significant influences on learning discussed in the MER responses and interviews

Personal Variables as a Source of Agency

The personal learning variable was represented by the students' learning motives. As explained earlier, the normal expectation would be for congruence between the motives and strategies, that is, students professing a deep (or surface) motive would also claim to use deep (or surface) strategies. This would be reflected in nonsignificant statistical differences between the motive and strategy scores.

However, the SPQ-S data here provided a counterintuitive set of results. The motive-strategy comparisons identified the following dissonances:

- Students as a group tended to have significantly lower surface strategies (SS) scores than surface motive (SM) scores.
- Students as a group tended to have significantly higher deep strategies (DS) scores than deep motive (DM) scores.

This is summarized in Table 1, which indicates that the differences are not only statistically significant but also have substantial effect sizes, again measured by Cohen's d.

This data challenges the current assumption of a correlation between motives and strategies with students less likely to adopt surface strategies and more likely to adopt deep strategies than their corresponding motives would suggest. Their approach to learning, underpinned as it is by the use of deep strategies and the avoidance of surface strategies, needs to be explained by factors other than their own personal or individual motives. Data that taps into the environmental influences may provide some insights into their salience as agencies for learning behavior.

Environmental Context as a Source of Agency

The data on the environmental influences on learning behavior was collected, as indicated above, through the PLEQ, the MER and interviews.

Data collected in TLEs using the PLEQ and detailed elsewhere (Clarke, 1995, 1998; T&LiTE, 1994) identified a large number of bipolar categories (i.e. positive and negative comments). The focus in the discussion here is on the responses associated with NLEs. The addition of the peer-learning and Web-based learning environments as new options gave rise to a number of new categories shown below in italics. As before, these new categories tended to be bipolar as indicated by the positive (+) and negative (–) comments.

Exposure to NLEs was characterized by, first, involvement with ICTs:

- *Electronic access to content or material* ("Lecture notes have been posted"; "Information can be retrieved" [+])
- *Availability of computer system* ("I sit for an on-line test" [+]; "Uni system is offline" [–])
- *Computer system design* ("User friendliness is optimized" [+]; "I don't understand something" [–])

and, second, involvement with group activities:

- *Group dynamics* ("We meet regularly"; "We work together to get answers" [+]; "Not able to find a group"; "We had conflict" [–])
- *Effect on group dynamics* ("Workload may be shared equally"; "Everybody gets a chance to participate" [+]; "Groups are already formed"; "Don't know who they are" [–])

Table 1. Motive-strategy comparisons

Comparison	t	df	p	d	
SM ↔ SS*	7.09	124	<.001	0.77	Dissonance
DM* ↔ DS	(6.06)	124	(<.001)	0.57	Dissonance

* Lower value

The significance of these contextual influences on students' learning was reiterated in their MER and interview responses and each of these clusters is discussed in turn, drawing on these various sources.

Technological Influences

Access to ICTs provided students with a conduit to sources of information. In the MER, when posed with resolving the problem of two different explanations being given for the same situation, one student responded that "I would question the actual author if possible by e-mail" and another that "an e-mail to a tutor or lecturer can sometimes reveal the truth." The access also provided learning experiences to complement the formal lectures. In addressing the role of the lecturer in learning, one student wrote, "It is good when the lecturer uses powerpoint presentation. The powerpoint can be printed out before the lecture and read so I've got an idea as to what the lecture is about and I can make notes on it during the lecture instead of writing it down—so it saves time." Interview comments also stressed the importance of electronic access: "[Subject name] is running a virtual classroom. . . . It was really good to have a virtual classroom where you could ask this guy . . . and he could point you exactly in the right direction. . . . [You had access to] someone who could tell you there and then because he was on just about every hour of the day." And again "[Tutor's name] gave me such invaluable help over the Internet."

The ICTs in turn by their very nature can influence how students go about their learning. As one interviewee noted,

> There's just so much information on there [the University Web site] that I've hardly opened my textbooks this semester. I've obviously had to go through and look up a few things but for [subject name], there's just been so much information given to you there that I think I've only opened the textbook three times and that was just to confirm something that had already been given to me in the lecture notes. So it's very thorough.

ICTs can also determine strategies as indicated by the MER responses related to the use of e-mail above and by the following response to how students handle the volume of electronic information available: "My personal way of doing it if I get the time then I read everything and then if I get more time, I'll join a discussion forum and then if I get more time I'll go further and do the publishers' tests and different textbooks. It's just time and priorities really. Everything is relevant."

Peer Influences

Involvement with peers was also seen as having a positive influence on learning as the following MER responses related to the role of peers in learning indicate. It is interesting to note that the responses often included an unsolicited comparison with formal learning through the lecturer: "Discussion with peers is good because mostly a student can explain things to me better than a teacher"; "As a group, you hear a wide variety of experiences and beliefs while the lecture often emphasized information." This emphasis is complemented by interview comments such as "the group discussion work has really accelerated my learning" and "I think most support comes informally [from peers]." The reciprocal interactive nature of peer support is exemplified by the interview comments: "With one subject, . . . I couldn't get any help from the lecturers [so] . . . I and a friend, we'd do an hour together every day"; "Me [sic] and my friend will go up to the library and we'll talk about it and we'll make concept maps and it really helps to understand it"; and "When I got everything finished . . . I've got a chance to help everybody else." Perhaps the most telling comments were interview responses to the question "Of all of the people who could challenge you at university, who challenges you the most?" The unequivocal response from one interviewee was "my peers," followed by another who said "definitely peers."

The differentiation of the roles of lecturers and peers intimated above is reinforced by MER responses related to the "role of the teacher." The bulk of the MER responses tended to reflect the absolutist view of knowledge that the teacher is the expert and the source of knowledge: "They teach. I learn"; "They show me step by step how things are done"; and "Lecturers are a source of info [sic]." This view was confirmed in interviews: "The lecturer's responsibility is to get as much of the information across as possible."

These comments indicate that students feel that the ICTs available in this NLE and their involvement with their peers not only are integral and salient to their learning but also provide an essential, if not dominant, complement to formal teaching-learning situations. They act as a source of action—agency—for their learning.

Summing up the Evidence

Students' professed use of deep strategies and avoidance of surface strategies cannot be explained by their own motives. The data suggest that the agency for this resides in the learning context itself. In the specific technology-rich learning environment being studied here,

- ICTs facilitated learning by providing access and learning opportunities beyond that possible from formal in-class contact,
- ICTs influenced the content and process of student learning,
- students attributed different roles to lecturers (source of facts) and peers (rich variety of experiences) as influences on their learning, and
- peers were seen as more valuable than lecturers when it came to the development of understanding.

In this particular learning setting, the complex and differentiated nature of the context significantly influenced learning. The evidence highlights the limitations of the current interpretation of agency discussed earlier and supports the need for a broader conception of agency. A consideration of this issue follows.

Agency in New Learning Environments

Learning, Context and Agency Revisited

The learning setting under scrutiny here is a complex mix of new teaching and learning tools or artifacts[4] (ICTs), strategies (informal and formal individual and group learning), philosophy of learning (learning to learn), and a further refinement of our understanding of existing substantive domain knowledge. This changing nature of learning environments challenges traditional notions with regard to the types of interaction possible and the manner in which learners engage with learning tasks. The proposal here is that there is a need to explore reciprocal causation and synchronous and asynchronous interaction when considering the interaction between the learner and the elements in these complex learning environments. This is in accord with Altman's (1988) argument that it is nonsensical to conceive of learning engagement as unidirectional and simply emanating from the learner either through direct interaction or interpretation of the learning context.

The findings in this study indicate that learning behavior (professed strategies) is more strongly influenced by a resource-rich and socially complex environment that involves an increase in the use of ICTs, learning from peers and the recognition of the roles of both informal and formal learning, than by personal characteristics such as espoused motives. It suggests a need to revisit the roots of Bandura's (1997) concept of "triadic reciprocal causation," which acknowledges that the environment could significantly and actively influence behavior. In the discussion that follows, this revisiting is accompanied by some insights from recent developments in learning theory which may provide an explanation for the reciprocal influence of a complex environment on learning behavior. It also focuses on the limitations of the current interpretation of agency, namely the singular focus on the learners as the basis for understanding the learning process and the limited attention given to the complexity of the environment.

First, the singular focus on the learner: The emerging literature on human learning suggests that artifacts in our learning environment have inherent meaning (Csikszentmihalyi & Rochberg-Halton, 1981; Verillon & Rabardel, 1995) and an epistemology (Bopry, 1999). Therefore, like the epistemology of knowledge, the epistemology of artifacts can structure how individuals interact with a learning task in a learning environment. Considering Bandura's work on triadic reciprocal causation, it is now becoming apparent that this reciprocal influence, as previously conceived, is not limited to the "agency" in individuals interpreting the environment but also includes the "agency" of the inherent meaning in the artifacts in the learning environment. Such reciprocal influence on the meaning-making process may complement individuals' personal characteristics and espoused beliefs in how they perceive and approach learning. Thus, individuals may engage with learning tasks in particular ways (in this case deeper ways) because of the reciprocal effect associated with an environment's artifacts. For example, Bolter (1984) argues that while human memory shaped the design of technologies and cultural tools, it is also reciprocally influenced by them: computers were constructed by humans, now they influence how humans live, think, and work. This means that it is difficult to locate agency only within individuals.

Extending the above argument, it could be suggested that the peer- and ICT-mediated learning experiences of the participants in this study were productive because of the characteristics of the physical environment and technological resources. With regard to the ICTs, the contention is that they were useful because of the selection of inherently user-friendly software and instructional materials. Such tools generate an attraction for users. The users' interpretation of software is not sufficient to make it user friendly; there has to be inherent quality in the software that gives it its meaning. Similarly, the use of physical space (such as the coffee shop) and objects in that space (such as peers) at this particular campus seems to have caused the increased informal peer interaction and learning. Again, the impetus for informal peer interaction around the coffee shops, we believe was just as much the affordances, or the provision of opportunities, in the use of space and culture of this campus as it was student choice. Aspects of these affordances were an outcome of quite specific design intentions, as reported by Taylor and Blaik (2002). Thus, agency-in-the-environment can be thought of as an outcome of the knowledge or intelligence, or both, designed into that environment.

Second, the limited attention given to the learning environment and its complexity: The current all-inclusive notion of learning environment has paid little regard to the micro elements within an environment and how they may influence the learning engagement. Also, most studies on learning environments have focused on formal classrooms and there has been little if any consideration of the role of informal learning environments. With regard to microelements, Boekaerts (2002) uses the analogy of tropical rainforests and the different microclimates that exist within them to illustrate the complexity inherent in an environment and the need to consider the microclimates separately and also in totality in order to appreciate the inherent sources of energy in an environment. The microclimates are similar to tools, strategies, physical spaces, and subject matter, which all have affordance that may exist in an environment and contribute to the learners' intentions and beliefs about their self-efficacy in working within such environments. When such affordances are responded to by learners and used as potential energy to drive learner engagement, we called it "personal agency." However, to acknowledge the locus of affordances in the environment, we would like to broaden the term beyond the person by introducing a more inclusive concept of "learning agency."

A Definition of Learning Agency

Learning agency is the effect on learning of the knowledge designed into and available within a learning context, and which acts to shape how learners engage in and with that context. This is more than motivation, as motivation is often located within the individual whereas learning agency can be located in ICT tools or the dominant ideology. For example, as indicated earlier, the inherent nature of some tools attracts learners whereas others do not. Such learner affinity for a tool is sometimes referred to as "user friendliness." Similarly, ideological positions such as the recognition of site-based learning may encourage learners to engage in different ways and at different levels of rigor. The learning agency inherent in the factors that go to make up the learning context together with the learner's self-efficacy provide a more holistic understanding of learner engagement and its consequences in a NLE or VLE.

Conclusion

This chapter has focused on the nature of the interdependent relationship between learners and the learning context. In doing so it challenges the conventional all-inclusive view of learning environments, and the unidirectional relationship between learning motives and strategies. Innovations in VLEs, including the NLE discussed in this chapter, open opportunities for new theorizing of the role of informal and formal learning environments, the influence of artifacts in a learning environment, and consequently the implications for designing intelligent learning environments. The study reported in this chapter has demonstrated the importance of the learning environment in determining learners' approach to and quality of learning. This is a postindividualist and therefore postconstructivist perspective consistent with Bandura's original theorizing. It acknowledges that an individual's approach to learning arises from the mutual interactions between individual and contextual agency. Given the considerable investment in the various elements that go to make up VLEs, recognition of their role in learning agency is essential if the potential of these learning environments is to be realized thing.

Endnotes

1   The research reported in this chapter was funded by the Australian Research Council grant DP0211854, with Hitendra Pillay and Peter Taylor as chief investigators.

2   The terms *environment* and context are used interchangeably throughout to mean the same thing.

3   The gender split in business was almost equal (F =30, 51.7%; M =28, 48.3%), while the education cohort was, as is traditional, dominantly female (F_{02} =39, 84.8%; F_{03} =18, 85.7%; M_{02} =7, 15.2%, M_{03} =3, 14.3%). The reporting of statistical probability follows the convention of Miller (1986), who recommends the reporting of values <.001 as just that.

4   The terms artifacts, tools, and objects are used in the literature to mean essentially the same thing.

References

Altman, I. (1988). Process, transaction/contextual, and outcome research: An alternative to the traditional distinction between basic and applied research. *Social Behaviour, 3,* 259-280.

Australian Vice Chancellors' Committee. (1996). *Exploiting information technology in higher education: An issues paper.* Author.

Bandura, A. (1989). Human agency in social cognitive theory. *American Psychologist, 44,* 1175-1184.

Bandura, A. (1997). *Self efficacy. The exercise of control.* New York: W. H. Freeman.

Bandura, A. (2001). The changing face of psychology at the dawning of the globalization era. *Canadian Psychology, 42*(1), 12-24.

Baxter Magolda, M. B. (1992). *Knowing and reasoning in college: Gender-related patterns in students' intellectual development.* San Francisco: Jossey-Bass.

Baxter Magolda, M. B. (2001). A constructivist revision of the measure of epistemological reflection. *Journal of College Student Development, 46*(6), 520-534.

Baxter Magolda, M. B., & Porterfield, W. D. (1988). *Assessing intellectual development. The link between theory and practice.* Alexandrina, VA: American College Personnel Association.

Biggs, J. B. (1987). *The Study Process Questionnaire (SPQ) user's manual.* Hawthorne, Australia: ACER.

Biggs, J. B., & Moore, P. J. (1993). *The process of learning* (3rd ed.). Sydney: Prentice Hall.

Boekaerts, M. (2002). Bringing about change in the classroom: Strengths and weaknesses of the self-regulated learning approach–EARLI presidential address, 2002. *Learning and Instruction, 12*(6), 589-604.

Bolter, D. J. (1984). *Turing's man: Western culture in the computer age.* Chapel Hill: University of North Carolina Press.

Bopry, J. (1999). The warrant for constructivist practice within educational technology. *Educational Technology Research and Development, 47*(4), 5-26.

Clarke, J. A. (1995). Tertiary students' perceptions of their learning environments: A new procedure and some outcomes. *Higher Education Research and Development, 14*(1), 1-12.

Clarke, J. A. (1998). Students' perceptions of different learning environments. *Higher Education Research & Development, 17*(1), 107-117.

Cohen, J. (1988). *Statistical power analysis for the behavioural sciences* (2nd ed.). Hillsdale, NJ: Lawrence Erlbaum.

Csikszentmihalyi, M., & Rochberg-Halton, E. (1981). *The meaning of things: Domestic symbols and the self.* New York: Cambridge University Press.

Eccles, J. S., & Wigfield, A. (2002). Motivational beliefs, values and goals. *Annual Review of Psychology, 53*, 109-132.

Entwistle, N., & Ramsden, P. (1983). *Understanding student learning.* London: Croom Helm.

Fox, R. A., McManus, I. C., & Winder, B. C. (2001). The shortened Study Process Questionnaire: An investigation of its structure and longitudinal stability using confirmatory factor analysis. *British Journal of Educational Psychology, 71*, 511-530.

Goddard, R. D., Sweetland, S. R., & Hoy, W. K. (2000). Academic emphasis of urban elementary schools and student achievement in reading and mathematics: A multilevel analysis. *Educational Administration Quarterly, 36*(5), 683-702.

Krapp, A. (2002). Structural and dynamic aspects of interest development: Theoretical considerations from an ontological perspective. *Learning and Instruction, 12*(4), 383-409.

Lent, R. W., & Lopez, F. G. (2002). Cognitive ties that bind: A tripartite view of efficacy beliefs in growth-promoting relationships. *Journal of Social and Clinical Psychology, 21*(3), 256-286.

Marton, F. (1975). On non-verbatim learning—I: Level of processing and level of outcome. *Scandinavian Journal of Psychology, 16*, 273-279.

Marton, F., & Säljö, R. (1976). On qualitative differences in learning. I—Outcome and process. *British Journal of Educational Psychology, 46*, 4-11.

Miller, R. C. (1986). *Beyond ANOVA. Basics of applied statistics*. New York: John Wiley & Sons.

Perry, W. G. (1970). *Forms of intellectual and ethical development in the college years: A scheme*. Troy, MO: Holt, Rinehart, & Winston.

Pillay, H., Clarke, J. A., & Taylor, P. G. (2003, August). *Learning agency in technological learning environments: What influences students' willingness to learn?* Paper presented at the Biennial Conference of the European Association for Research on Learning and Instruction, Padova, Italy.

Pintrich, P. R., Smith, D. A., Garcia, T., & McKeachie, W. J. (1991). *A manual for the use of the Motivated Strategies for Learning Questionnaire (MSLQ)* (Technical Report No. 91-B-004). Ann Arbor: University of Michigan.

Prosser, M., & Trigwell, K. (1999). *Understanding learning and teaching: The experience in higher education*. Buckingham, UK: SRHE and Open University Press.

T&LiTE. (1994). *The teaching and learning in tertiary education (T&LiTE) project*. Brisbane: School of Learning and Development, Queensland University of Technology.

Taylor, P. G., & Blaik, J. (2002). *Project report. What have we learned?* The Logan Campus 1998-2001. Brisbane: Griffith Institute for Higher Education.

Taylor, P. G., Pillay, H., & Clarke, J. A. (2002). Understanding the outcomes of change: Interrogating student adaptation to new learning environments. In J. Searle & R. Roebuck (Eds.), *Envisioning practice—Implementing change: Vol. 3. Proceedings of the 10th Annual International Conference on Post-Compulsory Education and Training* (pp. 185-191). Brisbane, Australia: Centre for Learning and Work Research, Griffith University.

Taylor, P. G., Pillay, H., & Clarke, J. A. (2003). Enriching the learning culture through peers and technology. In J. Searle, I. Yashin-Shaw, & R. Roebuck (Eds.), *Enriching learning cultures (Vol. 3). Proceedings of the 11th Annual International Conference on Post-Compulsory Education and Training* (pp. 140-146). Brisbane, Australia: Centre for Learning and Work Research, Griffith University.

Taylor, P. G., Pillay, H., & Clarke, J. A. (2004). Exploring student adaptation to new learning environments: Some unexpected outcomes. *International Journal of Learning Technology, 1*(1), 100-110.

Verillon, P., & Rabardel, P. (1995). Cognition and artifacts: A contribution to the study of thought in relation to instrumented activity. *European Journal of Psychology of Education, 10*(1), 77-101.

Watkins, D. A. (1983). Assessing tertiary students' study processes. *Human Learning, 2*, 29-37.

Chapter XIV

New Wine or New Bottles:
What's New about Online Teaching?

Michael Forret, University of Waikato, New Zealand

Elaine Khoo, University of Waikato, New Zealand

Bronwen Cowie, University of Waikato, New Zealand

Abstract

This chapter presents findings from research into the nature of successful, online tertiary teaching and learning. The project is part of a larger study aimed at establishing guidelines for the ongoing design and development of online courses within the authors' institution. The research findings, from interviews with tertiary online teachers, identify key characteristics of successful online teaching and learning that are consistent with a sociocultural view of learning. The authors recognize that online teaching and learning contexts present challenges for both teachers and learners but argue that quality pedagogy is founded on a well-considered view of learning and that the guiding pedagogical principles provided by such a view apply equally well in online and face-to-face contexts. Thus, they caution against confusing the need to respond flexibly to changing environments with the need for a new philosophy of learning.

Introduction

While it is clear that online technologies, through their greater facility for communication and interactivity, offer a wider repertoire of teaching opportunities than traditional forms of distance education (Curran, 2001), how this potential can be best realized for a particular educational task and student population remains the subject of continuing debate and research (Clark, 1994; Curran, 2001; Gibson, 1998; Windschitl, 1998). Recent reexamination of the development of online teaching and learning has underscored the importance of the teacher's role (Matuga, 2001; Palloff & Pratt, 1999; Salmon, 2000) as well as the differences between face-to-face and online teaching (Frey & Alman, 2001). LaMonica (2001) comments that "teaching online is a new and different experience from teaching in a classroom. It requires a different set of skills and a different pedagogy," and (Ells, 1999) has coined the term "webagogy" to describe the "art, craft, and science of using networked technologies, including the World Wide Web, to support teaching and learning."

It seems clear that learning to teach and learn in an asynchronous, online situation, as with any new context, requires both teachers and learners to develop new skills and strategies in order to take advantage of the opportunities afforded by these new learning contexts. Whether online teaching and learning requires us to redefine the principles guiding our pedagogy is, however, debatable. There is a danger that the novelty of the technologies used today may give rise to the impression that teachers need to develop completely new pedagogical principles in order to use the technology effectively—we question whether this is, in fact, so. We feel that pedagogy should be defined and guided by a well-articulated view of learning and the aims and intentions promoted by that view, and that these guiding principles remain constant regardless of context. While the strategies and skills developed to deal effectively with new teaching situations are clearly important, these strategies and skills derive their character and purpose from the teacher's underlying views of learning and associated aims and intentions. For this reason, the most important aspect of pedagogy is the establishment of its underlying guiding principles.

Moore (1998) argues that, while the opportunities of distance education have never been greater, neither has the gap of understanding between those who know how to design and deliver quality distance education programs and the policymakers and administrators who talk about the need for distance education. He goes on to say,

Distance education scholars must do better in sharing their knowledge more widely and make the results of their research and practise better known. An important part of this is to explain their learner-centred approach and to help conventional educators understand more about the complex process of designing, delivering and supporting learning at a distance. (Moore, 1998, p. 2)

With the above points in mind, we begin this chapter by developing a sociocultural view of learning as a useful account of the learning process and from this we identify the characteristics underpinning quality teaching and learning. Next, we present findings from our research into the nature of online tertiary teaching and learning that supports the applicability of these principles in an online context. We then examine some of the key differences between teaching and learning in a face-to-face context and online to highlight the affordances and constraints of an online context. The chapter concludes with a discussion of the issues raised by our research and we revisit the question of "new wine or new bottles?"

Establishing a View of Learning

In the early part of the last century, behaviorists saw learning as change in behavior brought about by trained responses to external stimuli. In the conditioning theories of Watson (1914) and Thorndike (1926), and in Skinner's (1954) "programmed instruction" approach to teaching, the learner was seen as playing little or no active part in the learning process, their behavior being reflexive responses to externally provided stimuli. With appropriately chosen stimuli, along with suitable positive and negative reinforcement, desirable behavior could be produced in anyone and undesirable behaviors extinguished.

In contrast, Piaget's work studied learning from the learner's point of view (Piaget, 1937) and challenged the simple, oneway, stimulus-response process of behaviorist learning. Piaget argued that experiences (stimuli) did not have generic, inbuilt meaning for the learner but rather, through experience and exploration, individuals developed their own perceptions and understandings of their world. In this view, learners constructed their own intellectual structures (or schemes) and thereby their perceptions of reality. New schemes develop by modifying existing ones and intellectual development is seen as the ongoing adaptation of an individual's cognitive structures to the physical environment. Although Piaget did not refer to his view of learning as constructivist until much later (Piaget, 1970), the view that knowledge is constructed by the learner and not transmitted ready-made was a central tenet of his work.

While Piaget's idea of developmental stages (early and late concrete, early and late formal operational) has been the source of much debate, the notion of learners as the constructors of knowledge has found support from educational researchers around the world. In science education, for example, research by Driver (1983) and Osborne and Freyberg (1985) began to show the range of ideas and understandings that different learners generate from similar learning situations, an outcome that would be difficult to explain in behaviorist terms. Subsequently, there have been thousands of studies identifying learners' views and ideas about a range of natural phenomena from electricity to animals and plants (see Pfundt & Duit, 2000). These studies have shown clearly that, not only do learners build personal explanations and perceptions of the world, but that their existing knowledge has a profound effect on their interpretation and subsequent understanding of new learning experiences.

By the late 1980s, constructivism had become a well-established philosophy of learning and much research now focused on examining learning from this point of view. That learners construct personal views of the world seemed clear, but it was also becoming evident that knowledge is characterized by the context within which it is constructed. The idea that knowledge and action are adapted to the physical and cultural settings from which they emerge has been described as "situated cognition" (Brown, Collins, & Duguid, 1989; Kirshner & Whitson, 1997). Brown et al. (1989) describe their view of situated cognition as follows:

> *The activity in which knowledge is developed and deployed . . . is not separable from or ancillary to learning and cognition. Nor is it neutral. Rather, it is an integral part of what is learned. Situations might be said to co-produce knowledge through activity. Learning and cognition . . . are fundamentally situated. (p. 32)*

The situation, or context, includes physical, emotional, intellectual, social, and cultural aspects of the learning environment.

While Piaget's work focused mainly on the physical context of learning, Vygotsky (1978) argued for the primacy of the social and linguistic context and that learning was socially mediated. The social character of learning is also central to Lave and Wenger's (1991) view of learning as the process by which learners progressively become active members of a "community of practice."

From this perspective, the unit of analysis is people in action, usually with others, using tools of some kind. Tools are seen as both physical and psychological with no artificial distinction between theory and practice. Learning at the interface between individual and culture is mediated by means of tools that are understood to be simultaneously physical and psychological. In Saljo's (1999, p. 149) words, "learning has to do with how people appropriate and master the *tools for thinking* and *acting* that exist in a given culture or society" (emphasis in original). Learning is viewed as inherently social (Wenger, 1998) and considered to involve a transformation of participation in the activities valued by the communities of which learners are a part (Lave & Wenger, 1991). In an educational setting, Brown, Ash,

Rutherford, Nakagawa, Gordon, and Campione (1993) suggest that teachers and students work together to develop a community of learners in which they are each intentional and self-motivated acquirers, users, and extenders of knowledge, individually and collaboratively.

Key Features of Learning from a Sociocultural Perspective

Our view of learning is based on the sociocultural perspective described above and rests on the following key, interrelated points:

- Knowledge is a not received ready-made but is actively developed by the learner through interaction with his or her cultural and physical environment. This interaction is aimed at appropriating the intellectual and physical tools of the learner's culture and is socially mediated through language and participation in culturally validated activities.

- Learners are active, intentional, thoughtful people with individual goals, values and ways of learning that are shaped by, and in turn shape, the communities of which they are members.

- Motivation, and the extent to which learning can be sustained over time, depends on the degree to which the learner's goals, values, and emotional well-being are supported by the learning context and the relationships established therein.

- Learning is situated; that is, the context—physical, emotional, intellectual, social, and so forth—within which knowledge is constructed influences the nature and meaning of that knowledge for the learner.

- Learning is developmental in that the learner's existing knowledge and values shape the way the learner perceives and makes sense of new learning experiences; that is, new knowledge is built on existing knowledge.

Characteristics of Quality Teaching and Learning

Pedagogy, viewed from this sociocultural perspective, is less concerned with learners' acquisition of discrete skills and techniques and focuses more on the construction and practices of learning communities (Leach & Moon, 1999). Students and teachers become partners in the interactive, developmental process of teaching and learning. The notion of partnership here implies that the goals, knowledge, and skills of the teacher and students evolve together in a mutually influential way. Although the teacher is clearly the 'senior' partner in knowledge and experience of the material being taught and learned, this notion of partnership implies that the aims, strategies, and expectations of the teacher are shared, and perhaps negotiated, with the learners. In this way, the teacher manages the planned and the emergent curriculum so that teaching and learning interact (Wenger, 1998).

An equally important aspect of the teacher's role is to create a learning environment that is both safe (physically, intellectually, and emotionally) and challenging; an environment in which learners are encouraged to express and explore their and others' ideas and to participate fully in the discourse of the learning community. To create such an environment, the teacher needs to understand and be able to access (or perhaps generate) the resources available within this environment, be attuned to the potential of these resources for teaching and learning, and be able to recognize when it is appropriate to use them. The teacher's interactions with learners need to be aimed at building students' self-esteem and identity as learners while simultaneously providing feedback that is constructive and enables students to be reflective, questioning, and critical.

It is our view that these characteristics underpin quality teaching in any face-to-face or online teaching and learning situation. Clearly, in an asynchronous, online teaching situation, the range and types of resources and possibilities for interaction and participation are different from those available in a conventional face-to-face situation. While this may require the teacher to adopt different practices in order to create the kind of learning environment described above, the underlying principles guiding the development of quality teaching and learning do not change when we move into an online context. As will be seen in the next section, research conducted in our university to examine online teaching and learning identified the above characteristics as qualities of effective online teaching and learning.

Investigating Online Teaching and Learning

New Zealand's University of Waikato first introduced its online supplemented courses (a combination of both face-to-face and online approaches) for teacher education at the School of Education in 1997. Known as the Mixed Media Program (MMP), it was the first of its kind in primary teacher education in New Zealand and since then online teaching and learning has grown steadily to encompass fully online courses offered by other schools and faculties at the university. To continue establishing its vision of quality online teaching and learning, the university has increased its efforts to advance research and development in areas such as online pedagogy, administration, management, and technical expertise (Campbell, 1997;

Campbell & Moodie, 1999; Campbell & Yates, 1997; Campbell, Yates, & McGee, 1998; McGee & Yates, 2000; Taylor & Biddulph, 1999; Taylor & Biddulph, 2000).

In line with this effort, our research reviewed and established a baseline of effective online pedagogy as perceived by lecturers and students. Our aim was to develop a pedagogically sound framework for the future development of online courses.

Part of the research involved case study interviews with ten lecturers from the School of Education at the University of Waikato, who have had online teaching experiences ranging from one to twelve years. The online courses taught involved a range of undergraduate and graduate levels and included MMP courses, and fully online distance courses.

While a wide range of issues and broad themes relating to the lecturers' online teaching practices emerged from the interviews, only the significant themes relevant to pedagogical strategies are discussed here.

The Importance of Social Interaction

All six lecturers with more than five years online teaching experience agreed that successful online teaching and learning was that which involved dialogue—the discussion and sharing of ideas in a way that construed learning as a social process. The following quotes illustrate their general perception that dialogue led to the generation of ideas in ways that did not necessarily happen through individual reading or reflection.

> *If you talk about a pedagogical perspective, that would be one that would be important to me. Dialogue has the potential for the creation of knowledge that individual thought never has anywhere near to the same degree. That's what online learning gives, the opportunity for people to have dialogues with each other which are generative rather than to sit in their own isolated study space and think things through in relation just to a book. So I guess that's the potential that I can see happening. Not all the time, but on certain occasions, people actually get into quite rich dialogue and that is the sense of which I meant, that I can see people's learning taking place. (Jake—a pseudonym)*

The lecturers in this study emphasized the development of students' skills and identities as contributors of ideas to online discussions.

> *You never feel shy about putting your idea forward because that's part of our whole learning experiences. We need to get all our ideas out there and talk about them. (Peter)*

In promoting students' experience of learning as a social process, the lecturers were aware of the need to actively promote and model collaborative activity in order to establish a sense of community within the class. The recommended means of doing this was to outline their expectations and provide guidance to help students become active participants. The lecturers considered their role (particularly at the beginning of a course) in setting the scene for a collaborative, participatory teaching and learning experience as crucial. One lecturer made explicit his hope that his classes become communities of inquiry.

> *Yeah, I always also teach my students in the online environment at the outset of the course about the concept of the Community of Inquiry. I try to encourage them to think about the fact that, in any of our online courses, we are a learning community and that means we need to be sharing our ideas with one another and agreeing and disagreeing with one another, but doing so in a respectful sort of a way . . . I've learnt they worked well if you get it set up right. And you have to get it set up right otherwise it's not going to work. (Peter)*

Explicit expectations for this social development were reported to be important by all those interviewed. They intimated that social interaction and participation in discussion was central to quality learning in the online context.

> *[What] I knew very, very clearly was that the social aspects of online learning are very, very important. Online learning will only work, or people will only take advantage of online learning media, if there is a kind of a pay off or purpose to what is going on. And again, this requires a strong participation, and preferably a participation within a community of other learners. Participation in a way which is not just an informational sort of accessing or information being thrown at you. (Gerard)*

The Importance of the Socioemotional Context

The lecturers elaborated on the importance of the socioemotional context in promoting, or otherwise, social interactivity among students. In particular, they stated the need to create a safe, tolerant, respectful, supportive climate for the sharing and discussion of ideas. This way, students in their courses are encouraged to overcome their shyness and inhibition of writing and sharing their ideas with others in the course. Their view was that they needed to model the types of helpful online interactions that conveyed a sense of respect and enthusiasm to achieve this climate online.

Online teachers need to value students and the little contributions that they make, affirm them as a person. (Nola)

I start out with establishing the Communities of Inquiry principles at the start. I do a fair bit of it. So then they are able to get into the discussions on the basis of knowing that that trust is there, respect is there, the tolerance for different thinking is okay. (Peter)

One way of doing this was through a regular presence online.

The other thing that I think is important is the attitude of the tutor. I do expect that we owe students at home a form of respect. They are sitting in an isolated community very many kilometers away from anywhere else and they asked a question. Well, I think they deserve a response. So to me that's absolutely critical, treating them and their questions seriously and actually giving them worthwhile responses. So that does mean regularly being online. (Marge)

One of the things as a staff member, when it's your turn to be online, is that you should actually have access wherever you are even if you have to go away for a few days to meetings or whatever. So you need to be there all the time for them. Of course you get a wee tempted but then again, it only has to be for a short time. So I think you have to change office hours. It's not just going to a classroom for 3 hours a week. So I think it is important that you are there for them. (Laura)

The development of trust and respect as a means of minimizing the risk of contributing was seen as being more important for an online class than a face-to-face class.

So that risk is being able to take the risk of trying something out, putting something up on the screen and seeing what others think without being too pressured about it. But also able to recognize that other people will do that too. It's a confidence thing, confident to talk with people, to interact with people, to try those things out. I think that's the key, more important than oral which is what you need on campus. (Basil)

Possibly because of the isolation the students faced.

But students often are isolated. You have to recognize their isolation. Whereas students who come on to campus have the ability to say, well I don't talk to a lecturer everyday. You mightn't talk to a lecturer every day but you talk to your classmates every day and you actually get something from them. I think we have to recognize that and compensate for that as best as you can. (Ralph)

Others also support the academic and personal advantages of incorporating and encouraging student collaboration to reduce this sense of acute social isolation when learning online (Bird & Morgan, 2003; Brown, 2001; Coulter, Konold & Feldman, 2000; Lai, 1997; Lake, 1999; McIssac, Blocher, Mahes, & Vrasidas, 1999).

An important element in achieving this climate is the appropriate use of language and knowing how and when to intervene at the most opportune moment.

> *That's where the teaching and learning comes in. Knowing what to pick up, knowing what out of their conversation is significant that I should be responding back to or trying to make a link of what somebody else has said. It's that knowledge about the things that they are saying in terms of content and linking those together and drawing them together and referring them to other readings. That's the important part of teaching. (Basil)*

> *Some of the language that we use is very important and that may sound stupid but sometimes just getting something so that its as you're talking not as you . . . not lecturing. So sometimes it can be very informal and there are other times when formality is better. (Marge)*

Consistent with a view of learning as a social process, the lecturers described their role as teacher as that of a partner with students in teaching and learning. One lecturer described how she saw herself as "part of that unit," that is, part of the class as a community that worked together to share ideas and solve problems.

> *I expect that we will support each other. I expect that we will share ideas and that we are not going to be sort of aloof from each other. Because if we are like that then it makes it very difficult working at home. I have the expectation that we will work together as a community. Not me here, them there as individuals, but they will work together solving problems, looking up things and that I'm just part of that unit. I'm not the head of that, that they've all got to contribute as a learner. (Marge)*

Another lecturer described teaching online as involving a change in role to work alongside students.

> *If you take lecturers for example, I think their adaptability has to be there. But at the same time, there has to be commitment and there has to be clear commitment to teach in this particular way. So, if you are talking about the changing role, I guess one of the things that the people need is to be seen as being learners alongside others. And I think its actually when students and lecturers were closer in a sense that if they could see the job actually*

engaging with them or not. So I suppose that would be really the main difference I think. (Ralph)

This change in role was seen as one of the more challenging aspects of moving to teach online.

One of the things that new staff find very difficult is that they have been the providers of knowledge. They see a discussion going in a certain direction and they think "I know the answer to that" and they want to leap on in. But you have to practice good wait time. You have to watch the flow, you have to look at who has contributed and you have to wait for exactly the right time to put it in. (Nola)

The Importance of Coherence and Purpose

Another characteristic of effective online teaching and learning was for lecturers to have carefully thought through their planning for learning.

Yeah, you can't wing it. Sometimes in terms of my [face-to-face] teaching, I usually try to be prepared and, you know, I can go with the general concept of what I'm wanting to discuss or talk about, but I can go with the flow and I can see what the group's doing. You can't do that on this online medium. You just can't do that. (Lesley)

Whereas, in the online environment, I find you've got to be a lot more structured and thoughtful about that then, you have to do more pre-planning, more thinking ahead on that than you do in the face-to-face environment. (Peter)

Careful planning for learning, and that students understood the relevance to their learning of each component of the course, was seen as a crucial element in facilitating student engagement and participation. The lecturers planned their online courses so that there was a coherency of purpose between the course materials sent out to students, the course tasks designed to engage students within the online environment, and the assignments or practical work that students were assigned. They made explicit how the components worked together.

You have to be prepared to, I think, think about things in a different sort of a way so that the components are coherent. So that your technology, your reading, and your practical work actually do fit together coherently. (Marge)

This was seen as a way of fostering active purposeful student engagement in the online component of the class with a benefit for any written or individual components or both.

> *The discussion topics have to relate to what the student is likely to be working on at that particular time. They don't want to go and talk about the cost of fish at the fish market if that's got nothing to do with the course. It has to be exactly what they'll be working on, so that that broadens their perspective and their answer is far better in the course work because of that discussion. (Nola)*

Teachers communicating their learning goals to students is currently recommended as important in face-to-face teaching (Black and William, 1998) but the lecturers considered this crucial in online teaching because students can and do choose not to participate or even log on to the class.

Acknowledging the Differences

Although we have argued that the guiding principles of quality teaching and learning remain the same regardless of context, we certainly acknowledge that asynchronous, online teaching and learning contexts are significantly different from conventional teaching situations and we now examine some of the important differences.

Changing Role of the Teacher

For teachers whose practice is already guided by the principles and characteristics we have described, there is likely to be minimal change in their role as guide, mentor, and facilitator. However, for teachers whose usual role has been that of the "sage on the stage" delivering information and content to their students, the move into an online context is likely to be uncomfortable and difficult. In conventional, face-to-face classrooms, teachers of this kind are able to verbally deliver (often at length) information to a captive (if not always captivated) audience and feel comforted that everyone present has received the message. In an asynchronous, online environment, however, there is no captive audience compelled to listen and watch at a particular time and place, and there is no stage. Students can opt in and out as they please choosing when to participate and what to attend to when they do. If what is happening in the "classroom" does not engage them then their "attendance" will be minimal. This concern is encapsulated in the following lecturer quote:

One of the great dangers of the Internet is that, for some people . . . the danger is that it becomes a very easy way of getting a degree, going through the motions. And I have no doubt that some people are going to come out the other side with their Bachelors, or indeed their Masters, and they have had far less confrontation with their prior ideas than those who have been on campus. (Gerard)

While there is always value in a motivating and inspiring presentation, for students to remain motivated and engaged over time, our research, and that of others (Bonk & Cunningham, 1998; Bonk & Dennan, 1999; Campos, LaFerriere, & Harashim, 2001), suggests that one of the most important aspects enhancing learners' motivation and learning is the degree to which they become involved in the activities, discussions, and debates within the online class. To support this, the teacher needs to be skilled in promoting discussion and debate, perhaps initially taking a prominent role but progressively moving to the sidelines as students become more involved and confident about participating in the learning community's discourse (Berge, 2000; Conceição, 2002; Salmon, 2000). One lecturer aptly highlighted this:

I have yet to see what I would consider a quality learning situation that doesn't have a quality teacher facilitating the discussion. The online teachers that students' say they value are those who know how to facilitate good discussion. (Nola)

Social and Nonverbal Cues

One of the most obvious differences between face-to-face and online teaching is the lack of social and nonverbal cues available in an online context. Within a face-to-face classroom, there are numerous social, nonverbal interactions between students and between students and teacher that contribute to the culture of the classroom and which cannot occur in an asynchronous, online "classroom" (Monolescu & Schifter, 2000). In a physical setting, individuals' appearance, dress, voice quality, mannerisms, and so forth all contribute to the teaching and learning context and assist the teacher in facilitating discussions, providing immediate real-time feedback and attending to the class' concerns. One of the lecturers in our study indicated her frustration with the lack of nonverbal cues to assist her in identifying students' learning in the online context:

In my class when I've got a group of students in front of me, I can tell by their body language and their hesitancy about who's done a real last minute rush job to meet the deadline. Or if I'm doing a reading in class, I can tell who's read the article, who knows what the critical points are. Whereas I cannot do that with the online stuff as well. (Lesley)

Real-Time Practical Activities

One concern about teaching online is the inability to conduct and implement real-time practical activities. This was highlighted by Basil as follows:

> *One of the real frustrations that I've had was that I've been in Physical Education and trying to get . . . trying to include that activity that physical education can and should be has always been a real challenge. We spend a lot of time talking about the teaching aspects of Physical Education and how to be an effective teacher in PE, without necessarily trying things out in a practical situation. On campus we'll talk about these things and we'll physically try them out down in the gym. I haven't mastered that, that's something that I've always been frustrated with here. (Basil)*

Online teachers have had to acknowledge this inadequacy and find ways to compensate for the inability to incorporate real-time practical activities in their curriculum. However, it is expected that as the technology evolves, face-to-face and online teaching differences will be further diminished as educational uses of the World Wide Web become more widespread (Hill, 1997).

Technologically Mediated Communication

Although new technologies are increasingly expanding the possible modes of communication available in online contexts, they are still currently dominated by text-based modes of communication (Garrison, Anderson, & Archer, 2000). This emphasis on text has advantages for students in terms of developing their writing abilities.

> *Being a technologically mediated communication, if in class on campus, for instance, students don't publish like that all the time. Their mode of communication is oral unless it's an assignment. These people, their mode of communication is definitely written. So at the end of the day, they'll probably be much better writers than the on-campus people. (Basil)*

It also advantages for them in terms of developing their reading abilities.

The difference, particularly if it involves reading, students do read that's what they've got to hook into when they're considering things. They will ask people, they will think about issues, and they do read in reference to the readings. Whereas some of the on-campus people, to encourage them to read sometimes is really difficult. (Marge)

A caveat, however, about text-based communication is the time it takes to teach online in comparison to the face-face context.

One of the other things is that it does take time. Teaching online does take longer than teaching on campus. (Basil)

So it takes quite a bit of time. It's not something that you can do. . . . Quite often, what I would do is read and then think and think how can I approach this. So I will type a statement and then I'll set it aside for a while to see whether that's going to actually encourage them to think more. So I take a bit of time to do that, its not something I can do straight-away. (Marge)

The time consuming nature of working online also extends to students learning online.

I find that students need time to hook in. I can set up a discussion face-to-face and it can happen within a few minutes. You'll have an activity, students will hook in, somebody will make a comment. But for the online aspect you have to wait for them to be able to read something, consider something, and put something back in. And so that notion of time becomes quite different. So to function you have to be prepared to wait. Say for example, on the face-to-face one might set up an activity, have a discussion and we can be moving on within half an hour, whereas it might take me a week online to get the same sorts of response. (Marge)

Despite the time involved in teaching online, an advantage is the time flexibility to conduct one's course.

And then the other real good bonus is flexibility. I get to say well I'll do my class later and it doesn't matter what time I hook in. Just as much as it doesn't matter what time they hook in. So that's a real bonus at times. Can be a burden too. But you can actually manipulate things to a certain extent to suit and plan for alternative ways of doing things. But having said that, you have just got to allocate the proper time to it. I do enjoy the flexibility of it. (Marge)

Dialogue is Available Over Time

Another advantage of text-based communication is its relative permanency in recording dialogue. Other researchers (Carnwell, 1999; Stratfold, 1998) highlight this advantage in terms of promoting student reflective thinking, and this was also noted by our lecturers.

> *The other thing is too, that online, one of the differences is because they are writing. Its actually committed. You can't run something off the cuff and its gone forever. Because what you say is actually recorded and its there forever and that in itself means that you have to be quite careful about you're are saying because it can be used outside the situation. (Marge)*
>
> *It is slightly less spontaneous but, in terms of developing careful thinking, that's actually helpful. Because what I want is students to be careful and critical and reflective in their thinking and so online discussion invites that kind of thinking forward more than top of the head spontaneous chat in class. And that I find is part of the learning value of it. (Jake)*

An added advantage is for the online teacher to simultaneously follow several student group discussions.

> *Often you have the luxury of being able to follow six groups at once. You can't do that face-to-face. You can't be in a classroom with six groups talking and know what's going on in every one. That's not possible. (Nola)*

Discussion

The themes emerging from our examination of online teaching and learning, such as the importance of social interaction and socioemotional security, resonate well with the sociocultural view of learning, discussed in the early part of this chapter. Although the underlying principles of this view have been derived in face-to-face contexts, our research suggests that these principles are just as applicable in online contexts and we question the need to develop new guiding principles for teaching and learning online. Quality teaching, regardless of the context, stems from the teacher's understanding of learning. This understanding underpins and characterizes the teaching strategies developed and employed by the teacher and, although unfamiliar teaching and learning contexts will always be challenging for both teachers and learners, the ability to achieve their goals by adapting their practices to suit the context has always been an important part of effective teaching. Adaptability is required when dealing with individual students, a new class of students, changes in curriculum, or the advent of new teaching technology. In coping with rapidly changing environments, a clear view of learning is imperative to anchor and guide teachers' approaches to new teaching and learning situations, otherwise there is a danger that teachers may be distracted by new technologies and loose sight of the core business of facilitating learning. Oliver and Herrington (2000), for example, have warned that if technological imperatives such as opportunity, competition, and efficiency drive the introduction of information and communication technologies in education rather than pedagogical imperatives, then new learning technologies are likely to be used in superficial ways akin to the notion of "gift-wrapping" (Fischer, 2003) where old content is delivered in new media with little or no benefit to learning.

While a well-considered view of learning will provide teachers with stability and guidance as they respond to new teaching and learning situations, views of learning are also subject to critique and change. It is important, however, that such changes are well informed by research and made with great care and consideration.

As in our metaphoric title "New Wine or New Bottles," we suggest that online teaching and learning represents yet another variety of wine bottled and charmingly packaged to attract attention and gain popularity in today's education marketplace. Online teaching and learning, in its different forms and uses, is but part of the many contemporary varieties of wine available for teachers and learners to explore and savor. In delighting in the wine's rich full-bodied flavor, however, we should not forget that, while our enjoyment of the wine is undoubtedly enhanced by its presentation, the wine's quality rests on the winemaker's mastery of the art, technology, and science of winemaking. Although it is possible to purchase expensive, attractively packaged wine that is mediocre in taste and experience, good quality wine, at a reasonable price, is also available. If we can identify and support good winemakers and encourage them to share their knowledge and skill then there is every chance that quality wines will continue to be available for everyone for years to come.

> *I don't think they [face-to-face and online] differ at all, I think the basic principles of teaching are still there. (Ralph)*

References

Berge, Z. (2000). New roles for learners and teachers in online higher education. In G. Hart (Ed.), *Readings and resources in global online education* (pp. 3-9). Melbourne: Whirligig Press.

Bird, J., & Morgan, C. (2003). Adults contemplating university study at a distance: Issues, themes and concerns. *International Review of Research in Open and Distance Learning, 4*(1), 1-14.

Black, P., & William, D. (1998). Assessment and classroom learning. *Assessment in Education, 5*(1), 7-74.

Bonk, C. J., & Cunningham, D. J. (1998). Searching for learner-centered, constructivist and sociocultural components of collaborative educational learning tools. In C. J. Bonk & K. S. Kim (Eds.), *Electronic collaborators: Learner centered technologies for literacy, apprenticeship and discourse* (pp. 25-50). Hillsdale, NJ: Laurence Erlbaum.

Bonk, C. J., & Dennan, V. P. (1999). Teaching on the Web: With a little help from my pedagogical friends. *Journal of Computing in Higher Education, 11*(1), 3-28.

Brown, A., Ash, D., Rutherford, M., Nakagawa, K., Gordon, A., & Campione, J. (1993). Distributed expertise in the classroom. In G. Salomon (Ed.), *Distributed cognitions: Psychological and educational considerations* (pp. 188-228). Cambridge: Cambridge University Press.

Brown, J. S., Collins, A., & Duguid, P. (1989). Situated cognition and the culture of learning. *Educational Researcher,* January-February, 32-42.

Brown, R. E. (2001). The process of community building in distance learning classes. *Journal of Asynchronous Learning Networks, 5*(2), 18-35.

Campbell, N., & Yates, R. (1997). *Meeting New Zealand's teacher shortage: A mixed medium approach to teacher education.* Paper presented at the Conference Proceedings of the 18th International Council for Distance Education World Conference, Pennsylvania.

Campbell, N. G. (1997). *Learning to teach online: An investigation of practice in teacher education.* Unpublished master's thesis, University of Waikato.

Campbell, N. G., & Moodie, P. (1999). *Getting the best out of your class forum* [Videorecording]. Hamilton, NZ: Teaching Technology Group.

Campbell, N. G., Yates, R., & McGee, C. (1998, October). *Bridging education in the classroom and distance education: An innovation in the delivery of a mixed media teacher education programme.* Paper presented at the Fourth Biennial New Zealand Conference on Teacher Education, University of Waikato, Hamilton.

Campos, M., Laferrière, T., & Harasim, L. (2001). The post-secondary networked classroom: Renewal of teaching practices and social interaction. *Journal of Asynchronous Learning Networks, 5*(2), 36-52.

Carnwell, R. (1999). Distance education and the need for dialogue. *Open Learning, 14*(1), 50-56.

Clark, R. E. (1994). Media will never influence learning. *Educational Technology Research and Development, 42*(2), 21-29.

Conceição, S. (2002). The sociocultural implications of learning and teaching in cyberspace. *New Directions for Adult and Continuing Education, 2002*(96), 37-47.

Coulter, B., Konold, C., & Feldman, A. (2000). Promoting reflective discussions: Making the most of online resources in your classroom. *Learning and Leading with Technology, 28*(2), 44-50.

Curran, C. (2001). The phenomenon of online learning. *European Journal of Education, 36*(2), 113-132.

Driver, R. (1983). *The pupil as scientist.* Milton Keynes: Open University Press.

Ells, R. (1999, June 20). 2000 UW computing & communications. *Webagogy.* Retrieved December 2, 2003, from http://staff.washington.edu/rells/webagogy/index.shtml

Fischer, G. (2003, May). *Learning paradigms of the 21st Century: New mindsets, new cultures, and new media for learning.* Paper presented at a talk at University of Waikato.

Frey, B. A., & Alman, S. W. (n. d.). *Lessons learned from online graduate students* [Web-site]. Retrieved June 24, 2002, from http://www.ipfw.edu/as/tohe/2001/Papers/frey.htm

Garrison, R., Anderson, T., & Archer, W. (2000). Critical thinking in a text-based environment: Computer conferencing in higher education. *The Internet and Higher Education, 2*(2), 87-105.

Gibson, C. C. (1998). *Distance learners in higher education: Institutional responses for quality outcomes.* Madison, WI: Atwood.

Hill, J. R. (1997). Distance learning environments via the World Wide Web. In B. H. Khan (Ed.), *Web-based instruction* (pp. 75-84). NJ: Educational Technology .

Kirshner, D., & Whitson, J. A. (1997). Editors' introduction to situated cognition: Social, semiotic, and psychological perspectives. In D. Kirshner & J. A. Whitson (Eds.), *Situated cognition: Social, semiotic, and psychological perspectives*. Mahwah, NJ: Lawrence Erlbaum.

Lai, K. W. (1997). Interactivity in Web-based learning: Some observations based on a Web-based course about CMC in education. In B. Collis & G. Knezek (Eds.), *Teaching and learning in the digital age* (pp. 211-230). Eugene, OR: International Society for Computers in Education (ISTE).

Lake, D. (1999). Reducing isolation for distance students: An online initiative. *Open Learning, 14*(3), 14-24.

LaMonica, L. (2001, July 17). *The role of the instructor in Web-based instruction: Are we practicing what we preach?* Retrieved December 2, 2003, from http://www.geocities.com/llamonica/instructorwbt.html

Lave, J., & Wenger, E. (1991). *Situated learning: Legitimate peripheral participation.* Cambridge: Cambridge University Press.

Leach, J., & Moon, B. (1999). Recreating pedagogy. In J. Leach & B. Moon (Eds.), *Learners and pedagogy* (pp. 265-276). Milton Keynes: Open University Press.

Matuga, J. M. (2001). Electronic pedagogical practice: The art and science of teaching and learning online. *Educational Technology & Society, 4*(3). Retrieved December 12, 2003, from http://ifets.ieee.org/periodical/vol_3_2001/matuga.html

McGee, C., & Yates, R. (2000). *Innovation in using telecommunications in pre-service teacher education and the impact upon distance learning student teachers.* Paper presented at the Society for Information Technology and Teacher Education (SITE 2000), 11th International Conference, San Diego, California.

McIssac, M. S., Blocher, J. M., Mahes, V., & Vrasidas, C. (1999). Student and teacher perceptions of interaction in online computer-mediated communication. *Educational Media International, 36*(2), 121-131.

Monolescu, D., & Schifter, C. (2000). Online focus group: A tool to evaluate online students' course experience. *Internet and Higher Education, 2*(2-3), 171-176.

Moore, M. G. (1998). Introduction. In C. C. Gibson (Ed.), *Distance learners in higher education: Institutional responses for quality outcomes* (pp. 1-8). Madison, WI: Atwood.

Oliver, R., & Herrington, J. (2000). Using situated learning as a design strategy for Web-based learning. In B. Abbey (Ed.), *Instructional and cognitive impacts of Web-based education* (pp. 178-191). Hershey, PA: Idea Group.

Osborne, R., & Freyberg, P. (1985). *Learning in science: The implications of children's science.* Auckland: Heinemann.

Palloff, R. M., & Pratt, K. (1999). *Building learning communities in cyberspace: Effective strategies for the online classroom.* San Francisco: Jossey Bass.

Pfundt, H., & Duit, R. (2000). *Bibliography: Students alternative frameworks and science education* (5th ed.). Kiel: Institut fur die Padagogik der Naturwissenschaften.

Piaget, J. (1937). *La construction de reel chez l'enfant.* Neuchatel, France: Delachaux et Nestle.

Piaget, J. (1970). *Genetic epistemology* (E. Duckworth, Trans.). New York: Columbia University Press.

Saljo, R. (1999). Learning as the use of tools: A sociocultural perspective on the human-technology link. In K. Littlejohn & P. Light (Eds.), *Learning with computers* (pp. 144-161). London: Routledge.

Salmon, G. (2000). *E-moderating: The key to teaching and learning online.* London: Kogan Page.

Skinner, B. F. (1954). The science of learning and the art of teaching. *Harvard Educational Review, 24,* 86-97.

Stratfold, M. (1998). Promoting learner dialogues in the Web. In M. Eisenstadt & T. Vincent (Eds.), *The knowledge web: Learning and collaborating on the net* (pp. 119-134). London: Kogan Page.

Taylor, M., & Biddulph, F. (1999). *A beast of burden or an exciting challenge? Examining the process of becoming an online educator.* Paper presented at the 14th Biennial Forum of the Open and Distance Learning Association of Australia, Australia.

Taylor, M., & Biddulph, F. (2000). *Can enactivist teaching be achieved online?* Paper presented at the annual conference of the New Zealand Association for Educational Research, Hamilton, New Zealand.

Thorndike, E. L. (1926). *The measurement of intelligence.* New York: Teachers College Press.

Vygotsky, L. S. (1978). *Mind in society: The development of higher psychological processes.* Cambridge, MA: Harvard University Press.

Watson, J. S. (1914). *Behavior, an introduction to comparative psychology.* New York: Holt, Rinehart, and Winston.

Wenger, E. (1998). *Communities of practice: Learning, meaning, and identity.* Cambridge: Cambridge University Press.

Windschitl, M. (1998). The WWW and classroom research: What path should we take? *Educational Researcher, 27*(1), 28-33.

Chapter XV

Quality Assurance During Distributed Collaboration:
A Case Study in Creating a Cross-Institutional Learning Community

Rita M. Vick, Quantum Leap Interactive Inc., United States

Brent Auernheimer, California State University, United States

Marie K. Iding, University of Hawaii, United States

Martha E. Crosby, University of Hawaii, United States

Abstract

This case study describes the design and delivery of a collaborative asynchronous-synchronous, graduate-level, cross-university computer science course designed to create a highly interactive learning environment that resulted in the emergence of multiple unique virtual learning communities. The pedagogical principles of situated and problem-based learning were combined in a distributed collaborative learning context where students' cognitive and metacognitive capabilities developed through the facilitative guidance of the instructors and through discourse with and observation of other students. The course was designed to motivate students to engage in interactive learning with others and to enhance transfer of knowledge gained through this learning experience to real-life situations. We describe the challenges inherent in creating and managing this type of learning context as well as how we deployed ongoing formative assessment to ensure the evolution of a dynamic learning environment. The result of our efforts was a unique learning experience for students and instructors.

Introduction

While there have been many cross-university distance learning efforts (e.g., Bunz, 2000; Gunawardena & Duphorne, 2001), it is important to note qualitative and functional differences between synchronous and asynchronous interactivity in order to deploy the interaction method that will best foster pedagogical goals throughout the stages of a course. The networking, courseware framework, and human and pedagogical components of an interactive learning environment (ILE) need to be persistent as well as flexible. While the appropriate mix of interactivity depends on the knowledge domain and the purpose of the course, learner engagement in a virtual context is often best achieved by deployment of a combination of asynchronous and synchronous course elements (Vick, 2002).

After delivering a number of online courses in asynchronous mode, it occurred to us that adding a synchronous phase to an otherwise asynchronous course would increase the level of human-human interaction resulting in an enhanced sense of participation on the part of students. It was hoped that this increased sense of community would, in turn, result in improved learning outcomes and greater satisfaction with the course.

In this chapter, we first discuss the overall strategy behind our design of a cross-institutional hybrid asynchronous-synchronous course that added exploratory (Wiedenbeck & Zila, 1997) and experiential (Dehler & Porras-Hernandez, 1998) synchronous elements to an asynchronous graduate-level computer science course in human-computer interaction (HCI). We focus on the synchronous part of this collaborative endeavor, how it was developed and deployed, and the results that were achieved. Our goal was to add value to an asynchronous course by embedding an interactive synchronous element to stimulate student engagement in knowledge exchange and create an active knowledge-building learning community. Interpretive and empirical analyses were used to assess learner participation and satisfaction with the course. We took advantage of a high level of student diversity and the potential of a hybrid course design to (a) enhance student understanding of core domain knowledge and (b) enable real-world use of this knowledge through problem-based and experiential learning.

Second, we explain our tactical division of students into multiple highly interactive local (same university) and global (cross-university) virtual learning communities. Our goal was to create a stimulating learning environment by enabling and encouraging interaction within and across team-based learning communities so that situated, cooperative learning could take place seamlessly.

Third, we discuss task, technology, and socially related challenges, costs, and benefits faced by learners and instructors. The nature and level of interactivity in the hybrid virtual learning environment used for this course amplified the effect of combining synchronous and asynchronous learning episodes. Separate and individual asynchronous periods of learning at two universities were followed; first, by synchronous team sessions at each university, and then by synchronous cross-university team sessions. This use of mixed contexts for learning presented a unique set of situational problems and opportunities.

Fourth, we present empirical analyses of student interactivity and satisfaction levels based on qualitative and interpretive analysis followed by an inventory of lessons learned and best practices discovered.

Types of Online Interactivity

Postings and responses to postings in asynchronous discussion groups may be required or optional. Although asynchronous discussions may result in "clutter" due to many vacuous entries (Sloffer, Dueber, & Duffy, 1999), this kind of "interactivity" enables reflective and self-paced learning. Also, the discussion may be shallow if participants talk around but fail to directly address the topic. At its best, however, asynchronous interactivity enables reflective and self-paced learning. Synchronous discussion groups, on the other hand, are dynamic in that interactivity is persistent, stimulates further interaction, and enables exploratory and experiential learning (Kang, 1998). When designing a framework for e-learning, it is necessary to consider such tradeoffs even though, as in face-to-face (FtF) communication, interaction improves as participants become more familiar with the designated interaction format.

It is also important to consider costs versus benefits for particular combinations of activity type. Given a fixed amount of time to devote to the endeavor, an increase in one type of interactivity will necessarily result in a decrease in another type of interactivity. The combination of interaction types and the percent of available course time devoted to each are dependent upon the goals of the course. Assuming a learner-centered design, content transfer may be self-paced, presupposing that time is required for reflection in order to achieve desired learning outcomes. On the other hand, dynamic collaborative interaction with peers may be important in achieving the goal of a course. Whether this dynamism is achieved by motivating asynchronous or synchronous discussion among participants is partly dependent upon the time and place configuration of participants and partly upon the value placed upon collaborative learning. More importantly, it is dependent upon expectations about the delivery of the course.

Synchronous collaboration can be an effective tool for encouraging problem-based and situated learning; that is, how information becomes applied knowledge. Balancing interactivity type and duration throughout a course is enabled by appropriate course and context design. Course outcomes are impacted by the pedagogical value of each kind of interactivity (Kang, 1998), the human scaffolding inherent in sociocultural learning (Wertsch, 1985a, 1985b), and the multiple perspectives afforded by learner diversity. Collaborative learning in a complex, interactive, open, cross-cultural context enables understanding to emerge and results in development of communities of learning, or communities of practice (Dillenbourg, 1999; Vick, 1998, 2002; Wenger, McDermott, & Snyder, 2002).

Designing a Value-Added Online Course

Successful management of a hybrid asynchronous-synchronous distance learning course requires flexible management of multiple interrelated contextual factors. Basic requirements for distance learning include dependable connectivity and flexible courseware. Design of online course content, however, requires clear understanding of the myriad ways in which context influences content and learner activity within the online environment. Effective design of a virtual learning environment requires understanding of the relational influences that exist between the learning context and learners, as well as how learner interaction changes these relationships (Lave & Chaiklin, 1993).

We have found that more effective delivery of content can be designed into a course by using basic technological capacity to support human-human interaction through use of technology-mediated collaborative projects. The collaborative nature of team projects serves to transform contextual liabilities, for example, the context of a single learner interacting with various media (Rogoff & Lave, 1984) into assets, for example, the context of a community of learners (Brown & Campione, 1994; Wenger, 1998; Wenger et al., 2002) actively engaged in knowledge building through interactive exchange of information. To accomplish this, however, quality assurance must be managed through ongoing formative assessment not only of content and student progress, but also of context and level of interactivity.

The described course was designed to combine the concepts of situated and problem-based learning in a distributed collaborative context. In this type of learning environment, students' cognitive and metacognitive capabilities develop through the facilitative guidance of the instructor and through discourse with and observation of other students (Collins, 1989; Collins, Brown, & Newman, 1987; Flavell, 1976; Wertsch, 1985a, 1985b). The context of the course was designed to motivate students to engage in interactive learning with others and to enhance transfer of knowledge gained through this learning context to real-life situations (Clements & Nastasi, 1988; Lave & Wenger, 1990; McLellan, 1995).

This case study represents a significant contribution to management of diverse pedagogical tools in a complementary way to advance the quality of what diverse student groups learn beyond the context of course material. It demonstrates maximal leveraging of collaborative Web-based interaction. Our analysis will benefit educators and trainers who will increasingly use information and communication technologies as connectivity improves and reliance on e-learning grows. Connectivity and courseware (e.g., WebCT, Blackboard [Bb]) enable persistent interaction among students and educators along with tools instructors can use to tailor content to the knowledge requirements of specific learning domains. The combination of e-learning and pedagogical tools (asynchronous WebCT and Bb, synchronous Bb, teamwork) that we utilized is an example of use of minimal resources to productively join culturally and geographically diverse students and educators in construction and transfer of implicit and explicit knowledge.

Case Study: Creating Cross-Institutional Learning Communities

Purpose of the Study

Basic challenges that influence the effectiveness of collaborative relationships among learners and with educators include (1) the nature and level of interactivity and how this bears on e-learning and (2) the issue of task-technology fit as this applies to design of distance learning courses. We tested the limits of the technology by using the Bb learning support system tools for synchronous as well as asynchronous interactivity. While the asynchronous aspects of the course provided content and interactive discussion between instructor and student, the synchronous phase of the course provided an intense and focused learning experience that spanned geographical location, as well as cultural and institutional boundaries. This same-time interaction engaged students in "learning by doing," learning from peers, and examining the extent of their knowledge to develop their capacity to "learn how to learn."

Methodology

Two HCI courses were offered separately, asynchronously, and in parallel to 36 globally distributed graduate-level computer science students at two geographically and temporally separate universities. The courses were conducted in asynchronous mode until the two classes joined at a common Bb site for the synchronous final project. Students worked synchronously online in same university teams to review their initial individual attempts at performing an HCI evaluation task. Subsequently, teams were paired with other-university teams to form tandems for a synchronous online final project presentation session where each team presented their project results to their counterpart team from the other university. Instructors attended each presentation as observers.

Classes consisted of culturally diverse students from the People's Republic of China (PRC), Taiwan, Northern Europe, Southeast Asia, the Continental United States, and Hawaii at one university and from the Indian Subcontinent, South America, South East Asia, and the Continental United States at the other university. During online presentations, students were geographically and temporally dispersed. Students were in Hawaii and California, one student was in the PRC, another in Chicago, and another in Boston. Students successfully met online for synchronous pre-presentation discussions as well as for the final presentations.

To develop students' understanding of HCI "principles-in-use," we introduced a final project that required students to perform a cognitive walkthrough (CW) of a Web site. The CW is an evaluation technique used by designers early in the design of a system to determine how well the features of the system support use through "exploratory learning." More information about the cognitive walkthrough as a technique for evaluating the design of a user interface can be found at http://www.acm.org/sigchi/chi95/Electronic/documnts/tutors/jr_bdy.htm.

The final project consisted of four phases: (1) Individual students performed CWs. (2) Four-member same-university teams carried out synchronous online review of their individual work, combining results into a single PowerPoint presentation. (3) Tandems (one team from each university) reciprocally presented and discussed results. During this course capstone, two teams and three instructors (11 participants) were present simultaneously in a Bb virtual classroom. Communication was via text chat, the support system proved robust, and sessions went smoothly. (4) Same-university teams discussed the presentations and critiqued the course as a whole.

Task Design

The synchronous phases were a critical part of the course design for three reasons. First, we wanted to provide students with the opportunity to actually experience the "doing" of a CW in real time. Second, we wanted to leverage the cultural and geographical diversity present in our student groups to afford students an online experience rich with varied perspectives. Third, the sequence of performing (a) individual, (b) team, and (c) tandem walkthroughs provided experiential learning by allowing time for reflection between CWs. This sequence served to scaffold the cross-university presentation by instilling sufficient confidence in the CW evaluation method and the support system to elevate the interuniversity presentations to the level of a meaningful, task-centered discussion with colleagues.

A list of suggested questions was placed on the common Bb Web site to help teams structure their final project discussions and to maximize collaborative learning. Teams determined which tandem would present first. The other team and the instructors asked questions at any point during the presentation.

Appropriateness of the Technology Used

In designing the courses' final project, we exploited the operational capability of the Bb virtual classroom to provide seamless interaction by having two student teams and three instructors in one room at the same time. Potentially, up to 11 participants could interact via chat simultaneously. However, it was generally the case that two or three participants were alternately active while other participants alternately observed. Also, more than one tandem meeting ran concurrently. The Bb support system provided for the synchronous use of multiple virtual classrooms with no major problems. Another concern was the optimum number of participants who could take part in the Bb virtual classroom at one time and still maintain a meaningful dialogue. The Bb virtual classroom interface itself was not a problem. Small individual participant screen size could be problematic due to having to sacrifice the size of the slide image in order to increase the size of the chat frame in Bb's virtual classroom window.

While text chat, used alone, is slow and may cause some confusion when multiple parties are "talking," the missing paralinguistic cues of FtF discussion causes people to attend to the "conversation" more intensely. This forces greater focus on conversation content because the mental time spent clarifying (perhaps unintentional or insignificant, or both) facial expression, tone of voice, and other cues in FtF discourse is eliminated. Text chat thus has a "distilling" effect on communication and the work process since it eliminates "noise" from other sensory sources. In spoken communication, people often use extra words accompanied by facial expression, body movement, and voice inflection to clarify meaning. When ideas must be expressed in writing, the communication task is much more difficult because meaning can only be achieved by using precise language supplemented, perhaps, by emoticons. Related findings have been found in other language-related research (Herring, 1996).

Other perspectives on "chat" as a lone communication channel include its lack of "richness" as a communication medium as well as the form in which it is presented. It has been found that trust, an important factor in establishing rapport with distant collaborators, is more quickly established using richer media (Bos, Olson, Gergle, Olson, & Wright, 2002). However, in the absence of FtF meeting before distance collaboration, it has been found that text chat or even a picture placed on the Web site helps to establish rapport (Zheng, Veinott, Bos, Olson, & Olson, 2002). If chat is the main means of communication, the form in which it appears on the interface has a significant impact on conversational turn taking as well as participation level. As a contextual element vital to communication, the Bb virtual classroom chat facility is less effective, for example, than that of NetMeeting due to its smaller size and "scrollability."

Outcomes of the Study

Teams held postpresentation summative assessment meetings in their private virtual team meeting rooms. Our concern was with (1) type and quality of interaction and (2) satisfaction with the team, task, and process elements of synchronous human-computer-human interaction during the tandem presentations. Many kinds of synchronous interactivity occurred during the tandem presentations. We focused on topic-related exchanges within, between, and across teams. We excluded extraneous activity (e.g., browsing to organize slides, exit to private team rooms for virtual caucuses, and subsequent reentry to the tandem presentation room).

Interaction Levels

For purposes of this study, interaction was analyzed by evaluating each line entry of the archived chat transcripts. Line entries consist of statements made by team members as well as Bb log entries indicating performance of an activity by a team member during the tandem presentations. Table 1 describes the categories used to define individuals' actions or statements. Categories were kept to a minimum because the goal was to gather a holistic view of the overall session. Before analyzing statement content, it is important to uncover the characteristics of conversational spread in order to assess evenness and directionality of participation.

Analysis of interactivity during the teams' presentations revealed that all tandems spent most of their meeting time conversing with their counterpart (other university) teams. Figure 1 shows that all teams devoted more time to interaction with their distributed counterparts than talking among themselves or speaking to everyone in general. This indicates that teams were very focused on the presentation and engaged in exchange of information related to the CW task. Each tandem presentation ranged in duration from 2.4 hours to 4.6 hours (average 3.1 hours) and generated from 443 to 1,051 lines of chat (average 795 lines). Because there were no upper or lower limits imposed on the tandem meetings, the instructors were encouraged by the amount of time and effort students were willing to devote to the project. The black bars in Figure 1 represent each tandem's total conversation as a percent of the total Bb log entries generated during the presentation shown as "On-Topic" in Figure 2, which separates "on-task" log entries from "Admin" (overhead) activities such as browsing or leaving the session.

Level of Satisfaction

Table 2 lists the codes used to identify statement categories and defines the elements that were assessed within each category. The categories to be assessed were counterpart team (C), task (T), and process (P). Statements referring to a category were also identified as favorable (F) or unfavorable (U) assessments on the part of the speaker. Complex statements that referred to multiple categories or expressed a combination of negative and positive assessments were coded to represent the overall intent of the statement given the conversational context in which the statement occurred.

Figure 3 shows a broad range of levels of satisfaction and dissatisfaction among the nine teams. The teams expressed greatest satisfaction with the overall work process leading up to the presentations. All teams were most dissatisfied with their counterpart tandem teams. This was partly due to students' (incorrect) perception that the tandem presentations were competitions. Also, lack of expected kinds of feedback from the counterpart team during the presentation led to a "large amount of subjective interpretation of the shared artifacts and of the other participants' thoughts about the same issues" (Baggetun & Mørch, 2002). These foiled expectations, which surfaced during the postpresentation debriefing sessions, were due in large part to the fact that teams had failed to "establish and maintain common ground" (Mäkitalo, Häkkinen, Salo, & Järvelä, 2002) prior to the final presentation. While the tandem meeting rooms provided the facility for getting acquainted with the counterpart team, teams did not avail themselves of this important contextual affordance. The result was that humorous remarks were often misunderstood and conflict arose due to teams' choice of an informal presentation style when the counterpart team anticipated a formal event. This was a "clash of contexts" in the sense that each team had become used to working and learning with the members of their same university team. When, during the cross-university presentation session, the accustomed learning context was suddenly faced with a new way of accomplishing the same task, participants were initially critical of the differences in approach taken. As the presentation continued with questions asked and explanations given, most often participants discovered potentially better ways

Table 1. Definitions of types of tandem interactivity during team presentations

Code	Type	Activity
1	Within Team	Conversation directed to a member of one's own university team
2	Between Teams	Conversation directed to a member of the other university's team
3	Across Teams	Conversation directed to anyone/everyone in the virtual classroom
4	Browsing	Calling up slides from the Bb (or an external) server
5	Entry/Exit	Entering or leaving the virtual classroom

Figure 1. The distribution of interactivity during each presentation shows that each set of paired teams (tandem) directed the majority of their comments to their counterpart team (Between Teams). Comments directed to members of the same team (Within Team) or to everyone present in the virtual classroom (To Everyone) varied in frequency by tandem.

Distribution of Statements by Tandem

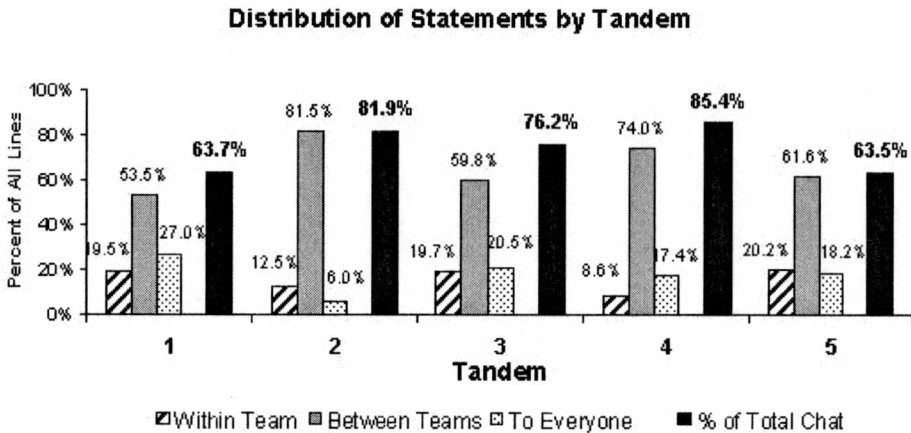

of accomplishing the task.

Summary

The synchronous phase of this case study involved recurring active learner engagement in zero-history group work. While there was some resistance to the more demanding time and place requirements of synchronous interaction, the overall outcome of the course was favorable. Because the project was limited to the last four weeks of the course, the assigned CW analysis focused on an existing rather than a prospective Web site. This, in conjunction with the usability study students had performed earlier in the course, caused students to assume an evaluative approach to the CW. Since the CW is an assessment method used by designers during the initial stages of product development, it is actually a formative method through which designers assume the role of a new user of the product. In doing this, designers engage in exploratory learning much as a new user might. This enables detection of design flaws before significant development expense has been incurred. Many students treated the CW as a usability assessment when they first performed the assignment as individuals. Once they joined their same-university teams, students collaboratively resolved initial misunderstandings about the difference between a usability study (evaluative) and a CW (formative).

Moving the class through individual, same university, and finally, cross university

Table 2. Definitions of statement categories and assessments

Category Code	Category	Category Elements
C	Counterpart Team	presentation content; protocol
T	Task Characteristics	cognitive walkthrough evaluation; specified Web site; collaborative production of PowerPoint slides; interactive presentation to counterpart team; interactive attention to counterpart team's presentation
P	Process	synchronous virtual context; interaction with own university team; understanding of objectives of and autonomous nature of assignment

Assessment Code		Assessment
F		Favorable Assessment of C, T, or P
U		Unfavorable Assessment of C, T, or P

Figure 2. Distribution of tandem interaction type for all teams as a percent of overall content

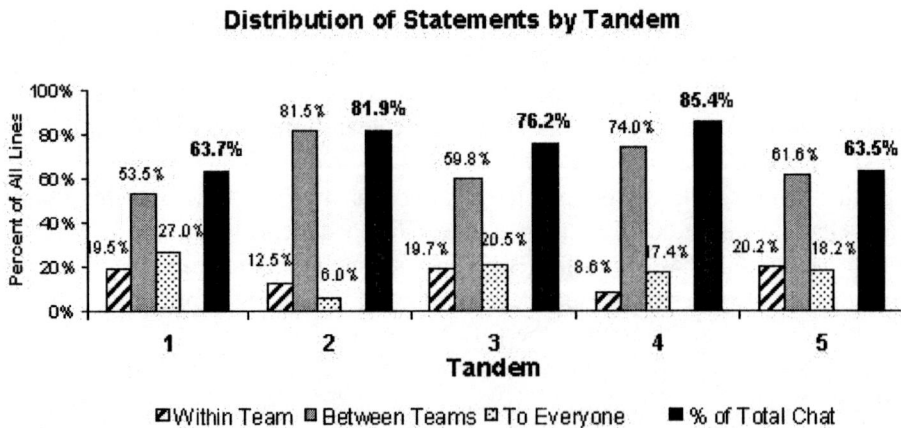

Distribution of Statements by Tandem

☑ Within Team ▤ Between Teams ☒ To Everyone   ■ % of Total Chat

Figure 3. Category assessments as percentages of the aggregate of all statements for all teams

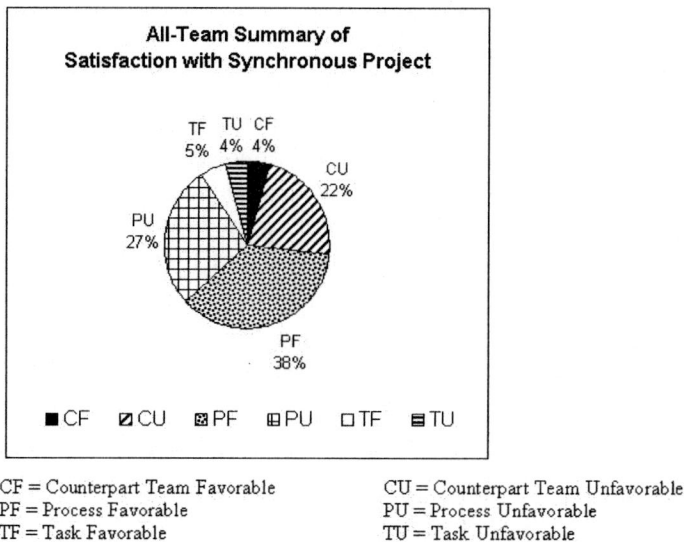

All-Team Summary of Satisfaction with Synchronous Project

TF 5% TU 4% CF 4% CU 22% PU 27% PF 38%

■ CF   ▨ CU   ▩ PF   ⊞ PU   ☐ TF   ☰ TU

CF = Counterpart Team Favorable   CU = Counterpart Team Unfavorable
PF = Process Favorable   PU = Process Unfavorable
TF = Task Favorable   TU = Task Unfavorable

design analysis using the CW methodology enabled the participating computer science students to understand how well the design of a system supports new users. Most users have neither the desire nor the time to study a manual. Students learned that a well-designed interface enables intuitive use of the system with minimal backtracking on the part of the user. This methodology requires the designer to step outside himself or herself and see the system from the point of view of the user. It is generally quite difficult for students to understand this methodology. Working collaboratively and with peers from another university provided a competitive element that motivated students to excel and at the same time, enabled them to learn from other students.

Lessons Learned

The innovative course discussed in this chapter provided many learning opportunities for the instructors. We developed a clearer understanding of several ways in which context influences learning. The following experience-based observations are an important first step in the seamless integration of technologybased learning and best practices for needs analysis, design and development, implementation, evaluation, and quality assurance of online learning environments.

A distributed synchronous collaborative effort is intensely demanding on the time and attention of both the instructor and the students. This is because quality assurance management in the form of ongoing formative assessment of the communal learning environment as well as student progress is integral to the success of the course.

The initial course description must clearly specify what the course will entail and what will be expected of the participants. During the design phase of this course, the instructors were uncertain as to whether it was feasible to conduct a complex synchronous exercise. The robustness of the technology and the capabilities of the students had yet to be tested. When the decision to implement the synchronous stage of the course was announced, a small minority of students was unhappy because their expectations were confounded. Their unhappiness persisted throughout the remainder of the project. We would recommend emphasizing to students at the outset that aspects of technology might be piloted, formatively assessed, and modified.

Accurate and timely communication between instructor(s) and course participants is critical. Whenever hardware or software problems were encountered or when students had discrepant understanding of content or task, the instructors immediately pursued and posted the remedy on the announcements bulletin board. This was quite effective for the majority of students who regularly read the announcements.

Close monitoring of participant interaction stimulates performance by motivating students to put forth their best efforts and to ask questions of peers as well as of the instructor. This results in a significant increase in collaborative knowledge building and growth of cohesion leading to transformation of a team into a community of learners.

Students must be given the opportunity to anonymously provide summative assessment of the overall course. In the present case, eight out of nine teams chose to conduct an open discussion in their virtual team room. This indicates that the value of community had become more important to participants than anonymity. It also demonstrates the fact that a high level of trust had been established among members of same university teams as well as with the instructors because students were clearly aware that all online discussions were archived and available to the instructors.

Conclusions

In this study, all students were exposed to greater diversity of thinking and different ways of working than they would have been within the context of an individual university's culture and cultural mix of students. The highly interactive nature of the course and the real-time work context of the final project worked together to leverage multiple learning contexts through activity to create an enhanced learning environment. This was not due to having the latest educational software and hardware technology available. Rather, it was due to (1) putting considered (and considerable) effort into the design of the course, (2) conducting meticulous and constant follow-through during delivery of the course, and (3) performing ongoing formative assessment of individual student and team social, cognitive, and metacognitive performance within the ever-changing context of the course.

Learner and instructor satisfaction is fundamental to learning and must be an explicit design goal for learner-centered online instructional support systems. Regardless of the "user-friendliness" of the courseware, instructors must devote considerable time to the initial design, regular updating, and constant facilitation of online courses to assure that course quality is maintained. Attention to design and delivery coupled with creative use of new technologies will result in multiple new paradigms for delivery of highly learner-centric education.

References

Baggetun, R., & Mørch, A. (2002, January). *Resources for coordination in collaborative telelearning.* Paper presented at Computer Support for Collaborative Learning , University of Colorado, Boulder.

Bos, N., Olson, J., Gergle, D., Olson, G., & Wright, Z. (2002, April 20-25). *Effects of four computer-mediated communications channels on trust development.* Paper presented at the proceedings of the Special Interest Group on Computer-Human Interaction (SIGCHI) Conference on Human Factors and Computing Systems, Minneapolis, MN.

Brown, A. L., & Campione, J. C. (1994). Guided discovery in a community of learners. In K. McGilly (Ed.), *Classroom lessons: Integrating cognitive theory and classroom practice* (pp. 229-270). Cambridge, MA: MIT Press/Bradford Books.

Bunz, U. K., (2000, April 1). *Teaching CMC through CMC: Experiences from a cross-university computer-mediated communication class.* Paper presented at the Southern States Communication Association Conference, New Orleans LA. Retrieved May 25, 2005, from http://www.scils.rutgers.edu/~bunz/SSCA2000ku_rpi.pdf

Clements, D. H., & Nastasi, B. K. (1988). Social and cognitive interactions in educational computer environments. *American Educational Research Journal, 25*(1), 87-106.

Collins, A. (1989, July). *Cognitive apprenticeship and instructional technology* (Technical Report No. 474). BBN Laboratories, Cambridge, MA. Centre for the Study of Reading, University of Illinois.

Collins, A., Brown, J. S., & Newman, S. E. (1987, January). *Cognitive apprenticeship: Teaching the craft of reading, writing and mathematics* (Tech. Rep. No. 403). Cambridge, MA: BBN Laboratories, Centre for the Study of Reading, University of Illinois.

Dehler, C., & Porras-Hernandez, L. H. (1998). Using computer mediated communication (CMC) to promote experiential learning in graduate studies. *Educational Technology, 38*(May-June), 52-55.

Dillenbourg, P. (Ed.). (1999). *Collaborative learning: Cognitive and computational approaches.* Oxford, UK: Elsevier Science.

Flavell, J. (1976). Metacognitive aspects of problem-solving. In L. Resnick (Ed.), *The nature of intelligence* (pp. 231-235). Hillsdale, NJ: Erlbaum.

Gunawardena, C.N., & Duphorne, P.L. (2001). *Which learner readiness factors, online features, and CMC related learning approaches are associated with learner satisfaction in computer conferences?* In Annual meeting of the American Educational Research Association. Seattle, WA.

Herring, S. C. (Ed.). (1996). *Computer-mediated communication: Linguistic, social, and cross-cultural perspectives.* Philadelphia: J. Benjamins.

Kang, I. (1998). The use of computer-mediated communication: Electronic collaboration and interactivity. In C. J. Bonk & K. S. King (Eds.), *Electronic collaborators: Learner-centered technologies for literacy, apprenticeship, and discourse* (pp. 315-337). Mahwah, NJ: Erlbaum.

Lave, J., & Chaiklin, S. (Eds.). (1993). *Understanding practice: Perspectives on activity and context.* Cambridge: Cambridge University Press.

Lave, J., & Wenger, E. (1990). *Situated learning: Legitimate peripheral participation.* Cambridge, UK: Cambridge University Press.

Mäkitalo, K., Häkkinen, P., Salo, P., & Järvelä, S. (2002, January 7-11). *Building and maintaining common ground in Web-based interaction.* Paper presented at Computer Support for Collaborative Learning, University of Colorado, Boulder.

McLellan, H. (1995). *Situated learning perspectives.* Englewood Cliffs, NJ: Educational Technology.

Rogoff, B., & Lave, J. (Eds.). (1984). *Everyday cognition: Its development in social context.* Cambridge: Harvard University Press.

Sloffer, S. J., Dueber, B., & Duffy, T. M. (1999). *Using asynchronous conferencing to promote critical thinking: Two implementations in higher education* (Center for Research on Learning and Technology Tech. Rep. No. 8-99). Bloomington, IN: Indiana University.

Vick, R. M. (1998). Perspectives on and problems with computer-mediated teamwork: Current groupware issues and assumptions. *Journal of Computer Documentation, 22*(2), 3-22.

Vick, R. M. (2002, January 7-10). Measuring performance and evaluating progress in a Web-based synchronous interactive learning environment. In R. H. Sprague, Jr.

(Ed.), *Proceedings of the Thirty-Fifth Hawaii International Conference on Systems Sciences* (pp. 135-144), Waikoloa, Hawaii. Los Alamitos, CA: IEEE.

Wenger, E. (1998). *Communities of practice: Learning, meaning, and identity.* Cambridge: Cambridge University Press.

Wenger, E., McDermott, R. A., & Snyder, W. M. (2002). *Cultivating communities of practice: A guide to managing knowledge.* Boston: Harvard Business School Press.

Wertsch, J. V. (1985a). *Vygotsky and the social formation of mind.* Cambridge, MA: Harvard University Press.

Wertsch, J. V. (1985b). Culture, communication, and cognition: Vygotskian perspectives. Cambridge: Cambridge University Press.

Wiedenbeck, S., & Zila, P. L. (1997). Hands-on practice in learning to use software: A comparison of exercise, exploration, and combined formats. *ACM Transactions on Computer-Human Interaction, 4*(2), 169-196.

Zheng, J., Veinott, E., Bos, N., Olson, J. S., & Olson, G. M. (2002, April 20-25). *Trust without touch: Jumpstarting long-distance trust with initial social activities.* Paper presented at the proceedings of the Special Interest Group on Computer-Human Interaction (SIGCHI) Conference on Human Factors and Computing Systems, Minneapolis, MN.

Chapter XVI

A Constructivist View of Knowledge Management in Open Source Virtual Communities

Sulayman K. Sowe, Aristotle University of Thessaloniki, Greece

Athanasis Karoulis, Aristotle University of Thessaloniki, Greece

Ioannis Stamelos, Aristotle University of Thessaloniki, Greece

Abstract

This chapter addresses a learning environment that is manifested in the domain of free/open source software development. It provides the base for the emergence, development, interactions, and management of a novel learning environment by taking a constructivist view of knowledge management. The learning activities of an online collaborative effort of a loosely and geographically disperse community of individuals is explored by looking at the interactions between members of the community, the tools used to communicate, and the interactions between the members of the community and the virtual learning context. The learning context as envisaged here refers to the free/open source software development environment in

which learning actually takes place. The main focus is on the resources and pur-
poseful activities that promote collaborative learning in this context, as well as the
transfer of learning from the virtual setting to the real-life situation by involving in
a collaborative activity.

Introduction

The general concept behind *open source software* is in making the source code of computer programs freely available to anyone who wants to obtain it. However, many people use the term *free software* or *libre software* instead of open source software. According to the Free Software Foundation (FSF, http://www.gnu.org/), free software (F/S) gives the user the freedom to study what the program does, change it to suit his or her needs, distribute copies to other people, and publish improved versions of the program. Of course, access to the source code is a precondition of this freedom. However, the term *free software* has raised linguistic ambiguities such as the use of the term *free* as in "freedom," "free beer," or "gratis." *Libre software* is another term used to refer to user's freedom of use, redistribution, and so forth. In this chapter, we use the term *free/open source software* (F/OSS) to refer to user's freedom to use, modify, distribute, or even sell the software with little obligations as in propriety software. Users can either choose to keep changes made private, or altruistically return them to the community.

F/OSS is better understood if one looks beyond the horizon of source codes and licenses agreements to focus on *inter* and *intra* community activities within a project and across projects. The *contextual focus* is more than just F/OSS; it is about the communities that have created the software. The purpose of this chapter is to explore the learning activities of the F/OSS virtual community by utilizing a constructivist view of knowledge management. The approach of combining constructivism and knowledge management to investigate how F/OSS might revolutionize learning, assists in formulating a model of sound educational practices. Constructivism helps us explore the context in which participants individually and collectively take responsibility not only of their own learning, but also of the collective construction of knowledge and meaning. The F/OSS paradigm of collaborative software development is not a new phenomenon. What is new and needs addressing is the understanding of a sound and improved context in which learning occurs.

The organization of this chapter is as follows. In the second section, we discuss what virtual communities are, focusing on their characteristics, activities, and roles. Furthermore, the section will examine how the infrastructure on which virtual communities are built continues to support learning, content quality and delivery in the F/OSS virtual community. The third section concentrates on the

F/OSS learning environment. Advantages and disadvantages of the virtual learning context, the behaviors of a new generation of learners in a virtual context, and the significance of F/OSS to education are discussed. Knowledge and knowledge management concepts are explained in the fourth section, with main focus on knowledge sharing, and the introduction of the F/OSS Knowledge Sharing Model (KSM). In the fifth section, we put forward a constructivist view of learning and argue that learning in the context of F/OSS development is purely based on constructivism. In our concluding remarks, in the sixth section, we propose some guidelines for educators and researchers who would venture into educational issues in F/OSS and signal future research guidelines in this new area.

What is a Virtual Community?

Howard Rheingold (1993) defined virtual communities as "social aggregations that emerge from the net when enough people carry on those public discussions long enough, with sufficient human feeling, to form webs of personal relationships in cyberspace." Thus, there is social interaction taking place in cyberspace, resulting in the establishment of relationships among the participating *personas*. Dowdy (2001) sees this as an intimate secondary relationship: an informal, frequent, and supportive type of community relationship that operates only in one specialized sphere of influence, such as F/OSS. As a good source for acquiring and sharing information (Rheingold, 1993; Lapachet, 1994), virtual community members may be involved in practical *information seeking* (seeking answers to specific questions in the form of postings). In some communities, members undertake a more general activity characterized by frequent visits to monitor the information neighborhood and what goes on in various communities (Burnett, 2000). Erdelez (1999) likens this activity to *information encountering*: a memorable experience of an unexpected discovery of useful or interesting information. As agents of socialization and information providers, virtual communities serve as important learning environments.

Characteristics of Virtual Communities

Virtual communities exhibit some common characteristics that, at least, differentiate them from real world communities. Their participants are generally geographically dispersed. They employ many-to-many means of communication. Community interaction is mainly text-based and participants have active as well as passive membership roles.

Roles and Activities of Virtual Community Members

In every community, a small group of people form the *core members* and provide a large proportion of online activity. They decide who and what comes in and what goes out of the community, acting as *knowledge stewards* (Brazelton & Gorry, 2003). Others participate as *lurkers* or consumers of information, acquiring knowledge, skills, and aptitudes. Lurkers may not "adopt knowledge and practice from the community" (Brazelton & Gorry, 2003), but they represent a huge pool of potential active members. New to virtual community life and the Internet in general is a group of people referred to as *newbies, novices,* or *beginners*. As inexperienced participants, often, their starting point is the frequently asked questions or FAQs, where they can learn community norms. This cohort forms the future users and beneficiaries of online interaction. The virtual learning environment is not devoid of hostilities. Participants may encounter hostile, unprovoked, messages or *flames*. In all its forms, flaming breaks community norms, distorts genuine conversation, and is often shunned by community members.

The F/OSS Virtual Community

The Internet, particularly the Web, continues to support the emergence and proliferation of [virtual] communities of diverse interest (Sowe, Karoulis, Stamelos, & Bleris, 2004). Virtual communities are attracting a lot of attention as valuable communities through which both learners and instructors can try new approaches. The pedestal on which they are built continues to influence teaching and learning, and content quality and delivery. This bifurcation has in recent years converged onto the F/OSS virtual community.

The F/OSS community is a learning community in which individuals interact with collaborating peers to solve a particular problem and exchange ideas. Collaborative learning and the peer review process emphasize the importance of shared dialogue. The community consists of individuals, commonly referred to as *hackers*, who contribute to, write, and build a particular application by means of the F/OSS development or *bazaar model* (Raymond, 1998). The general view is that of an egalitarian network of programmers developing software in a decentralized environment free of hierarchical control structures.

One of the most visible and researched F/OSS communities is the Linux community (Figure 1). It is composed of highly dedicated online groups of hackers, collaboratively tinkering to produce a high-quality open source operating system (*GNU/Linux OS*) and many other utility programs. The F/OSS community is composed of loosely organized ad hoc communities of contributors from all over the world who share a strong sense of commitment (Kim, 2003). Programming cognoscenti dominate the community and development activities constitute few individual efforts rather than community. In their study of F/OSS community activities, Krishnamurthy (2002) and Kim (2003) found out that most development activities do not generate a lot of discussion. These findings run contrary to most F/OSS evangelists' view, which does not take into consideration a typical F/OSS project having what Krishnamurthy (2002) called a "cave type" developer community. Nor did early F/OSS advocates anticipate a classic project to generate less discussion. In a cave-type community the only eyeballs, according to "Linus's Law" ("*Given enough eyeballs, all bugs are shallow*"), looking at the code is that of the project developer. F/OSS community activities are inscribed in many and varied projects. Participants develop software online, relying on extensive peer collaboration through the Internet (using project's mailing list, emails, discussion forums, etc). However, in certain projects, communities have been found to provide support services such as suggestions for products features, act as distributing agents, help new members, and so forth.

Free/Open Source Software Development (F/OSSD) Activities

F/OSS projects provide a rich field to explore the process of software knowledge creation, accumulation, and dissemination. Moreover, they represent decentralized *project-based learning* through which participants learn coding techniques by having access to a large *codebase*. Stallman (2002) conjectured that to learn to write software well you have to read and write a lot of software. Furthermore, the novice needs to observe professional writing good software and to learn from their art. The cyclic nature of source code acquisition, modification, distribution, and reacquisition is an important aspect of F/OSSD. Figure 2 shows typical F/OSSD activities with possible exits from the cycle.

Participants *checkout* code from the project repository to begin the software development activity. Some just acquire the source code and no longer take part in project activity (Exit 1). Others continue the development process by modifying code, bug fixing, and adding new functionalities. Participants dissatisfied with a project's development, or how it is managed and coordinated may exit the cycle with the modified code to start their own "mutant" version of the project, in what is called *forking* (Exit 2). Still, active members may continue to participate in the project through *commits*. Some may terminate their involvement after some time (Exit 3). The development activity continues in perpetuity, generating knowledge from which community members can learn.

Figure 1. Communication pathway and interactions between different facets in the Linux community

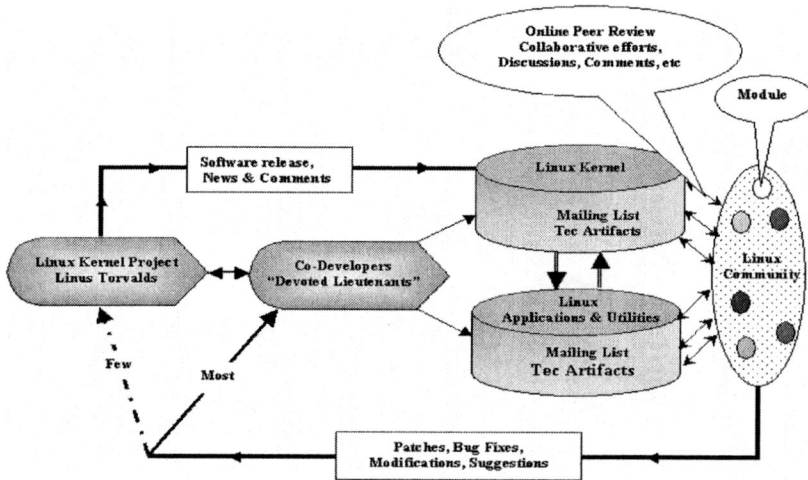

Free/Open Source Software Development Learning Environment (F/OSSDLE)

F/OSS is making a large impact on many aspects of society including computer science education. The F/OSSDLE is a virtual setting that is receiving a lot of attention as a genuine and meaningful learning context. Jelkner (2003) pronounces such a context thus:

> *Students learn everything I have to teach them. . . . They start asking more and more questions for which I have no ready answers . . . they are ready to take their study of computer science to new levels, to forge ahead to places I've never been . . . busy schedule [didn't] permit me to go there with them. I am not a computer scientist, and I have papers to grade and lessons to plan. [The F/OSSDLE] provides opportunities for . . . students to grow and develop while still in [college and university] to levels that would not be possible without it. [The context] also provides me with a way to continue to take part in the growth of these . . . students, thus keeping the teacher in me happy. (Jelkner, 2003)*

This pronouncement demonstrates the need to search for sound educational paradigms to support genuine renewal in education. A renewal that will make learning

Figure 2. F/OSSD activities

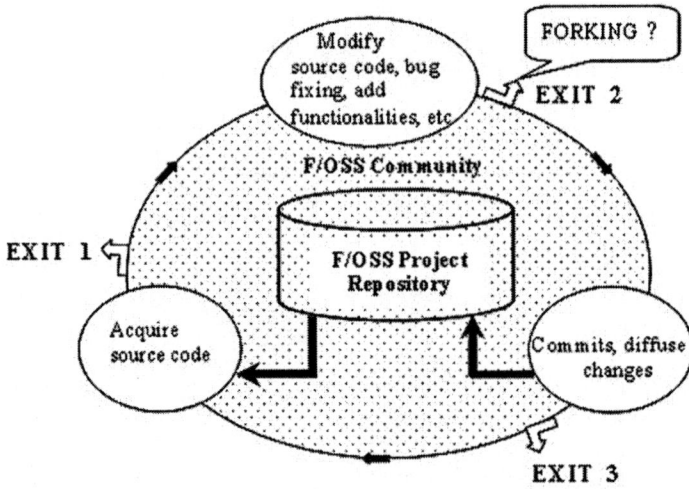

more meaningful by accommodating the climate that present day technologies are able to deliver. This in turn raises certain questions:

1.   Have learners of today outgrown most curricular initiatives?

2.   What context can we present to learners so that they learn by reflecting on their experiences?

3.   What opportunities do we have for motivated students who find most curricular contents and pedagogies not just inadequate but also out of tune with real-life situations?

4.   Learners are browsing and sampling, boldly going where many teachers never ventured either because of their busy schedules, or lack of skills and competence in the use of computers. Does the F/OSSDLE provide opportunities for learners to grow and develop while still in college or university to levels that would not be possible without it?

Most of these questions are hard to answer, considering the contemporary research findings on the domain. However, there is interesting discussion on these issues.

Methodologically, F/OSS is collaboratively built software that is shared by developers and users as they co-create a product (Faber, 2002). On the educational front, F/OSS provides an example not only of a viable software development approach, but also of a model for the creation of learning experiences in which students and instructors both yield some control to create a more dynamic learning environment (Scharff, 2002). In presenting an educational model for open source, Faber (2002) sighted F/OSS as an alternative form of innovation and product development against the context of expanding commercial interest in innovation, education, and knowledge creation and dissemination. However, Hippel (2001) contends that engaging in innovation, development, and consumption can only flourish when certain conditions are met: (a) at least some users have sufficient incentive to innovate, (b) at least some users have an incentive to voluntarily reveal their innovation, and (c) would-be innovators have access and the tools to help them collaborate and share their knowledge.

Advantages of the Virtual Learning Context

The virtual learning context benefits learners by leveraging their knowledge and information access repertoire, enabling them to participate at their own convenience and learn at their own pace. Furthermore, learners are exposed to complex social issues from a disperse and geographically diverse community of participants. In this setting, anonymity (gender, race, sexual orientation, disabilities, etc.) allows students to freely participate in the discussion.

The already described structure of the F/OSS community and the F/OSSD activities taking place in it are an environment based on the pillars of constructivism to support learning: learners can control the pace and amount of learning, they are in charge of their personal decisions, and they decide their own learning styles and strategies. Most of all, they conclude on the learning scope themselves (*what to do*) and decide on the method of acquiring the knowledge (*how to do it*). Knowledge acquisition is accomplished, for example, by studying online documentations visiting the frequently asked questions (FAQs), asking more experienced members for assistance, or *learning by doing*, which represents the *drill-and-practice* approach in "normal" constructivist environments.

Disadvantages of the Virtual Learning Context

Apart from isolation and detachment of learners from *face-to-face* interaction, commonly associated with virtual learning environments, learning in this context requires access to the Internet and computer facilities. In addition, a high degree of literacy in reading, writing, and typing is required to participate effectively. The environment is also not conflict free. Flaming, the feeling of being ignored in a dominated discussion and disinterestedness are all major concerns in the management of such a context. What is more, it is not free for all community members. Access rights are needed to participate in some community activities. Moderated sites limit freedom of expression by deciding what and what not a member can post. Contents of unmoderated sites might be irrelevant, unstructured, and badly presented.

New Generation of Learners in a Virtual Context

Associated with the roles and activities already described, is a new generation of learners whose behaviors are largely shaped by the virtual learning context. In a venture to understand how to create a new context in which learning occurs and how it can become omnipresent in the future, Brown (2003) observed that today's learners are always multiprocessing and multitasking. Learners in a virtual context need to feel comfortable navigating through information spaces, where surfing fuses learning with entertainment to create *infotainment* (Brown, 2003). In this context, discovery and judgement all come to play in situ. Learning becomes situated in action, intertwined with judgement and exploration.

What Motivates F/OSSD Participants?

Researchers strive to understand what motivates people to participate in F/OSSD and the overwhelming interest of software firms and educationists (among others, Hippel, 2001; Lerner & Tirole, 2001; O'Hara & Jennifer, 2003). Lakhani and Wolf (2003) see it as an irrational altruistic behaviour by participants. Participants may be attracted by the mere joy of participating in an intellectually stimulating activity (coding) in which they share their knowledge and learn new skills. Others participate in F/OSSD in order to improve job opportunities, or to gain recognition from peers and community of F/OSS programmers. Ye and Kishida (2003) noted two forms of learning as motives for F/OSSD participants—*explorative learning* and *learning by doing*, both known pillars of constructivism. Explorative learning in F/OSSD is a way of solving a problem or satisfying an itch. In learning by doing, the learner may wish to consolidate his or her understanding of a concept by engaging community members, allowing him or her to apply his or her existing knowledge and expertise.

Significance of F/OSS in Education

F/OSS issues in education often focus attention on F/OSS as an inexpensive alternative to commercial software (Scharff, 2002). F/OSS provides low-cost technology to teach and learn computer science and has the potential to expand group work beyond the classroom to include much larger projects and more distributed teams. In this context, computer science educators and students can develop and improve existing software code. The context not only provides students with a world-size laboratory and support staff, but also gives them experience in large-scale software collaboration and development (O'Hara & Jennifer, 2003). By learning in this environment students participate in a distributed software community and learn the corpuses of online peer review. What is more, students can be encouraged to build projects on top of existing ones rather than developed software projects from scratch. Pedagogically, F/OSS provides the opportunity to extend the methodology by which we learn, apply, and teach computer science thereby keeping the teacher happy.

Knowledge and Knowledge Management

Collaborative project-based learning in the F/OSSDLE demonstrates that the transfer of learning from virtual settings to real-life situation is a daunting task. What kinds of knowledge are there that we need to identify and teach so that students will get to know? For an answer, we need to understand something about knowledge and the nature of knowing. Schools often end up concentrating on facts because it is easy to state and grade the facts we know. When it comes to processes and skills, various factors (e.g., how well the learning context elucidates the concept being learned) come into play that makes it harder to identify and assess the processes and skills of our pupils.

In the context of knowledge and knowledge management, three terms need to be clarified, data, *information*, and *knowledge*. Data are basically discrete facts representing an item. Information is data that have been processed and made meaningful and relevant to the context or situation under consideration. Zack (1998) defined knowledge as "that which we come to believe and value based on the meaningful organized accumulation of information (messages) through experience, communication or inference." Knowledge can be viewed both as a thing to be stored (in the learners head) and manipulated (by the learning process) and as a *process* of simultaneously knowing and acting—where the learner constructs knowledge by being involved. Practically, schools need to manage knowledge both as a thing and as a process to generate a meaningful learning context.

Types of Knowledge

When talking about knowledge, difference is made between *explicit* and *tacit* knowledge. Explicit knowledge can be expressed or articulated into signs, text, and words. It can be more easily codified and documented. As such, explicit knowledge is transmitted and shared in the F/OSSDLE via the Internet and through personal communication means (direct exchange of e-mail between participants). In this context, the learner must interact with the entities (e.g. websites, forums, to-do lists, etc) in which explicit knowledge is contained to have mastery of concepts and principles. However, it does not follow that the receiving party can comprehend and correctly value the knowledge due to differences in language, level of maturity, or lack of required capabilities (Stenmark, 2002). Tacit knowledge, in contrast, is more difficult to code, articulate, and transfer since it is often deeply rooted in the "owners head." Zack (1998) argued that tacit knowledge is subconsciously understood and applied, developed from direct experience and action. Unearthing tacit knowledge is profoundly difficult in teaching and learning, since understanding requires familiarity with both the concepts themselves and the context to which they normally belong (Stenmark, 2002). Other types of knowledge often discussed are (1) *declarative knowledge*, knowledge about something; (2) *procedural knowledge*, knowledge of how something occurs or is performed; and (3) *strategic knowledge*, the basis of problem solving, such as actions to be taken if a proposed solution fails, and how to respond if necessary information is absent (Harris, Korsakova, Wakefield, Baxter, & Farinha , 1998).

Approaches to Knowledge Management in F/OSSD

In their approach to knowledge management (KM), cognitivists and organizational learning specialists consider how well organizational structures and processes promote *collaborative learning* and sharing of knowledge (Dieter, 2002). The goal of knowledge management, as put forward by Dieter (2002), is to supersede barriers imposed by organizational structures, format restrictions, and conceptual limitations, so that the acquisition, transfer, and sharing of knowledge can be facilitated. Thus, KM helps us understand tools, roles, and activities we need to develop in order to help individuals learn from F/OSS related activities. KM in F/OSSD incorporates all of the community's shared assets that can be directly or indirectly applied to knowledge generation, sharing, and accumulation. These include software codes, licenses agreements, projects Web sites, community members, and collaborative software development tools.

To address KM issues in F/OSSD, one needs to consider a *paradigm shift* from organizational attention and knowledge making as a manufacturing process to online interactive systems where knowledge making is characterized by *co-presence* rather than physical presence. The community approach to KM sees knowledge as consisting of dynamic processes and *know-how* that are constantly changing. This approach calls for the need to facilitate a collaborative process at the community level by applying expertise; that is, knowing and acting (Sveiby, 1997).

The management of information approach recognizes knowledge as an object to be identified and handled in information systems. The F/OSSD process not only highlights a different way of developing and acquiring software knowledge but also acquiring knowledge is a complicated process and building on existing knowledge takes time. As an educational exercise for computer students, we need a new approach to manage learning in this context. To manage this context is to focus on guided learning (e.g. instruct and guide F/OSS participants for further involvement). In addition, learning is increasingly becoming online information-based, with educational establishments uniting rather than competing on the basis of knowledge. These realities conspicuously alter the methods by which we must manage, learn, represent knowledge, interact, solve problems, and act. This in turn poses new challenges that call for improved management strategies.

The F/OSSD Knowledge Sharing Model (KSM)

Knowledge transfer is the transmission or representation of knowledge to a potential recipient and the absorption by that person or group. Through knowledge transfer and absorption, members of an organization learn (Dieter, 2002). Knowledge acquisition is the result of an activity, personal interaction, which would be better described as a process of knowing (Sveiby, 1997). Knowledge acquisition symbolizes the act of learning where the learner, as a result of interaction with the F/OSSD environment, acquires knowledge. The "new" knowledge resulting from such interaction is better in quality than the previous "old knowledge"—it is at a higher level and more functional.

In the context of the F/OSSDLE, we shall demonstrate, using KSM, how individuals share knowledge and learn. In this model, individuals will exchange ideas and recognize their differences in the perception of a concept. And after multiple iterations of this process, they will come to a mutual agreement. In his cybernetic theory of machine learning, Gordon Pask (1928-1996) proposed that such mutual agreements could be archived into an "*entailment mesh.*" The archive forms a collection of shared and publicly available concepts known as general or public knowledge. Ryder (1995) posits that mutually agreed concepts become a community asset.

The F/OSSD context is a "*symbiotic cognitive system,*" where the community learns from its participants, and each individual learns from the community. Ongoing interactions and activities are a means of acquiring valuable knowledge that is worth archiving. Participants learn advanced and basic concepts associated with collaborative software development. Novice and lurkers alike learn by browsing the knowledge base. The *legitimate peripheral participant* learns as an apprentice, observing and participating. Having learned the basics of the peer review process, the legitimate peripheral participant may then begin to participate as a peer (Ryder, 1995; Ye & Kishida, 2003), offering his own perspectives and constructing new knowledge in the process. In this learning environment, the process of finding and inventing patterns and relationships is not straightforward. Tellen (1997) substantiated that if we start with an ordered understanding we cannot learn, because we already know the patterns and relationships. Thus, as a bricoleur, the learner is continuously involved in a discovery, trying to put order where there is disorder, structure where there is no structure, fitting his or her knowledge with the project's knowledge base.

The F/OSSD KSM in Figure 3 shows knowledge transfer between a learner or knowledge seeker (KS) and an expert or mentor or knowledge provider (KP) in a F/OSSDLE.

Three terms deserve a focus in this model. *Externalization* is the transfer of knowledge, expertise, or know-how from the learner or expert to the knowledge base (KB) to provide for knowledge sharing. Internalization is the process of acquiring knowledge from the KB and "filtering of that knowledge, to provide greater relevance" (Davidson, 1998) to the learner or expert.

The KB contains the community's knowledge.

Knowledge Sharing Model Algorithms

The potential KS confronts an unfamiliar concept within the F/OSSDLE. There are two ways he can learn:

by *reflecting* on his or her experience {Route: $KS \Rightarrow KS^A \Rightarrow KS^B \Rightarrow KS^C$} and *navigating* the project's knowledge base to seek for answers.

If the *concept has been encountered* before, it will be captured and stored in the KB in the form of FAQs, archives, or in "live" discussion threads. The learner then learns directly from the KB {Route: $KS \Rightarrow KS^C \Rightarrow KS^D \Rightarrow KP^E$}. Even the expert or instructor or teacher is continuously reflecting and learning from the KB in this model:

Reflecting {Route: $KP \Rightarrow KP^A \Rightarrow KP^B \Rightarrow KP^C$} and

Navigating {Route: $KP \Rightarrow KP^C \Rightarrow KP^D \Rightarrow KS^E$}

If the *concept has not been encountered*, strategic knowledge comes into play. The learner may post questions to a forum and exchange ideas in a process of continuous *composition* and *decomposition* with members of the F/OSS community. Alternatively, he may also be engaged in private online or off-line discussions that do not get posted or publicly disclosed due to their perceived sensitive content (Scacchi, 2002).

Figure 3. F/OSS knowledge sharing model

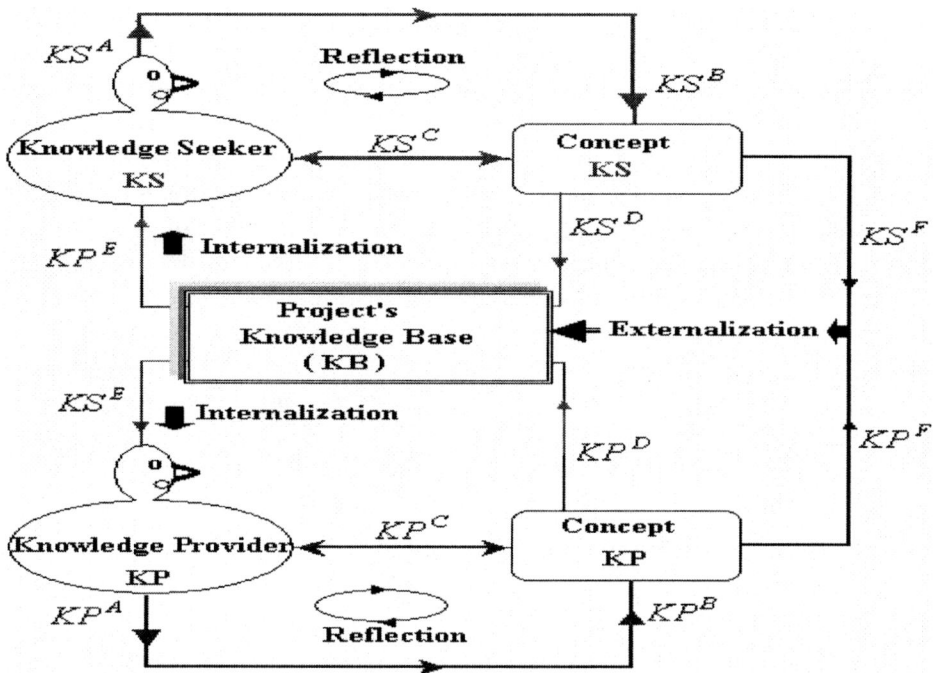

Forward {Route $KS \Rightarrow KS^C \Rightarrow KS^D \Rightarrow KS^E \Rightarrow KP$} and

Backward {Route $KP \Rightarrow KP^C \Rightarrow KP^D \Rightarrow KP^E \Rightarrow KS$}.

The backward route or feedback as well as the forward route are influenced by

(1) location of information on the project's Web site,

(2) speed of net access, and

(3) contents and nature of the information acquired or solicited (e.g. graphics or text).

Knowledge "gained" is externalized into the KB from which others can learn by internalization.

({Route $KS \Rightarrow KS^C \Rightarrow KS^F \Rightarrow KB$} & {Route $KP \Rightarrow KP^C \Rightarrow KP^F \Rightarrow KB$}).

In the process of creating new knowledge, the learner will experiment with available options or routes and record processes. Structurally accomplished task becomes action research for the learner. If such a creative process is random, knowledge creation becomes hit-and-miss or *accidental learning* process (Tellen, 1997).

Constructivist View of Learning in F/OSSDLE

The F/OSSDLE relies on extensive peer collaboration and knowledge building activities. The theory of learning underpinning the F/OSSDLE is obviously one of constructivism. A constructivist theory of learning lays great emphasis on an active and autonomous role for the learner. The F/OSS participant constructs meaning by interacting with the environment in which the knowledge of the domain is not separated from the context in which it applies. The KSM model, by design, facilitates a constructivist approach to online learning. In this context, the learner through his or her interaction with the learning environment constructs knowledge, and his or her prior knowledge impacts the learning process. Meaningful learning by *scaffolding* requires purposeful activity where a novice learner has direct access to experts. Originating from social constructivism, scaffolding is a process of guiding the learner from the known to the unknown. The principles of constructivist learning in this context, as highlighted by Hein (1991), are as follows:

Learning is an active process. Learning is not passive acceptance of knowledge that exists "out there," but it rather involves the learner interacting with the context.

People learn to learn as they learn. Learning consists of constructing both meaning and constructing systems of meaning (Hein, 1991). As a social activity, our ability to learn is intimately associated with our connection with others, in the real as well as the virtual world. The F/OSSDLE recognizes the social aspects of learning and uses technological artifacts, interaction with others, and the application of knowledge as an integral aspect of learning.

Learning is contextual. We do not learn isolated facts and theories in some abstract way, but we learn concepts in relation to what we know and build and improve on the knowledge of others. Learning in this environment means constantly reflecting on what has been learned, adjusting our experiences, and accommodating that of others.

One needs knowledge to learn. Learning involves assimilating new knowledge. The context needs to provide the learner with the opportunity to build on his or her previous experiences. The F/OSSD model is that of use and reuse, building on reusable components, codes, and programs built by others. The more we know, the more we can learn.

It takes time to learn. Learning is not whimsical and instantaneous. To be effective, the learner needs to revisit ideas, ponder, and experiment. More often, in F/OSSD, learners need to revisit the project's Web site to constantly keep abreast with project activities and be up to date with releases.

Motivation is a key component in learning. The learner in F/OSSD is extrinsically as well as intrinsically motivated. The context needs to sustain learner motivation by engaging him or her in a meaningful and intellectually stimulating activity.

Concluding Remarks

The preceding sections established the F/OSS virtual community as a community composed of users and for users (Hippel, 2001) who cooperate to create and sustain a complex learning environment as a by-product of their main activity. Using constructivism both as a learning theory and epistemology, we are able to have an in-depth understanding of how learning occurs in the F/OSSDLE and of the nature of knowledge. In this context, learners can construct knowledge for themselves by reflecting on previous experience and use the F/OSSD community as a springboard to further refine their ideas. Each learner or expert individually and socially constructs meaning as he or she learns (Hein, 1991). Thus, F/OSS virtual communities are constructivist-oriented environments and learning takes place in a pure constructivist fashion. F/OSS developers work on projects they find interesting and, by so doing, they acquire knowledge associated with their profession. Similarly, an educational classroom could be based around specific projects that students find interesting and challenging. These projects could integrate experiences from other fields of endeavor associated with their studies. Students would choose projects they want to work on and in the process they will learn other course relevant material and correlative skills and aptitudes. Furthermore, educators and software enterprises wanting to educate their personnel in an effective and productive manner should pay close attention to the way learning occurs in F/OSS communities.

However, a lot of research into the F/OSSDLE is needed (Hein, 1991; Hippel, 2001; Kim, 2003) so that learners and experts alike can better take advantage of what the context has to offer. The collaborative project-based learning needs better analysis to understand how discussions are posted and rejected and the influence this has on learners. The F/OSSD activities, although being a crucial aspect of the overall F/OSSD model, fall short of enumerating how forking affects the dynamics of project-based learning, the cultivation of *critical mass* and how all these impinge on the learner's motivation and the quality of interaction. While being an initial work in this area, a better KSM is needed to understand the techniques F/OSS developers use to manage knowledge (Kim, 2003) and how people learn by sharing knowledge. Furthermore, there is the need to understand the information-seeking behavior posited by Burnett (2000) and Erdelez (1999) in the context of different F/OSSDLEs and report on the experience of learners because such serendipitous behaviors are directly correlated with the activities and roles we have described. This will give us better understanding of not only the F/OSSDLE but the holistic behaviors of learners in virtual settings. This in turn will help us better plan and manage learning in a virtual setting.

References

Brazelton, J., & Gorry, G. A. (2003). Creating a knowledge-sharing community: If you build it, will they come? *Communications of the ACM, 46*(2), 23-25.

Brown, S. J. (2003). *Learning, working, & playing in the digital age serendip.* Retrieved October 9, 2003, from http://serendip.brynmawr.edu/sci_edu/seelybrown/seelybrown4.html

Burnett, G. (2000). Information exchange in virtual communities: A typology. *Information Research, 5*(4). Retrieved September 9, 2003, from http://informationr.net/ir/5-4/paper82.html

Davidson, S. (1998). Knowledge management: An overview. *DM Review.* Retrieved August 18, 2003, from http://www.dmreview.com/master.cfm?NavID=198&EdID=904

Dieter, G. M. (2002). *Knowledge management.* Retrieved August 8, 2003, from http://tigger.uic.edu/~miked/KM_Pathfinder.htm

Dowdy, E. (2001, May 28). B*irth pangs of a new learning environment: Collective representation, network technology, and communities of place.* A Paper Submitted for presentation at the Conference of International Communication Association, Washington, DC, US.

Erdelez, S. (1999). Information encountering: It's more than just bumping into information. *American Association for Information Science, 25*(3), 25-29.

Faber, D. B. (2002). Educational models and open source: Resisting the proprietary university. *Journal of Technical Writing and Communication, 32*(4), 319-348.

Harris, A., Korsakova, M., Wakefield, M., Baxter, M., & Farinha, D. (1998). *Knowledge based systems: Acquisition, design, and interfaces* (Coursework 1). Retrieved July 28, 2003, from http://www.scism.sbu.ac.uk/inmandw/tutorials/ka/g1/

Hein, E. G. (1991). *Constructivist learning theory.* Retrieved September 2, 2003, from http://www.exploratorium.edu/IFI/resources/constructivistlearning.html

Hippel, V. E. (2001). Innovation by user communities: Learning from open- source software. *MIT Sloan Management, 42*(4), 82-86.

Jelkner. (2003, April). (Contributed). *When students know more than the teacher. Schoolforge.* Retrieved September 10, 2003, from http://opensourceschools.org/article.php?story=20030407074154690

Kim, E. E. (2003). *An introduction to open source communities.* Blue Oxen Associates. Retrieved September 20, 2003, from Blue Oxen University Web site: http://www.blueoxen.org/research/00007/BOA-00007.pdf

Krishnamurthy, S. (2002). Cave or community? An empirical examination of 100 mature open source projects. *Firstmonday*. Retrieved August 21, 2003, from http://www.firstmonday.dk/issues/Issue7_6/krishnamurthy/

Lakhani, R. K., & Wolf, G. R. (2003). *Why hackers do what they do: Understanding motivation effort in free/open source software projects.* Retrieved October 1, 2003, from http://opensource.mit.edu/papers/lakhaniwolf.pdf

Lapachet, J. A. H. (1994). *Virtual communities: The 90's mind altering drug or facilitator of human interaction?* Retrieved September 20, 2003, from http://is.gseis.ucla.edu/impact/s94/students/jaye/jaye_asis.html

Lerner, J., & Tirole, J. (2001). The open source movement: Key research questions. *European Economic Review, 45*(5), 819-826.

O'Hara, J. K., & Jennifer, S. K. (2003). Open source software and computer science education. *ACM Digital Library, 18*(3), 1-7.

Pask, G. (1980). Developments in conversation theory—Part 1. *International Journal of Man-Machine Studies, 13*(1), 357-411

Raymond, S. E. (1998). *The cathedral and the bazaar.* Retrieved from http://www.firstmonday.dk/issues/issue3_3/raymond/

Rheingold, H. (1993). *The virtual community.* Retrieved July 6, 2003, from http://www.rheingold.com/vc/book/2.html

Ryder, M. (1995). *USENET: A constructivist learning environment.* Retrieved August 4, 2003, from http://carbon.cudenver.edu/~mryder/aect_95.html

Scacchi, W. (2002). *Understanding the requirement of developing open source software systems.* Retrieved August 8, 2003, from http://www1.ics.uci.edu/~wscacchi/Papers/New/Understanding-OS-Requirements.pdf

Scharff, E. (2002). *Applying open source principles to collaborative learning environments.* Retrieved August 8, 2003, from http://newmedia.colorado.edu/cscl/61.pdf

Sowe, K. S, Karoulis, A., Stamelos, I., & Bleris, G. L. (2004). Free or open source software learning community and Web-based technologies. *IEEE Learning Technology Newsletter, 6*(1), 26-29.

Stallman, R. (2002, April 3). *Why software should be free.* [Interview with Alfred Hermida, BBC Online.]. Retrieved July11, 2003, from http://news.bbc.co.uk/1/hi/sci/tech/1898803.stm

Stenmark, D. (2002, January 7-10). Information vs. knowledge: The role of intranets in knowledge management. In *Proceedings of HICSS-35*, Hawaii. Retrieved August 20, 2003, from http://w3.informatik.gu.se/~dixi/publ/ddom102.pdf

Sveiby, E. K. (1997). *Tacit knowledge.* Retrieved July 22, 2003, from http://www.sveiby.com/articles/Polanyi.html

Tellen, L. S. (1997). *Internet as knowledge management systems basic concepts and definitions.* Retrieved August 20, 2003, from http://www.iorg.com/papers/knowledge.html

Ye, Y., & Kishida, K. (2003, May). Towards an understanding of the motivation of open source software developers. *Proceedings of the 25th International Conference on Software Engineering,* Portland, OR (pp. 419-429).

Zack, H. M. (1998). Developing a knowledge strategy. *Sloan Management Review, 41*(3), 125-145.

Chapter XVII

Building a Learning Community Online

Tessa Owens, Liverpool Hope University College, United Kingdom

Petra Luck, Liverpool Hope University College, United Kingdom

Abstract

This chapter reviews a pilot e-learning project at Liverpool Hope University College. It will illustrate an approach to online learning aimed at students working in the early years education and care sector and attempts to demonstrate the development of a "community of practice." This chapter will discuss how the context informed the rationale for the approaches taken by the staff team and provides commentary from student evaluations highlighting their experiences.

Introduction

Liverpool Hope University College has a 150-year tradition of widening participation and has over the last decade expanded degree provision to a number of Network of Hope locations across the northwest of England to further provide access to those groups of students currently still underrepresented in higher education in the United Kingdom. Against this institutional backdrop the Bachelor of Arts (BA) Nursery Management commenced as a taught part-time programme for early years educare practitioners in September 2001. To date this degree remains the only one of its kind in the United Kingdom, providing a higher level management qualification in a rapidly expanding service sector.

Service Sector Demands

The market in the United Kingdom for such a programme is large and is growing in line with U.K. Government initiatives. For example, childcare spending is set to double to £1.5 billion in 2005-06. This expansion of childcare places is only possible through a rapid increase in the childcare workforce. According to the Department for Education and Science (DfES) the number of professionals in the childcare sector grew by 21% between 1998 and 2001, while the numbers of workers in nursery and after school provision doubled over the same period. This rise in provision and staff involved in the sector is leading to a demand for higher level management qualifications. Publicity in *Nursery World* and *Nursery Management Today* during 2002 about Liverpool Hope's BA Nursery Management generated more than 100 enquiries from across the United Kingdom and abroad.

To enable Liverpool Hope to respond to the demand from individuals and organizations in the early years educare sector, the programme team explored a number of distance and e-learning modes such as paper based learning materials or the transfer of existing lecture notes to Web pages. The team debated whether such methods could be adopted to enable interested practitioners from across the United Kingdom to participate in the degree programme. An adoption of a format that would allow students to participate from a distance is also in line with Liverpool Hope's mission to widen participation to previously disadvantaged groups. As stated by Hedge (1996, p. 7), "distance education . . . represents opportunities for continuing education that are, already, enabling notions of lifelong learning to advance beyond rhetoric and into reality." Employer and employee organizations in the sector such as the National Day Nurseries Association are concerned that such programmes are available.

Tricia Pritchard (2000), professional officer of the Professional Association of Nursery Nurses said, "The government should be investing in training, developing a career ladder, improving salaries, tightening regulations, and attracting the right quality of person into childcare." The educare sector is set to continue to grow as though the private sector for nursery provision has increased by 400% over the last 10 years, it still only meets 2% of the current demand.

Significant child carer recruitment targets have been set by the UK government and this will require a considerable amount of training provision, much of which will need to be distance learning orientated. Due to the nature of this employment sector, it is evident from the Organization for Economic Co-operation and Development (OECD) research that the current provision for training and development of child care staff is only of a pedagogic or vocational nature, with no specific training and development opportunities in childcare management. Increasingly, though early years staff are expected to perform these management roles, "In countries with complex funding streams, staff are expected to be social entrepreneurs to juggle various funding sources, compete for scarce resources and grants" (OECD, 2001, p. 96). This research further shows the need for open and distance learning (ODL) training: "Workers face many practical challenges to access in-service training, especially the difficulty of obtaining release time with pay to attend courses" (2001, p. 98). In addition to the training and management skills development, there are issues of equality of opportunities to address. The U.K. labour force survey 1991-1995 reveals that nursery nurses are 99.2% female with only 1% educated to degree level. These areas of development are further highlighted in the House of Commons Education and Employment Committee "Early Years" report submitted on December 12, 2000. Section 108 calls for all nursery managers to be qualified to degree level for professional management of the childcare facilities and provision.

E-Learning Rationale

The BA Nursery Management programme team decided on an e-learning mode, as this was seen to provide the best vehicle to widen participation. Offering online learning would provide an accredited route for the attainment of a relevant degree level qualification for carers and managers within the childcare sector, and assist in attracting suitable people into this employment sector to meet the childcare demand over the next 10 years. It would provide a vehicle that enhances the skills in management which are now needed in this expanding sector and prepare students to meet the demands of future employment.

The modification from a face-to-face mode to an e-learning mode embraces the use of computer technology and communication systems through use of a virtual learning environment (VLE) and critical use of the World Wide Web. This allows the broadening of access to the target group, as delivery is achieved while students continue to be active within the workplace. This enhances the learning experience and the employability factors, as the knowledge will be directly transferable to the work environment.

Offering the programme online means that instead of the students moving to the location of the resource provider (i.e. Liverpool Hope) and studying at times convenient for the institution, the programme is taken to the students and they can study at times convenient to them. Through this mode, the BA Nursery Management e-learning would contribute towards achieving one of Liverpool Hope's prime strategic objectives, widening participation by providing study opportunities for groups of students previously excluded from higher education.

The participants enrolled on this programme are, to date, all female. This is typically seen in the childcare sector in the United Kingdom. The provision of this programme therefore enables us to pursue our mission further as "women returners" are seen to be one of the underrepresented groups in higher education today. Offering the BA Nursery Management online to an overwhelmingly female target group also concurs with the rise of female Internet participation. This participation rose from 5.1% of all users in 1995 to 31.43% of Internet users in 1998. (Bockermann, Masaneck, & Wiesner, 2001). But, as Spender (1995) states, "For more than a century, women have been engaged in a battle for equal educational rights, and the struggle must now been transferred to the virtual society" (p. 210).

In deciding on an e-learning mode the team was aware that e-learning can be misunderstood as an "information dump" and not as a process. This is in response to Honey's assertion that "the common thread running through . . . forms of e-learning is that it offers the possibility of learning from information delivered to us electronically" (2001, p. 200). Honey furthermore asserts that "e-learning more often than not amounts to e-reading" (2001, p. 202).

Learning and Teaching Rationale

It is the stated aim of this programme that students will develop knowledge and understanding of the educational and management issues pertinent to their sector, and that they will also develop the requisite skills to critically analyse, evaluate, and apply this knowledge. As professional knowledge requires functioning knowledge that can be put to work immediately the management team choose to adopt a "problem-based learning" approach for the programme. This approach has been widely used in higher education in recent years particularly in health related professions and has been found to facilitate the acquisition of professional knowledge along with the requisite practitioner skills (see, e.g., Newble & Clarke, 1986).

Problem-based learning simulates everyday learning and problem solving. Knowledge is acquired in a working context and is put back to use in this context. Students learn the skills for seeking out the required knowledge when the occasion arises. They are motivated immediately by the interaction with a "real" problem and are active early in the process. There is a large body of literature to support the motivational aspects of collaboration on learning (Dobos, 1996; Johnson & Johnson, 1989; Sharan & Shaulov, 1990). Students are assigned to small problem-solving groups and begin cooperating with tutors and peers to build up a knowledge base of material; they learn where to go and check it and seek out more. They are guided to a wide variety of resources. Knowledge is developed, strengthened, and applied.

The university college's chosen VLE is Granada's Learnwise. This VLE has as one of its features collaborative "forums" in which students take part in asynchronous discussion in small teams and work on specific management and education problems. Wenger (1998) provides a view on learning that highlights social learning processes within communities of practice where students debate meaning and mutually construct knowledge. This contrasts with theories of learning that emphasises individual and isolated cognitive processes and where learning is viewed as the absorption of an abstract body of knowledge that stands apart from its practice.

In the first session the students are presented with a problem. This will frequently take the form of a written "case study" but could also be a video or audio format. Simmons (2000) identifies the powerful role of stories in learning. Students attempt to broadly identify the problem and its key features and using their own experience and existing knowledge, they generate a number of potential causes and solutions. This "brainstorming" of ideas is permanently recorded in the forums and allows the students to create a picture of their group's collective understanding of the issues. They then convert their questions into learning objectives for the problem.

Once the learning goals have been identified, students share these out. They individually use the available resources to develop an understanding of the information, which they bring back to the group for the second phase. The students are strongly encouraged to get information and develop understandings relevant to the problem as their group defined it. The information they gather must be subsequently presented to the group in an easily understood and relevant format.

After further discussions the implications of the new information allows the group to refine their early assumptions and uncover their knowledge gaps. Students therefore develop their explanations of the problem and discover more pertinent information for resolving it.

The final session is followed by a period of reflection where students identify some of the barriers to their learning and issues they will encounter when dealing with "real" problems. Students are also given an opportunity for two-way feedback: tutor to students and students to tutor. They describe the things they think worked well and those that could be improved upon. These can be incorporated into the learning objectives for this group with their next problem.

The tutor's role throughout this process is that of a facilitator. The tutor encourages the students to explore their own knowledge and determine their own learning needs and generally refrains from providing information, instead prompting discussion among the students. The tutor will illuminate discussion asking pertinent questions and checking all lines of enquiry, the currency, and validity of the information they provide (e.g., Goldsborough, 2001) and encouraging students to consider their priorities. They will also intervene in negative group dynamics to examine what may be going wrong and determine how to proceed.

Using a problem-based learning approach is seen to be particularly important as these students are working at a distance and it was anticipated that the students will maintain their sense of belonging to the group and the programme by working together on shared problems. In so doing their skills of communication, self-direction, team working, problem solving, and creativity will be developed.

Collaborative learning is a natural process of social interaction and communication (Flannery, 1994; Gerlach, 1994) and by using problems to define the curriculum, students acquire necessary knowledge and skills. Honey (2001) identifies that "learning has always flourished when it has been actively encouraged and supported." The learning and assessment on the programme is aligned (Biggs, 1999) to their everyday work experiences. This type of social interaction, learning, and decision making is expected in the workplace today and this approach should ultimately therefore promote a desire for and ability to partake in "life-long learning." Students will have gained the skills for acquiring new knowledge and for evaluating it, while also understanding the necessity of analysing and reflecting upon the outcomes of their proposed solutions.

The Pilot Group

The first cohort of students has been recruited, and this pilot group started in February 2003.

The team has monitored and evaluated the early student experiences and attainment encouraging open and frank comment from the participating students. This is particularly pertinent as students are at a distance and "we need a way of giving our invisible and silent students a voice so that they can contribute to public evaluation processes" (Gilroy, Long, Rangecroft, & Tricker, 2001, p. 17). Students have contributed to module evaluations as is standard practice at Liverpool Hope University College, in conjunction with a continuous review of the programme's coherence, which is undertaken via the VLE'S anonymous evaluation tool. To illustrate the experiences of students, the writers will present in the next section the unanimously positive evaluation comments from anonymous formal module evaluations, forum contributions, and chat room seminars.

Results

The results gained have been illuminating in many ways and the authors feel that, in particular, the role of context is highly significant, specifically as it relates to student success on this type of programme. Three main contexts have been identified: (1) the context of common professional field, (2) the context of community, and (3) the context of gender.

All participants are working within the same professional field. What they learn is of significance to their other work as well as their studies. By using an online environment these "special interest" groups have a medium in which to communicate (Preece, 2000). All the modules have used case studies in the nursery management sector, which is in line with a classic problem based learning philosophy, which requires students to learn, and access information, on a "need to know" basis. The key here appears to be that students start from a position of confidence, they look at a given problem, and state what they know about the problem. As each group has a wide and varied experience the "pooling" of these initial considerations is in itself informative and edifying for the group. In identifying where the gaps exist in their knowledge, each group of students will suggest a large variety of means of accessing the information and possible sources of information, which they require.

Context therefore is providing the rich backdrop and focus in which the student can learn. Context enhances not only the student's academic studies but also their everyday practical knowledge and acquisition of skills, which can be used in their everyday employment.

Students comment on the knowledge gained:

> *I am constantly using the information gained in my setting and have been able to download a good deal for the presentation I am giving to about 50 of my parents on Thursday in line with my Partners as Parents policy which has made my life very easy. Sad to say I even keep on reviewing the DfES site for any new news!! Looking forward to starting back again and having looked at the problems feel that this will once again help me in my day to day working.*

> *I am loving the challenge of the modules, as well as knowing that the information I gain on this course will be helpful now and in my future career (wherever it takes me).*

The importance of the professional context is also apparent in the following student's comment during a group live chat:

I prefer to do 4 and 5 (parts of the group task) as I may need to look at it as\I am working with a school at the moment so to freshen up on any latest funding would be good research for me.

Another student describes her approach to choosing a work situation for academic analysis in a chat discussion with her tutor:

I have already started thinking about this individual task and with my current reading and research of problem 3—I will be putting some of my reading into practice as early as Monday!!! The nice thing about this is that I can actually evaluate any academic theory I may decide to try and apply.

I will keep you updated.

While Donohue (2002) asserts that the childcare field tends to be a low tech/high touch field, distance learning and particularly online learning can be perceived as a high tech/no touch activity. Staff employed in the early years sector often have limited experience with technology and might lack technological literacy. This demands opportunities for students for hands-on technology experiences and skills development such as provided in the Induction Residential for the BA Nursery Management. Students built on this induction during their first modules and comment on skills enhancement:

I have learnt loads and have really enjoyed the challenge of beating the internet in my quest for information on French education amongst other things.

I had a fair bit of IT training and experience—but had not done much research on the web! Boy what info you can find. I certainly became addicted. Problem I think though—is when do you decide you have enough info—N. will ditto that!

The team attempted to make the technology as transparent as possible by giving technical as well as academic support so that students can focus on the content, not worry about fighting the technology to access information and communicate with each other. Students' skills development is apparent in these quotes from reflective evaluations:

I had also never entered chat rooms or even sent attachments with my e-mails yet suddenly I'm like a computer wiz kid (well perhaps not!)

What an experience the last few months have been—it has certainly been an eye opener and most of the time an enjoyable way of learning. I really enjoy doing research into the different types of provisions and countries—searching the web. Can't wait to get started again!

The second context identified is that the students have now formed a community. They show loyalty and care towards one another and frequently comment on the importance of the "team" to their continuation on the programme. As time has passed the groups have grown in confidence, their contributions in the forums have become more frequent and fulsome. They have shared not only knowledge but also ways of looking at problems, which Rowntree (1995) suggests is to be part of this mutually beneficial process:

> *Participants are liable to learn as much from one another as from course material or from the interjections of the tutor. What they learn of course is not so much product (e.g. information) as process—in particular the creative cognitive process of offering up ideas, having them criticized or expanded on, and getting the chance to reshape them (or abandon them) in the light of peer discussion. The learning becomes not merely active . . . but also interactive. (Rowntree, 1995, p. 207)*

Getting out of the early years setting and being together, and fighting the isolation family childcare providers often feel, are important reasons for participating in training. This desire for an online learning community is evident in this student's comments:

> *Like everyone else I found the whole experience better than I initially anticipated. When I first heard that we were going to work in groups I had my doubts, yet this has been fantastic because we all support each other.*

> *Hi everyone, I am still struggling to get my head round all this technology! Would anyone else feel it valuable to meet in the chat room to discuss work in progress (conversation flows easier in chat room). Look forward to replies.*

According to Gilligan (1982) women students have a preference to share their studies with classmates, however, she asserts that this preference for a community of learners is not due to any type of inferiority, but to a positive stance of participation and "dependent connection."

The students themselves recognise the benefits of working together:

> *All I can say is that it would be great to get together again. Having originally thought working alongside a group was going to be difficult really glad we are as it does give you a bit of a kick up the proverbial to ensure that you get your piece done and you are not letting down your colleagues.*

> *Working with groups really helped me a lot. It enabled me to gain confidence in my work and it was great to have the support of the rest of the group. . . . It would be nice to meet up again . . . What do you think Hope?*
>
> *I have really enjoyed the course so far and made great friends . . . now definitely in my book of best buddies! We can spend hours sharing ideas and thoughts . . .*

Donohue (2002) implores instructional designers and e-tutors to create a learning environment that emphasises visual learning, hands-on activities, individual reflection, and group activities and collaborative learning. Students echo the importance of that collaborative activity:

> *The group commitment is the only thing that works for me ensuring that I get my work in on time otherwise I would always find something else to do!*
>
> *These last few months have been quite enjoyable and enlightening. . . . I am pleasantly surprised how much I have enjoyed working with groups of people whom I have only ever met (face to face) once.*
>
> *Thanks . . . but I feel I need to pull my weight and put my lot in otherwise I will feel guilty.*

The third context important to the programme is that of gender and particularly the impact of students' situation as working mothers. Keegan (2000, cited in Aggelli, 2003) states that women prefer distance learning because of its nature, since studies of this type allow them to fulfil their family and career commitments. Furthermore, it enables them to learn at their own pace, while minimizing costs—saving money and time on commuting and childcare. As mentioned earlier, women's access to IT is still significantly lower than that of males, while in addition many staff working in the early years sector only have access to slow tech/old tech IT equipment in their work places.

Despite the dedication and motivation of online learners, many are still made to feel that they are letting their families down when they try to further their education (Kramarae 2000):

> *I will (I promise) be on line for a bit at 9 pm tonite—need to pick 3 of the children up by 9.30—so 20 mins should do it.*

Many students' involvement in the study programme has been impeded by lack of affordable childcare, while the lack of wider family support presents a barrier to participation:

> *The more notice (for the next residential) the better as childcare is a major issue for a whole weekend.*

Now need to work on childcare!!!! If you only know the problems I had last year—nearly didn't manage to make it—even with 6 months notice it collapsed at the last minute. Blended families!!!

Ok, I will look at suppliers, but it will be tomorrow, if that is ok, I have to work tonite, having kids home from school is a pain, I get nothing done.

Conflicting responsibilities causes women learners to declare anxiety and many others (especially mothers of young children) often do their coursework while the other family members are sleeping, working mothers adding on a "third shift" to their responsibilities (according to Kramarae, 2000). This is evident in the following excerpts from chat room group meetings:

It is a busy week for me and have been so tired each night.

Can I leave you to it? have to get a very tired little boy to bed now, but yes S. your definition of EVR is right.

Gotta go and pick up my son—presumably D. is out and about picking up kids somewhere.

Conclusions

Context has been a powerful influence and motivating force for the students on this programme. By recreating a "virtual world" which replicates their own "real life" the team believe they have created the most appropriate environment in which the students can learn. The programme creates a coherent whole, with a targeted professional curriculum for those currently working in this domain, using readily understood and meaningful problems and simulations as a framework for learning.

Formal student groups were created with the expectation that students would work together on complex tasks and that this group activity would stimulate creativity, provide multiple viewpoints and enable the students to solve problems and "implement" quality decisions. The groups have also, however, begun to serve more informal, though no less important, functions. The groups have formed into communities, which fulfil social needs for friendship, support, and interaction. The participants have been able to develop in a safe environment offering their expertise and confirming their own self-worth. The online synchronous and asynchronous discussion allows them to question their beliefs, illustrate their realities, experiences, and understandings. The virtual community of learners have become a robust and self-reliant reality.

The context of gender adds to this already powerful and unifying mix. All students are female, most are mothers. Their particular set of difficulties are instinctively known by their peers. The struggle to fulfil their multiple roles is well evidenced but these women know that they need not concern themselves with the judgement of their peers, in this particular community lengthy excuses are not required. These factors provide real strength and cohesion for the group, making their struggle an individual and joint endeavour that they seem determined to overcome together.

References

Aggeli, A., & Vassala, P. (2003). Women in distance learning: 2nd chance or 3rd shift. *Proceedings of the 2003 EDEN Annual Conference*, Rhodes, Greece.

Biggs, J. (1999). Teaching for quality learning at university. SRHE: Open University.

Bockermann, I., Masanneck, M., & Wiesner, H. (2001). Expect the best - Prepare for the worst; Virtuelle Lernumgebungen im Kontext von gender and cultural studies [Virtual learning environments in the context of gender and cultural studies]. In *Querelles-Net Rezensionszeitschrift für Frauen und Geschlechterforschung.* Retrieved from http://www.querelles-net.de/forum/forum4-1.html

Dobos, J. (1996). Collaborative learning: Effects of students' expectations and communication apprehension on student motivation. *Communication Education, 45,* 118-34.

Donohue, C. (2002). It is a small world: Taking your first steps into online teaching and learning. *Childcare Information Exchange, 9,* 20-25.

Flannery, J. (1994). Teacher as co-conspirator: Knowledge and authority in collaborative learning. *New directions in Teaching and Learning, 59*(Fall), 15-23.

Gerlach, J. (1994). Is this collaboration? *New directions in Teaching and Learning, 59*(Fall), 5-14.

Gilligan, C. (1982). *In a different voice: Psychological theory and women's development.* Cambridge, MA: Harvard University Press.

Gilroy, P., Long, P., Rangecroft, M., & Tricker, T. (2001). Evaluation and the invisible student: Theories, practice, and problems in evaluating distance education provision. *Quality Assurance in Education, 9*(1), 14-22.

Goldsborough, R. (2001). Personal computing. *Black Issues in Higher Education, 11*(October), 40.

Hedge, N. (1996). Introduction. In N. Hedge (Ed.), *Going the distance: Teaching, learning, and researching in distance education* (pp. 7-10). Sheffield: USDE.

Honey, P. (2001). E-learning: A performance appraisal and some suggestions for improvement. *The Learning Organization, 8*(5), 200-202.

Johnson, D. W., & Johnson, R. T. (1989). *Cooperation and competition: Theory and research.* Edina, MN: Interaction Book Company.

Keegan, D. (2000). *The basic principles of open distance learning* (A. Melista, Trans.). Athens: Metaixmeio.

Kramarae, C. (2000). *The third shift: Women learning on-line. American association of University Women (AAUW),* Educational Foundation.

Newble, D., & Clarke, R. (1986). The approaches to learning of students in a traditional and in an innovative problem-based medical school. *Medical Education, 20,* 267-273.

OECD. (2001). *Starting strong-early childhood education and care.* Paris: OECD.

Preece, J. (2000). Empathic communities: Balancing emotional and factual communication. *Interacting with Computers, 12,* 63-77.

Pritchard, T. (2000, September 12). Baby boom. *Guardian.*

Rowntree, D. (1995). Teaching and learning online: A correspondence education for the 21st century. *British Journal of Educational Technology, 26*(3), 205-215.

Sharan, S., & Shaulov, A. (1990). Cooperative learning, motivation to learn, and academic achievement. In S. Sharan (Ed.), *Co-operative learning: Theory and research* (pp. 173-202). New York: Praeger.

Simmons, A. (2000). *The story factor: Secrets of influence from the art of storytelling.* Cambridge, MA: Perseus.

Spender, D. (1995). *Nattering on the net.* North Melbourne: Spinnifex Press.

Wenger, E. (1998). *Communities of practice: Learning, meaning and identity.* Cambridge, MA: Cambridge University Press.

About the Authors

António Dias de Figueiredo is professor of information systems at the Universidade de Coimbra, Portugal, since 1984. He integrated the NATO Special Program Panel on Advanced Educational Technology, Brussels, and was vice-president of the Intergovernmental Informatics Program of UNESCO, Paris. He was the chair of PROMETEUS (PROmoting Multimedia access to Education and Training in EUropean Society), of the European Commission. He has collaborated with the European Commission and the OECD on initiatives regarding strategies for ICT in education. He was awarded an Honoris Causa by the Portuguese Open University and the Sigillum Magnum by the University of Bologna, Italy.

Ana Paula Afonso was born in Mozambique in 1973. She is a doctoral student in educational sciences, major in educational technology, at the Faculty of Psychology and Educational Sciences, Universidade de Coimbra, Portugal. She is also a researcher at the Center for Informatics and Systems of the UC since 2000. She obtained her master's degree in educational sciences, major in educational psychology, from UC in 2000. She graduated in educational sciences at the same university in 1996. Her main scientific areas of research interest include educational sciences, educational psychology, organizational psychology and learning, knowledge management, Web-based Learning, e-learning, adults education, learning communities, and information systems.

* * *

Patricia Arnold studied mathematics and educational science in Hamburg and London and worked in grammar schools and in adult education. For a long period her focus was on teaching information technology and particularly facilitating women's appropriation of technology. She coordinated several transnational adult learning projects funded by European programs, again with a focus on gender issues and technology. Within this context her interest in online education and collaborative computer-supported leaning grew. She took up research in the field and received a PhD in educational science. Communities of practice, online and off-line, and designing for learning in virtual settings are at the heart of her professional interests right now.

Brent Auernheimer is interim director of Digital Campus and professor of computer science at California State University, Fresno (USA). His professional interests are software engineering and human-computer interaction. He received three degrees in computer science from the University of California, Santa Barbara. Auernheimer held visiting appointments at the Software Engineering Institute (SEI) at Carnegie Mellon University, NASA Jet Propulsion Laboratory (JPL), and the University of Hawaii, Manoa. He was a summer research fellow at both NASA Kennedy Space Center (KSC) and JPL.

Bernard Blandin, a PhD in sociology, is senior consultant, head of the CESI-Online Department, and adviser to the managing director of CESI Group, France (http://www.cesi.fr). His expertise is rooted in research on the uses of information technologies in education and training and in evaluations of more than a hundred open and distance learning, collaborative learning, or e-learning projects funded by the French Ministry of Employment, by the European Commission within the framework of the Leonardo da Vinci program, and by the European Social Fund programs. Since 1987, he has contributed to several books and has published a large number of papers in French and in English.

Ellen Christiansen is a PhD in humanistic computer science and has since 1985 been a university teacher and researcher of context representation in design and use of computerized information systems. Her research comprises ethnographic fieldwork, experimental design in the area of CSCW and CSCL, and the development of pattern languages.

John A. Clarke is currently a senior research assistant in the School of Learning and Professional Studies at the Queensland University of Technology, Australia. He has a history of working and researching in the fields of classroom learning and interaction and learning environments, particularly at the tertiary level. He also has an interest in research methodology and has integrated this with learning environment research through the development and refinement of an instrument for gathering students' perceptions of what helps and hinders their learning. His current research interests include flexible, distance, and online learning environments.

Bronwen Cowie is a senior lecturer in the Centre for Science and Technology Education Research at the University of Waikato, Hamilton, New Zealand. She is cur rently teaching master's papers in science education and educational research methodologies. Her research interests include assessment, student views, curriculum implementation, and environmental education. She is currently involved in a range of projects focusing on classroom teaching and learning and the impacts of ICT on teachers' work and student learning.

Martha E. Crosby is a professor and associate chair in the Department of Information and Computer Sciences at the University of Hawaii, in Manoa (USA). She conducts research in the areas of the human use of computing systems, individual differences of users (particularly cultural), cognitive styles, and evaluation of innovative educational environments, particularly those using multimedia. She has conducted several empirical studies of reading comprehension and problem solving. She is particularly interested in developing user models and in the evaluation of human use of computer interfaces for educational applications.

John Davey is learning technology development manager at Edge Hill College of Higher Education, UK. He is responsible for the management and development of learning technology and e-learning developments across the institution, and contributes to college-wide e-learning initiatives and strategies. John works with academic and learning support staff to advise and support them in the development of teaching and learning materials and approaches to facilitate learning in online environments, including the delivery of a staff development e-learning program, which encompasses relevant pedagogic, practical, and technical skills. He writes and facilitates on CPD e-learning modules, and has a particular research interest in supporting students and preparing them for e-learning experiences.

Philip Duchastel is working in the emerging area of information design, at the crossroads of information, cognition, and computer technology. The Information Design Atelier (Canada) serves to structure these efforts in information design theory. He obtained his doctorate in the field of instructional systems. His interests in knowledge and information systems and technologies led him to a dynamic career that involved him in organizational innovation within universities and corporations, in innovative uses of computers for learning and instruction, in new forms of distance education, in online education, and in Internet development.

Laura G. Farres is a professor in sport science and coaching at Douglas College, Canada. She specializes in the area of sport psychology, psychopedagogy, and the psychology of performance. Her research extends into the field of e-learning as she explores the concept and possibilities of e-learning in sport health and mental skills training.

Michael Forret is a senior lecturer at the University of Waikato, Hamilton, New Zealand. He holds a joint position in the School of Education and the Centre for Science and Technology Education Research (CSTER). Mike is currently teaching undergraduate papers in science and technology education and a master's paper in technology education. His research interests lie in developing effective learning environments through a clearer understanding of learning and the ways in which learners engage with learning situations. He is currently involved in a range of research and development projects focusing on online learning, technology education, and physics education.

Xun Ge is an assistant professor in the program of instructional psychology and technology, Department of Educational Psychology, at the University of Oklahoma (USA). She earned her doctorate in instructional systems from the Pennsylvania State University in 2001. Her primary research interest is in designing and developing instructional scaffolds, tools, and learning environment to support students' reasoning, problem-solving, and metacognitive skills. Her other research areas include the dynamics of online collaborative learning, community of learners and practice, and technology integration in K-12 and higher education. She can be reached via e-mail at xge@ou.edu.

Marie K. Iding is an associate professor in Educational Psychology at the University of Hawaii (USA). Her research interests involve aspects of text processing and visualization with multimedia and computer-based instructional tools. She is also interested in how people make determinations about credibility of information on the Web.

Athanasis Karoulis holds a BSc in mathematics from Aristotle University of Thessaloniki, Greece, a degree in educational technology from the University of Macedonia (Greece), a degree in open and distance learning from the Greek Open University, an MSc in information systems from the University of Macedonia (Greece), and a PhD in informatics in the domain of human-computer interaction from the Aristotle University of Thessaloniki, Greece. He is the author of two books and coauthor of five, which are published in Greece, and he has managed more than six multimedia projects. His scientific interest concern human-computer interaction, multimedia and Web design, educational technologies, and distance learning.

Elaine Khoo is currently completing her PhD at the University of Waikato, New Zealand. Her research interests include Web-based learning, specifically pedagogical issues in designing collaborative Web-based learning environments to facilitate teaching and learning at the tertiary level. She led the Learning Technology Group while lecturing in the area of cognitive sciences and education at University

Malaysia Sarawak, and she has been involved in several e-learning initiatives at the national and university level in Malaysia.

Petra Luck is principal lecturer in Management and Business Centre at Liverpool Hope University College, UK. She is also the project manager for the Leonardo-funded European Enhancement of Early Years Management Skills project. Her background has been in community development, informal education, and project management in the not-for-profit sector. She took up her first post in higher education in 1989 at Liverpool John Moore's University, training youth and community workers. From 1993, at Liverpool Hope University College, she initially managed "widening participation" initiatives and been the award director for the innovative BA Nursery Management since 2001. Her research interests include e-learning, Web-based communities, and communities of practice.

Colla J. MacDonald is a professor in curriculum design and evaluation in the Faculty of Education at the University of Ottawa, Canada. Much of her research has advanced the field of curriculum development, evaluation, and e-learning. She has published many book chapters and refereed and professional articles on various aspects of e-learning. The Demand Driven Learning Model (DDLM), which she designed in collaboration with E. Stodel, L. Farres, K. Breithaupt, and M. A. Gabriel in 2001, is being used as a quality standard to design, develop, deliver, and evaluate teacher education and graduate online courses at the University of Ottawa in various education programs across Canada and the United States, as well as for health care teams working in long-term care facilities.

Kathy L. Milhauser lives in the Pacific Northwestern United States with her husband and children. She is a graduate of Pepperdine University's (USA) Online Master of Arts in Educational Technology program, a degree that she completed while balancing work and family. She has more than 20 years of experience in business and local government, with a focus on information technology and corporate training. Kathy's most recent work involves leading e-learning efforts for a global consumer product marketing company, where she hopes to bridge the gaps between space, time, and culture to enable collaborative learning online.

Markus Molz, trained as an organizational and educational psychologist, has been adviser, lecturer, and researcher in instructional design and technology and in intercultural communication at different universities in Germany and France, as well as co-founder of an innovative training company. Currently he is working as an independent consultant for nonprofit organizations, leveraging their capacity to take advantage of the transnational knowledge age; at the same time he is pursuing his long-term interest in integral adult and higher education.

Tessa Owens is a senior lecturer in Management and Business at Liverpool Hope University College, UK. She also holds the post of Learning and Teaching Fellow for the Deanery of International Business Information Technology and Enterprise. Her background is in the financial services sector within the United Kingdom, specifically within banking and insurance, where she held posts in lending, systems analysis, management development, and administration management. She joined higher education in 1999 to pursue her love of teaching and research. Her research interests include assessment and appraisal, personal development, e-learning, problem-based learning, human resource development, and learning through work.

Hitendra Pillay is an associate professor in the School of Learning and Professional Studies at the Queensland University of Technology, Australia. He has researched and consulted in the areas of information technology and learning. His ongoing research has highlighted the significance of cognitive interactions within ICT-rich learning environments by focusing on the understanding of cognitive maneuvers, such as inferential reasoning and anticipation, and has aimed at developing a more holistic understanding of human learning. To this end, he is also researching and publishing on learners' conceptions, beliefs, and approaches to learning in traditional learning environments.

Licínio Roque obtained a PhD in informatics engineering from the Universidade de Coimbra while developing a sociotechnical approach to information systems development. He has been practicing participatory action research and technological development in such diverse fields as management information systems, administration, individual and organizational learning, interactive entertainment, and Internet technologies for online communities. For the last 10 years he has been teaching software engineering and human-computer interaction as part of engineering curricula by promoting contextual approaches to learning in studio and project-based contexts.

Andrew Sackville established the Postgraduate Certificate and MA in teaching and learning in clinical practice at Edge Hill College of Higher Education, UK. He has qualifications in social work, postcompulsory education and training, a BA in political institutions and social studies, an MSc in urban studies, and a PhD in a historical study of professional associations in social work. He has studied at Keele, Wales in Swansea, Salford, Manchester, and the Open Universities. He has practiced as a probation officer, area social services manager, and a local authority trainer and taught social policy, management studies, and continuing education. He currently teaches and researches online teaching and learning.

Mark Schofield is head of Teaching and Learning at Edge Hill College of Higher Education, UK and reader in Educational Development. He contributes to teaching and curriculum design in undergraduate and postgraduate programs in education, health, and teaching and learning in clinical practice and provides consultancy in education in the school and university sectors. His interests include constructivism and learning, pedagogy and widening participation, and the use of technologies to enrich learning. He is a member of the Higher Education Academy and chair of Staff and Educational Development Association publications committee. He is chair of Edge Hill's Centre for Learning and Teaching Research, which focuses on postcompulsory education policy and practice.

John D. Smith is a technologist, developer, and coach for communities of practice. In collaboration with Etienne Wenger, he has offered the "Foundations of Communities of Practice" workshop over the last five years. He was instrumental in the launch of CPsquare, an international community of practice on communities of practice. He speaks and writes on topics related to communities of practice, including improvisation, narrative, community self-assessment, and community design. He received a bachelor's degree from St. John's College in Annapolis, MD, and a master's degree in planning and architecture from the University of New Mexico in 1976.

Sulayman K. Sowe is a registered PhD student at the Department of Informatics, Aristotle University of Thessaloniki, Greece. He received a BEd in science education from University of Bristol, United Kingdom (1991) and an advanced diploma and MSc in computer science from Sichuan University, People's Republic of China (1997). He taught physics, chemistry, and mathematics at various high schools in The Gambia (1988-1998). He was a lecturer in information technology at the University of The Gambia (2002). He worked as the director of the Information Technology and Human Resource Development (IT/HRD) unit at The Gambia's Department of State for Education (1998), as a system administrator for the West African Exams Council (1998-2002), and as a database manager for the Medical Research Council (2002-2003). His PhD research topic is free or open source development and knowledge management.

Ioannis Stamelos is an assistant professor at the Department of Informatics, Aristotle University of Thessaloniki, Greece. He joined the department in 1997 as a lecturer. He received a BSc in electrical engineering (1983) and a PhD in computer science (1988) from Aristotle University of Thessaloniki. He worked as a senior researcher at Telecom Italia from 1988 to 1994 and as a system integrator director at STET Hellas, a mobile telecom operator, from 1995 to 1996. He is the course coordinator of a number of undergraduate and graduate courses and teaches language and automata theory, object-oriented analysis and design, software engineering, and information systems. His research interests include software evaluation, measurement, cost estimation, testing, and software education. He is a member of the IEEE and Computer Society.

Peter G. Taylor is a professor and director of Bond University's Institute for Learning Communities, Australia. His interests and expertise are focused on the application of constructivist thinking about learning to a range of issues including the design of effective learning environments and the promotion of learning within communities of practice. In the last five years, this has involved projects on the design of learning spaces, organization level evaluation of innovations, and the use of information and communication technologies to support learning.

Beverly Trayner teaches at School of Business Sciences in Setúbal, Portugal. She has also designed and taught online modules for courses in online education and training at the University of London and the University of Bocconni, Milan. Her PhD research focuses on designing for communication and learning in international online communities. She has a first degree in business and holds a master of science in development studies. Beverly is an active member of CPSquare, an online community for communities of practice, and is involved in several Portuguese projects on learning in communities of practice.

Rita M. Vick is research and development coordinator for Quantum Leap Interactive, Honolulu, Hawaii, United States. Quantum Leap Interactive focuses on user-centered design and development of adaptive collaborative software and is a sister company of Quantum Leap Innovations, Newark, Delaware, United States, a pioneer in the emerging field of intelligent software for decision making and new knowledge creation. Her work in human-computer interaction, distributed collaborative decision- making, virtual teamwork, and distance learning reflects her research interests in ubiquitous computing, distributed cognition, multi-agent systems, and distributed collaborative technologies. Vick also holds an MBA from the University of Hawaii.

Martin Weller is a senior lecturer at the Institute of Educational Technology at the Open University (OU) in the United Kingdom. He is also the project director for the VLE project at OU. His research interests are in learning objects, open architecture learning environments, and the implications of e-learning for higher education. He is the author of the book Delivering Learning on the Net and numerous articles on e-learning.

Ke Zhang is assistant professor of instructional technology at the Texas Tech University, United States. Her major research interests include e-learning, virtual teams, problem solving, computer-supported collaborative work, and the social impacts of emerging technologies. She can be reached by e-mail at ke.zhang@ttu.edu

Index